Chambe
rhyming
dictionary

Chambers

CHAMBERS
An imprint of Chambers Harrap Publishers Ltd
7 Hopetoun Crescent
Edinburgh, EH7 4AY

www.chambers.co.uk

This edition published by Chambers Harrap Publishers Ltd 2008

Previous edition published 2003

A CIP catalogue record for this book is available from the British Library.

ISBN 978 0550 10347 5

Typeset by The Charlesworth Group
Printed and bound in Great Britain by CPI Cox & Wyman, Reading, RG1 8EX.

Contents

Preface	v
The Use of Rhyme	vii
How to Use This Book	ix
Chambers Rhyming Dictionary	**1**
Index	261
Some Common Non-Rhyming Words	421

Contributors

Editors
Ian Brookes
Liam Rodger
Andrew Holmes

Publishing Manager
Vivian Marr

Data Management
Patrick Gaherty

Prepress
Nicolas Echallier
Andrew Butterworth

Preface

by **Benjamin Zephaniah**

If you have bought this book or are just checking it out in a bookshop, you are probably interested in using poetry as a way of expressing your thoughts and feelings, or you may just want to change the world. You are not the only one; there are millions of us. People have always found poetry a particularly satisfying form of expression, and people like me continue to argue that in its oral form it is probably the oldest and most accessible art form known to mankind, and still we continue to use it in new and original ways. I started to create poetry because of my love of words, the rhythms of poetry excited me, and I was fascinated by the way words could be given various meanings depending on where they were placed on the page. When I walk into bookshops and libraries I still have to remind myself that there are only 26 letters in the alphabet, and that the books I see simply contain various arrangements of those 26 letters. How great the word! And this is just the English language!

A fellow poet once referred to me in a radio interview as a walking rhyming dictionary. What a great idea, I thought: a book full of rhymes! It wasn't until I began to phone friends to tell them of this new publishing idea I had that I was told that such things already existed. Having discovered them, I refused to use them. After all, why should I, the walking rhyming dictionary, require the use of such a book? Then I received one as a present (honest), and I have since learnt that they can be a great help when you are constructing tricky rhymes. I have found them most useful just when I feel that what I'm writing is not working. I am often surprised by their suggestions and then I find myself full of new ideas.

Chambers already have a reputation for producing great conventional dictionaries, but here they have adopted a completely new approach. Rhymes are grouped by the stressed syllables; phrases are given as well as individual words, and thousands of proper names have been included. So it's now official, you can rhyme *Johnny Cash* with *balderdash*, or *Ben Nevis* with *crevice*. The future is bright, it's a rapper's delight. By acknowledging words that have come into use via films, television, music, and other forms of popular culture, this new approach has brought the rhyming dictionary into the 21st century, so that experienced writers can enjoy finding new ways of doing things and younger writers will be familiar with many of its references.

Use this book as a starting point, a source for new ideas, and as a way of finishing those poems that will not be done by head-scratching alone, but remember there are no boundaries to the things that you can do in poetry. You have my permission to use words outside the list provided. By breaking the rules you may make new discoveries and you may very well find yourself contributing to a new edition of this very dictionary.

Benjamin Zephaniah

The Use of Rhyme

Is rhyme important?

Poetry does not have to rhyme. However, there are often good reasons for using rhyme to give your poem shape and structure. If you are writing poetry or songs to be performed in public, rhyme helps the audience to pick up the structure of the piece easily, a point which is important when the words are not written down.

Verses that rhyme are easier to remember than ones that don't. That is why rhymes are used in so many popular sayings. Your parents and grandparents probably told you rhymes to make you remember things, such as:

> *An apple a day*
> *Keeps the doctor away.*

Rhyme is also a great way to make people stop and take notice, especially when it is used in a creative or unusual way. The more unexpected and original the rhyme, the better. Writers such as Ogden Nash and W S Gilbert (of Gilbert and Sullivan fame) were expert at producing unexpected rhymes to give a comic effect, making *turtle* rhyme with *fertile* and *Hungary* rhyme with *ironmongery*.

Different forms of rhyme

Rhyme occurs when two lines of verse end with a similar sound. However, there are various different types of rhyme. Often there will be a stress or accent on the final syllable of the rhyming words. This is called "masculine rhyme" and is found, for example, when you rhyme *fox* with *socks*. However, you can also have rhymes when there is an extra unstressed syllable at the end of the line, such as when you rhyme *dancer* with *answer*. This is called "feminine rhyme". You can sometimes even have two unstressed syllables after the main stressed syllable, as in *charity* and *hilarity*.

Another form of rhyme happens when the ends of the words sound almost but not exactly identical. This is called "half-rhyme" or "near-rhyme". An example of this occurs if you rhyme *home* and *alone*. You will find that some pairs of letters, for example *m* and *n* or *d* and *t*, can be used almost interchangeably for rhyming purposes. Using half-rhymes greatly increases the number of words you can use to rhyme with any word. It

also allows you to surprise and amuse by introducing unexpected words as rhymes.

Common rhyme schemes

Many types of verse use rhyme as an essential part of their structure. The simplest regular patterns or "rhyme schemes" involve using rhyme at the end of every two lines of a poem (AABBCCDD etc) or by using rhyme at the end of alternating lines of a poem (ABABCDCD etc). However, there are many ways of using rhyme in more elaborate patterns. The Elizabethan poet Edmund Spenser devised a verse-form (the Spenserian stanza) that interweaves three different sounds in the pattern ABABBCBCC, and there are any number of other patterns you could adopt.

One powerful rhyming technique is to repeat the same sound at the end of three, four, or even more successive lines of verse. Another variation is to use "internal rhyme" where the same sound is repeated at the middle and end of a line.

Some types of poem employ a specific pattern of rhymes to give them their structure. One of the most popular is the **sonnet**, a favourite of Shakespeare, which always has fourteen lines and follows a regular rhyme scheme (either ABBAABBA CDCDCD or ABABCDCD EFEFGG).

Another common verse form is the **limerick**. The limerick uses the pattern AABBA with the third and fourth lines being shorter than the others. The reappearance of the original rhyme in the last line often has a comic effect:

> *There once was a fellow called Patrick*
> *Who had limbs that were made of elastic.*
> *He could butter some bread*
> *While still lying in bed.*
> *All his friends were astonished at that trick!*

The comic possibilities of rhyme are also exploited by the **clerihew**. This type of poem uses a sequence of two rhyming couplets, often of different lengths, and contains (usually bogus) biographical content:

> *Alexander Graham Bell,*
> *As far as anyone can tell,*
> *Wasn't wearing cologne*
> *When he invented the telephone.*

These are just a few of the ways that you can work with rhyme. However, you don't need to follow the patterns that other people have used, and it can often be more interesting to experiment with your own rhyme schemes. Enjoy your rhyming!

How to Use this Book

How the lists in the book are arranged

This book contains lists of words that rhyme. Each list is headed by a common word in bold type:

> **rabble**
> babble
> dabble
> gabble
> scrabble

The lists of rhyming words are grouped together according to the main stressed syllable in a word. There are 19 different sections in the book corresponding to the 19 different vowel sounds used in Standard English. Thus all of the words in Section 8 have the sound *-er-* as their main stressed syllable, but within that section you will find lists of words that rhyme with *herb*, *work*, *word*, and so on.

Each section is divided into numbered subsections. Each subsection contains words that have the same consonant sound after the main vowel sound. Thus Subsection 8.2 contains words with the sound *-erb-*, Subsection 8.3 contains words with the sound *-erk-*, and so on.

Each subsection may also contain lists of words that have unstressed syllables at the end of the word. Thus under the list of words in Subsection 8.8 that rhyme with *term*, you will find lists of words that rhyme with *murmur*, words that rhyme with *thermal*, words that rhyme with *German*, and so on.

Where an explanation of the meaning of a word is required, this is supplied in brackets after the word:

> tarry (= *like tar*)

Explanations are given to distinguish between easily confused words, or words that may be pronounced in different ways. For example, *tarry* only rhymes with *starry* when it means "like tar". When it means "to dawdle" it rhymes with *carry*.

Explanations are also given to show the full form of abbreviations:

> VCR (= *video cassette recorder*)

How to find a rhyme for a word

Look up the word in the index at the back of the book. The index lists every rhyming word in alphabetical order and tells you where in the book you can find it. For example, if you look up the word *jammy* you will be told to look in Subsection 1.7.

Now go to the part of the book indicated by the index, using the subsection numbers at the top of each page to help you. You will find a list of words that rhyme with your word. The list may include not only common words, but also names of famous people and places, abbreviations, and common idioms or figures of speech, all of which may suggest a way of completing the rhyme. For example, you will find nine possible rhymes listed for *jammy*: *chamois, clammy, double whammy, gammy, hammy, mammy, Miami, Sammy* and *Tammy*.

The subsection may also contain lists of other words that have the same main stressed syllable, but a slightly different ending. Some of these lists may give near-rhymes for your word. For example, words in Subsection 1.7 that rhyme with *gammon* form near-rhymes with words that rhyme with *famine*.

In some lists you will see rhymes are made using words like *it* (e.g. *catch it* under *hatchet* in 1.13), *her* (e.g. *forsake her* under *baker* in 3.3) and *us* (e.g. *enrage us* under *courageous* in 3.4), and you can make many more rhymes like this.

Sometimes a note is added at the end of a list to give you a hint about how to add to the range of rhymes. Some of these notes indicate words in another list which some people pronounce in a way that will also form a rhyme (e.g. the note after the list of rhymes for *back* in Subsection 1.2 refers to words like *Iraq* in Subsection 2.3). You will have to test these words in your own accent to see if they work as rhymes for you!

You can also browse around the other lists in the section. These will not offer exact rhymes, but you may get some ideas for near-rhymes that will serve your purpose. For example, words in Section 8 that rhyme with *work* may form near-rhymes with words that rhyme with *shirt*.

'a'

cat, badger, Japan

All the words in this section use the sound 'a' in their main stressed syllable

1.1

cab
blab
crab
dab
drab
fab
flab
gab
gift of the gab
grab
hackney cab
jab
kebab
lab
minicab
nab
pick up the tab
scab
Skylab
slab
stab
tab

blabber
Abba
jabber

rabble
babble
dabble
gabble
Margaret Drabble
scrabble

collaborate
elaborate (= to explain)

shabby
abbey
Abby
cabby
crabby
flabby
Gab(b)y
scabby
tabby

rabid
crabbed

habit
blab it
cohabit
dab it
grab it
inhabit
jab it
nab it
rabbit
stab it

vocabulary
constabulary

1.2

back
aback
almanac
anorak
aphrodisiac
attack
back-to-back
bivouac
black
blow your stack
bric-à-brac
Cadillac
cardiac
Cilla Black
counterattack
crack
cul-de-sac
flak
get your own back
hack
haemophiliac
hard nut to crack
haversack
heart attack
hit the sack
hypochondriac
insomniac
in the black
Jack
jack
Jack Kerouac
Jacques Chirac
knack
lack
laid-back
lumberjack
mac
Mach

pack
paperback
piggyback
quack
quarterback
rack
sac
sack
Sassenach
shack
slack
smack
snack
stack
steeplejack
stickleback
tack
track
unpack
water off a duck's back
whack
WRAC (= *Women's Royal Army Corps*)
yack (= *to talk*)
yak (= *a Tibetan ox*)
Za(c)k
zodiac

Many English speakers pronounce some words in section **2.3** (eg *Iraq*) in such a way that they rhyme with these words

backer
alpaca
attacker
attack her
back her
backpacker
blacker
counterattacker
cracker

Dakar
Dhaka
firecracker
hacker
knacker
lacquer
Michael Schumacher
packer
sacker
sack her
slacker
smacker
smack her
snacker
tracker
track her
whacker
whack her

tackle
cackle
crackle
cut the cackle
jackal
ramshackle
rugby-tackle
shackle
tabernacle

blacken
bracken
slacken

crackers
alpacas
attackers
backers
backpackers
Caracas
counterattackers
firecrackers
hackers
maracas
nutcrackers
slackers

smackers
trackers

tackier
Czechoslovakia
Slovakia
wackier

tacky
baccy
Jackie
lackey
wacky

backing
attacking
counterattacking
cracking
get cracking
hacking
lacking
nerve-(w)racking
packing
piggybacking
quacking
sacking
slacking
smacking
snacking
stacking
tacking
tracking
unpacking
whacking

jacket
attack it
bracket
cost a packet
crack it
packet
racket
smack it
stack it
track it
unpack it

acne
Hackney

hackneyed
arachnid

slackness
blackness

jackpot
crackpot

tax
almanacs
anoraks
aphrodisiacs
attacks
axe
battleaxe
bivouacs
blacks
Cadillacs
counterattacks
cracks
cul-de-sacs
fax
Filofax®
flax
hacks
haemophiliacs
Halifax
haversacks
heart attacks
hypochondriacs
insomniacs
jacks
lax
Mad Max
Max
max
lumberjacks
packs
pax
paperbacks
piggybacks
quacks

quarterbacks
racks
relax
sacs
sacks
Sassenachs
sax
sealing wax
shacks
slacks
smacks
snacks
stacks
steeplejacks
sticklebacks
tacks
tracks
wax
whacks

waxen
Anglo-Saxon
flaxen
Jackson
Jesse Jackson
klaxon
Michael Jackson
Saxon

axis
praxis (= *the practice
of a profession*)

taxing
axeing
faxing
relaxing
waxing

waxed
axed
faxed
overtaxed
relaxed
waxed

action
abstraction
attraction
contraction
delayed-action
dissatisfaction
distraction
extraction
faction
Fatal Attraction
fraction
inaction
interaction
reaction
satisfaction
subtraction
traction
transaction

act
abstract
artefact
attacked
attract
blacked
cataract
compact
contract (= *to become
smaller*)
counteract
cracked
detract
distract
enact
exact
extract
fact
hacked
impact
inexact
intact
interact
jacked
jam-packed
matter-of-fact

overact
overreact
packed
pact
quacked
racked
react
re-enact
refract
retract
sacked
smacked
snacked
stacked
subcontract
subtract
tacked
tact
tracked
tract
unpacked
vacuum-packed
whacked

actor
attract her
benefactor
contractor
detractor
distract her
extract her
factor
malefactor
protractor
reactor
subcontractor
tractor
windchill factor

tractable
intractable
refractable
retractable

factory
olfactory
refractory
satisfactory
unsatisfactory

tactic
climactic
didactic
galactic
prophylactic

practical
impractical
tactical

distracted
abstracted
attracted
compacted
contracted
counteracted
detracted
distracted
enacted
exacted
extracted
impacted
interacted
overacted
overreacted
protracted
reacted
re-enacted
refracted
retracted
subcontracted
subtracted

acting
abstracting
attracting
compacting
contracting (=
  becoming smaller)
counteracting

detracting
distracting
enacting
exacting
extracting
impacting
interacting
overacting
overreacting
play-acting
reacting
re-enacting
refracting
retracting
subcontracting
subtracting

active
attractive
hyperactive
inactive
interactive
overactive
proactive
radioactive
retroactive
unattractive
underactive

actress
benefactress

fracture
manufacture

actual
contractual
factual

spectacular
Dracula
vernacular

1.3

bad
ad

add
Baghdad
barking mad
bit of a lad
Brad
cad
Chad
clad
dad
fad
gad
glad
had
hopping mad
jihad
lad
Leningrad
like mad
mad
pad
plaid
rad
Riyadh
SAD (= seasonal affective disorder)
sad
Stalingrad
tad
Trinidad
Volgograd

ladder
adder
add her
bladder
gladder
lowest rung of the ladder
madder
sadder
stepladder
top rung of the ladder

haddock
Fanny Cradock

paddock
shaddock

saddle
addle
paddle
side-saddle
straddle
unsaddle

madam
Adam
add 'em
had 'em
pad 'em

sadden
Aladdin
gladden
madden

daddy
baddie
caddie (= a golfer's assistant)
caddy (= a container for tea)
grandaddy
laddie
Paddy
paddy

nomadic
sporadic

radish
laddish
saddish

shadow
foreshadow
overshadow
saddo

badly
Bradley
gladly
madly

sadly

madman
ad-man
Bradman

badness
gladness
madness
midsummer madness
sadness

badge
cadge
hadj
Madge

magic
tragic

magically
tragically

agile
fragile

1.4

naff
blow the gaff
caff
carafe
decaf(f)
faff
gaff (= a fishing pole)
gaffe (= a blunder)
WAAF (= Women's Auxiliary Air Force)

➕

You can also make rhymes for these words by using words in section **1.15** that rhyme with *homeopath*

➡

Many English speakers pronounce some words in section

2.5 (eg laugh) in such a way that they rhyme with these words

gaffer
Jaffa
Staffa

baffle
raffle
snaffle

café
cybercafé
daffy

Mafia
daffier
raffia

graphic
demographic
geographic
photographic
pornographic
telegraphic
traffic
typographic

You can also make rhymes for these words by using words in section **1.15** that rhyme with *telepathic*

---

geographical
autobiographical
biographical
typographical

graphics
affix

BAFTA
NAFTA (= *North American Free Trade Agreement*)

→

Many English speakers pronounce some words in section **2.5** (eg *laughter*) in such a way that they rhyme with these words

---

1.5

bag
brag
crag
drag
fag
flag
gag
hag
Jag
jag
Jiffy® bag
lag
lose your rag
mag
nag
rag
saddlebag
sag
scallywag
slag
snag
stag
swag
tag
wag

dagger
bragger
dragger
cloak-and-dagger
drag her
gag her
jag her
nag her
ragga
slag her

---

snag her
stagger
swagger
tagger
tag her

haggard
laggard
staggered
swaggered

gaggle
haggle
straggle
waggle

dragon
fall off the wag(g)on
flagon
on the wag(g)on
pendragon
wag(g)on

diagonal
hexagonal
octagonal

antagonist
protagonist

maggot
braggart
faggot

baggy
craggy
jaggy
Maggie
saggy
scraggy
shaggy

ragged
jagged

nagging
bragging
dragging

flagging
jagging
lagging
nagging
ragging
sagging
slagging
snagging
tagging
unflagging

Magnus
Agnes

jaguar
Nicaragua

1.6

pal
Al
alimentary canal
cabal
Cal
canal
Chantal
corral
et al
gal
Hal
Sal
shall
Suez Canal
Val

Many English speakers pronounce some words in section **2.8** (eg *morale*) in such a way that they rhyme with these words

ballet
Calais
chalet
valet

valour
Allah
Valhalla

salad
ballad

analogy
allergy
genealogy
metallurgy

gallon
Al(l)an
talon
Woody Allen

balance
imbalance
overbalance
valance

balanced
unbalanced
valanced
well-balanced

talent
gallant

gallery
calorie
high-calorie
low-calorie
salary
Valerie

callous
callus
Dallas
Maria Callas
palace
Wynton Marsalis

galleon
Italian

rally
alley
Ally
dally
dilly-dally
galley
pally
Sally
sally
tally
valley

Many English speakers pronounce some words in section **2.8** (eg *finale*) in such a way that they rhyme with these words

metallic
Alec
Gallic
italic

valid
dallied
dilly-dallied
invalid (= *not valid*)
pallid
rallied
sallied
tallied

malice
Alice
aurora borealis
chalice
poisoned chalice

analysis
dialysis
paralysis
psychoanalysis

mallet
ballot
palate (= *the roof of the mouth*)
palette (= *a tray for mixing paint*)
pallet (= *a mattress*)

reality
abnormality
banality
brutality
confidentiality
eventuality
fatality
formality
generality
geniality
hospitality
illegality
immorality
immortality
impartiality
impracticality
individuality
informality
legality
locality
mentality
morality
mortality
municipality
nationality
neutrality
normality
originality
partiality
personality
plurality
practicality
principality
punctuality
sensuality
sentimentality

sexuality
speciality
spirituality
superficiality
technicality
totality
unpunctuality
vitality

shallow
callow
fallow
hallow
mallow
marshmallow
sallow
tallow

Alf
Ralph

Alma
halma
Palma

alto
contralto

valve
salve

stallion
battalion
galleon
medallion

1.7

jam
Abraham
ad nauseam
aerogram(me)
am
Amsterdam
anagram
battering ram
cam

centigram(me)
clam
cram
dam
damn
diagram
diaphragm
dram
electrocardiogram
epigram
exam
gram(me)
ham
histogram
hologram
Hoover Dam
jamb
Jean-Claude Van Damme
kilogram(me)
kissogram
lamb
marjoram
milligram(me)
money for jam
monogram
not give a damn
Omar Khayyám
Pam
parallelogram
pram
pro-am
RAM (= *random access memory*)
ram
Rotterdam
Sam
scam
scram
sham
slam
spam
Surinam
swam

'a'

Tam
telegram
tram
Vietnam
Wham!
wham
yam

hammer
Alabama
clamour
crammer
enamour
Franz Klammer
gamma
glamour
grammar
rammer
scammer
slammer
spammer
stammer
the slammer
yammer

flammable
inflammable
nonflammable
programmable

enamoured
clamoured
hammered
Muhammad
stammered
yammered

camel
enamel
mammal
Tamil

gammon
backgammon
salmon
with jam on

glamorous
amorous
clamorous

defamatory
amatory
declamatory
exclamatory

jammy
chamois
clammy
double whammy
gammy
hammy
mammy
Miami
Sammy
Tammy

dynamic
aerodynamic
ceramic
Islamic
panoramic

dynamics
aerodynamics
ceramics
thermodynamics

family
extended family
hammily
jammily
one-parent family

famine
cross-examine
examine
re-examine

contaminate
decontaminate
laminate

stamina
cross examine her
examiner
examine her
re-examine her

jamming
clamming
damming
damning
hamming
lambing
ramming
scamming
scramming
shamming
spamming

diameter
ammeter
parameter
pentameter

amber
Amber
clamber
samba

gamble
amble
bramble
gambol
preamble
ramble
scramble
shamble
unscramble

Zambia
Gambia

Bambi
namby-pamby

gambler
rambler

scrambler
unscrambler

gambling
rambling
scrambling
unscrambling

lamp
amp
camp
champ
clamp
cramp
damp
ramp
revamp
rising damp
rubber-stamp
scamp
stamp
Terence Stamp
tramp
vamp

hamper
camper
clamper
clamp her
cramp her
damper
pamper
revamper
revamp her
rubber-stamper
scamper
stamper
stamp her
Tampa
tamper
tramper

ample
trample

Many English speakers pronounce some words in section **2.9** (eg *sample*) in such a way that they rhyme with these words

champion
campion
Grampian

tampon
camp on
clamp on
crampon
stamp on
tramp on

1.8

man
Aberfan
also-ran
an
anchorman
angry young man
Ann(e)
artisan
ASEAN (= *Association of Southeast Asian Nations*)
ban
began
billy-can
bipartisan
bogeyman
bran
businessman
Caliban
cameraman
can
Cannes
caravan
carry the can
Catalan
catamaran

clan
Dan
Dian(n)e
divan
extractor fan
fan
flan
flash in the pan
frying pan
gran
handyman
Has(s)an
hosepipe ban
in the can
Isle of Man
Jan
Japan
jerrican
Joanne
Kirg(h)izstan
Kurdistan
ladies' man
Leanne
man-to-man
Marianne
marzipan
middleman
Milan
muscleman
Nan
newspaperman
non-partisan
Oman
open-plan
Oran
outran
overran
pan
Parmesan
partisan
Peter Pan
plan
Princess Anne
ran

reran
Roseanne
Roxan(n)e
scan
sedan
self-made man
signalman
snowman
span
spick-and-span
Stan
Sudan
superman
tan
than
trimaran
van
weatherman
Yerevan
yuan

Many English speakers pronounce some words in section **2.10** (eg *Iran*) in such a way that they rhyme with these words

manner
Anna
bandan(n)a
ban her
banner
Deanna
Diana
fan her
Fermanagh
Hannah
Havana
Indiana
Joanna
Louisiana
manor
Montana
outran her

planner
Pollyanna
Savannah
savanna(h)
scanner
spanner
Susanna(h)
tanner

Many English speakers pronounce some words in section **2.10** (eg *Guyana*) in such a way that they rhyme with these words

channel
cross-Channel
flannel
panel

panelling
channelling

panellist
analyst
psychoanalyst

cannon
canon
Rhiannon
Shannon

cannery
granary
tannery

Britannia
cannier
pannier
Tanya

nanny
Afghani
Annie
canny
cranny
Danny

Fanny
granny
Omani
trannie
uncanny

panic
Germanic
Hispanic
inorganic
Koranic
manic
mechanic
messianic
oceanic
organic
satanic
Titanic
titanic
volcanic

mechanical
botanical
puritanical
tyrannical

unanimous
magnanimous

planning
banning
Bernard Manning
canning
caravanning
fanning
overmanning
planning
spanning
tanning
undermanning

ban(n)ister
canister

vanish
banish
Spanish

planet
gannet
ban it
began it
can it
fan it
granite
Janet
outran it
overran it
pan it
plan it
pomegranate
ran it
reran it
scan it
span it
tan it

sanitary
interplanetary
planetary

vanity
Christianity
humanity
inanity
inhumanity
insanity
profanity
sanity
urbanity

bank
Anne Frank
blank
Blankety Blank
clank
crank
dank
drank
flank
franc
Frank
frank

Girobank
Hank
J Arthur Rank
lank
outflank
plank
point-blank
prank
rank
sank
shank
shrank
spank
stank
swank
tank
thank
Yank
yank

banker
anchor
Bianca
blank her
canker
Casablanca
flanker
franker
hanker
lanker
lingua franca
rancour
ranker
Ravi Shankar
sank her
shanker
spanker
spank her
Sri Lanka
supertanker
tanker
thank her
yanker

ankle
rankle

lanky
cranky
Frankie
hanky
hanky-panky
Jimmy Krankie
manky
swanky
Yankee

spanking
blanking
clanking
flanking
franking
outflanking
planking
ranking
spanking
tanking
telebanking

frankly
Bill Shankly
blankly
dankly
lankly
rankly

hand
ampersand
and
band
banned
bland
borderland
brand
canned
band
caravaned
cash in hand
close at hand
contraband

crash-land
disband
Euroland
expand
fanned
fat of the land
Ferdinand
gland
grand
hand-to-hand
hinterland
inland
land
lend a hand
lie of the land
Maryland
misunderstand
motherland
near at hand
Newfoundland
no man's land
offhand
one-night stand
overland
panned
pituitary gland
planned
rand
Rio Grande
sand
scanned
second-hand
sleight of hand
spanned
stagehand
stand
strand
Swaziland
Switzerland
tanned
underhand
understand
unmanned
unplanned

vanned
withstand
Wonderland

Many English speakers pronounce some words in section **2.10** (eg *command*) in such a way that they rhyme with these words

panda
Amanda
backhander
blander
brander
brand her
bystander
candour
coriander
dander
disbander
expander
expand her
gander
grander
Icelander
lander
land her
Laplander
left-hander
meander
memoranda
Miranda
misunderstand her
oleander
overlander
pander
philander
propaganda
right-hander
Rwanda
salamander
stander
stand her

strand her
tanned her
Uganda
understand her
veranda(h)
withstand her

Many English speakers pronounce some words in section **2.10** (eg *slander*) in such a way that they rhyme with these words

standard
meandered
pandered
substandard

handle
candle
dandle
Derek Randall
fly off the handle
Handel
mishandle
sandal
scandal
vandal

vandalize
scandalize

random
brand 'em
disband 'em
expand 'em
land 'em
memorandum
misunderstand 'em
stand 'em
strand 'em
tandem
tanned 'em
understand 'em
withstand 'em

abandon
Rwandan
Ugandan

handy
Andy
bandy
brandy
Candy
candy
dandy
Indira Gandhi
Mahatma Gandhi
Mandy
Randy
Sandy
sandy
shandy

landed
backhanded
banded
branded
cack-handed
candid
candied
crash-landed
disbanded
empty-handed
even-handed
expanded
heavy-handed
high-handed
landed
left-handed
red-handed
right-handed
stranded
underhanded

candidly
single-handedly

landing
banding
branding

crash-landing
disbanding
expanding
landing
long-standing
misunderstanding
notwithstanding
outstanding
overlanding
standing
stranding
understanding
upstanding

brandish
outlandish

handbag
sandbag

grandly
blandly

Sandra
Cassandra

Andrea
Alexandria

handstand
bandstand
grandstand

hang
bang
boomerang
clang
fang
gang
go with a bang
harangue
meringue
orang-outan(g)
overhang
pang
rang
sang
slang

sprang
tang
twang

anger
banger
Bangor
clanger
cliffhanger
hangar
hanger
harangue her
languor
rang her
sprang her

angle
bangle
dangle
disentangle
entangle
jangle
mangle
quadrangle
rectangle
spangle
strangle
tangle
untangle
wangle
wide-angle
wrangle

tangled
dangled
disentangled
entangled
jangled
mangled
newfangled
spangled
strangled
tangled
untangled
wangled

mango
quango
tango

angling
dangling
gangling
jangling
wrangling

anguish
languish

angular
rectangular
triangular

manhandle
panhandle

manly
Stanley
unmanly

expanse
askance
finance
manse
Penzance
romance

Many English speakers pronounce some words in section **2.10** (eg *dance*) in such a way that they rhyme with these words

cancer
Cancer
necromancer
romancer

Many English speakers pronounce some words in section **2.10** (eg *answer*) in such a way that they rhyme with these words

ransom
handsome
king's ransom
transom

fancy
chancy
Clancy
flights of fancy
Nancy
nancy
necromancy
trancey

financial
circumstantial
insubstantial
substantial

financially
substantially

mansion
expansion

pant
ant
cant
commandant
decant
extant
gallivant
rant
recant
scant
sycophant

Many English speakers pronounce some words in section **2.10** (eg *plant*) in such a way that they rhyme with these words

banter
Atlanta
canter

decanter
gallivanter
manta
ranter
recanter
Santa
scanter
Tam o' Shanter

phantom
bantam

scanty
Alicante
ante
anti
Dante
dilettante
shanty
vigilante

Many English speakers pronounce some words in section **2.10** (eg *auntie*) in such a way that they rhyme with these words

frantic
Atlantic
gigantic
pedantic
romantic
semantic
sycophantic
transatlantic
unromantic

antics
semantics

elephantine
Byzantine

tantrum
Antrim

'a'

pantry
gantry

pants
ants
commandants
flying by the seat of
  one's pants
Hants
Northants
rants
smarty-pants
sycophants
underpants

panther
Samantha

philanthropist
misanthropist

spaniel
Daniel
Nathaniel

canyon
companion

annual
manual
Victor Emmanuel

annually
manually

bonanza
extravaganza
Mario Lanza
panzer
stanza

stanzas
extravaganzas
Kansas
panzers
stanzas

1.9

cap
bap
booby-trap
chap
clap
feather in one's cap
flap
gap
handicap
lap
Lapp
map
nap
overlap
pap
put on one's thinking
  cap
rap
sap
scrap
slap
snap
strap
take the rap
tap
thunderclap
trap
unwrap
wrap
yap
zap

rapper
Ayia Napa
clapper
dapper
flapper
handicap her
handicapper
mapper
napper
rapper
sapper

scrap her
scrapper
slap her
slapper
snapper
strap her
strapper
tap her
tapper
trap her
trapper
whippersnapper
wrap her
wrapper
zap her
zapper

apple
chapel
dapple
grapple

happy
chappie
flappy
gappy
happy-clappy
make it snappy
nappy
sappy
scrappy
snappy
unhappy
zappy

rapid
vapid

happily
sappily
scrappily
snappily
unhappily

happiness
sappiness

snappiness
unhappiness

wrapping
clapping
booby-trapping
flapping
handicapping
lapping
mapping
napping
overlapping
rapping
sapping
scrapping
slapping
snapping
strapping
tapping
trapping
unwrapping
wrapping
yapping
zapping

strapless
hapless

shrapnel
grapnel

lapse
collapse
elapse
perhaps
relapse

You can add to this list by
adding *-s* to some words that
rhyme with *cap*, as in *snaps*

caption
contraption

apt
adapt

chapped
handicapped
inapt
rapt
unwrapped

You can add to this list by
adding *-ped* to some words that
rhyme with *cap*, as in *trapped*

chapter
adapter
captor
raptor

capture
enrapture
rapture
recapture

1.10

Barra
Far(r)ah

Arab
carob

parable
arable

paragon
tarragon

barrel
apparel
carol
Carol(e)
Darryl
Lewis Carroll

Carolyn
Marilyn

Harold
barrelled
double-barrelled

carolled

barren
Arran
baron
Darren
Karen
Sharon

apparent
transparent

embarrass
harass

embarrassed
harassed

carrot
carat
claret
garret
parrot

narrative
comparative

barrier
carrier
carry her
farrier
harrier
harry her
marry her
miscarry her
parry her
remarry her

Marion
carrion

chariot
Harriet

carry
Barry
Carrie
Gar(r)y
Harry

harry
intermarry
J M Barrie
Kalahari
Larry
marry
miscarry
parry
remarry
tarry (= *to dawdle*)

barbaric
Balearic
Tariq

married
arid
carried
harried
parried
tarried
unmarried

marriage
carriage
disparage
garage
hackney carriage
miscarriage
shotgun marriage
undercarriage

Harris
An American in Paris
Bomber Harris
Paris
Rolf Harris

garrison
comparison

charity
barbarity
Charity
clarity
disparity
dissimilarity

familiarity
hilarity
irregularity
parity
peculiarity
polarity
popularity
regularity
similarity
solidarity
subsidiarity
unpopularity
vulgarity

arrow
barrow
harrow
Hercule Poirot
Jarrow
marrow
Mia Farrow
narrow
sparrow
tarot
wheelbarrow

1.11

ass
alas
amass
bass (= *a fish*)
Calor Gas®
crass
en masse
gas
jackass
lass
mass
morass

Many English speakers pronounce some words in section **2.13** (eg *class*) in such a way that they rhyme with these words

Nasser
Mombasa
NASA (= *National Aeronautics and Space Administration*)

hassle
tassel

Vaseline
gasoline

gassy
Cassie
chassis
Haile Selassie
Tallahassee

Many English speakers pronounce some words in section **2.13** (eg *classy*) in such a way that they rhyme with these words

classic
boracic
Jurassic
thoracic
Triassic

acid
flaccid
placid

classify
declassify
pacify

assassinate
fascinate

asset
basset
facet
tacit

acetate
incapacitate

capacity
audacity
incapacity
overcapacity
sagacity
tenacity
veracity
vivacity

massive
impassive
passive

massively
impassively
passively

Picasso
Burkina-Faso
El Paso

Alaska
ask her
Madagascar
mask her
Nebraska
task her
unmask her

gasket
blow a gasket
mascot

Many English speakers
pronounce some words in
section **2.13** (eg *basket*) in such
a way that they rhyme with
these words

lambast
amassed
enthusiast
gassed
massed

Many English speakers
pronounce some words in
section **2.13** (eg *last*) in such a
way that they rhyme with these
words

pasta
alabaster
aster

Many English speakers
pronounce some words in
section **2.13** (eg *master*) in such
a way that they rhyme with
these words

pasty
osteoplasty
rhinoplasty

Many English speakers
pronounce some words in
section **2.13** (eg *nasty*) in such a
way that they rhyme with these
words

plastic
bombastic
drastic
dynastic
ecclesiastic
elastic
enthusiastic
fantastic
gymnastic
iconoclastic
monastic
overenthusiastic
sarcastic
scholastic
spastic
unenthusiastic

sarcastically
drastically
enthusiastically
fantastically

1.12

smash
ash
balderdash
bash
brash
cache
cash
clash
crash
cut a dash
dash
flash
gash
gnash
hard cash
hash
have a bash
Johnny Cash
lash
mash
moustache
panache
pebbledash
quick as a flash
rash
rehash
sash
slapdash
slash
splash
stash
thrash
trash
Wall Street Crash

sachet
papier-mâché

rasher
basher
bash her
brasher
crasher
crash her
dasher
dash her
flasher
flash her
Gnasher
gnasher
gnash her
lasher
lash her
masher
mash her
Natasha
rasher
rehasher
slasher
slash her
smasher
smash her
splasher
splash her
stasher
thrasher
thrash her
trash her

passion
ashen
compassion
fashion
parrot-fashion
ration

fashionable
rationable
unfashionable

national
international
irrational

multinational
rational
supranational

rationally
internationally
irrationally
nationally

nationalist
rationalist

nationalism
rationalism

nationalize
denationalize
rationalize

passionate
compassionate
dispassionate

old-fashioned
fashioned
impassioned
rationed

flashy
ashy
trashy

smashing
bashing
cashing
clashing
crashing
dashing
flashing
gnashing
hashing
lashing
mashing
pebbledashing
rehashing
slashing
splashing
stashing

thrashing
trashing

flashback
cashback

rashly
Ashley

smashed
abashed
bashed
cashed
clashed
crashed
dashed
flashed
gashed
gnashed
hashed
lashed
mashed
pebbledashed
rehashed
slashed
splashed
stashed
thrashed
trashed
unabashed

1.13

cat
acrobat
Anwar Sadat
aristocrat
at
autocrat
automat
bat
brat
bureaucrat
chat
Cheshire cat
copycat

cravat
Democrat
democrat
diplomat
drat
drowned rat
expat
fat
fat cat
flat
GATT (= General
    Agreement on Tariffs
    and Trade)
gnat
Gujarat
habitat
hat
just like that
mat
Matt
matt
Montserrat
Mount Ararat
Nat
Pat
pat
Photostat®
pit-a-pat
plait
Postman Pat
prat
Rabat
rat
rat-a-tat
resat
sat
scat
slat
spat
sprat
Take That
tat
that
thermostat

tit-for-tat
VAT
vat

pâté
latte
satay

matter
bat her
batter
bespatter
chat her
chatter
clatter
drat her
fatter
flatter
Jomo Kenyatta
latter
mad as a hatter
Mad Hatter
natter
pat her
patter
platter
Qatar
regatta
ratter
resat her
sat her
scatter
shatter
spat her
spatter
splatter
tatter

battered
bespattered
chattered
clattered
flattered
mattered
nattered

pattered
scattered
shattered
spattered
splattered
tattered

battle
cattle
chattel
embattle
half the battle
prattle
rattle
Seattle
tattle
tittle-tattle

latterly
Natalie
philately

atom
at 'em
bat 'em
chat 'em
drat 'em
EURATOM (=
    European Atomic
    Energy Community)
pat 'em
rat 'em
resat 'em
sat 'em
spat 'em

flatten
baton
batten
fatten
General Patton
Lord Mountbatten
Manhattan
pattern
Staten

battery
cattery
flattery
Qatari

flattering
battering
bespattering
chattering
clattering
earth-shattering
mattering
nattering
pattering
scattering
shattering
smattering
spattering
splattering
tattering
unflattering

chatty
batty
Bugatti
catty
Cincinnati
fatty
Hattie
Maserati
natty
Patty
ratty
scatty
tatty

static
acrobatic
Adriatic
aquatic
aristocratic
aromatic
Asiatic
asthmatic
attic

autocratic
automatic
axiomatic
bureaucratic
charismatic
climatic
democratic
diplomatic
dogmatic
dramatic
ecstatic
emphatic
enigmatic
erratic
fanatic
idiomatic
idiosyncratic
lymphatic
melodramatic
operatic
phlegmatic
pneumatic
pragmatic
problematic
psychosomatic
rheumatic
schematic
semiautomatic
symptomatic
systematic
thematic
traumatic
undemocratic
undiplomatic
unemphatic
unsystematic

fanatical
grammatical
mathematical
problematical
sabbatical

dramatically
automatically

democratically
emphatically
grammatically

mathematics
acrobatics
aromatics
attics
automatics
fanatics
melodramatics
pragmatics
rheumatics
semiautomatics

gratify
ratify

satin
Latin
sat in
spat in

gratitude
attitude
ingratitude
latitude
platitude

plateau
château
gâteau

plateaux
châteaux
gâteaux

catfish
flatfish

atlas
hatless

flatly
Clement Attlee

psychiatric
geriatric
hat trick

paediatric
Patrick

geriatrics
paediatrics

matrimony
patrimony

catch
attach
batch
detach
dispatch
hatch
latch
man of the match
match
meet one's match
patch
purple patch
scratch
slanging match
snatch
thatch

oystercatcher
attach her
catcher
catch her
detach her
dispatcher
dispatch her
hatcher
hatch her
matcher
match her
patcher
patch her
scratcher
scratch her
snatcher
snatch her
thatcher
Margaret Thatcher

catchy
patchy
scratchy

matching
attaching
batching
catching
detaching
dispatching
eye-catching
hatching
latching
matching
patching
scratching
snatching
thatching

hatchet
attach it
batch it
Bob Cratchit
catch it
detach it
dispatch it
hatch it
latch it
match it
patch it
ratchet
scratch it
snatch it
thatch it

attachment
catchment
detachment

detached
attached
batched
dispatched
hatched
latched
matched

patched
scratched
semidetached
snatched
thatched
unattached

1.14

gather
blather
lather

1.15

homeopath
Kath
osteopath
psychopath

You can also make rhymes for
these words by using words in
section **1.4** that rhyme with **naff**

Many English speakers
pronounce some words in
section **2.18** (eg *path*) in such a
way that they rhyme with these
words

telepathic
homeopathic
osteopathic
psychopathic
telepathic

You can also make rhymes for
these words by using words in
section **1.4** that rhyme with
graphic

1.16

cadaver
slaver

➜

Many English speakers pronounce some words in section **2.19** (eg *palaver*) in such a way that they rhyme with these words

travel
gavel
gravel
unravel

traveller
unraveller

travelling
unravelling

cavern
Cavan
Gavin

tavern

ravenous
cavernous

savage
ravage

lavish
ravish

gravity
cavity
depravity

1.17

jazz
as
Gaz
has

La Paz
razzmatazz
whereas

dazzle
Basil
basil
frazzle
razzle dazzle

chasm
enthusiasm
spasm

jazzy
snazzy

jasmine
Jasmine
Yasmin

'ar'

cart, barber, alarm

All the words in this section use the sound '**ar**' in their main stressed syllable

---

2.1

car
abattoir
Accra
afar
ajar
APR (= *annual percentage rate*)
are
Armagh
armoured car
au revoir
baa
bah
bar
bazaar
below par
bizarre
Bogotá
bra
budgerigar
catarrh
caviar(e)
char
cigar
czar
Daily Star
debar
ER
Eurostar®
fa(h)
far

GDR (= *German Democratic Republic*)
guitar
hurrah
hussar
isobar
jar
Jimmy Carr
Kandahar
la(h)
Loire
ma
mar
Mark Lamarr
MLR (= *minimum lending rate*)
motorcar
Myanmar
OCR (= *optical character reader*)
Omaha
OR (= *operating room*)
pa
papa
par
PR (= *public relations*)
R
R & R (= *rest and recreation*)
registrar
repertoire
reservoir
scar

seminar
shah
Shangri-La
SLR (= *single-lens reflex*)
spa
spar
star
Stranraer
superstar
ta
tar
ta-ta
tsar
um and aah
UNHCR (= *UN High Commissioner for Refugees*)
USSR
VCR (= *video cassette recorder*)
VTR (= *video tape recorder*)
Zanzibar

cacao
Bilbao

2.2

garb
barb

barber
harbour
macabre

Pearl Harbor

marble
garble
Kabul

garbled
marbled

Barbie
Abu Dhabi
Derby
derby
Robert Mugabe

Barbara
candelabra
Santa Barbara

2.3

mark
arc
ark
Bach
bark
black mark
clerk
Cutty Sark
dark
disembark
double-park
embark
hark
in the dark
Iraq
Joan of Arc
Jurassic Park
lark
leap in the dark
macaque
Mark
Mansfield Park
miss the mark
narc
nark

park
plaque
quark
remark
Sark
shark
spark
stark
trademark
watermark

marker
barker
bookmarker
Charlie Parker
darker
disembarker
embarker
harker
larker
Lusaka
markka
narker
nosy parker
Osaka
parka
remarker
sparker
starker

sparkle
debacle
matriarchal
patriarchal

carcass
double-park us
Marcus
mark us
nark us
park us
spark us

narky
hierarchy
Iraqi

khaki
matriarchy
Nagasaki
oligarchy
patriarchy
sparky

marking
arcing
barking
disembarking
double-parking
embarking
harking
larking
narking
parking
remarking
sparking
trademarking
watermarking

marked
arced
barked
disembark
double-parked
embarked
harked
larked
narked
parked
remarked
sparked
trademarked
unmarked
watermarked

2.4

card
Abelard
avant-garde
baaed
bard
barred

battle-scarred
bodyguard
bombard
boulevard
charade
charred
debarred
discard
disregard
façade
guard
hard
Hyderabad
Islamabad
jarred
lard
leotard
Marquis de Sade
marred
parred
promenade
regard
retard
rock-hard
scarred
shard
sparred
starred
tarred
yard

larder
ardour
Auchterarder
cicada
charred her
discarder
discard her
disregarder
disregard her
Douglas Bader
Granada
guard her
harder

Lada
Lake Garda
Nevada
RADA (= *Royal Academy of Dramatic Art*)
regarder
regard her
retarder
retard her
Sierra Nevada
Torquemada

garden
harden
Osama bin Laden
pardon

pardonable
hardenable
unpardonable

hardened
battle-hardened
pardoned

hardy
Bacardi®
foolhardy
Keir Hardie
Laurel and Hardy
tardy
Yardie

guarded
bombarded
discarded
disregarded
guarded
larded
promenaded
regarded
retarded
unguarded

bravado
avocado

Colorado
cruzado
incommunicado
The Mikado

cardboard
hardboard

large
barge
charge
discharge
enlarge
in charge
marge
overcharge
recharge
undercharge

enlarger
barger
barge her
charger
charge her
discharger
enlarger
larger
overcharger
overcharge her
recharger
undercharger
undercharge her
supercharger
turbo-charger

2.5

graph
autograph
barf
behalf
calf
cardiograph
cenotaph
chaff
choreograph

electrocardiograph
epitaph
giraffe
half
laugh
lithograph
monograph
paragraph
photograph
scarf
seismograph
staff
telegraph

You can also make rhymes for these words by using words in section **2.18** that rhyme with **path**

Many English speakers pronounce some words in section **1.4** (eg *carafe*) in such a way that they rhyme with these words

staffing
autographing
barfing
chaffing
choreographing
epitaphing
graphing
halfing
laughing
lithographing
monographing
overstaffing
paragraphing
photographing
scarfing
telegraphing
understaffing

craft
abaft
aft
autographed
barfed
chaffed
choreographed
daft
draft
draught
epitaphed
graphed
graft
halfed
handicraft
hovercraft
laughed
lithographed
monographed
needlecraft
overdraft
overstaffed
paragraphed
photographed
raft
redraft
scarfed
shaft
staffed
telegraphed
understaffed

after
grafter
happily ever after
hereafter
laughter
rafter
sought-after
thereafter

Many English speakers pronounce some words in section **1.4** (eg *BAFTA*) in such a way that they rhyme with these words

crafty
draughty

craftsman
draughtsman

2.6

saga
Aga®
lager

jargon
bargain

cargo
Chicago
embargo
Iago
largo
Margo(t)
Santiago

2.7

Oahu
Binyamin Netanyahu

2.8

snarl
banal
Basle
Bhopal
Caledonian Canal
canal
corral
Guadalcanal
Jamal
Kamal
Karl
locale
marl
morale
Natal
Neanderthal
Roald Dahl

'ar'

Thor Heyerdahl
Transvaal

gnarled
snarled

koala
Carla
gala
Guatemala
Kampala
Mahler
parlour

Harlem
corral 'em
slalom

Marlon
Guatemalan

Bali
barley
Bob Marley
Boutros-Boutros Ghali
Carly
Charlie
finale
Kali
Mali
Muhammad Ali
parley
Salvador Dali
Somali
Svengali

darling
corralling
marling
snarling
starling
Will Carling

scarlet
Charlotte
John Arlott

Scarlett
starlet
starlit
Will Scarlet

Harlow
Carlow
Jean Harlow
Monte Carlo
St Malo

Charles
Arles
corrals
locales
marls
Ray Charles
snarls

2.9

arm
alarm
Animal Farm
balm
calm
chance one's arm
charm
Dar es Salaam
disarm
embalm
farm
give one's right arm
grease someone's palm
Guam
harm
ma'am
palm
psalm
qualm
rearm

charmer
armer
arm her

alarmer
alarm her
armour
balmer
calmer
calm her
charmer
charm her
Dalai Lama
disarmer
disarm her
drama
embalmer
embalm her
farmer
harmer
harm her
llama
melodrama
Osama
palmer
panorama
Parma
rearmer
self-harmer
Vasco da Gama
Yokohama

barman
Carmen
Tutankhamen

pyjamas
armers
Bahamas
charmers
disarmers
dramas
embalmers
farmers
llamas
melodramas
panoramas
rearmers
self-harmers

army
balmy
barmy
macramé
origami
pastrami
salami
smarmy

charming
alarming
arming
balming
calming
charming
disarming
embalming
farming
harming
palming
Prince Charming
rearming
self-harming

armed
alarmed
balmed
becalmed
calmed
charmed
disarmed
embalmed
farmed
harmed
palmed
rearmed
unarmed
unharmed

sample
example

alms
alarms
arms

balms
Brahms
charms
disarms
embalms
farms
Glamis
harms
palms
psalms
qualms
rearms
up in arms

2.10

barn
Afghanistan
Aga Khan
Aswan
Azerbaijan
Bhutan
darn
Don Juan
elan
Genghis Khan
Imran Khan
Iran
Kazak(h)stan
Koran
Kublai Khan
Kyrgyzstan
Moshe Dayan
naan
Pakistan
Ramadan
San Juan
Sian
spin a yarn
Tadzhikistan
Taiwan
Teh(e)ran
Turkmenistan
Uzbekistan
yarn

banana
Botswana
Dana
Ghana
Guyana
gymkhana
iguana
Ivana
Juliana
Ljubljana
marijuana
nirvana
piranha
sultana
Tijuana
Tirana

blarney
Armani
Azerbaijani
Barney
Hindustani
Killarney
Pakistani
sarnie

varnish
garnish
tarnish

garnet
Alf Garnett
Barnet
incarnate

soprano
oregano

demand
command
countermand
darned
remand
reprimand

yarned

slander
Alexander
commander
command her
countermander
countermand her
remander
remand her
reprimander
reprimand her

commanding
countermanding
demanding
remanding
reprimanding
undemanding

dance
advance
Afrikaans
chance
enhance
entrance (= *to charm*)
France
glance
lance
prance
stance
trance

Many English speakers
pronounce some words in
section **1.8** (eg *askance*) in such
a way that they rhyme with
these words

dancer
answer
advancer
advance her
chancer
enhancer

enhance her
entrancer
entrance her
glancer
lancer
lance her
prancer

dancing
advancing
chancing
enhancing
entrancing
glancing
lancing
prancing

plant
aren't
aunt
can't
Cary Grant
chant
confidante
débutant(e)
enchant
Hugh Grant
grant
Immanuel Kant
implant
Robert Plant
shan't
slant
supplant
transplant

Many English speakers
pronounce some words in
section **1.8** (eg *commandant*) in
such a way that they rhyme
with these words

auntie
slanty

Many English speakers
pronounce some words in
section **1.8** (eg *Dante*) in such a
way that they rhyme with these
words

slanting
chanting
enchanting
granting
implanting
planting
slanting
supplanting
transplanting

branch
avalanche
blanch
Blanche
carte blanche
ranch

2.11

sharp
carp
harp
razor-sharp

2.12

mascara
Che Guevara
Clara
Guadalajara
Lara
Sahara
Sara
Tamara
Tara
tiara
Zara

aria
Gran Canaria
starrier

starry
Campari
Ferrari
Harare
Marie
safari
sari
tarry (= *like tar*)

scenario
impresario
Lothario
worst-case scenario

barring
baaing
charring
debarring
hurrahing
jarring
marring
scarring
sparring
starring
tarring

guitarist
tsarist

Faro
Kilimanjaro

2.13

pass
bold as brass
brass
class
farce
fibreglass
first-class
glass
grass

hourglass
Madras
middle-class
outclass
overpass
second-class
snake in the grass
sparse
stained glass
supergrass
surpass
underclass
underpass
upper-class
working-class

passable
classable
impassable
surpassable
unsurpassable

castle
parcel

parson
arson
fasten
unfasten

classy
brassy
glassy
grassy

glasses
classes
eyeglasses
farces
grasses
hourglasses
middle classes
overpasses
sunglasses
supergrasses
surpasses

underclasses
underpasses
upper classes
working classes

ask
bask
Basque
cask
flask
mask
task
unmask

basket
ask it
breadbasket
casket
mask it
unmask it

parsley
sparsely

grasp
clasp
gasp
rasp

last
aghast
Belfast
blast
blast from the past
breathe one's last
cast
caste
classed
contrast
Elastoplast®
fast
glassed
grassed
Gormenghast
half-mast
hard-and-fast

mast
miscast
nail one's colours to
  the mast
opencast
outclassed
outlast
overcast
past
repast
surpassed
too good to last
unsurpassed
vast

master
bandmaster
blaster
blast her
broadcaster
castor
contrast her
court disaster
disaster
Doncaster
faster
headmaster
housemaster
Lancaster
miscast her
newscaster
outlast her
pastor
paymaster
plaster
postmaster
quartermaster
ringmaster
schoolmaster
scoutmaster
taskmaster
vaster

plastered
mastered

nasty
contrasty

lasting
blasting
broadcasting
casting
contrasting
everlasting
fasting
long-lasting
masting
outlasting

cast-off
blast-off

ghastly
lastly
vastly

2.14

mirage
arbitrage
barrage
camouflage
corsage
entourage
espionage
fuselage
massage
sabotage

2.15

harsh
marsh

Many English speakers
pronounce some words in
section **1.12** (eg *moustache*) in
such a way that they rhyme
with these words

partial
court-martial

impartial
marshal
martial

2.16

part
apart
applecart
art
Bart
cart
change of heart
chart
counterpart
dart
depart
heart
heart-to-heart
impart
outsmart
poles apart
scart
smart
start
state-of-the-art
tart
young at heart

starter
barter
carter
charter
chart her
darter
departer
Djakarta
errata
garter
imparter
Jakarta
Jimmy Carter
La Traviata
martyr
nonstarter

outsmart her
pro rata
Renata
self-starter
smarter
sonata
Sparta
start her
stigmata
strata
Tartar
tartar

smarten
carton
hearten
kindergarten
spartan
tartan

heartening
disheartening
smartening

party
Abigail's Party
arty
chapati
hale and hearty
hearty
karate
Kiribati
multiparty
one-party
tarty

article
particle

downhearted
big-hearted
brokenhearted
carted
charted
cold-hearted
darted

departed
faint-hearted
half-hearted
hard-hearted
imparted
kind-hearted
light-hearted
lion-hearted
outsmarted
smarted
softhearted
started
stouthearted
tenderhearted
uncharted
warm-hearted
wholehearted

parting
carting
charting
darting
departing
imparting
outsmarting
smarting
starting

partly
smartly
tartly

heartless
artless

department
apartment
compartment

Sumatra
Frank Sinatra
Sartre

cartridge
partridge

march
arch
larch
March
parch
starch

archer
departure
Jeffrey Archer
marcher

starchy
Archie
Karachi

2.17

father
farther
founding father
rather

Many English speakers
pronounce some words in
section **1.14** (eg *lather*) in such a
way that they rhyme with these
words

2.18

path
aftermath
Bath
bath
hearth
lath

You can also make rhymes for
these words by using words in
section **2.5** that rhyme with
graph

Arthur
General MacArthur
Martha

2.19

carve
calve
halve
Slav
starve
suave
Yugoslav

lava
balaclava
Bratislava
cassava
Cava
guava
Java
larva

palaver

Harvey
Ravi

starving
calving
carving
halving

halves
calves
go halves
scarves

2.20

Okinawa
Peshawar

2.21

Mars
handlebars
parse
vase

You can add to this list by
adding **-s** to some words that
rhyme with *car*, as in **bars**

plaza
Gaza

Swazi
Benghazi
kamikaze

'ay'

bay, player, away

All the words in this section use the sound '**ay**' in their main stressed syllable

3.1

day

A
a (= *emphatic form of the indefinite article*)
AA
AAA (= *American Athletic Association*)
AEA (= *Atomic Energy Authority*)
affray
aka (= *also known as*)
allay
alleyway
all work and no play
anyway
array
astray
away
BA
bay
betray
blasé
BMA (= *British Medical Association*)
Bombay
Botany Bay
bouquet
bray
Cabaret
cabaret
caraway
carriageway

Cassius Clay
castaway
Chevrolet
child's play
CIA
clay
CNAA (= *Council for National Academic Awards*)
Colwyn Bay
convey
CSA (= *Child Support Agency*)
DA (= *District Attorney*)
day-to-day
decay
defray
delay
disarray
dismay
disobey
display
DNA
Dorian Gray
Doris Day
dossier
Earl Grey
émigré
Ernest Hemingway
ETA (= *estimated time of arrival*)
everyday

FA (= *Football Association*)
faraway
Fay(e)
flay
foldaway
foul play
fray
gainsay
Galloway
gay
Gay(e)
General Pinochet
getaway
giveaway
going-away
grey
halfway
hay
hey
Hogmanay
hooray
Hudson Bay
Hyacinth Bucket
IAEA (= *International Atomic Energy Agency*)
IBA (= *Independent Broadcasting Authority*)
IFA (= *independent financial adviser*)
interplay

inveigh
IPA (= *International Phonetic Alphabet*)
IRA (= *Irish Republican Army*)
J
Jacqueline du Pré
Jay
jay
K
Kay(e)
LA
Lady Jane Grey
lamé
latter-day
lay
LEA (= *Local Education Authority*)
live for the day
MA (= *Master of Arts*)
Malay
Mandalay
Man Ray
Marseilles
matinée
May
may
MBA (= *Master of Business Administration*)
Michael Faraday
midday
Milky Way
mislay
Montego Bay
Monterey
motorway
née
negligée
neigh
Nineveh
NRA (= *National Rifle Association*)
obey

OK
out-of-the-way
outstay
outweigh
overstay
PA
parquet
passageway
passé
pay
pay one's way
Peter Kay
play
portray
pray
present-day
prey
protégé
PTA
RA (= *Royal Academy*)
railway
Ray
ray
RDA (= *recommended daily allowance*)
red-letter day
relay
repay
replay
résumé
ricochet
RNA (= *ribonucleic acid*)
RSA (= *Royal Scottish Academy*)
RSPCA
runaway
St-Tropez
Santa Fe
save the day
say
SEA (= *Single European Act*)
seize the day

SFA (= *Scottish Football Association*)
slay
sleigh
spay
splay
spray
stay
Stornoway
straightaway
stray
survey
sway
TA (= *Territorial Army*)
take-home pay
tearaway
the devil to pay
they
today
tourniquet
tray
UDA (= *Ulster Defence Association*)
UK
underlay
USA
V&A (= *Victoria and Albert Museum*)
Vanessa Mae
VOA (= *Voice of America*)
waterway
way
waylay
WBA (= *World Boxing Association*)
WEA (= *Workers' Educational Association*)
weigh
whey
workaday
yea
yesterday

YMCA
YWCA

layer
betray her
bricklayer
delay her
dismay her
disobey her
Eritrea
Marbella
obey her
pay her
player
portray her
prayer
purveyor
ratepayer
repay her
slay her
soothsayer
surveyor
taxpayer

You can add to this list by adding -er to some words that rhyme with day, as in **betrayer**

payable
conveyable
decayable
defrayable
playable
portrayable
repayable
surveyable
swayable
unplayable
unsayable
weighable

betrayal
portrayal

Himalayan
Eritrean
Ghanaian
Guinean

conveyance
abeyance

archaic
Judaic
mosaic
prosaic

saying
allaying
baying
betraying
braying
decaying
defraying
delaying
dismaying
disobeying
displaying
flaying
gainsaying
greying
laying
mislaying
obeying
outstaying
outweighing
overstaying
paying
playing
portraying
praying
preying
relaying
repaying
replaying
saying
slaying
spaying
splaying

spraying
staying
straying
surveying
swaying
waylaying

laity
deity
spontaneity

payoff
lay-off
play-off

spray-on
crayon
rayon

Mayo
Galileo
Idomeneo
KO (= knockout)
mayo
Montevideo
Simon Mayo

3.2

labour
caber
neighbour
sabre
toss the caber

able
Abel
Betty Grable
cable
Clark Gable
disable
enable
fable
gable
label
Mabel
sable

38

stable
table
Tower of Babel
unable
under the table
unstable
Vince Cable

fabled
cabled
disabled
enabled
fabled
gabled
labelled
tabled

labouring
neighbouring

rabies
scabies

baby
Abie
crybaby
maybe

3.3

make
ache
awake
bake
bellyache
brake
break
cake
drake
fake
flake
for goodness' sake
for heaven's sake
for Pete's sake
forsake
Francis Drake

give-and-take
hake
Jake
lake
mistake
on the make
opaque
overtake
partake
quake
rake
rattlesnake
remake
retake
sake
shake
sheik(h)
Sir Francis Drake
slake
snake
stake
steak
Swan Lake
take
undertake
wake

baker
acre
awake her
bellyacher
bookmaker
breaker
break her
cabinet-maker
caretaker
clockmaker
dressmaker
faker
forsake her
holidaymaker
housebreaker
icebreaker
Jamaica

lawmaker
maker
matchmaker
meet one's maker
mistake her
moneymaker
overtake her
pacemaker
partaker
quaker
Quaker
raker
remaker
remake her
retaker
shaker
shake her
shirtmaker
shoemaker
slaker
strikebreaker
taker
take her
troublemaker
undertaker
waker
wake her
watchmaker

breakable
mistakable
shakeable
unbreakable
unmistakable
unshakeable

taken
awaken
bacon
bring home the bacon
forsaken
godforsaken
Jamaican
mistaken
overtaken

partaken
reawaken
retaken
shaken
undertaken
waken

takeaway
breakaway

shaky
achy
flaky
wakey wakey

shaking
aching
awaking
backbreaking
baking
bellyaching
braking
breaking
breathtaking
caking
decision-making
dressmaking
epoch-making
faking
flaking
forsaking
ground-breaking
heartbreaking
housebreaking
in the making
leave-taking
loss-making
lovemaking
making
mistaking
moneymaking
muckraking
non-profit-making
overtaking
painstaking

partaking
profit-making
quaking
raking
record-breaking
remaking
retaking
slaking
snaking
staking
stocktaking
taking
undertaking
waking

takeover
makeover

stakeout
breakout
takeout

make-up
break-up
shake-up
take-up

baked
ached
bellyached
caked
faked
flaked
half-baked
quaked
raked
slaked
snaked

3.4

shade
accolade
Adelaide
afraid
aid

aide
arcade
bade
balustrade
barricade
Belgrade
blade
blockade
braid
brayed
brigade
brocade
cascade
cavalcade
centigrade
chambermaid
cockade
colonnade
crusade
custom-made
degrade
dissuade
downgrade
escapade
esplanade
evade
fade
first-aid
forbade
fusillade
glade
grade
grenade
handmade
home-made
inlaid
invade
Jade
jade
laid
lemonade
made
maid
make the grade

man-made
marinade
marmalade
masquerade
mislaid
motorcade
overlaid
overpaid
paid
palisade
parade
persuade
pervade
prepaid
raid
ready-made
relaid
remade
renegade
repaid
retrograde
Rollerblade®
serenade
Sinéad
Slade
spade
staid
stockade
suede
tailor-made
they'd
tirade
trade
unafraid
underpaid
unmade
unpaid
upbraid
upgrade
wade
waylaid
well-made
well-paid

You can add to this list by
adding **-ed** to some words that
rhyme with **day**, as in **delayed**

heyday
Mayday
payday

trader
Ada
aid her
cicada
crusader
Darth Vader
degrade her
dissuade her
evade her
forbade her
Grenada
invader
laid her
made her
mislaid her
overpaid her
paid her
parade her
persuader
persuade her
raider
repaid her
upbraid her
wader
waylaid her

degradable
biodegradable
evadable
upgradable

cradle
ladle

maiden
Aden
Aidan

doom-laden
laden

stadia
nadir

stadium
radium

Canadian
Barbadian

radiant
gradient

lady
My Fair Lady
Sadie
shady
Slim Shady

faded
aided
barricaded
cascaded
cavalcaded
computer-aided
crusaded
degraded
dissuaded
downgraded
evaded
graded
invaded
jaded
marinaded
paraded
persuaded
pervaded
raided
serenaded
shaded
traded
unaided
upgraded
waded

fading
aiding
barricading
cascading
cavalcading
crusading
degrading
dissuading
downgrading
evading
fading
grading
invading
marinading
parading
persuading
pervading
raiding
serenading
shading
trading
upgrading
wading

tornado
Toledo

Adrian
Adrienne
Hadrian

age
assuage
backstage
cage
disengage
engage
enrage
gauge
offstage
on-stage
over-age
page
Pa(i)ge
rage

rampage
rattle someone's cage
sage
stage
under-age
upstage
wage

wager
engage her
enrage her
John Major
major
old stager
pager
page her
rampager
sergeant-major
stager
teenager
upstage her

courageous
advantageous
assuage us
cage us
contagious
disengage us
engage us
enrage us
guage us
outrageous
page us
upstage us

courageously
advantageously
contagiously
outrageously

raging
ageing
assuaging
caging
disengaging
engaging

enraging
gauging
paging
rampaging
staging
upstaging
waging

waged
aged (as in *aged 10*)
assuaged
caged
disengaged
engaged
enraged
gauged
middle-aged
paged
raged
rampaged
staged
upstaged
unwaged

shades
AIDS
Crusades
Everglades
Rollerblades®

You can add to this list by
adding **-s** to some words that
rhyme with **shade**, as in
parades

3.5

safe
chafe
Ralph
strafe
unsafe
waif

You can also make rhymes for these words by using words in section **3.16** that rhyme with *faith*

wafer
chafer
safer
UEFA (= *Union of European Football Associations*)

3.6

vague
Craig
Daniel Craig
Earl Haig
Hague
plague
renege
The Hague
William Hague

bagel
Hegel
inveigle

pagan
Copenhagen
Ronald Reagan

Las Vegas
plague us
Tagus

Fagin
Menachem Begin

lumbago
sago
San Diego
Tierra del Fuego
Trinidad and Tobago

fragrant
flagrant

vagrant

3.7

mail
Abigail
abseil
ail
ale
assail
avail
bail
bale
bewail
Braille
curtail
dale
derail
entail
exhale
fail
fairytale
fight tooth and nail
fingernail
flail
frail
full-scale
Gail
gale
hail
hale
impale
inhale
jail
kale
male
monorail
nail
nightingale
pail
pale
ponytail
prevail
quail
rail

regale
resale
Richter Scale
sail
sale
scale
shale
snail
stale
tail
tale
they'll
trail
travail
unveil
vale
veil
wail
whale

sailor
abseiler
assailer
baler
bewail her
curtailer
derailer
entailer
exhaler
failer
fail her
frailer
hailer
hail her
impaler
inhaler
jailer
jail her
Leila
loudhailer
Michaela
mailer
nailer
paler

43

scaler
staler
tailor
trailer
trail her
unveiler
Venezuela
wailer
whaler
wholesaler

available
assailable
saleable
unassailable
unavailable

Australia
azalea
dahlia
paraphernalia
regalia

alien
Alien
Australian
episcopalian
Pygmalion

daily
Benjamin Disraeli
capercaillie
ceilidh
Eilidh
gaily
Hayley
Israeli
scaly
ukulele

sailing
abseiling
ailing
assailing
availing
bailing

baling
bewailing
curtailing
derailing
entailing
exhaling
failing
flailing
hailing
impaling
inhaling
jailing
mailing
nailing
plain sailing
prevailing
quailing
railing
regaling
scaling
tailing
trailing
travailing
unavailing
unfailing
unveiling
veiling
wailing
whaling

railings
failings
impalings
jailings
mailings
nailings
scalings
unveilings
veilings

failed
abseiled
ailed
assailed
availed

bailed
baled
bewailed
curtailed
derailed
entailed
exhaled
failed
flailed
hailed
impaled
inhaled
jailed
nailed
paled
prevailed
quailed
railed
regaled
sailed
scaled
tailed
trailed
travailed
unveiled
veiled
wailed

ailment
derailment

scales
Gaels
telesales
Wales

You can add to this list by
adding -s to some words that
rhyme with **mail**, as in **prevails**

game
acclaim
aim

became
blame
came
claim
dame
declaim
defame
disclaim
exclaim
fame
flame
frame
inflame
in heaven's name
lame
maim
much the same
name
old flame
overcame
proclaim
put to shame
reclaim
rename
same
shame
tame
what's-her-name
what's-his-name

You can also make rhymes for these words by using words in section **3.9** that rhyme with *pain*

gamer
acclaim her
aimer
blame her
claimer
claim her
declaimer
defame her
disclaimer

flamer
framer
Kramer vs Kramer
name her
namer
proclaimer
reclaimer
shame her
shamer
tame her
tamer

layman
Bremen
Damon
Eamonn
shaman
stamen

payment
claimant
down payment
non-payment
overpayment
prepayment
repayment
underpayment

famous
blame us
frame us
ignoramus
inflame us
overcame us
Seamus
shame us
tame us
world-famous

Amy
cockamamie
gamy
Jamie

famed
above-named

ashamed
acclaimed
aimed
blamed
claimed
declaimed
defamed
disclaimed
exclaimed
flamed
framed
gamed
inflamed
maimed
named
proclaimed
reclaimed
renamed
shamed
tamed
unashamed
unclaimed
unnamed
untamed

namely
gamely
lamely
tamely

shameless
aimless
blameless
nameless

games
acclaims
aims
blames
claims
dames
declaims
defames
disclaims
exclaims
fan the flames

flames
frames
inflames
James
Jesse James
maims
names
old flames
proclaims
reclaims
renames
shames
tames

3.9

pain
abstain
aeroplane
arraign
ascertain
attain
Bahrain
bane
brain
Cain
campaign
cane
Cellophane®
chain
champagne
Charlemagne
Charmaine
Citizen Kane
Cleo Laine
cocaine
complain
constrain
contain
counterpane
crane
Dame Margot Fonteyn
Dane
deign
detain

disdain
domain
down the drain
drain
Duane
Dunblane
El Alamein
Elaine
entertain
explain
feign
gain
Germaine
germane
grain
humane
hurricane
Hussein
hydroplane
inane
inhumane
insane
Jane
Joan Fontaine
John Wayne
lain
lane
Lois Lane
Lorraine
main
Maine
maintain
mane
Margot Fonteyn
Mark Twain
Michael Caine
mundane
obtain
ordain
pane
Penny Lane
pertain
plain
plain Jane

plane
polyurethane
profane
rain
raise Cain
refrain
regain
reign
rein
remain
restrain
retain
retrain
right as rain
Saddam Hussein
sane
scatterbrain
Seine
Shane
slain
Spain
sprain
stain
strain
sustain
terrain
train
Ukraine
underlain
urbane
vain
vane
varicose vein
vein
wane
windowpane
with might and main
✛

You can also make rhymes for these words by using words in section **3.8** that rhyme with *game*

trainer
attain her
campaigner
chain her
complainer
container
disdain her
entertainer
entertain her
explainer
Gaynor
no-brainer
obtainer
obtain her
pain her
plainer
regain her
restrainer
retainer
retain her
retrainer
saner
strainer
sustainer
trainer
vainer

attainable
containable
obtainable
retainable
retrainable
sustainable
trainable
unattainable
uncontainable
unobtainable
unsustainable

Janus
cane us
chain us
disdain us
entertain us
heinous

Uranus

mania
Albania
crania
kleptomania
Lithuania
Mauritania
megalomania
nymphomania
Pennsylvania
pyromania
Romania
Ruritania
Tasmania
the Lusitania
Transylvania

cranium
geranium
titanium
uranium

Romanian
Albanian
Iranian
Jordanian
Lithuanian
Mauritanian
Mediterranean
Panamanian
Pennsylvanian
Ruritanian
subterranean
Tasmanian
Transylvanian
Ukrainian

spontaneous
extraneous
instantaneous
miscellaneous
simultaneous

rainy
Ayatollah Khomeini

Bahraini
brainy
Eugenie
grainy
zany

maniac
brainiac
dipsomaniac
kleptomaniac
megalomaniac
nymphomaniac
pyromaniac

training
entertaining
explaining
raining
reigning
remaining
retraining

You can add to this list by
adding **-ing** to some words that
rhyme with **pain**, as in
restraining

trained
attained
complained
disdained
ingrained
pained
potty-trained
restrained
scatterbrained
self-contained
stained
strained
sustained
unexplained
untrained

You can add to this list by adding **-ed** to some words that rhyme with **pain**, as in **remained**

strange
arrange
change
chop and change
exchange
free-range
interchange
long-range
mange
medium-range
range
rearrange
short-change
short-range

danger
arranger
changer
change her
endanger
exchanger
exchange her
hydrangea
Lone Ranger
manger
ranger
rearranger
short-change her
stranger

changeable
arrangeable
exchangeable
interchangeable

mangy
rangy

changing
arranging

exchanging
interchanging
ranging
rearranging
short-changing
unchanging
wide-ranging

deranged
arranged
changed
estranged
exchanged
interchanged
prearranged
ranged
rearranged
unchanged

painful
disdainful
gainful

painfully
disdainfully
gainfully

mainly
humanely
inhumanely
insanely
plainly
sanely
ungainly
urbanely
vainly

painless
brainless

attainment
arraignment
ascertainment
containment
detainment
entertainment

brainstorm
rainstorm

paint
acquaint
ain't
complaint
constraint
faint
feint
quaint
repaint
restraint
saint
self-restraint
taint
try the patience of a saint

untainted
acquainted
fainted
feinted
painted
repainted
tainted
unacquainted

faintly
quaintly
saintly

remains
brains
pick someone's brains
rack one's brains
Staines
varicose veins

You can add to this list by adding **-s** to some words that rhyme with **pain**, as in **chains**

3.10

ape
cape
crêpe
drape
escape
gaffer tape
gape
grape
in shape
insulating tape
jape
masking tape
measuring tape
nape
out of shape
parcel tape
rape
reshape
scrape
Sellotape®
shape
tape

paper
blotting paper
caper
crêpe paper
draper
flypaper
glasspaper
greaseproof paper
newspaper
notepaper
reshape her
sandpaper
scrape her
scraper
shape her
skyscraper
tape her
taper
tapir
toilet paper

vapour
wallpaper
wastepaper
wrapping paper
writing paper

capable
escapable
incapable
inescapable
shapable

staple
maple
papal

staples
maples
Naples

capon
misshapen

3.11

face
abase
about-face
ace
anyplace
at a snail's pace
base
bass (= *deep voice*)
brace
breathing space
case
chase
commonplace
cyberspace
database
debase
deface
disgrace
displace
efface
embrace

encase
face-to-face
Grace
grace
interface
in-your-face
lace
Mace®
mace
make a face
marketplace
misplace
not a hair out of place
outer space
pace
pillowcase
place
plaice
pull a face
race
replace
retrace
slap in the face
space
steeplechase
trace
unlace
waste of space
W G Grace
Will and Grace

racer
chase her
chaser
disgrace her
displace her
embrace her
place her
racer
replace her
steeplechaser
trace her
tracer

mason
basin
chasten
encase in
freemason
hasten
Jason
place in
stonemason
washbasin
wash-hand basin

adjacent
complacent

bases
oases
précis (= *summaries*)

racy
Count Basie
Kevin Spacey
lacy
pac(e)y
spacey
Stac(e)y
Trac(e)y

racing
abasing
all-embracing
bracing
casing
chasing
debasing
defacing
disgracing
displacing
effacing
embracing
encasing
facing
gracing
interfacing
lacing
misplacing

north-facing
pacing
placing
replacing
retracing
self-effacing
south-facing
spacing
steeplechasing
tracing
unlacing

basis
oasis

racist
antiracist
bassist
non-racist

evasive
abrasive
invasive
non-invasive
persuasive
pervasive

wayside
Speyside
Tayside

say-so
peso

graceful
caseful
disgraceful

gracefully
disgracefully

faceless
baseless
graceless
spaceless
traceless

basement
casement
debasement
displacement
effacement
encasement
outplacement
placement
replacement

taste
aftertaste
baby-faced
baste
chaste
cut-and-paste
distaste
foretaste
hard-faced
haste
no accounting for taste
paste
poker-faced
posthaste
red-faced
shamefaced
straight-faced
straitlaced
waist
waste

You can add to this list by adding **-d** to some words that rhyme with **face**, as in **embraced**

taster
paster
turkey baster
waster

tasty
hasty
pasty (= *pale*)

pasting
basting
time-wasting
wasting

Hastings
Battle of Hastings
pastings

tasteful
distasteful
wasteful

3.12

beige
Liège

Asia
Australasia
Eurasia

Many English speakers pronounce some words in section **3.18** (eg *aphasia*) in such a way that they rhyme with these words

Asian
abrasion
Australasian
Caucasian
equation
Eurasian
evasion
invasion
occasion
persuasion
quadratic equation

3.13

racial
facial
interracial
multiracial
palatial

spatial

nation
abbreviation
abdication
aberration
abomination
acceleration
acclamation
accommodation
accumulation
accusation
adaptation
adjudication
administration
admiration
adoration
adulation
adulteration
affectation
affiliation
affirmation
afforestation
aggravation
agitation
allegation
alliteration
allocation
Alsatian
alteration
altercation
amputation
animation
annexation
annihilation
anticipation
application
appreciation
appropriation
approximation
arbitration
articulation
artificial insemination
asphyxiation

aspiration
assassination
assignation
assimilation
association
authorization
automation
aviation
beatification
brutalization
calculation
cancellation
capitalization
carnation
castration
casualization
celebration
cessation
characterization
circulation
citation
civilization
clarification
classification
cohabitation
collaboration
combination
commemoration
commendation
commiseration
communication
compensation
compilation
complication
computation
computerization
concentration
conciliation
condemnation
condensation
confederation
configuration
confirmation
confiscation

51

confrontation
congregation
conjugation
connotation
consecration
conservation
consideration
consolation
consolidation
constellation
consternation
constipation
consultation
contamination
contemplation
continuation
conurbation
conversation
cooperation
coordination
copulation
coronation
corporation
correlation
corroboration
creation
cremation
Croatian
cross-examination
crustacean
culmination
cultivation
Dalmatian
damnation
decentralization
decimalization
declaration
decoration
dedication
defamation
deflation
deforestation
deformation
degeneration

degradation
dehydration
deindustrialization
delegation
deliberation
demarcation
demobilization
demonstration
denationalization
denomination
denunciation
depopulation
deportation
depravation
deprecation
depreciation
deprivation
deputation
deregulation
derivation
desalination
desecration
desegregation
designation
desolation
desperation
destination
deterioration
determination
detonation
detoxification
devaluation
devastation
deviation
dictation
dilapidation
dilation
discrimination
disinclination
disinformation
disintegration
dislocation
disorganization
disorientation

dispensation
disqualification
dissertation
dissipation
diversification
documentation
domination
donation
duplication
duration
edification
education
ejaculation
elation
electrification
elevation
elimination
emancipation
emendation
emigration
equivocation
escalation
estimation
evacuation
evaluation
evaporation
evocation
exaggeration
examination
exasperation
excavation
exclamation
excommunication
exhalation
exhortation
expectation
explanation
exploitation
exploration
exportation
expropriation
extermination
extrapolation
fascination

'ay'

federation
fermentation
fixation
flotation
fluctuation
formation
fornication
fortification
foundation
frustration
further education
generalization
generation
gentrification
germination
gestation
globalization
gradation
graduation
gratification
gyration
habitation
Haitian
hallucination
harmonization
hesitation
hibernation
higher education
humiliation
hyperinflation
identification
illumination
illustration
imagination
imitation
immigration
immunization
impersonation
implementation
implication
importation
impregnation
improvisation
inauguration

incantation
incarceration
incarnation
incineration
inclination
incubation
indentation
indication
indignation
indoctrination
infatuation
infiltration
inflammation
inflation
information
inhalation
initiation
innovation
inoculation
insemination
insinuation
inspiration
installation
instigation
instrumentation
insubordination
insulation
integration
interpretation
interrogation
intimidation
intonation
intoxication
investigation
invitation
in vitro fertilization
irradiation
irrigation
irritation
isolation
jollification
jubilation
justification
laceration

lamentation
legalization
legation
legislation
levitation
liberation
limitation
liquidation
litigation
location
lubrication
magnification
manifestation
manipulation
matriculation
mediation
medication
meditation
menstruation
migration
misappropriation
miscalculation
misinformation
mispronunciation
misrepresentation
mistranslation
mitigation
moderation
modernization
modification
modulation
mortification
motivation
mouth-to-mouth
  resuscitation
multiplication
mutation
mutilation
nationalization
naturalization
navigation
negation
negotiation
nomination

normalization
notation
notification
no-win situation
obfuscation
obligation
observation
occupation
operation
oration
ordination
organization
orientation
ostentation
ovation
overgeneralization
overpopulation
ovulation
pagination
pale imitation
participation
penetration
perforation
permutation
personification
perspiration
pigmentation
plantation
polarization
pollination
poor relation
population
precipitation
predestination
preoccupation
preparation
presentation
preservation
prevarication
privation
privatization
probation
proclamation
procrastination

procreation
proliferation
pronunciation
propagation
protestation
provocation
publication
punctuation
purification
qualification
quotation
radiation
ramification
ratification
rationalization
reafforestation
recitation
reclamation
recommendation
reconciliation
recreation
recrimination
recuperation
reflation
reforestation
reformation
refrigeration
refutation
regeneration
regimentation
regionalization
registration
regulation
rehabilitation
reincarnation
reinterpretation
reiteration
relation
relaxation
relegation
relocation
remuneration
renovation
reorganization

reparation
repatriation
representation
repudiation
reputation
reservation
resignation
respiration
restoration
resuscitation
retaliation
reunification
revelation
reverberation
rotation
salvation
sanitation
saturation
sedation
segmentation
segregation
self-deprecation
self-determination
self-preservation
sensation
separation
sequestration
simplification
simulation
situation
sophistication
specialization
specification
speculation
stagflation
stagnation
standardization
starvation
station
sterilization
sticky situation
stimulation
stipulation
strangulation

stratification
subordination
suffocation
superannuation
supplication
synchronization
syncopation
taxation
temptation
termination
titillation
tit(t)ivation
toleration
transformation
translation
transplantation
transportation
trepidation
tribulation
undulation
unification
urbanization
vacation
vaccination
validation
valuation
variation
vegetation
veneration
ventilation
verification
vexation
vibration
victimization
vilification
vindication
violation
visualization
vocation

stationer
probationer
vacationer

sensational
coeducational
conversational
denominational
educational
gravitational
navigational
non-denominational
occupational
operational
recreational
representational
vocational

stationary
deflationary
inflationary
probationary
stationery

palpitations
celebrations
congratulations
globalizations
Good Vibrations
Great Expectations
machinations
negotiations
telecommunications

You can add to this list by
adding -s to some words that
rhyme with **nation**, as in
sensations

gracious
audacious
capacious
curvaceous
efficacious
fallacious
flirtatious
loquacious

ostentatious
perspicacious
pugnacious
rapacious
sagacious
salacious
sebaceous
spacious
tenacious
ungracious
vivacious
voracious

satiate
ingratiate

3.14

date
abate
abbreviate
abdicate
accelerate
accentuate
accommodate
accumulate
activate
adjudicate
adulterate
advocate (= to
  recommend)
affiliate
aggravate
agitate
Alexander the Great
alienate
allocate
alternate
amalgamate
amputate
animate (= to enliven)
annihilate
annotate
anticipate

appreciate
appropriate (= *to take*)
approximate (= *to be close*)
arbitrate
articulate (= *to speak clearly*)
asphyxiate
assimilate
associate (= *to connect with*)
ate
authenticate
automate
await
backdate
bait
bantamweight
berate
bicarbonate
blind date
Brandenburg Gate
calculate
calibrate
candidate
capitulate
captivate
carbonate
castigate
castrate
Catherine the Great
celebrate
chlorinate
circulate
circumnavigate
coagulate
cogitate
collate
commemorate
commentate
commiserate
communicate
compensate
complicate

concentrate
confiscate
congratulate
congregate
conjugate
consecrate
consolidate
consummate
contemplate
cooperate
coordinate (= *to match*)
copperplate
correlate
corroborate
counterweight
crate
create
cremate
cultivate
debate
debilitate
decapitate
decelerate
decimate
decorate
defecate
deflate
deliberate (= *to ponder*)
delineate
denigrate
deprecate
depreciate
deregulate
desecrate
designate
deteriorate
detonate
devastate
dictate
differentiate
dilate
directorate

disintegrate
dislocate
disorientate
disseminate
dissociate
domesticate
dominate
donate
duplicate (= *to make a copy of*)
educate
eight
elevate
elongate
elucidate
emanate
emancipate
emasculate
emigrate
emirate
emulate
encapsulate
enervate
enumerate
enunciate
equate
equivocate
eradicate
escalate
estate
estimate (= *to guess*)
evacuate
evaluate
evaporate
exacerbate
exaggerate
exasperate
excavate
excommunicate
exonerate
expiate
expostulate
expropriate
expurgate

extirpate
extrapolate
extricate
fabricate
fate
featherweight
fête
first-rate
flagellate
fluctuate
flyweight
formulate
freight
frustrate
fumigate
gait
gate
germinate
graduate
grate
gravitate
great
gyrate
hallucinate
hate
heavyweight
hesitate
hibernate
hundredweight
hyphenate
ice-skate
illustrate
imitate
immigrate
impersonate
implicate
impregnate
inaugurate
incarcerate
incinerate
incorporate
incubate
inculcate
indoctrinate

infiltrate
inflate
infuriate
innate
innovate
inoculate
insinuate
instigate
insulate
integrate
interpolate
interrogate
intimate (= to suggest)
intimidate
inundate
invalidate
investigate
invigilate
invigorate
irate
irradiate
irrigate
irritate
isolate
Kate
Kiss Me Kate
Kuwait
lacerate
late
legislate
legitimate
levitate
liberate
liquidate
locate
lubricate
luxuriate
magistrate
mandate
marinate
mate
mediate
meditate
menstruate

middleweight
migrate
miscalculate
moderate (= to ease)
modulate
motivate
mutate
mutilate
narrate
nauseate
navigate
necessitate
negate
negotiate
nominate
numberplate
obviate
one over the eight
operate
orchestrate
orientate
originate
ornate
oscillate
out-of-date
overcompensate
overestimate
overrate
overstate
overweight
ovulate
palpate
palpitate
paperweight
pate (= head)
penetrate
percolate
perforate
permeate
perpetrate
perpetuate
placate
plate
pollinate

pontificate
postulate
potentate
precipitate
predate
predominate
prevaricate
procrastinate
procreate
proliferate
propagate
prostrate
pulsate
punctuate
radiate
rate
reactivate
reanimate
recapitulate
reciprocate
re-create
recuperate
redecorate
reflate
refrigerate
regulate
regurgitate
reinstate
rejuvenate
relate
relocate
remunerate
renovate
repatriate
replicate
reprobate
repudiate
resonate
resuscitate
retaliate
reverberate
roller-skate
rotate
salivate

sate
saturate
second-rate
sedate
segregate
sell-by date
separate (= *to part*)
skate
slate
solid-state
spate
speculate
stagnate
state
straight
strait
subjugate
sublimate
subordinate (= *to make subservient*)
substantiate
suffocate
sulphate
suppurate
tabulate
tempt fate
Terry Waite
tête-à-tête
third-rate
titillate
tit(t)ivate
tolerate
trait
translate
truncate
ulcerate
underestimate
underrate
underweight
undulate
update
up-to-date
urinate
use-by date

vacate
vaccinate
vacillate
validate
vegetate
ventilate
vibrate
wait
weight
welterweight

later
abator
abbreviator
abdicator
accelerator
accumulator
activator
adjudicator
administrator
adulterator
advocator
agitator
alligator
alternator
amputator
animator
annihilator
annotator
anticipator
appreciator
appropriator
arbitrator
articulator
asphyxiator
assimilator
authenticator
baiter
calculator
calibrator
castigator
cater
celebrator
circulator

'ay'

collaborator
collator
commemorator
commentator
communicator
compensator
confiscator
congratulator
consecrator
consolidator
consummator
contemplator
coordinator
corroborator
crater
creator
cremator
cultivater
data
debater
decelerator
decimator
decorator
delineator
denigrator
demonstrator
denominator
deprecator
depreciator
deregulator
desecrater
designator
detonator
devastator
dictator
differentiator
dilator
disintegrator
disseminator
domesticator
dominator
dumb waiter
duplicator
educator

elevator
elucidator
emanator
emancipator
emasculator
emulator
enumerator
enunciator
equator
equivocator
eradicator
escalator
estimator
evacuator
evaluator
evaporator
exaggerator
exasperator
excavator
excommunicator
exonerator
expiator
expostulator
expropriator
expurgator
extirpator
fabricator
flagellator
formulator
freighter
fumigator
gaiter
generator
gladiator
grater
hater
hesitator
illustrator
imitator
impersonator
inaugurator
incarcerator
incinerator
incorporator

incubator
inculcator
indicator
indoctrinator
infiltrator
inflator
innovator
inoculator
instigator
insulator
integrator
interpolator
interrogator
intimidator
investigator
invigilator
irrigator
irritator
isolator
legislator
levitator
liberator
liquidator
locator
lubricator
mandator
mater
mediator
moderator
modulator
motivator
mutilator
narrator
navigator
negator
negotiator
nominator
numerator
operator
orchestrator
oscillator
pater
penetrator
percolator

perforator
perpetrator
perpetuator
peseta
pollinator
pontificator
postulator
precipitator
propagator
pulsator
punctuator
radiator
rater
reciprocator
recuperator
refrigerator
regulator
rejuvenator
remunerator
renovator
repatriator
replicator
repudiator
respirator
resuscitator
rotator
separator
skater
slater
spectator
speculator
subjugator
titillator
tolerator
traitor
translator
ventilator
vibrator
vaccinator
ventilator
waiter

You can add to this list by adding -(e)r to some words that rhyme with **date**, as in **straighter**

You can also make rhymes for these words by using **her** after some words that rhyme with **date**, as in **hate her**

debatable
inflatable
translatable
untranslatable

fatal
antenatal
postnatal
prenatal

verbatim
ultimatum

You can add to this list by adding 'em to some words that rhyme with **date**, as in **hate 'em**

straighten
Len Deighton
Satan
straiten

latent
blatant
patent

blatantly
latently
patently

compensatory
regulatory

status
apparatus
hiatus

You can also make rhymes for these words by using **us** after some words that rhyme with **date**, as in **hate us**

matey
eighty
Haiti
Katie
Kuwaiti
slatey
weighty

fated
agitated
animated
antiquated
associated
authenticated
bated
belated
calculated
carbonated
celebrated
coin-operated
complicated
constipated
corrugated
cultivated
decaffeinated
deflated
dehydrated
dilapidated
educated
elasticated
elated
electroplated
elevated
emaciated
emancipated
exaggerated
exhilarated
frustrated
gold-plated

graduated
ill-fated
inebriated
infatuated
inflated
integrated
interrelated
intoxicated
invigorated
isolated
liberated
opinionated
outdated
overrated
perforated
performance-related
polyunsaturated
prefabricated
premeditated
related
serrated
silver-plated
simulated
situated
sophisticated
unadulterated
unaffiliated
unappreciated
uncomplicated
uncontaminated
uncoordinated
uncorroborated
uncultivated
undated
underpopulated
uneducated
uninitiated
unrelated
unsophisticated
unsubstantiated
variegated
zero-rated

You can add to this list by adding **-d** to some words that rhyme with **date**, as in **hated**

waiting

accommodating
aggravating
alternating
appreciating
calculating
captivating
debilitating
deprecating
depreciating
devastating
enervating
exasperating
excruciating
exhilarating
fascinating
frustrating
grating
humiliating
ice-skating
illuminating
infuriating
ingratiating
intimidating
invigorating
irritating
lady-in-waiting
liberating
mating
operating
penetrating
rating
roller-skating
scintillating
skating
stimulating
unhesitating
weighting

You can add to this list by adding **-ing** to some words that rhyme with **date**, as in **abating**

native
creative
dative
stative

daytime
playtime

NATO
Plato
potato

grateful
fateful
hateful
ungrateful

lately
greatly
irately
sedately
stately

stateless
dateless
weightless

statement
abatement
overstatement
reinstatement
understatement

lateness
greatness
irateness
sedateness

matron
patron

matriarch
patriarch

3.15

bathe
lathe
swathe

scathing
bathing

3.16

faith
Faith
in good faith
wraith

You can also make rhymes for these words by using words in section **3.5** that rhyme with **safe**

pathos
bathos

3.17

save
aftershave
behave
beyond the grave
brave
cave
concave
crave
Dave
dig one's own grave
early grave
engrave
enslave
forgave
from the cradle to the grave
gave
grave
knave
microwave
misbehave

nave
pave
rant and rave
rave
shave
slave
stave
they've
waive
wave

quaver
braver
crave her
demisemiquaver
disfavour
engraver
enslave her
enslaver
favour
flavour
forgave her
gave her
life-saver
microwave her
paver
raver
save her
saver
savour
semiquaver
shave her
shaver
slaver
waiver
waver

flavourless
savourless

raven
Avon
clean-shaven
graven
haven

shaven
unshaven

bravery
quavery
savoury
slavery
unsavoury

wavering
disfavouring
favouring
flavouring
quavering
savouring
slavering
unwavering

Moldavia
Octavia
Scandinavia

navy
Davy
gravy
wavy

saving
craving
energy-saving
engraving
enslaving
face-saving
life-saving
paving
raving
shaving
staving
time-saving
waving
waiving

Mavis
Bette Davis
Miles Davis
Steve Davis

depraved
behaved
braved
craved
engraved
enslaved
microwaved
misbehaved
paved
ranted and raved
raved
saved
shaved
slaved
staved
waived
waved
well-behaved

bravely
gravely

saviour
behaviour
misbehaviour

3.18

gaze
ablaze
amaze
appraise
baize
blaze
bolognese
braise
craze
daze
émigrés
erase
faze
glaze
graze
halcyon days
haze

laze
liaise
maize
malaise
mayonnaise
maze
nowadays
one of these days
paraphrase
phase
phrase
polonaise
praise
raise
raze
reappraise
rephrase
the good old days
the Krays
to coin a phrase
waifs and strays
waterways
yesterdays

➕

You can add to this list by adding -s to some words that rhyme with **day**, as in **plays**

laser
amaze her
blazer
delays her
disobeys her
displays her
eraser
Fraser
gazer
glazer
grazer
obeys her
pays her
praise her
raise her
razor

taser

nasal
appraisal
Hazel
hazel

brazen
emblazon
raisin

glazier
Anastasia
aphasia
brazier
crazier
euthanasia
Fantasia
hazier
lazier
Malaysia

Many English speakers pronounce some words in section **3.12** (eg *Australasia*) in such a way that they rhyme with these words

lazy
crazy
Daisy
daisy
hazy
Maisie
Patrick Swayze

phrasing
amazing
appraising
blazing
braising
crazing
dazing
double-glazing
erasing
fazing

gazing	**dazed**	hazed
glazing	amazed	lazed
grazing	appraised	liaised
liaising	blazed	phased
navel-gazing	braised	phrased
phasing	crazed	praised
praising	erased	raised
raising	fazed	razed
razing	gazed	reappraised
reappraising	glazed	rephrased
rephrasing	grazed	unfazed

'air'

chair, fairy, despair

All the words in this section use the sound '**air**' in their main stressed syllable

4.1

rare

Aberdare
affair
aftercare
air
anywhere
au pair
aware
Ayr
Ballyclare
bare
bear
beware
beyond compare
billionaire
blare
Burke and Hare
camelhair
care
chair
Cher
Cla(i)re
commissionaire
compare
County Clare
Dan Dare
dare
debonair
declare
Delaware
despair
devil-may-care
disrepair

doctrinaire
earthenware
eclair
ensnare
everywhere
fair
fair and square
fanfare
fare
flair
flare
forbear
forswear
Fred Astaire
glare
go spare
Hair
hair
hare
heir
impair
in good repair
Jane Eyre
Kildare
kitchenware
lair
laisser-faire
legionnaire
Leicester Square
mare
mayor
midair
millionaire
multimillionaire

open-air
ovenware
pair
pare
pear
prayer
premiere
prepare
questionnaire
Red Square
repair
rocking chair
scare
share
silverware
snare
solitaire
spare
square
stair
stare
swear
tableware
tear (= *to rip*)
their
there
the worse for wear
they're
thoroughfare
Tiananmen Square
Tony Blair
Trafalgar Square
unaware
underwear

unfair
Vanity Fair
Voltaire
walk on air
Walter De La Mare
wear
Weston-super-Mare
where
yeah
Yogi Bear

4.2

scared
aired
bared
black-haired
blared
brown-haired
cared
chaired
curly-haired
compared
dared
dark-haired
declared
despaired
ensnared
fair-haired
fanfared
fared
flared
glared
grey-haired
impaired
laird
Logie Baird
long-haired
paired
pared
premiered
prepared
red-haired
repaired

shared
short-haired
snared
spared
squared
stared
straight-haired
unimpaired
unprepared
white-haired

4.3

rarely
barely
debonairly
fairly
squarely
unfairly

airlift
chairlift
stairlift

airless
careless
hairless

airline
hairline

4.4

chairman
repairman
vice-chairman

4.5

cairn
bairn
Nairn
Pitcairn

fairness
awareness

bareness
squareness
unawareness
unfairness

4.6

carer
barer
bearer
carer
compare her
Éamon de Valera
Eire
ensnare her
fairer
pallbearer
prepare her
rarer
Riviera
Sara(h)
scare her
scarer
seafarer
share her
sharer
snare her
snarer
spare her
sparer
squarer
starer
swearer
tearer
torchbearer
wayfarer
wearer

bearable
repairable
unbearable

Aries
caries

area
Bavaria
Bulgaria
malaria
planetaria

aerial
secretarial

barium
aquarium
planetarium

Aryan
agrarian
antiquarian
authoritarian
barbarian
Bavarian
Bulgarian
Caesarean
centenarian
disciplinarian
egalitarian
grammarian
humanitarian
Hungarian
libertarian
librarian
nonagenarian
octogenarian
ovarian
parliamentarian
proletarian
sectarian
septuagenarian
sexagenarian
totalitarian
utilitarian
vegetarian
veterinarian

sectarianism
agrarianism
antiquarianism

authoritarianism
egalitarianism
humanitarianism
libertarianism
parliamentarianism
totalitarianism
utilitarianism
vegetarianism

various
Aquarius
gregarious
hilarious
multifarious
nefarious
precarious
Sagittarius
vicarious

variously
hilariously
multifariously
nefariously
precariously
vicariously

secretariat
proletariat

vary
airy
airy-fairy
Azeri
Canary
canary
chary
contrary (= *perverse*)
dairy
fairy
General Galtieri
hairy
Mariah Carey
Mary
prairie
scary

Tipperary
unwary
wary

daring
airing
baring
blaring
bearing
caring
chairing
child-bearing
comparing
declaring
despairing
disrepairing
ensnaring
fanfaring
faring
flaring
forbearing
forswearing
glaring
hard-wearing
haring
impairing
pairing
paring
overbearing
preparing
profit-sharing
raring
repairing
scaring
seafaring
sharing
snaring
sparing
squaring
staring
swearing
tearing (= *to rip*)
uncaring
unsparing

wearing

sparingly
despairingly
glaringly
overbearingly

heiress
mayoress
millionairess

Pharaoh
bolero
Rio de Janeiro
sombrero

4.7

stairway
airway
fairway

4.8

theirs
downstairs
split hairs

You can add to this list by adding -*s* to some words that rhyme with *rare*, as in *stairs*

'e'

bet, credit, impress

All the words in this section use the sound '**e**' in their main stressed syllable

5.1

web
at a low ebb
ebb
Maghreb
pleb
Zagreb

pebble
rebel
treble

Debbie
Entebbe

Deborah
zebra

5.2

neck
Ant and Dec
beck
bedeck
bottleneck
check
cheque
Czech
deck
discotheque
double-check
fleck
get it in the neck
Gregory Peck
halterneck
heck
high-tech
millstone round one's
  neck
nervous wreck
pain in the neck
peck
polo neck
quarterdeck
Quebec
Shrek
spec
speck
Toulouse-Lautrec
trek
turtleneck
up to one's neck
V-neck
wreck

wrecker
Boris Becker
bedeck her
check her
Chubby Checker
deck her
Desmond Dekker
double-check her
double-decker
exchequer
Mecca
peck her
Rebecca
single-decker
spell-checker
trekker

woodpecker

freckle
Dr Jekyll
heckle
shekel
speckle

beckon
Brecon
reckon

second
beckoned
nanosecond
reckoned
split-second

reckless
feckless
necklace

flex
annex
bedecks
bottlenecks
checks
cheques
circumflex
convex
Czechs
decks
discotheques
double-checks
ex
flecks
halternecks

Malcolm X
multiplex
necks
Oedipus Rex
pecks
pecs
perplex
polo necks
Posh and Becks
quarterdecks
Rex
sex
specs
Tex-Mex
treks
turtlenecks
unisex
vex
V-necks
wrecks
X

dyslexia
alexia
anorexia
sexier

sexy
apoplexy

anorexic
dyslexic

complexity
convexity
perplexity

text
annexed
circumflexed
convexed
flexed
from one day to the
   next
hypertext
next

perplexed
teletext
vexed

section
affection
antivivisection
by-election
collection
complexion
connection
convection
correction
cross-section
defection
deflection
dejection
detection
direction
disaffection
ejection
election
erection
imperfection
infection
injection
inspection
insurrection
interjection
intersection
introspection
objection
perfection
projection
protection
recollection
re-election
reflection
rejection
resurrection
selection
subsection
vivisection

perfectionist
antivivisectionist
projectionist
protectionist
vivisectionist

sect
affect
after-effect
architect
aspect
bedecked
bisect
checked
circumspect
collect
connect
correct
decked
defect (= to desert
   one's country)
deflect
detect
dialect
direct
disconnect
disinfect
disrespect
dissect
double-checked
effect
eject
elect
erect
expect
flecked
genuflect
incorrect
indirect
infect
inflect
inject
inspect
intellect

interconnect
interject
intersect
knock-on effect
misdirect
necked
neglect
object (= *to make an objection*)
pecked
perfect (= *to make perfect*)
project
prospect
protect
recollect
redirect
re-elect
reflect
reject
respect
resurrect
retrospect
select
self-respect
subject (= *to cause to experience something*)
suspect
trekked
turtle-necked
unchecked
Utrecht
wrecked

sector
bisect her
collect her
collector
connector
conscientious objector
correct her
defector
deflector

detector
director
disrespect her
ejector
elect her
elector
executive director
expect her
film director
Hannibal Lecter
Hector
hector
injector
inspector
interconnector
managing director
nectar
neglect her
nonexecutive director
objector
Phil Spector
projector
prospector
protect her
protector
rector
reflector
reject her
respect her
respecter
selector
spectre
suspect her
vector

respectable
collectable
connectable
correctable
delectable
detectable
disrespectable
electable
erectable

injectable
inspectable

vasectomy
hysterectomy
mastectomy

expectant
disinfectant

pectoral
electoral

rectory
directory
ex-directory
refectory
trajectory

hectic
apoplectic
dialectic
eclectic

expected
affected
bisected
collected
connected
corrected
defected
deflected
dejected
detected
directed
disconnected
disinfected
disrespected
disaffected
dissected
effected
ejected
elected
erected
genuflected
infected
inflected

injected
inspected
interconnected
interjected
intersected
misdirected
neglected
objected
perfected
projected
prospected
protected
recollected
redirected
re-elected
reflected
rejected
respected
resurrected
selected
subjected
suspected
unaffected
unconnected
undetected
unexpected
unprotected
unsuspected
well-respected
write-protected

rectify
objectify

unsuspecting
affecting
bisecting
collecting
connecting
correcting
defecting
deflecting
detecting
directing
disconnecting

disinfecting
disrespecting
dissecting
effecting
ejecting
electing
erecting
expecting
genuflecting
infecting
inflecting
injecting
inspecting
interconnecting
interjecting
intersecting
misdirecting
neglecting
objecting
perfecting
projecting
prospecting
protecting
recollecting
redirecting
re-electing
reflecting
rejecting
respecting
resurrecting
retrospecting
selecting
self-respecting
subjecting
suspecting

detective
collective
corrective
defective
directive
effective
elective
ineffective

introspective
invective
irrespective
objective
perspective
prospective
protective
reflective
respective
retrospective
selective
subjective

effectively
collectively
objectively
respectively
retrospectively

respectful
disrespectful
neglectful

directly
correctly
incorrectly
indirectly

spectra
Electra

spectrum
plectrum

lecture
architecture
conjecture

effectual
ineffectual
intellectual

secular
molecular

consecutive
executive

5.3

bed
ahead
arrowhead
BEd (= *Bachelor of Education*)
behead
black bread
bled
bottle-fed
bread
bred
brown bread
centre spread
cut someone dead
dead
DipEd (= *Diploma in Education*)
dread
drop dead
Ed
ed
embed
Erik the Red
Fed
fed
figurehead
fled
flowerbed
force-fed
Fred
gainsaid
gingerbread
go-ahead
go to someone's head
head
Holyhead
ill-bred
infrared
instead
Judge Dredd
knock 'em dead
lead (= *the metal*)
led

letterhead
like a bear with a sore head
lose one's head
MEd (= *Master of Education*)
misled
misread (= *past tense of misread*)
naan bread
Ned
not right in the head
out of one's head
overhead
paint the town red
Peterhead
pitta bread
quadruped
read (= *past tense of read*)
red
riverbed
said
see red
shed
shred
sled
sliced bread
soda bread
sped
spread
stead
stone-dead
streets ahead
Ted
the best thing since sliced bread
the Med
thoroughbred
thread
tread
underfed
unsaid
unshed

watershed
wed
well-bred
well-fed
well-read
white bread
wholemeal bread
Z

shredder
bedder
Cheddar
dread her
header
led her
misled her
wed her

medal
back-pedal
meddle
pedal
peddle
soft-pedal
treadle

deaden
Armageddon
leaden
redden

pedantry
sedentary

ready
already
Eddie
eddy
Freddie
heady
oven-ready
rough-and-ready
steady
Teddy
teddy
unsteady

edible
credible
incredible
inedible

dedicate
medicate
predicate (= *to proclaim*)

dedicated
medicated
predicated

dreaded
bareheaded
bedded
beheaded
bigheaded
breaded
clear-headed
cool-headed
embedded
empty-headed
hard-headed
headed
hotheaded
leaded
level-headed
light-headed
muddleheaded
pig-headed
shedded
shredded
sledded
threaded
unleaded
wedded
wrong-headed

readily
headily
steadily
unsteadily

sediment
impediment

wedding
bedding
beheading
breading
dreading
embedding
heading
leading (= *the metal*)
shedding
shredding
sledding
spreading
steading
threading
treading

edit
behead it
credit
discredit
dread it
embed it
force-fed it
head it
led it
read it (= *past tense of read*)
shred it
spread it
subedit

editor
creditor
subeditor

headboard
breadboard

meddler
peddler
pedlar

deadly
medley

headline
breadline
deadline

wedlock
deadlock
dreadlock

bedpan
deadpan

Cedric
Frederic(k)

bedroom
headroom

edge
allege
dredge
hedge
ledge
on edge
pledge
Reg
sedge
sledge
veg
wedge

ledger
dredger

edgy
Reggie
veggie

double-edged
alleged
dredged
edged
fully-fledged
hedged
ledged
pledged
sedged
sledged
vegged

wedged

overheads
loggerheads
newlyweds
tear to shreds
zeds

You can add to this list by adding -s to some words that rhyme with **bed**, as in **threads**

5.4

chef
BAF (= *British Athletic Federation*)
cf (= *compare*)
clef
deaf
eff
F
Geoff
IMF (= *International Monetary Fund*)
IVF
RAF
ref
Rudolf Nureyev
stone-deaf
tone-deaf
treble clef
UHF (= *ultrahigh frequency*)
UNICEF
USAF (= *United States Air Force*)
VHF (= *very high frequency*)
WWF (= *Worldwide Fund for Nature; World Wrestling Federation*)

[+]
You can also make rhymes for these words by using words in section **5.16** that rhyme with **death**

zephyr
heifer

reference
cross-reference
deference
preference

left
bereft
cleft
deft
theft
weft

5.5

leg
an arm and a leg
beg
break a leg
egg
Eigg
keg
Meg
nest egg
Peg
peg
Winnipeg

beggar
Arnold Schwarzenegger
Ewan McGregor

leggy
Peggy

eggs
begs
boiled eggs

dregs
fried eggs
hard-boiled eggs
kegs
legs
nest eggs
on one's last legs
pegs
poached eggs
scrambled eggs
soft-boiled eggs
sure as eggs is eggs

5.6

tell
Adele
Alexander Graham Bell
Annabel(l)e
ASL (= *American Sign Language*)
befell
bell
Belle
belle
Brunel
caramel
caravel
carousel
cartel
cell
Charles Parnell
citadel
clientele
compel
Danielle
decibel
Del
dispel
dwell
EFL (= *English as a foreign language*)
Estelle
excel

expel
farewell
fell
foretell
Gabrielle
gazelle
gel
Gisèle
give someone hell
hell
hotel
HTML (= *hypertext markup language*)
impel
Isabel(le)
jell
Jezebel
kiss and tell
knell
L
lapel
like a bat out of hell
like hell
Mel
Michelle
misspell
motel
Nell
NFL (= *National Football League*)
Noël
Noel(l)e
not have a hope in hell
outsell
parallel
pell-mell
personnel
propel
quell
Raquel
Ravel
razor-shell
rebel (= *to revolt*)
repel

San Miguel
Scafell
sell
shell
smell
sound as a bell
spell
swell
Tinkerbell
tortoiseshell
unwell
URL (= *uniform resource locator*)
well
XL (= *extra large*)
yell

melee
Pele

seller
Arabella
befell her
Bella
bestseller
bookseller
cellar
Cinderella
compel her
Daniella
Della
dweller
Ella
expel her
Fenella
fortune-teller
impel her
Isabella
Nelson Mandela
Nigella
outsell her
propel her
propeller
Prunella
quell her

repel her
rubella
salmonella
saltcellar
sell her
smell her
speller
spell her
Stella
storyteller
Tarantella
teller
tell her
umbrella
yeller

vellum
antebellum
befell 'em
cerebellum
compel 'em
dispel 'em
excel 'em
expel 'em
impel 'em
outsell 'em
propel 'em
quell 'em
repel 'em
sell 'em
shell 'em
smell 'em
spell 'em
swell 'em
tell 'em

melon
Ellen
felon
Ferdinand Magellan
Helen
watermelon

Melanie
felony

miscellany

jealous
bestsellers
booksellers
cellars
compel us
dwellers
expel us
fortune-tellers
propellers
saltcellars
sellers
sell us
smell us
spellers
storytellers
tellers
tell us
umbrellas
zealous

pellet
zealot

jelly
belly
Delhi
deli
Ellie
Gene Kelly
George Melly
Grace Kelly
Kelly
Liza Minnelli
Machiavelli
Ned Kelly
Nellie
New Delhi
not on your nelly
Sandro Botticelli
Shelley
smelly
tagliatelle
telly

welly

relic
angelic
psychedelic

eligible
ineligible
intelligible
unintelligible

relegate
delegate (= to depute)

telling
belling
best-selling
compelling
dispelling
dwelling
evil-smelling
excelling
expelling
felling
foretelling
gelling
impelling
jelling
knelling
misspelling
outselling
parallelling
propelling
quelling
rebelling
repelling
selling
shelling
smelling
spelling
sweet-smelling
swelling
welling
yelling

wellington
Duke Ellington
Duke of Wellington
Wellington

trellis
Ellis
Ruth Ellis

hellish
embellish
relish

yellow
bedfellow
bellow
cello
Donatello
Elvis Costello
fellow
Ivor Novello
Longfellow
mellow
Othello
schoolfellow

elk
whelk

held
beheld
belled
compelled
dispelled
dwelled
excelled
expelled
felled
gelled
impelled
jelled
jet-propelled
knelled
misspelled
propelled
quelled
rebelled

repelled
shelled
smelled
spelled
swelled
unparalleled
upheld
weld
welled
withheld
yelled

elder
Imelda
welder
Zelda

welding
gelding

self
do-it-yourself
elf
herself
himself
itself
myself
oneself
shelf
yourself

selfish
elfish
shellfish
unselfish

elm
helm
overwhelm
realm

helmet
pelmet

help
self-help
whelp
yelp

Elsie
Chelsea

belt
at full pelt
Celt
conveyor belt
dealt
dwelt
felt
Franklin D Roosevelt
heartfelt
knelt
melt
misspelt
pelt
smelt
spelt
svelte
tighten one's belt
under one's belt
welt

shelter
belter
dealt her
delta
felt her
helter-skelter
melt her
misspelt her
pelt her
smelter
spelt her
swelter
welter

belch
squelch

health
Commonwealth
ill-health
stealth
wealth

healthy
stealthy
unhealthy
wealthy

twelve
delve
shelve

Kelvin
Melvin

Elvis
pelvis

elves
ourselves
selves
shelves
themselves
yourselves

Seychelles
Book of Kells
H G Wells
Orson Welles
Tunbridge Wells
URLs (= *uniform resource locators*)
wedding bells

You can add to this list by adding **-s** to some words that rhyme with **tell**, as in **smells**

5.7

gem
AGM (= *annual general meeting*)
AM (= *amplitude modulation*)
am (= *ante meridiem, before noon*)
ATM (= *automated teller machine*)

Bethlehem
CAM (= *computer-aided manufacture*)
condemn
diadem
Eminem
ERM (= *Exchange Rate Mechanism*)
FHM
FM (= *frequency modulation*)
GM (= *genetically modified*)
hem
IBM
Jerusalem
La Bohème
Lib Dem
M
NUM
phlegm
PM
pm (= *post meridiem, after noon*)
REM
rpm
stem
them
wpm (= *words per minute*)

You can also make rhymes for these words by using words in section **5.8** that rhyme with **pen**

Emma
dilemma
Gemma
tremor

lemon
Jack Lemmon
Yemen

lemony
anemone
Yemeni

demonstrate
remonstrate

memory
emery

jemmy
semi

epidemic
academic
endemic
polemic

chemical
biochemical
petrochemical
polemical

blemish
Flemish

demo
memo

member
December
dismember
non-member
November
remember
September

tremble
assemble
dissemble
reassemble
resemble

gremlin
Kremlin

solemnity
indemnity

hemp
temp

redemption
exemption

tempt
attempt
contempt
exempt
last-ditch attempt
pre-empt
unkempt

5.8

pen
again
amen
Ben
Big Ben
born-again
cayenne
comedienne
den
fen
gen
glen
Glen(n)
Gwen
hen
ISBN (= *International Standard Book Number*)
ITN
Ken
ken
LAN (= *local area network*)
Len
men
N
News at Ten
once again
Phnom Penh

pigpen
playpen
RN (= *Royal Navy*)
Sean Penn
Sir Christopher Wren
ten
then
Tony Benn
UN
USN (= *United States Navy*)
WAN (= *wide area network*)
when
wren
yen
Zen

✚

You can also make rhymes for these words by using words in section **5.7** that rhyme with **gem**

henna

antenna
Ayrton Senna
Jenna
Siena
tenner
tenor
Vienna

kennel

fennel

tenant

flight lieutenant
lieutenant
pennant

generate

degenerate (= *to deteriorate*)
regenerate
venerate

perennial

bicentennial
biennial
centennial

penny

any
a pretty penny
Benny
Jenny
Kenny
Kilkenny
Lenny
many
Penny
spend a penny
ten-a-penny

schizophrenic

allergenic
carcinogenic
hallucinogenic
hypoallergenic
photogenic
telegenic
transgenic

tennis

Den(n)is
Dennis the Menace
Glenys
menace
The Merchant of Venice
Venice

venison

Alfred Lord Tennyson

rennet

Elizabeth Bennet
Gordon Bennett
Senate
tenet

obscenity

serenity

Kenneth

zenith

end

amend
append
apprehend
ascend
at a loose end
attend
befriend
bend
blend
Bridgend
commend
comprehend
condescend
contend
defend
depend
descend
dirty weekend
distend
dividend
emend
extend
fend
friend
intend
Land's End
lend
make someone's hair stand on end
mend
offend
on the mend
Ostend
overspend
People's Friend
portend
pretend
recommend
rend
round the bend

send
Southend
spend
superintend
suspend
tend
to the bitter end
transcend
trend
upend
weekend
wend

gender

agenda
amender
ascender
attender
bartender
befriend her
bender
blender
Brenda
contender
defender
defend her
descender
engender
extender
fender
Glenda
Gwenda
hacienda
lender
lend her
mender
moneylender
offender
offend her
pretender
recommend her
render
sender
send her

slender
spender
splendour
surrender
suspender
tender
weekender

dependable

amendable
commendable
emendable
expendable
extendable

tendon

Brendan

attendance

dependence
independence
nonattendance
overdependence
resplendence
transcendence

tendency

ascendancy
dependency
resplendency
transcendency

pendant

ascendant
attendant
defendant
dependant
dependent
independent
interdependent
overdependent
resplendent
superintendent

tremendous

attend us
befriend us

end us
horrendous
lend us
offend us
recommend us
send us
superintend us
stupendous
suspend us
transcend us
upend us

tremendously

horrendously
stupendously

trendy

bendy
Sister Wendy
Wendy

splendid

intended
offended
open-ended
overextended
suspended
undefended
unintended

You can add to this list by adding **-ed** to some words that rhyme with **end**, as in **pretended**

ending

amending
appending
apprehending
ascending
attending
befriending
bending
blending
commending
comprehending

condescending
contending
defending
depending
descending
distending
emending
ending
extending
fending
heartrending
impending
intending
lending
mending
never-ending
offending
overspending
parascending
pending
portending
pretending
recommending
rending
sending
spending
superintending
suspending
tending
transcending
unbending
uncomprehending
unending
upending
weekending
wending

crescendo
decrescendo
diminuendo
innuendo
kendo
Nintendo®

endless
friendless

revenge
avenge
Stonehenge

strength
at arm's length
full-length
length

strengthen
lengthen

fence
coincidence
commence
condense
consequence
decadence
defence
dense
diffidence
diligence
disobedience
dispense
eloquence
eminence
evidence
excellence
expense
frankincense
hence
immense
impertinence
impotence
impudence
incense
incontinence
inference
innocence
insolence
intense
intransigence
magnificence

negligence
offence
omnipotence
pence
penitence
permanence
pestilence
precedence
pretence
providence
recompense
residence
self-defence
sense
suspense
tense
thence
turbulence
vehemence
violence
whence

censor
condenser
denser
dispenser
fencer
Lech Walesa
sensor
suspenser
tenser

pencil
stencil
utensil

sensory
dispensary
extrasensory

census
consensus
incense us
recompense us
sense us
tense us

sensible
comprehensible
defensible
incomprehensible
indefensible
insensible
ostensible
reprehensible

sensibly
comprehensibly
defensibly
incomprehensibly
indefensibly
insensibly
ostensibly
reprehensibly

density
immensity
intensity
propensity

pensive
apprehensive
comprehensive
counteroffensive
defensive
expensive
extensive
inexpensive
inoffensive
intensive
labour-intensive
offensive

pensively
apprehensively
comprehensively
defensively
expensively
extensively
inexpensively
inoffensively
intensively
offensively

senseless
defenceless

densely
immensely
intensely
tensely

essential
confidential
consequential
deferential
differential
existential
exponential
inconsequential
inessential
influential
nonessential
potential
preferential
presidential
providential
quintessential
residential
reverential
sequential
torrential
vice-presidential

essentially
confidentially
consequentially
deferentially
inconsequentially
potentially
providentially
quintessentially
reverentially

mention
abstention
apprehension
Ascension
attention
bone of contention

comprehension
condescension
contention
contravention
convention
declension
detention
dimension
dissension
extension
hypertension
inattention
incomprehension
intention
intervention
invention
misapprehension
pension
pretension
prevention
retention
suspension
tension

pensionable
mentionable
unmentionable

conventional
intentional
one-dimensional
three-dimensional
two-dimensional
unconventional
unintentional

well-intentioned
above-mentioned
aforementioned
dimensioned
ill-intentioned
intentioned
mentioned
pensioned
undermentioned

pretentious
conscientious
contentious
licentious
sententious
tendentious
unpretentious

tent
accent (= *to stress*)
Arthur Dent
ascent
assent
augment
bent
cement
cent
circumvent
consent
content
dent
descent
discontent
disorient
dissent
event
extent
ferment
50 Cent
foment
forewent
fragment (= *to shatter*)
frequent (= *to visit*)
gent
Ghent
Gwent
happy event
heaven-sent
indent
intent
invent
Kent
lament
leant

Lent
lent
meant
misrepresent
misspent
nonevent
orient
overspent
peppercorn rent
percent
present (= *to introduce*)
prevent
reinvent
relent
rent
repent
represent
resent
scent
segment (= *to divide*)
sent
spent
Stoke-on-Trent
Tashkent
torment
underwent
vent
went

The following words will also tend to rhyme with these when they come at the end of a line:
accident
accompaniment
acknowledg(e)ment
advertisement
argument
astonishment
banishment
belligerent
beneficent

betterment
bewilderment
complement
compliment
condiment
consequent
continent
corpulent
decadent
detriment
development
diffident
diligent
dissident
document
element
eloquent
embarrassment
embezzlement
embodiment
enlightenment
entanglement
entitlement
environment
establishment
excellent
excrement
exigent
filament
fraudulent
grandiloquent
imminent
impenitent
implement
impotent
imprisonment
improvident
impudent
incident
increment
indolent
innocent
insolent
instrument

intelligent
intransigent
irreverent
magnificent
management
measurement
monument
negligent
nourishment
omnipotent
opulent
ornament
parliament
penitent
permanent
precedent
predicament
presentiment
punishment
recipient
redolent
regiment
reticent
sacrament
sentiment
settlement
somnolent
subsequent
supplement
temperament
tenement
testament
tournament
turbulent
vehement
virulent

enter

centre
complement her
compliment her
content her
dissenter
epicentre

fermenter
fomenter
frequenter
inventor
Jobcentre
lament her
magenta
placenta
presenter
present her
preventer
prevent her
re-enter
renter
repenter
resenter
torment her

presentable

augmentable
fermentable
inventable
lamentable
preventable
rentable
unpresentable

mental

accidental
coincidental
continental
dental
departmental
detrimental
elemental
environmental
experimental
fundamental
gentle
governmental
incidental
incremental
instrumental
intercontinental
judg(e)mental

lentil
monumental
occidental
oriental
ornamental
parental
regimental
rental
sentimental
temperamental
transcendental
transcontinental
unsentimental

mentally

accidentally
coincidentally
departmentally
detrimentally
elementally
environmentally
experimentally
fundamentally
governmentally
incidentally
incrementally
instrumentally
judg(e)mentally
monumentally
occidentally
orientally
ornamentally
parentally
regimentally
sentimentally
temperamentally
transcendentally
transcontinentally
unsentimentally

instrumentalist

environmentalist
fundamentalist
Orientalist
sentimentalist

sentence
repentance

documentary
complementary
complimentary
elementary
parliamentary
rudimentary
supplementary
testamentary
uncomplimentary
unparliamentary

momentous
content us
discontent us
disorient us
misrepresent us
portentous
present us
prevent us
represent us
resent us
sent us

tentative
argumentative
preventative
representative
unrepresentative

plenty
aplenty
twenty

demented
contented
discontented
regimented
unrepresented

You can add to this list by adding -*ed* to some words that rhyme with *tent*, as in *resented*

dissenting
unrelenting

You can add to this list by adding -*ing* to some words that rhyme with *tent*, as in *resenting*

entity
identity
nonentity

incentive
attentive
disincentive
inattentive
inventive
preventive
retentive

memento
lento
pimento
Sacramento

eventful
resentful
uneventful

gently
Bentley
contently
intently

contentment
resentment

entry
gentry
re-entry
sentry

French
bench
blench
clench
Dame Judi Dench

drench
quench
retrench
stench
tench
trench
wench
wrench

venture
adventure
backbencher
clench her
drench her
misadventure
quench her
retrench her
wrench her

tenth
nth

menu
pull-down menu
venue

strenuous
disingenuous
ingenuous
tenuous

lens
cleanse
comediennes
dens
fens
glens
hens
pens
pigpens
playpens
telephoto lens
wrens
zoom lens

cleanser
cadenza

influenza

5.9

step
crêpe
Dieppe
Johnny Depp
overstep
PEP
pep
prep
rep
steppe
yep

pepper
high-stepper
leper

leopard
shepherd

separable
inseparable
irreparable

tepid
intrepid

reception
apperception
conception
contraception
deception
exception
Immaculate
   Conception
inception
interception
misconception
perception
preconception
self-deception

kept
accept

adept
crept
except
inept
intercept
leapt
overslept
overstepped
pepped
prepped
slept
stepped
swept
well-kept
wept

septic
antiseptic
aseptic
epileptic
Eurosceptic
sceptic

5.10

error
sierra
terror

Herod
Gerard

peril
Beryl
Cheryl
Errol
imperil
Meryl

necessarily
ordinarily
temporarily
voluntarily

herald
Ella Fitzgerald
Gerald

errand
gerund

deterrent
inherent

cherry
berry
Bryan Ferry
bury
Chuck Berry
Derry
ferry
Fred Perry
Halle Berry
Gerry
glacé cherry
Jerry
Kerry
Londonderry
make merry
merry
Perry
sherry
Terry
Tom and Jerry
very

cleric
atmospheric
Derek
derrick
Eric
esoteric
generic

Erica
America

clerical
hysterical
numerical
spherical

hysterically
numerically

terrify
verify

merriment
experiment

terrace
Nerys

perish
cherish

merit
demerit
disinherit
ferret
inherit

sincerity
asperity
austerity
dexterity
insincerity
posterity
prosperity
severity
temerity

5.11

dress
acquiesce
address
anybody's guess
assess
bad press
baroness
battledress
Bess
bless
Caithness
caress
chess
coalesce
compress
confess
convalesce

couldn't-care-less
cress
deaconess
depress
digress
dispossess
distress
DSS (= *Department of Social Security*)
duress
excess
express
finesse
guess
HMS
impress
Inverness
IRS (= *Internal Revenue Service*)
Jess
largesse
less
lioness
Loch Ness
manageress
mess
nevertheless
NHS
nonetheless
NUS (= *National Union of Students*)
OAS (= *Organization of American States*)
obsess
OHMS (= *On Her Majesty's Service*)
oppress
overdress
peeress
Porgy and Bess
POS (= *point of sale*)
possess
press
princess

profess
progress
PS
reassess
redress
regress
repossess
repress
RS (= *Royal Society*)
Rudolf Hess
S
SAS
second-guess
shepherdess
Sheerness
Skegness
SOS
stewardess
stress
success
suppress
Tess
transgress
trouser press
undress
unless
US
USS (= *United States Ship*)
VHS
watercress
yes

The following words will also tend to rhyme with these when they come at the end of a line:
absent-mindedness
assertiveness
backwardness
barrenness
bashfulness
bitterness

carelessness
cautiousness
cleanliness
cleverness
clumsiness
colourless
consciousness
drowsiness
eagerness
easiness
effectiveness
effortless
emptiness
expressionless
featureless
gentleness
giddiness
governess
greediness
holiness
humourless
idleness
indebtedness
inventiveness
jauntiness
judiciousness
lawlessness
laziness
limitless
liveliness
loneliness
manliness
meaningless
merciless
motionless
nastiness
nervousness
nosiness
odourless
openness
penniless
pitiless
powerless
precociousness

pretentiousness
quietness
selfishness
shabbiness
silliness
sorceress
stubbornness
suddenness
tenderness
thoroughness
ticketless
togetherness
unpleasantness
untidiness
usefulness
valueless
wariness
weariness
wickedness
wilderness

dresser
aggressor
assessor
bless her
caress her
compressor
confessor
impress her
lesser
obsess her
Odessa
oppress her
oppressor
possessor
predecessor
professor
stress her
successor
TESSA
Tessa
Vanessa

wrestle
Cecil

nestle
pestle
TESL (= *Teaching English as a Second Language*)
trestle
vessel

lesson
delicatessen
lessen

essence
acquiescence
adolescence
convalescence
effervescence
excrescence
fluorescence
incandescence
luminescence
obsolescence
phosphorescence
quiescence
quintessence

crescent
acquiescent
adolescent
antidepressant
convalescent
effervescent
fluorescent
incandescent
incessant
luminescent
phosphorescent
quiescent

pessary
accessory

messy
Bessie
dressy
Jesse

Jessie

accessible
expressible
inaccessible
inexpressible
irrepressible

message
presage

decimal
infinitesimal

dressing
blessing
depressing
distressing
prepossessing
pressing
unprepossessing
window-dressing

You can add to this list by adding *-ing* to some words that rhyme with **dress**, as in *guessing*

excessive
aggressive
depressive
expressive
impressive
inexpressive
manic-depressive
obsessive
oppressive
possessive
progressive
regressive
repressive
successive

excessively
aggressively
depressively

expressively
impressively
inexpressively
obsessively
oppressively
possessively
progressively
regressively
repressively
successively

desk
burlesque
grotesque
picturesque
statuesque

fresco
alfresco
Tesco
UNESCO

stressful
successful
unsuccessful

wrestling
nestling

yes-man
chessman

rest
abreast
acquiesced
addressed
arrest
assessed
attest
behest
bequest
best
blessed
blest
breast
Bucharest
Budapest

caressed
chest
coalesced
compressed
confessed
contest
convalesced
crest
depressed
detest
digest
digressed
dispossessed
distressed
divest
do one's level best
dressed
expressed
feather one's own nest
George Best
guessed
guest
hard-pressed
hornet's nest
impressed
infest
interest
invest
jest
Kanye West
lest
love nest
Mae West
manifest
Marie Celeste
messed
Mid-West
molest
nest
north-northwest
northwest
obsessed
oppressed
overdressed

pest
possessed
pressed
professed
progressed
protest
quest
reassessed
redressed
regressed
reinvest
repossessed
repressed
request
second-best
second-guessed
self-confessed
self-possessed
south-southwest
southwest
stressed
suggest
suppressed
test
transgressed
Trieste
undressed
unimpressed
unrest
unstressed
vest
well-dressed
west
wrest
zest

pester
blessed her
caressed her
Chester
Cirencester
detest her
Esther
fester

Hester
impressed her
investor
jester
Leicester
Lester
molestor
nester
north-northwester
northwester
polyester
protestor
questor
semester
sequester
south-southwester
southwester
sou'-wester
stressed her
Sylvester
tester
trimester

western
Charlton Heston
Mid-Western
north-northwestern
northwestern
Preston
south-southwestern
southwestern

contestant
decongestant

bestial
celestial

domestic
majestic

vested
arrested
attested
bequested
bested

chested
congested
contested
crested
detested
digested
divested
double-breasted
flat-chested
guested
infested
interested
invested
jested
manifested
molested
nested
protested
quested
reinvested
requested
rested
single-breasted
suggested
tested
tried-and-tested
uncontested
undigested
unrested
untested
wrested

destine
clandestine
intestine
predestine

jesting
arresting
attesting
bequesting
besting
chesting
contesting
cresting

detesting
digesting
divesting
guesting
infesting
interesting
investing
manifesting
molesting
nesting
protesting
questing
reinvesting
requesting
resting
suggesting
testing
unresting
wresting
zesting

festive
digestive
restive
suggestive

kestrel
ancestral
orchestral

pedestrian
equestrian

question
beyond question
congestion
digestion
indigestion
suggestion
without question

tempestuous
incestuous

5.12

pleasure
countermeasure
displeasure
leisure
measure
tape measure
treasure

measurable
immeasurable
pleasurable

5.13

fresh
afresh
Bangladesh
crèche
enmesh
flesh
Marrakesh
mesh
refresh
thresh

fresher
high-pressure
pressure
refresher
thresher

session
accession
aggression
compression
concession
confession
decompression
depression
digression
discretion
expression
freshen
immunosuppression
impression

indiscretion
intercession
manic depression
obsession
oppression
possession
procession
profession
progression
recession
regression
repression
secession
self-expression
self-possession
succession
suppression

professional
confessional
obsessional
processional
unprofessional

concessionary
discretionary

fleshy
Bangladeshi

5.14

set
abet
aid and abet
alphabet
Annette
Antoinette
baronet
barrette
Bernadette
beset
bet
Brett
brunette
cadet

cassette
cigarette
clarinet
Claudette
close-set
Colette
coquette
Corvette
courgette
croquette
debt
diskette
duet
epaulette
epithet
etiquette
forget
fret
gazette
Georgette
get
Internet
Intranet
Jean(n)ette
jet
Juliet
kitchenette
Lafayette
laundrette
layette
let
Lynette
maisonette
Marie Antoinette
marionette
met
minaret
minuet
motet
Nanette
Net
net
netiquette
no sweat

octet
Odette
overate
parapet
Paulette
pet
Phuket
pipette
pirouette
play hard to get
preset
quadruplet
quartet
quintet
regret
reset
Romeo and Juliet
rosette
roulette
septet
serviette
sextet
silhouette
Somerset
statuette
sublet
suffragette
sweat
thickset
threat
Tibet
turbojet
upset
usherette
vet
vignette
wet
whet
yet
Yvette

letter
abet her
aid and abet her
beset her

better
bettor
carburettor
debtor
fetter
forget her
for the better
get her
go-getter
Greta
Henrietta
jet-setter
let her
Loretta
met her
newsletter
operetta
pet her
setter
subletter
sweater
trendsetter
typesetter
upset her
Valetta
vendetta
vet her
wet her
wetter

regrettable
forgettable
unforgettable

settle
Dettol®
fettle
grasp the nettle
kettle
metal
mettle
nettle
petal
Popocatepetl
unsettle

threaten
Breton
cretin
Tibetan

petty
Betty
confetti
Hetty
Jean Paul Getty
jetty
machete
Serengeti
Shilpa Shetty
spaghetti
sweaty
Tom Petty
yeti

athletic
aesthetic
anaesthetic
apathetic
apologetic
ascetic
cosmetic
diabetic
emetic
energetic
frenetic
genetic
hermetic
kinetic
magnetic
pathetic
phonetic
poetic
prophetic
sympathetic
synthetic
unapologetic
unsympathetic

poetical
alphabetical
arithmetical

heretical
hypothetical
theoretical

genetically
alphabetically
apathetically
apologetically
athletically
cosmetically
energetically
frenetically
hermetically
hypothetically
pathetically
phonetically
poetically
prophetically
sympathetically
synthetically
theoretically
unapologetically
unsympathetically

athletics
aesthetics
anaesthetics
cosmetics
cybernetics
diabetics
emetics
genetics
hermetics
kinetics
phonetics
poetics
synthetics

indebted
abetted
aided and abetted
betted
duetted
fetid
fretted

jetted
netted
petted
regretted
sweated
vetted
wetted
whetted

betting
abetting
aiding and abetting
besetting
bloodletting
duetting
forgetting
fretting
getting
jetting
letting
netting
petting
pirouette
presetting
regretting
resetting
setting
silhouetting
subletting
sweating
upsetting
vetting
wetting
whetting

ghetto
falsetto
libretto
Rigoletto
Soweto
stiletto

set-up
get-up
het up

let-up

fretful
forgetful
regretful

Petra
et cetera

Betsy
tsetse

fetch
etch
lech
retch
sketch
stretch
vetch
wretch

stretcher
etcher
etch her
lecher
sketcher
sketch her
stretcher
stretch her

lecherous
treacherous

lechery
treachery

sketchy
stretchy
tetchy

fetching
etching
leching
retching
sketching
stretching

5.15

tether
altogether
at the end of one's
tether
blether
feather
get-together
Heather
heather
leather
together
under the weather
weather
whether

feathery
heathery
leathery

5.16

death
Beth
breath
Elizabeth
flog to death
hang on like grim
death
Lady Macbeth
Macbeth
Nazareth
Seth
worried to death

You can also make rhymes for
these words by using words in
section **5.4** that rhyme with
chef

5.17

clever
endeavour
ever

forever
however
never
never-never
same as ever
sever
Trevor
whatever
whatsoever
whenever
wherever
whichever
whoever
whosoever

level
bedevil
bevel
daredevil
devil
go to the devil
high-level
low-level
Neville
revel
top-level

reveller
leveller

prevalence
benevolence
malevolence

prevalent
benevolent
malevolent

cleverly
Beverley

seven
Aneurin Bevan
Devon
eleven
Evan
heaven

'e'

in seventh heaven
Kevin
leaven
Severn

seventh
eleventh

reverence
irreverence
severance

heavy
bevvy
bevy
levy

top-heavy

crevice
Ben Nevis

brevity
levity
longevity

5.18

pleasant
omnipresent
peasant
pheasant
present (= *here*)

unpleasant

pleasantly
presently
unpleasantly

president
nonresident
resident
vice-president

Lesley
Elvis Presley
John Wesley
Leslie

'ee'

green, cheeky, indeed

All the words in this section use the sound '**ee**' in their main stressed syllable

6.1

tree

A & E (= *accident and emergency*)

AB (= *able-bodied seaman*)

ABC

absentee

AD

ADC (= *aide-de-camp*)

agree

Ali G

ANC (= *African National Congress*)

asap

B

B & B

BBC

BC

be

Bea

bee

bonhomie

bootee

bourgeoisie

Bruce Lee

BSc

BSE

BST (= *British Standard Time*)

bug-free

bumblebee

C

CAB (= *Citizens' Advice Bureau*)

CAD (= *computer-aided design*)

CAP (= *Common Agricultural Policy*)

Capri

CB (= *citizens' band*)

CBE (= *Commander of the (Order of the) British Empire*)

cc

CD

CFC

Cherie

chimpanzee

CID

C-in-C (= *Commander-in-Chief*)

CJD

CND

COD

C of E (= *Church of England*)

CSE (= *Certificate of Secondary Education*)

CV

D

DC

decree

deep-sea

degree

detainee

devotee

disagree

divorcee

DOE (= *Department of the Environment*)

DTP (= *desktop publishing*)

Dundee

duty-free

DVD

E

ECG

ECT

EDP (= *electronic data processing*)

EEC

EFT (= *electronic funds transfer*)

eg

ELT (= *English Language Teaching*)

ENT (= *ear, nose and throat*)

EOC (= *Equal Opportunities Commission*)

escapee

ESP (= *extrasensory perception*)

EST (= *Eastern Standard Time*)

ET

Euro-MP

evacuee

examinee
fait accompli
fee
filigree
first-degree
flea
flee
foresee
formulae
free
fricassee
FTP (= *file transfer protocol*)
G
Galilee
GB
GCE
GCSE
GDP (= *gross domestic product*)
gee
glee
GMT
GNP (= *gross national product*)
GP
Grand Prix
guarantee
Gypsy Rose Lee
Harper Lee
he
HGV
HIV
HMG (= *Her Majesty's Government*)
HNC
HND
HP
HRT
HTTP (= *hypertext transfer protocol*)
ID
ie
interest-free

internee
interviewee
ISP (= *Internet Service Provider*)
IT
ITV
Jack Dee
jamboree
Joshua Tree
JP
jubilee
KB (= *kilobyte*)
kedgeree
key
KGB
knee
Laurie Lee
LCD (= *liquid crystal display*)
lea
lead-free
LED (= *light-emitting diode*)
Lee
low-key
LP
LSD
lychee
Marie
marquee
marrowfat pea
MBE
MC
MD (= *managing director*)
ME
me
MEP
mg (= *milligram(me)*)
mi
MOD
monoski
MOT
mother-to-be

MP
mpg (= *miles per gallon*)
MSc
MSG (= *monosodium glutamate*)
MSP (= *Member of the Scottish Parliament*)
NB
NME
nominee
NSPCC
NUT
OAP
OBE
OD
OECD (= *Organization for Economic Cooperation and Development*)
off-key
OHP (= *overhead projector*)
OTC (= *Officers' Training Corps*)
OTT
oversee
P
p & p
PAYE
payee
PC
PE
pea
pedigree
PG
PhD
plc
plea
PMT
PT
PVC
QC
QED

'ee'

quay
RAC
R & D (= *research and development*)
RC (= *Roman Catholic*)
RE
re (= *about*)
referee
refugee
rent-free
repartee
RIP
Robert E Lee
RP (= *Received Pronunciation*)
RRP (= *recommended retail price*)
RSPB
RSPCC
RSVP
RUC (= *Royal Ulster Constabulary*)
rupee
RV (= *Revised Version*)
SAE
scot-free
scree
SDLP
SDP
SE
sea
see
SET (= *selective employment tax*)
settee
she
ski
SNP (= *Scottish National Party*)
Spike Lee
spree
sugar-free
T
tax-free

TB
te
tea
tee
Tennessee
thee
three
Tiree
TLC
TNT
toll-free
Torquay
trainee
Tralee
trouble-free
trustee
TV
TVP (= *textured vegetable protein*)
twee
Tweedledee
UAE (= *United Arab Emirates*)
UHT
USP (= *unique selling proposition*)
UV
V
VAT
VC
vCJD (= *variant-CJD*)
VIP
virtuosi
vis-à-vis
Vivien Leigh
water-ski
WC
we
wee
whoopee
WP (= *word processing; word processor*)
WPC

ye
yippee
Z
Zebedee

The following words will also tend to rhyme with these when they come at the end of a line:
aborigine
absurdity
abundantly
academy
accompany
accordingly
accountability
accountancy
accuracy
accurately
acrimony
actively
actually
actuary
adequacy
adequately
Admiralty
admittedly
adultery
adversary
adversity
agency
agony
alacrity
Albany
alchemy
alimony
allegedly
allegory
alternately
alternatively
amnesty
anarchy
anatomy

'ee'

ancestry
anchovy
Anglesey
angrily
anomaly
Ant(h)ony
antipathy
anxiously
apathy
apostrophe
apparently
appropriately
approximately
arbitrary
archery
arguably
aristocracy
armoury
artery
artistry
assuredly
atrophy
attentively
auditory
autopsy
auxiliary
aviary
avidly
Aylesbury
balcony
bankruptcy
basically
beautifully
beneficiary
Bethany
bigamy
bigotry
biodiversity
biology
biopsy
blackberry
blasphemy
blissfully
bloodthirsty

blustery
bodily
breviary
brilliantly
broccoli
brotherly
budgetary
buoyancy
bureaucracy
burglary
busily
butchery
calamity
Calgary
calligraphy
calumny
candidacy
canopy
Canterbury
capably
captaincy
carefully
carelessly
carpentry
casually
casualty
catastrophe
category
cautiously
cavalry
ceaselessly
celebrity
celery
celibacy
cemetery
centrally
century
ceremony
certainly
chaplaincy
chastity
cheerfully
chemistry
chiropody

chivalry
Cicely
clemency
colliery
colony
comedy
comfortably
commercially
commonly
company
complacency
compulsory
conceivably
conciliatory
concurrently
conditionally
confectionery
confederacy
confidently
congratulatory
consciously
consequently
conservatory
conspiracy
constituency
consultancy
contemporary
contingency
contrary
controversy
corollary
coronary
Coventry
cowardly
cranberry
credulity
Cromarty
crotchety
culinary
currency
currently
custody
customary
cutlery

'ee'

dangerously
debauchery
deceptively
decidedly
deliberately
delicacy
delicately
delinquency
deliriously
democracy
dentistry
deputy
derogatory
desperately
despondency
destiny
desultory
diametrically
dictionary
differently
difficulty
digitally
dignitary
diplomacy
disciplinary
discrepancy
discriminatory
disorderly
distastefully
diversity
Dorothy
dreadfully
dromedary
drudgery
dynasty
dysentery
dystrophy
earnestly
easterly
eatery
ebony
economically
ecstasy
efficacy

efficiency
effortlessly
effrontery
elderly
electrically
electronically
elegantly
elegy
embassy
embroidery
Emily
eminently
emissary
emotionally
empathy
emphatically
enemy
energy
enmity
enormously
entirely
entirety
enviously
epitome
equally
estuary
ethically
ethnically
eulogy
evenly
eventually
evidently
exceedingly
excellency
exceptionally
excitedly
exemplary
expectancy
expediency
expertly
explanatory
explicitly
exquisitely
extraordinarily

extraordinary
fabulously
facsimile
faculty
faithfully
falconry
fallacy
famously
fantasy
fatally
fatherly
fearlessly
February
fidgety
fiendishly
figuratively
finally
finicky
flagrantly
fluently
foolishly
forcibly
forestry
forgery
fortunately
frantically
frequency
frequently
functionary
funnily
furiously
gaiety
galaxy
gallantry
gaudily
generally
generously
genially
gentlemanly
genuinely
Germany
gimmicky
gingerly
Glastonbury

'ee'

glossary
gluttony
gooseberry
gossipy
graciously
gradually
graphically
gratefully
gratuitously
gravelly
grievously
grocery
grudgingly
gruesomely
grumpily
guardedly
guiltily
haberdashery
habitually
half-heartedly
hallucinatory
handsomely
haphazardly
harmony
hastily
hazily
heartily
heavenly
heavily
helpfully
helplessly
heraldry
hereditary
heredity
heresy
heroically
hesitancy
hideously
historically
homeopathy
homily
honestly
honorary
hopefully

hopelessly
horizontally
horribly
hosiery
hospitably
humanly
humorously
humourlessly
Hungary
hungrily
hurriedly
husbandry
hypocrisy
idiocy
idiosyncrasy
idolatry
illegitimacy
illegitimately
illiberally
illogically
illusory
imagery
imaginary
immediacy
immediately
immodestly
immodesty
immorally
imperceptibly
imperfectly
impersonally
importantly
impotency
inadequacy
inadequately
inadvertently
incendiary
inclemency
increasingly
incredibly
independently
individually
industry
inefficacy

inefficiency
inevitably
inextricably
infamy
infancy
infantry
infinitely
infirmary
infirmity
inflammatory
inflationary
inhospitably
inhumanly
injury
innumeracy
insanitary
insignificantly
insolvency
instantly
intangibly
integrity
intentionally
intermediary
intimacy
intimately
intravenously
intricacy
introductory
invariably
inventory
invisibly
involuntary
inwardly
irony
itinerary
ivory
January
jealously
jealousy
jeopardy
Jeremy
jerkily
jewellery
jittery

jokily
jokingly
jovially
joyfully
judiciary
justifiably
Kennedy
knowingly
laboratory
lamentably
languidly
larceny
lavatory
lavishly
laxity
legacy
legality
legally
legitimacy
legitimately
leisurely
lengthily
leprosy
lethargy
liberally
liberty
library
lifelessly
lingerie
literally
literary
liturgy
locally
logically
longingly
lovely
luminary
lunacy
luxury
mahogany
majesty
malady
Malagasy
mammary

mandatory
manfully
manifestly
marginally
Marjorie
markedly
masonry
masterly
mastery
materially
mediocrity
melody
menagerie
mercenary
mercifully
merrily
messily
mightily
migratory
military
mimicry
ministry
miserably
miserly
misery
moderately
modestly
modesty
momentary
monarchy
monastery
monetary
monogamy
moodily
morally
morbidly
mortuary
mulberry
mutually
naivety
narrowly
nastily
naturally
needlessly

negatively
negligently
neighbourly
nervously
niggardly
noiselessly
noisily
Normandy
northerly
nostalgically
notably
noticeably
novelty
nudity
nugatory
numeracy
obesity
obituary
obligatory
observatory
obstinacy
obviously
occasionally
odyssey
Offaly
ominously
openly
orally
orderly
ordinarily
ordinary
originally
outwardly
overwhelmingly
pageantry
palmistry
panicky
panoply
papacy
papery
paramilitary
parody
partially
particularly

'ee'

patiently
peccary
peculiarly
pecuniary
penalty
Penelope
penitentiary
penury
peony
peppery
perceptibly
peremptory
perfectly
perfunctory
perilously
perpetually
personally
persuasively
pharmacy
philanthropy
philosophy
physically
piously
piracy
pitifully
plaintively
planetary
pleasantly
pleasantry
pleurisy
poetry
poignancy
pointedly
policy
politically
polygamy
popularly
positively
posthumously
potency
poverty
powdery
practically
precipitately

predatory
predictability
predictably
predominantly
preferably
pregnancy
preliminary
preparatory
presidency
presumably
previously
primacy
primarily
primary
privacy
privately
probably
probity
prodigy
profitably
profundity
progeny
prohibitively
prominently
property
prophecy
proprietary
provisionally
psychiatry
puberty
publicly
pulmonary
punctually
purgatory
purposely
quandary
quantity
quietly
rapidly
rarity
raspberry
reactionary
reasonably
recipe

redundancy
reformatory
regency
relatively
religiously
remarkably
remedy
repeatedly
repertory
reportedly
repository
reputedly
respectably
respiratory
reverie
rhapsody
rivalry
Romany
Rosalie
rosary
Rosemary
rosemary
Salisbury
salutary
sanctity
sanctuary
sanitary
savagely
Saxony
scantily
scarcity
scholarly
scruffily
scrupulously
scullery
secondary
secondly
secrecy
secretly
sesame
seventy
sexually
shabbily
shadowy

'ee'

shakily
shamefully
shamelessly
showery
Shrewsbury
Sicily
signatory
significantly
silently
silvery
similarly
simile
simultaneously
sinewy
singularly
sisterly
sketchily
sleepily
slippery
slovenly
socially
solidly
soliloquy
solitary
solvency
sophistry
sorcery
southerly
sovereignty
specifically
statutory
stealthily
Stephanie
stonily
strategy
strawberry
strenuously
structurally
stupidly
sub judice
subsequently
subsidiary
subsidy
subtlety

suddenly
successfully
sugary
suitably
summarily
suppository
supremacy
surprisingly
swimmingly
sympathy
symphony
synergy
syrupy
tacitly
tactfully
tactlessly
tangibly
tapestry
tardily
tastefully
tastelessly
tearfully
technically
telepathically
telepathy
temporary
tenancy
tenderly
tentatively
terminally
terribly
terrifically
territory
tertiary
testily
testimony
thankfully
thanklessly
therapy
thingummy
thoroughly
thoughtfully
thoughtlessly
timidly

Timothy
tomfoolery
totally
tragedy
tragically
transitory
travesty
treasury
trilogy
Tripoli
Tuscany
typically
tyranny
ultimately
unanimously
unconditionally
unconsciously
understandably
undoubtedly
uneconomically
unfortunately
unhurriedly
unimportantly
unintentionally
unitary
universally
university
unknowingly
unlovely
unnaturally
unpredictability
unreasonably
unscrupulously
unsubtlety
unsuccessfully
unsuitably
unsurprisingly
untypically
unusually
unwillingly
unwittingly
upholstery
uppity
urgently

urinary
usefully
uselessly
usually
usury
vacancy
vacantly
vagary
vagrancy
valency
valiantly
velvety
vertically
veterinary
villainy
violently
virtually
visibly
visionary
visually
vitally
vividly
vociferously
volubly
voluntary
wallaby
warranty
watery
westerly
wilfully
willingly
wittily
wittingly
womanly
Zachary

idea
foresee her
free her
freer
guarantee her
knee her
Lea(h)
Mia

Nicosia
oversee her
overseer
Ria
see her
seer
sightseer
skier
Sophia
trachea

agreeable
disagreeable
foreseeable
unforeseeable

Liam
foresee 'em
free 'em
guarantee 'em
knee 'em
mausoleum
oversee 'em
see 'em

Ian
Aegean
Caribbean
Crimean
epicurean
European
Fijian
Hebridean
Jacobean
Korean
paean
plebeian
Pyrenean
Tanzanian

seeing
agreeing
being
decreeing
disagree
fleeing

foreseeing
freeing
guaranteeing
keying
overseeing
refereeing
sightseeing
skiing
teeing
water-skiing
weeing
wellbeing

Leo
Cleo
Rio
Theo
trio

6.2

amoeba
RIBA (= *Royal Institute of British Architects*)
The Queen of Sheba

feeble
enfeeble
Keble

You can make rhymes for these words by using words in section **6.17** that rhyme with *evil*

keyboard
seaboard

Libra
zebra

6.3

week
antique
batik
beak
bezique

bleak
boutique
cheek
chic
clique
creak
creek
critique
eke
freak
geek
Greek
hide-and-seek
leak
leek
Martinique
meek
midweek
Mozambique
mystique
oblique
off-peak
peak
peek
physique
pique
reek
seek
shriek
Sikh
sleek
sneak
speak
squeak
streak
teak
technique
tweak
unique
weak
wreak

kneecap
recap

e-card
keycard

speaker
asylum-seeker
beaker
bleaker
cheek her
Costa Rica
eureka
freak her
leaker
Lake Tanganyika
loudspeaker
meeker
seeker
seek her
sleeker
sneaker
squeaker
streaker
Topeka
tweaker
Ulrika
weaker

beacon
archdeacon
Costa Rican
deacon
Mozambican
pecan
Puerto Rican
weaken

sneaky
cheeky
creaky
freaky
leaky
peaky
squeaky
streaky

speaking
cheeking
creaking
freaking
French-speaking
leaking
peaking
peeking
reeking
seeking
shrieking
sneaking
squeaking
streaking
tweaking
wreaking

weekly
bi-weekly
bleakly
meekly
sleekly
weakly

equal
sequel
unequal

6.4

seed
accede
Adam Bede
agreed
aniseed
bead
bleed
bottle-feed
breast-feed
breed
cede
centipede
concede
creed
decreed

'ee'

deed
disagreed
exceed
feed
force-feed
freed
Ganymede
geed
greed
guaranteed
he'd
heed
high-speed
impede
indeed
intercede
keyed
knead
kneed
knock-kneed
lead (= to guide)
millipede
mislead
misread (= to read
   wrongly)
need
Oliver Reed
plead
precede
proceed
read
recede
reed
refereed
secede
she'd
ski'd
speed
stampede
succeed
supersede
Swede
swede
teed

tweed
water-ski'd
we'd
weak-kneed
weed

reader
Aida
bleeder
breeder
cedar
cheerleader
feeder
feed her
Freda
freed her
leader
mindreader
mislead her
need her
newsreader
pleader
proofreader
ringleader
seeder
speeder
weeder

readable
machine-readable
pleadable
unreadable

needle
wheedle

Eden
Anthony Eden
Sweden

media
encyclop(a)edia
greedier
mass media
multimedia
needier

seedier
speedier
weedier

medium
tedium

median
comedian
tragedian

obedient
disobedient
expedient
ingredient

immediate
intermediate

greedy
beady
needy
seedy
speedy
weedy

orthop(a)edic
encyclop(a)edic

greedily
seedily
speedily

lead-in
Dunedin
feed in
intercede in
keyed in
lead in(= to guide)
succeed in

reading
breeding
leading
misleading
preceding
speeding

succeeding
weeding

You can add to this list by
adding **-ing** to some words that
rhyme with **seed**, as in **feeding**

torpedo
libido
lido
speedo
tuxedo

needless
heedless
seedless

siege
besiege
liege

DJ
Vijay

region
Glaswegian
legion
Norwegian

gee-gee
Fiji
squeegee

strategic
paraplegic
quadriplegic

Bognor Regis
aegis
Lyme Regis

weeds
Leeds
tweeds

You can add to this list by
adding **-s** to some words that
rhyme with **seed**, as in **needs**

6.5

chief
aperitif
Barrier Reef
bas-relief
beef
belief
brief
corned beef
debrief
disbelief
Georgia O'Keefe
grief
handkerchief
leaf
Lee Van Cleef
motif
overleaf
reef
relief
roast beef
sheaf
Tenerife
thief

You can also make rhymes for
these words by using words in
section **6.16** that rhyme with
teeth

prefect
defect (= a flaw)

beefy
leafy

briefing
debriefing
leafing

chiefly
briefly

6.6

league
fatigue
intrigue

eager
meagre
Riga

legal
beagle
eagle
illegal
regal

legally
eagerly
illegally
meagrely
regally

6.7

steal
Achilles' heel
Anil
appeal
automobile
Batmobile
conceal
congeal
daisywheel
deal
eel
feel
ferris wheel
genteel
heal
heel
he'll
imbecile
Ismail

John Peel
keel
Kiel
Kim Jong Il
kneel
Lille
Lucille
meal
Neil
peal
peel
reel
repeal
reveal
seal
she'll
Sir Robert Peel
snowmobile
spiel
squeal
stainless steel
steel
Sunil
the Bastille
three-course meal
veal
weal
we'll
wheel
zeal

Many English speakers
pronounce some words in
section **7.4** (eg *ordeal*) in such a
way that they rhyme with these
words

dealer

concealer
conceal her
feeler
feel her
healer
heal her

heeler
Jamila
kneeler
newsdealer
peeler
reeler
repealer
revealer
reveal her
sealer
Sheila
spieler
squealer
stealer
steal her
tequila
three-wheeler
wheeler
wheel her

Celia

Amelia
camellia
Cecilia
Cordelia
Delia
Ophelia
steelier

freely

mealy
steely
touchy-feely
tweely
wheelie

feeling

appealing
ceiling
concealing
congealing
Darjeeling
dealing
double-dealing
free-wheeling

healing
heeling
keeling
kneeling
pealing
peeling
reeling
revealing
sealing
squealing
stealing
steeling
unappealing
unfeeling
wheeling
wheeling and dealing

dealings

ceilings
feelings
peelings

beeline

feline

field

afield
appealed
battlefield
concealed
congealed
four-wheeled
healed
heeled
high-heeled
Huddersfield
ill-concealed
keeled
kneeled
left-field
low-heeled
midfield
pealed
peeled
reeled

repealed
revealed
sealed
shield
squealed
three-wheeled
two-wheeled
unconcealed
wedge-heeled
well-heeled
wheeled
wield
yield

6.8

dream

A Midsummer Night's
   Dream
beam
blaspheme
bream
clotted cream
cream
deem
double cream
downstream
esteem
extreme
gleam
harem
Ibrahim
ice-cream
Julian Bream
kibbutzim
let off steam
midstream
ream
redeem
regime
scheme
scream
seam
seem
self-esteem

single cream
sour(ed) cream
steam
stream
supreme
team
teem
theme
The Scream
upstream
whipped cream
whipping cream

You can also make rhymes for
these words by using words in
section **6.9** that rhyme with
dean

female
e-mail

dreamer
beamer
blasphemer
creamer
esteem her
femur
Hiroshima
Iwo Jima
lemur
Lima
reamer
Redeemer
redeem her
schemer
screamer
seamer
steamer
streamer

demon
seaman

anaemia
creamier
dreamier

leukaemia
seamier
septicaemia
steamier

dreamy
creamy
seamy
steamy

seeming
beaming
blaspheming
creaming
deeming
dreaming
esteeming
gleaming
reaming
redeeming
scheming
screaming
seaming
steaming
streaming
teaming
teeming
theming

seemingly
screamingly

Seymour
Timor

seemly
extremely
supremely
unseemly

6.9

clean
Aberdeen
Aileen
answering machine
aquamarine

aubergine
bean
been
beguine
Benin
between
big screen
black-eyed bean
bottle-green
broad bean
butter bean
caffeine
canteen
Charlene
Charlie Sheen
Charlotte Green
clementine
Colleen
contravene
convene
cuisine
David Lean
Dean
dean
demean
Dixie Dean
dopamine
dry-clean
eighteen
Eileen
emerald-green
evergreen
fifteen
fine bean
foreseen
Forest of Dean
fourteen
Francis Wheen
gabardine
gelatine
Gene
gene
Geraldine
glean

glycerine
go-between
Goose Green
green
grenadine
Gretna Green
guillotine
Hallowe(')en
has-been
Idi Amin
in-between
intervene
iodine
Jacqueline
jade-green
James Dean
Janine
Jean
jellybean
Jock Stein
Jolene
Josephine
Justine
Kathleen
keen
kerosene
kidney bean
knitting machine
latrine
lean
lima bean
limousine
machine
magazine
margarine
marine
Martine
Martin Sheen
Maxine
mean
mezzanine
Mr Bean
Nadine
naphthalene

navy bean
nectarine
nicotine
nineteen
nitroglycerine
obscene
overseen
oxyacetylene
pinto bean
polythene
preen
quarantine
Queen
queen
quinine
ravine
Roisin
routine
Roy Keane
runner bean
sardine
scene
screen
seen
serene
seventeen
sewing machine
sheen
Shereen
silver screen
sixteen
Slovene
small screen
soya bean
spleen
spring-clean
Steve McQueen
string bean
submarine
tambourine
tangerine
teen
terrine
The African Queen

thirteen
trampoline
tureen
ultramarine
umpteen
unclean
unforeseen
unseen
vaccine
velveteen
vending machine
village green
washing machine
wean
wide screen
Yitzhak Rabin

You can also make rhymes for these words by using words in section **6.8** that rhyme with **dream**

cleaner

Angelina
arena
Argentina
ballerina
Bosnia-Herzegovina
between her
Catriona
Christina
concertina
contravener
convener
Cortina
Davina
demeanour
dry-cleaner
Edwina
Ford Cortina
foreseen her
Georgina
Gina
gleaner

greener
guillotine her
hyena
Katrina
keener
leaner
Lena
Marina
marina
Martina
meaner
mean her
Messalina
misdemeanour
Nina
Pasadena
preen her
Pristina
retsina
Ribena®
Rowena
Sabrina
Saint Helena
screen her
seen her
Selina
semolina
Serena
Sheena
spring-clean her
subpoena
Tina
wean her
Wilhelmina
Zena

penal

duodenal
renal
venal

scenery

bicentenary
centenary
greenery

machinery
plenary
tercentenary

Venus

between us
genus
intravenous
mean us
seen us

Slovenia

Armenia
schizophrenia

menial

congenial
genial
venial

Slovenian

Armenian

lenient

convenient
inconvenient

teeny

Bikini
bikini
genie
Isabella Rossellini
Jean(n)ie
Lamborghini
meanie
Mussolini
Puccini
Queenie
Rene
Rossini
Santorini
teeny-weeny
zucchini

scenic

hygienic
unhygienic

phoenix
hygienics
Phoenix

meaning
cleaning
contravening
convening
demeaning
dry-cleaning
gleaning
guillotining
intervening
keening
leaning
machining
preening
quarantining
screening
spring-cleaning
weaning
well-meaning

casino
albino
Al Pacino
Angeleno
beano
cappuccino
Filipino
Lee Trevino
neutrino
palomino
Quentin Tarantino
Reno
Rudolph Valentino
San Marino
The Beano
vino

keenly
cleanly
meanly
obscenely
routinely

serenely

senior
Kenya
Monsignor

means
baked beans
jeans
Milton Keynes
New Orleans
Philippines
Queens
smithereens
teens

You can add to this list by
adding -s to some words that
rhyme with *clean*, as in *screens*

6.10

deep
asleep
beep
bleep
cheap
cheep
creep
dirt-cheap
heap
Jeep®
keep
knee-deep
leap
Meryl Streep
oversleep
peep
put to sleep
reap
seep
sheep
sleep
steep
sweep

Uriah Heep
weep

sleeper
barkeeper
beekeeper
beeper
bleeper
carpet-sweeper
cheaper
cheeper
creeper
deeper
doorkeeper
gamekeeper
gatekeeper
goalkeeper
housekeeper
innkeeper
keeper
keep her
leaper
leap her
minesweeper
peeper
reaper
shopkeeper
steeper
sweeper
the grim reaper
timekeeper
wicketkeeper

people
steeple
townspeople

cheapen
deepen
steepen

sleepy
creepy
weepy

sleeping
beeping
bleeping
bookkeeping
creeping
goalkeeping
heaping
housekeeping
keeping
leaping
oversleeping
peacekeeping
peeping
reaping
safe-keeping
seeping
sweeping
timekeeping
weeping

6.11

crease
apiece
Bernice
breach of the peace
caprice
cease
centrepiece
decease
decrease
Dumfries
fleece
frontispiece
geese
Grease
grease
Greece
Henri Matisse
increase
lease
mantelpiece
masterpiece
mounted police

Nice
niece
obese
peace
piece
police
release
Rhys
War and Peace

recent
decent
indecent

recently
decently
indecently

rhesus
Croesus
decrease us
fleece us
grease us
increase us
lease us
police us
release us

faeces
prostheses
theses

fleecy
greasy
St Francis of Assisi

leasing
ceasing
creasing
decreasing
fleecing
greasing
increasing
piecing
policing
releasing
unceasing

thesis
amniocentesis
prosthesis

seaside
Deeside
quayside
Teesside

east
beast
ceased
creased
deceased
decreased
feast
fleeced
greased
increased
leased
least
northeast
north-northeast
pieced
priest
released
southeast
south-southeast
yeast

Easter
barista
Batista
fashionista

6.12

seizure
freesia
Indonesia
Melanesia
Micronesia
Polynesia

Many English speakers
pronounce some words in
section **6.19** (eg *amnesia*) in
such a way that they rhyme
with these words

lesion
adhesion
cohesion
Fri(e)sian
Indonesian

6.13
leash
fiche
hashish
Kenny Dalglish
microfiche
niche
pastiche
quiche
unleash

Esher
Aisha
Nisha

completion
deletion
depletion
Grecian
secretion
Tahitian
Venetian

facetious
specious
unleash us

6.14
sweet
Arthur's Seat
beat
beet

bittersweet
bleat
cheat
compete
complete
conceit
cracked wheat
Crete
deceit
defeat
delete
deplete
discreet
discrete
downbeat
Downing Street
eat
effete
ejector seat
elite
en suite
entreat
excrete
feat
feet
fleet
greet
heat
ill-treat
incomplete
indiscreet
maltreat
meat
meet
mete
mistreat
neat
obsolete
overeat
overheat
parakeet
peat
Pete
petite

pleat
preheat
receipt
repeat
replete
retreat
seat
secrete
sheet
sleet
street
suite
teat
the patter of tiny feet
treat
tweet
unseat
upbeat
Wall Street
wheat
white as a sheet

detail
retail

heater
Anita
beater
beat her
centilitre
centimetre
cheater
cheat her
cheetah
complete her
defeat her
eater
entreat her
Evita
Gita
greeter
greet her
heater
ill-treat her
litre

Lolita
maltreat her
man-eater
meat-eater
meet her
meter
metre
millilitre
millimetre
mistreat her
neater
Nita
Peter
peter
repeater
Rita
saltpetre
seater
seat her
secretor
sweeter
teeter
treat her
tweeter
unseat her
windcheater
world-beater

beetle
Beatle
Beetle
betel
deathwatch beetle
decretal
f(o)etal

beaten
Buster Keaton
Cretan
eaten
Eton
moth-eaten
neaten
overeaten
sweeten

unbeaten
uneaten
weatherbeaten
wheaten
worm-eaten

treaty
entreaty
meaty
Nefertiti
sweetie
Tahiti

heated
bleated
cheated
competed
completed
conceited
deep-seated
defeated
deleted
depleted
entreated
excreted
greeted
ill-treated
maltreated
meted
mistreated
overheated
pleated
preheated
repeated
retreated
seated
secreted
sleeted
treated
tweeted
undefeated
unseated

beating
bleating

cheating
competing
completing
defeating
deleting
depleting
eating
entreating
excreting
fleeting
greeting
heating
ill-treating
maltreating
man-eating
meat-eating
meeting
meting
mistreating
overeating
overheating
pleating
preheating
repeating
retreating
seating
secreting
self-defeating
sheeting
sleeting
treating
tweeting
unseating

defeatist
elitist

defeatism
elitism

veto
burrito
Hirohito
incognito
Marshal Tito

'ee'

mosquito
Quito
SEATO (= *South-East
Asia Treaty
Organization*)

sweetly
completely
discreetly
indiscreetly
neatly

sweetness
neatness

eats
beats
beets
bleats
cheats
competes
completes
conceits
deceits
defeats
deletes
depletes
ejector seats
elites
entreats
excretes
feats
fleets
greets
heats
ill-treats
Keats
maltreats
meats
meets
metes
mistreats
overeats
overheats
parakeets

pleats
preheats
receipts
reheats
repeats
retreats
seats
secretes
sheets
sleets
streets
suites
sweets
teats
treats
tweets
unseats

reach
beach
beech
beseech
bleach
Bondi Beach
breach
breech
each
impeach
leech
overreach
Palm Beach
peach
preach
screech
speech
teach

teacher
beach her
beseech her
bleach her
creature
feature
Friedrich Nietzsche
impeach her

preacher
reach her
schoolteacher
screecher
teach her

teaching
beaching
bleaching
beseeching
breaching
far-reaching
impeaching
leeching
overreaching
preaching
reaching
schoolteaching
screeching

6.15

breathe
bequeath
Meath
seethe
sheathe
teethe
unsheathe
Westmeath
wreathe

breather
bequeather
either
neither

teething
bequeathing
breathing
seething
sheathing
unsheathing
wreathing

6.16

teeth
beneath
buckteeth
Edward Heath
heath
Keith
sheath
underneath
wreath

You can also make rhymes for these words by using words in section **6.5** that rhyme with *chief*

Aretha
beneath her
ether
Ibiza
sheath her
underneath her
wreath her

6.17

leave
achieve
Adam and Eve
believe
cleave
conceive
deceive
disbelieve
Eve
eve
Genevieve
grieve
heave
make-believe
naive
Niamh
overachieve
peeve

perceive
Rajiv
receive
relieve
reprieve
retrieve
sleeve
Steve
Tel Aviv
thieve
underachieve
weave
we've

fever
achiever
beaver
believer
believe her
cantilever
cleaver
cleave her
conceive her
deceiver
deceive her
disbeliever
disbelieve her
Eva
Geneva
grieve her
hayfever
heave her
leaver
leave her
lever
peeve her
perceive her
overachiever
receiver
receive her
relieve her
reprieve her
retriever
retrieve her

rheumatic fever
scarlet fever
unbeliever
underachiever
weaver

believable
achievable
conceivable
inconceivable
irretrievable
retrievable
unbelievable

evil
medieval
primeval
upheaval

even
Stephen
Steven
uneven

previous
devious

deviate
abbreviate
alleviate

weaving
grieving
heaving
receiving
thieving

bereaved
achieved
aggrieved
believed
cleaved
conceived
deceived
disbelieved
grieved
heaved

long-sleeved
overachieved
peeved
perceived
preconceived
received
relieved
reprieved
retrieved
short-sleeved
sleeved
thieved
underachieved
unrelieved
weaved

achievement
bereavement
overachievement
underachievement

leaves
achieves
Anne of Cleves
as thick as thieves
believes
cleaves
conceives
deceives
disbelieves
eaves
grieves
heaves
Jeeves
Jimmy Greaves
Keanu Reeves
Maldives
overachieves
peeves
perceives
receives
relieves
reprieves
retrieves
sheaves

sleeves
thieves
underachieves
weaves

6.18
freeway
leeway
seaway

kiwi
wee(-)wee

6.19
freeze
antifreeze
Antipodes
Balinese
Belize
breeze
Burmese
Cantonese
Celebes
cheese
Chinese
Congolese
deep-freeze
Denise
DTs
dungarees
ease
expertise
frieze
Gabonese
Guyanese
he's
Hebrides
Heloise
Hercules
Japanese
Javanese
jeez
John Cleese
journalese

Lebanese
legalese
like chalk and cheese
Los Angeles
Louise
Maltese
manganese
MEPs
monoskis
MPs
MSPs (= *Members of the Scottish Parliament*)
Nepalese
officialese
overseas
Pekinese
please
Portuguese
Pyrenees
Rameses
re-freeze
seize
Senegalese
she's
Siamese
Sinhalese
sleaze
sneeze
Socrates
squeeze
Sudanese
Taiwanese
tease
these
Togolese
trapeze
Ulysses
unease
unfreeze
valise
Valkyries
Viennese
Vietnamese

wheeze

You can add to this list by adding -s to some words that rhyme with *tree*, as in *agrees*

freezer
appeaser
appease her
crowd pleaser
displease her
ease her
foresees her
fridge-freezer
geezer
geyser
guarantees her
Julius Caesar
Leaning Tower of Pisa
Louisa
Mother Teresa
Pisa
please her
seize her
sneezer
squeeze her
squeezer
tease her
teaser
T(h)eresa
unfreeze her
visa
wheezer

weasel
diesel
easel
teasel

reason
off-season
season
treason

reasonable
seasonable
treasonable
unreasonable
unseasonable

reasoning
seasoning

amnesia
breezier
easier
queasier
sleazier

Many English speakers pronounce some words in section **6.12** (eg *Polynesia*) in such a way that they rhyme with these words

easy
breezy
queasy

sleazy
sneezy
uneasy
Zambezi

easily
breezily
queasily
sleazily
uneasily

pleasing
appeasing
displeasing
easing
freezing
seizing
sneezing
squeezing
teasing
wheezing

pleased
appeased
breezed
cheesed
diseased
displeased
eased
seized
sneezed
squeezed
teased
wheezed

'ear'

fear, weary, appear

All the words in this section use the sound '**ear**' in their main stressed syllable

7.1

dear
adhere
all-clear
appear
atmosphere
auctioneer
austere
beer
Benazir
bier
bioengineer
biosphere
black marketeer
blear
Boadicea
brigadier
Brighton Pier
buccaneer
career
cashier
cashmere
cavalier
chandelier
cheer
Chick Corea
clear
commandeer
Crimea
crystal-clear
deer
diarrhoea
disappear
Dorothea

ear
Edward Lear
endear
engineer
fear
gazetteer
gear
Golda Meir
gondolier
grenadier
Guinevere
hear
hemisphere
here
insincere
interfere
jeer
Kampuchea
Kashmir
King Lear
Korea
leer
lithosphere
Mamma Mia!
Maria
mere
mishear
mountaineer
musketeer
mutineer
near
North Korea
overhear
overseer

panacea
peer
persevere
pier
pioneer
profiteer
pyorrhoea
queer
racketeer
reappear
rear
revere
Richard Gere
scrutineer
sear
seer
severe
shear
sheer
sincere
smear
sneer
Sofia
South Korea
souvenir
spear
sphere
steer
stratosphere
Tangier
Tanzania
tear (= *a drop of moisture*)
tier

7.1

Tyne and Wear
unclear
veer
veneer
Vermeer
volunteer
Wear
weir
we're
Windermere
year
Zaire

7.2

weird
beard
tiered
veneered

You can add to this list by adding **-ed** to some words that rhyme with **dear**, as in **appeared**

7.3

tearful
cheerful
earful
fearful

7.4

real
ideal
ordeal
surreal
unreal

Many English speakers pronounce some words in section **6.7** (eg **deal**) in such a way that they rhyme with these words

really
austerely
clearly
dearly
half-yearly
ideally
insincerely
merely
nearly
queerly
severely
sincerely
unclearly
yearly

fearless
cheerless
peerless

realist
idealist
surrealist

realism
idealism
surrealism

realize
idealize

7.5

Vera
adherer
Alan Shearer
cheerer
cheer her
clearer
clear her
endear her
Elvira
era
hearer
hear her
interferer
jeerer

lira
lire
Madeira
nearer
queerer
rearer
revere her
shearer
smearer
sneerer
steerer

serum
cheer 'em
fear 'em
hear 'em
mishear 'em
near 'em
overhear 'em
theorem

clearance
adherence
appearance
coherence
disappearance
incoherence
interference
perseverance
reappearance

bacteria
Algeria
anterior
cafeteria
cheerier
criteria
diphtheria
drearier
eerier
exterior
hysteria
Iberia
inferior
interior

Lake Superior
Liberia
Nigeria
posterior
Siberia
superior
ulterior
wearier

serial
bacterial
cereal
ethereal
immaterial
imperial
magisterial
managerial
material
ministerial

materialism
imperialism

serialize
materialize

Nigerian
Algerian
criterion
Iberian
Liberian
Presbyterian
Shakespearean
Siberian
Zairean

serious
deleterious
imperious
mysterious

seriously
imperiously
mysteriously

weary
beery

bleary
cheery
dreary
eerie
eyrie
Kashmiri
Lake Erie
query
theory
world-weary

eerily
cheerily
drearily
wearily

hearing
adhering
appearing
buccaneering
careering
cashiering
cheering
clearing
commandeering
disappearing
earring
electioneering
endearing
engineering
fearing
gearing
God-fearing
interfering
jeering
leering
mishearing
mountaineering
nearing
orienteering
overhearing
peering
persevering
pioneering

profiteering
racketeering
reappearing
rearing
revering
searing
shearing
smearing
sneering
spearing
steering
tiering
veering
volunteering

hero
Joan Miró
Local Hero
Nero
Rio de Janeiro
Robert De Niro
sub-zero
zero

7.6

fierce
pierce

7.7

shears
Algiers
arrears
Britney Spears
in tears
Piers
Tangiers

You can add to this list by
adding -s to some words that
rhyme with **dear**, as in **appears**

'er'

herb, German, emerge

All the words in this section use the sound 'er' in their main stressed syllable

8.1

her
aver
blur
burr
concur
confer
connoisseur
defer
demur
deter
entrepreneur
err
fir
fur
incur
infer
inter
Louis Pasteur
masseur
myrrh
non sequitur
occur
per
prefer
purr
recur
refer
saboteur
sir
slur
spur
stir
transfer
voyeur
were
whirr

8.2

herb
blurb
curb
disturb
kerb
perturb
Serb
superb
verb

herbal
burble
gerbil
nonverbal
verbal

verbally
hyperbole
nonverbally

urban
bourbon
Durban
suburban
turban

sherbet
Herbert
turbot

Serbia
suburbia

disturbed
curbed
herbed
kerbed
perturbed
undisturbed
unperturbed

8.3

work
berk
berserk
bodywork
Dirk
dirk
Dunkirk
F W de Klerk
handiwork
irk
jerk
Kirk
kirk
latticework
lurk
metalwork
needlework
overwork
paperwork
perk
quirk
rework

shirk
silverwork
smirk
Turk
wickerwork

worker
berserker
bodyworker
circa
coworker
Gurkha
irk her
jerker
jerk her
lurker
metalworker
needleworker
overwork her
shirker
smirker
tearjerker

workable
reworkable
shirkable
unworkable

jerky
Albuquerque
murky
perky
quirky
Turkey
turkey

working
dirking
irking
jerking
hard-working
kirking
lurking
metalworking
overworking
perking

reworking
shirking
smirking

circuit
jerk it
rework it
shirk it
short-circuit
work it

heard
absurd
averred
bird
blurred
Cape Verde
concurred
conferred
curd
deferred
demurred
deterred
Dicky Bird
Douglas Hurd
erred
four-letter word
furred
gird
herd
incurred
inferred
interred
hummingbird
Kurd
ladybird
misheard
nerd
occurred
overheard
preferred
purred
recurred

referred
reword
Richard III
slurred
spurred
stirred
surd
the last word
third
Thora Hird
transferred
undeterred
whirred
word

Many English speakers
pronounce some words in
section **19.2** (eg *assured*) in such
a way that they rhyme with
these words

murder
deterred her
Gerda
girder
herder
heard her
interred her
misheard her
overheard her
preferred her
spurred her
stirred her
transferred her

hurdle
curdle
girdle

sturdy
birdie
hurdy-gurdy
nerdy
Verdi
wordy

verge
converge
dirge
diverge
emerge
merge
purge
scourge
Serge
serge
submerge
surge
urge

merger
perjure
purge her
urge her
verger

surgeon
burgeon
sturgeon
virgin

emergence
convergence
divergence

urgency
emergency
insurgency
resurgency

urgent
detergent
divergent
emergent
insurgent
resurgent

surgery
microsurgery
neurosurgery
perjury

8.5

turf
Astroturf®
serf
surf

You can also make rhymes for these words by using words in section **8.16** that rhyme with **earth**

surfing
turfing
windsurfing

8.6

Luxembourg
Brandenburg
erg
Gettysburg
Gothenburg
Heidelberg
Johannesburg
Nuremberg
St Petersburg

burgle
gurgle

8.7

curl
earl
furl
girl
hurl
mother-of-pearl
Pearl
pearl
purl
swirl
twirl
unfurl
whirl

---

surly
burly
curly
curly-wurly
early
Elizabeth Hurley
girlie
hurly-burly
pearly
Shirley

sterling
curling
furling
hurling
pearling
purling
Stirling
swirling
twirling
unfurling
whirling

girlish
churlish

world
curled
furled
hurled
News of the World
pearled
purled
swirled
twirled
underworld
unfurled
whirled

8.8

term
affirm
confirm
firm
full-term

germ
half-term
infirm
perm
reaffirm
sperm
squirm
worm

You can also make rhymes for these words by using words in section **8.9** that rhyme with ***turn***

murmur
affirmer
Burma
firmer
Irma
squirmer
wormer

thermal
geothermal

You can make rhymes for these words by using words in section **8.9** that rhyme with ***kernel***

German
Herman
sermon

vermin
determine
ermine
predetermine

terminate
exterminate
germinate

hermit
affirm it
confirm it
Kermit

permit (= *a licence*)
perm it
reaffirm it

confirmed
affirmed
firmed
permed
reaffirmed
squirmed
termed
unconfirmed

8.9

turn
about-turn
adjourn
Bannockburn
Bern(e)
burn
churn
concern
discern
earn
fern
intern
Jules Verne
Lake Lucerne
learn
overturn
pay-as-you-earn
return
spurn
stern
taciturn
tern
urn
yearn

You can also make rhymes for these words by using words in section **8.8** that rhyme with ***term***

learner
Bunsen burner
burner
burn her
churner
concern her
earner
intern her
Kathleen Turner
overturn her
returner
return her
spurn her
sterner
turner
turn her
yearner

returnable
discernible

kernel
colonel
eternal
external
fraternal
infernal
internal
journal
maternal
nocturnal
paternal

eternally
externally
fraternally
internally
maternally
nocturnally
paternally

sternum
burn 'em
concern 'em
earn 'em
intern 'em

laburnum
overturn 'em
return 'em
spurn 'em
turn 'em

journey
attorney
Bernie
Ernie

turning
adjourning
burning
churning
concerning
discerning
earning
interning
learning
overturning
returning
spurning
yearning

earnest
Ernest
The Importance of
  Being Earnest
sternest

furnish
burnish

eternity
fraternity
maternity
paternity

inferno
Salerno

concerned
about-turned
adjourned
burned
churned

discerned
earned
hard-earned
interned
learned
overturned
returned
spurned
turned
unconcerned
unearned
well-earned
yearned

adjournment
discernment
internment

learnt
burnt
weren't

8.10

slurp
burp
chirp
twerp
usurp

turpentine
serpentine

8.11

stirring
averring
blurring
concurring
conferring
deferring
demurring
deterring
erring
furring
incurring
inferring

interring
occurring
preferring
purring
recurring
referring
slurring
spurring
stirring
transferring
unerring
whirring

8.12

verse
adverse
averse
coerce
converse
curse
disburse
disperse
diverse
hearse
immerse
intersperse
nurse
perverse
purse
rehearse
reimburse
reverse
terse
transverse
traverse
universe
worse

cursor
bursar
coerce her
converser
curse her
disburser

disperser
immerser
immerse her
nurse her
precursor
purser
rehearser
reimburse her
reverser
reverse her
terser
traverser
vice versa

rehearsal
dispersal
reversal
universal

person
chairperson
non-person
salesperson
spokesperson
sportsperson
worsen

nursery
anniversary
bursary
cursory

mercy
Percy

subversive
discursive

tersely
adversely
conversely
perversely

first
burst
coerced
cursed

Damien Hirst
disbursed
dispersed
Geoff Hurst
headfirst
immersed
interspersed
nursed
pursed
rehearsed
reimbursed
reversed
thirst
transversed
traversed
versed
worst

thirsty
Kirsty

8.13

commercial
controversial
infomercial
uncontroversial

version
assertion
aversion
coercion
conversion
desertion
diversion
excursion
exertion
immersion
incursion
insertion
Persian
perversion
reversion
submersion
subversion

8.14

dirt
advert (= *to refer*)
assert
avert
Bert
blurt
cert
convert
curt
desert (= *to leave*)
dessert (= *a sweet course*)
disconcert
divert
exert
extrovert
flirt
girt
hurt
inert
insert
introvert
invert
John Hurt
Kurt
miniskirt
overt
pert
pervert (= *to lead astray*)
reinsert
revert
shirt
skirt
spurt
squirt
subvert
underskirt
unhurt

deserter
Alberta
asserter

converter
convert her
desert her
disconcert her
divert her
hurter
hurt her
inserter
inverter
perter
Roberta
skirter
squirter
subverter
subvert her

turtle
hurtle
Myrtle
myrtle

certain
curtain
uncertain

dirty
flirty
Gertie
shirty
thirty

deserted
asserted
averted
blurted
concerted
converted
disconcerted
diverted
exerted
extroverted
flirted
inserted
introverted
inverted
perverted

reinserted
reverted
skirted
spurted
squirted
subverted

furtive
assertive

hertz
adverts
asserts
averts
blurts
certs
converts
deserts (= what one
   deserves)
desserts
disconcerts
diverts
exerts
extroverts
flirts
hurts
inserts
introverts
inverts
just deserts
kilohertz
megahertz
miniskirts
perverts
reinserts
reverts
shirts
skirts
spurts
squirts
subverts
underskirts

search
besmirch

birch
church
lurch
perch
research

nurture
besmirch her
lurcher
percher
researcher
research her
searcher
search her

searching
besmirching
birching
lurching
perching
researching

8.15

worthy
airworthy
blameworthy
newsworthy
noteworthy
praiseworthy
roadworthy
seaworthy
trustworthy
untrustworthy
unworthy

You can make rhymes for these
words by using words in section
8.17 that rhyme with *nervy*

8.16

earth
afterbirth
berth
birth

dearth
down-to-earth
Fort Worth
girth
Middle Earth
mirth
Perth
rebirth
unearth
worth

You can also make rhymes for these words by using words in section **8.5** that rhyme with **turf**

Bertha
Eartha

8.17

nerve
conserve
curve
derv
deserve
observe
preserve
reserve
serve
swerve
unnerve
verve

fervour
conserver
deserve her
observer
observe her
preserver
preserve her
server

serve her
swerver
unnerve her

servant
fervent
observant
unobservant

nervy
scurvy
topsy-turvy

You can make rhymes for these words by using words in section **8.15** that rhyme with **worthy**

serving
conserving
curving
deserving
observing
preserving
reserving
swerving
undeserving
unnerving
unswerving

curved
conserved
deserved
observed
preserved
reserved
served
swerved
undeserved
unnerved
unobserved
unreserved

8.18

hers
avers
blurs
burrs
concurs
confers
connoisseurs
defers
demurs
deters
entrepreneurs
errs
firs
furs
incurs
infers
inters
masseuse
non sequiturs
occurs
prefers
purrs
recurs
refers
saboteurs
secateurs
slurs
spurs
stirs
transfers
voyeurs
whirrs

jersey
Jersey
Mersey
New Jersey

'**i**'

ship, city, admit

All the words in this section use the sound 'i' in their main stressed syllable

9.1

rib
ad-lib
bib
crib
drib
fib
glib
jib
nib
squib
women's lib

fibber
ad-libber
bibber
cribber
gibber
glibber
women's libber

dribble
nibble
quibble
scribble
Sibyl

ribbon
gibbon

Libya
Namibia
tibia

Libyan
amphibian

Namibian

exhibit
gibbet
inhibit
prohibit

9.2

quick
Arabic
arithmetic
arsenic
bishopric
Bolshevik
brick
candlestick
chick
click
crick
Dick
Dominic
double-quick
flick
get on someone's wick
get-rich-quick
heretic
hick
in good nick
kick
lick
Limerick
limerick
lunatic
maverick

Mick
Moby Dick
Nick
nick
nonstick
pick
politic
prick
Reykjavik
rhetoric
Rick
rick
Roderick
sic
sick
slick
stick
thick
three-card trick
tic
tick
travel-sick
trick
turmeric
Vic
wick

flicker
bicker
clicker
flick her
kicker
kick her
licker
lick her

liquor
nicker
nick her
nit-picker
picker
pick her
picnicker
pricker
prick her
quicker
rainslicker
ricker
sicker
slicker
snicker
sticker
thicker
ticker
tricker
trick her
vicar
Alan Whicker
wicker

knickers
Snickers®
Vickers

despicable
applicable
explicable
inexplicable

fickle
nickel
pickle
prickle
sickle
tickle
trickle

chicken
grief-stricken
horror-stricken
no spring chicken
panic-stricken

poverty-stricken
quicken
sicken
stricken
terror-stricken
thicken

trickery
chicory
flickery
hickory

tricky
Billericay
brickie
dicky
Mick(e)y
mickey
Nicky
Nikki
piccy
picky
quickie
Ricky
sticky
Vicki

ticking
bricking
clicking
cricking
flicking
kicking
licking
nicking
nit-picking
picking
politicking
pricking
ricking
sicking
sticking
tricking
wicking

ticket
click it
cricket
flick it
kick it
lick it
nick it
picket
pick it
prick it
rick it
stick it
thicket
tick it
wicket

rickety
pernickety

pick-up
hiccup
stick-up

quickly
prickly
sickly
thickly
trickly

sickness
airsickness
carsickness
homesickness
quickness
seasickness
thickness
travel-sickness

fix
affix
Beatrix
bishoprics
Bolsheviks
bricks
candlesticks
chicks

clicks
cricks
crucifix
fiddlesticks
flicks
geopolitics
Harvey Nicks
heretics
hicks
in the sticks
Jimi Hendrix
kicks
licks
like a ton of hot bricks
limericks
lunatics
MI6
mavericks
mix
nicks
picks
politics
pricks
ricks
six
sticks
Styx
suffix
three-card tricks
tics
ticks
transfix
tricks
wicks

mixer
elixir
fixer
fix her
sixer

vixen
Richard Nixon

mixed
affixed
fixed
suffixed
transfixed

mixture
fixture

fiction
addiction
affliction
benediction
constriction
contradiction
conviction
crucifixion
depiction
dereliction
diction
eviction
friction
jurisdiction
non-fiction
prediction
Pulp Fiction
restriction

strict
addict
afflict
bricked
Benedict
clicked
conflict (= to disagree)
constrict
contradict
convict
cricked
depict
derelict
evict
flicked
inflict
kicked

licked
nicked
picked
Pict
predict
pricked
restrict
ricked
sicked
slicked
ticked
tricked
wicked

victor
boa constrictor
depicter
inflicter
predictor
stricter
Victor

predictable
contradictable
convictable
inflictable
unpredictable

victory
contradictory
self-contradictory

addicted
afflicted
conflicted
constricted
contradicted
convicted
depicted
evicted
inflicted
predicted
restricted
self-inflicted
unrestricted

vindictive
addictive
restrictive

ubiquitous
iniquitous

antiquity
iniquity
ubiquity

gesticulate
articulate (= *to speak*)
matriculate

particular
curricular
extracurricular
perpendicular
vehicular

ridiculous
meticulous

9.3

lid
amid
bid
Billy the Kid
chid
did
El Cid
flip one's lid
forbid
grid
hid
inhabited
inhibited
kid
limited
Madrid
mid
outbid
outdid
overdid
prohibited

pyramid
quid
redid
rid
skid
slid
squid
talented
undid
uninhibited

bidder
consider
forbid her
hid her
kidder
kid her
outbid her
outdid her
reconsider
skidder
undid her

middle
diddle
fiddle
griddle
idyll
riddle
twiddle

hidden
bedridden
bidden
chidden
forbidden
midden
overridden
ridden
stridden
unbidden

hideous
fastidious
insidious
invidious

perfidious

bidding
forbidding
kidding
outbidding
skidding

stupidity
acidity
fluidity
humidity
liquidity
rapidity
rigidity
solidity
timidity
validity

fiddler
riddler
tiddler

fiddly
tiddly
twiddly

kidney
Sidney
Sydney

bridge
abridge
anchorage
average
beverage
Brooklyn Bridge
foliage
Forth Rail Bridge
Forth Road Bridge
fridge
haemorrhage
heritage
Humber Bridge
lineage
London Bridge
Menai Bridge

midge
ridge
Tay Bridge
Tower Bridge

religious
irreligious
prestigious
prodigious
sacrilegious

rigid
frigid

pigeon
pidgin
smidgen
wigeon

fidget
Bridget
digit
midget

abridged
averaged
bridged
haemorrhaged
ridged
unabridged

residual
individual

9.4

stiff
biff
bored stiff
Cliff
cliff
if
niff
quiff
riff
sniff
tiff

whiff

You can also make rhymes for these words by using words in section **9.16** that rhyme with *pith*

differ
sniffer
stiffer

differed
Clifford

stiffen
griffin
gryphon

Tiffany
Epiphany

vociferous
coniferous

periphery
midwifery

jiffy
iffy
sniffy

terrific
horrific
Pacific
prolific
scientific
soporific
South Pacific
specific
unscientific

You can also make rhymes for these words by using words in section **9.16** that rhyme with *neolithic*

gift
adrift
drift
GIFT (= *gamete intrafallopian transfer*)
lift
rift
shift
shrift
sift
swift
thrift
uplift

drifter
grifter
lifter
lift her
shifter
shoplifter
sifter
snifter
swifter
uplifter
uplift her
weightlifter

shifty
fifty
nifty
thrifty

uplifting
drifting
gifting
lifting
rifting
shifting
sifting

shiftless
thriftless

9.5

dig
big
fig
gig
infra dig
jig
pig
prig
rig
sprig
swig
twig
wig
WYSIWYG

digger
bigger
disfigure
figure
four-figure
gold-digger
gravedigger
jigger
prefigure
rigger
rigour
snigger
swigger
transfigure
trigger
vigour

giggle
jiggle
niggle
squiggle
wiggle
wriggle

ligament
disfigurement

vigorous
rigorous

bigot
frigate

piggy
biggie
biggy
Twiggy

stigma
enigma

figment
pigment

indignant
malignant
non-malignant

signify
dignify

dignified
signified
undignified

digs
Bay of Pigs
figs
gigs
jigs
pigs
prigs
rigs
Ronnie Biggs
Ryan Giggs
sprigs
swigs
syrup of figs
twigs
wigs

9.6

still
Benny Hill
Bill
bill
Brazil

brazil
chill
chlorophyl(l)
Cruella De Vil
daffodil
dill
distil
downhill
drill
fill
frill
fulfil
Gil
gill
go downhill
goodwill
Grange Hill
grill
grille
hill
if looks could kill
ill
instil
Jill
Jimmy Hill
kill
Kill Bill
Louisville
mill
nil
overkill
overspill
over the hill
Phil
pill
quill
refill
Rhyl
run-of-the-mill
Seville
shrill
sill
skill
spill

stand still
stock-still
swill
thrill
till
trill
until
uphill
vaudeville
Will
will
windowsill

killer
Arthur Miller
Attila
bill her
Camilla
caterpillar
cedilla
chiller
chill her
distiller
driller
drill her
filler
fill her
fulfil her
Glenn Miller
gorilla
griller
grill her
guer(r)illa
instil her
kill her
lady-killer
Manila
miller
painkiller
pillar
Priscilla
shriller
spiller
swiller

thriller
thrill her
tiller
triller
vanilla
villa
weedkiller
will her

syllable
monosyllable
refillable
tillable

villain
Bob Dylan
Dylan
Harold Macmillan

pillory
ancillary
artillery
capillary
distillery
Hilary
Sir Edmund Hillary

Phyllis
bacillus
bill us
chill us
drill us
fill us
fulfil us
grill us
kill us
refill us
thrill us
villus
will us

dilatory
depilatory

familiar
Brasília
haemophilia

unfamiliar

Brazilian
Chilean
Gillian
Lil(l)ian
pavilion
reptilian
Sicilian

bilious
punctilious
supercilious

silly
arum lily
Billy
Caerphilly
Chile
chilli
chilly
Dennis Lillee
filly
frilly
hillbilly
hilly
Lily
lily
Millie
Scilly
silly-billy
tiger lily
Tilly
water lily
Willie
willy-nilly

humiliate
affiliate
conciliate

idyllic
acrylic

silica
basilica

village
pillage
spillage

penicillin
Enniskillen

willing
billing
chilling
distilling
drilling
filling
fulfilling
grilling
instilling
killing
milling
refilling
schilling
shilling
skilling
spilling
spine-chilling
swilling
thrilling
tilling
trilling
unwilling

willingness
thrillingness
unwillingness

billet
fillet
millet
skillet

You can also make rhymes for
these words by using *it* after
some words that rhyme with
still, as in *spill it*

militate
debilitate

facilitate
rehabilitate

ability
accessibility
agility
availability
capability
civility
compatibility
credibility
debility
disability
durability
eligibility
facility
fallibility
feasibility
fertility
flexibility
fragility
futility
gullibility
hostility
humility
immobility
impossibility
improbability
inability
inaccessibility
incapability
incivility
incompatibility
ineligibility
inevitability
infallibility
infertility
inflexibility
instability
irresponsibility
liability
mobility
nobility
possibility

probability
profitability
reliability
respectability
responsibility
senility
stability
sterility
suitability
tranquillity
unavailability
unfeasibility
unprofitability
unreliability
unsuitability
utility
versatility
viability
virility
visibility
vulnerability

pillow
Amarillo
armadillo
billow
willow

willowy
billowy

bilberry
Tilbury

silk
buttermilk
ilk
milk
semi-skimmed milk
skimmed milk

silky
milky

build
billed
chilled

distilled
drilled
filled
frilled
fulfilled
grilled
gild
guild
instilled
killed
milled
overspilled
rebuild
refilled
skilled
spilled
strong-willed
swilled
thrilled
tilled
trilled
unfulfilled
unskilled
weak-willed
willed

builder
bewilder
guilder
Hilda
Mat(h)ilda
St Kilda

building
gilding
rebuilding

skilful
unskilful
wilful

skilfully
unskilfully
wilfully

fulfilment
instilment

illness
shrillness
stillness

tilt
built
custom-built
gilt
guilt
hilt
jerry-built
jilt
kilt
lilt
purpose-built
quilt
rebuilt
silt
spilt
stilt
well-built
wilt

filter
built her
jilt her
kilter
rebuilt her
tilt her

zilch
filch

million
billion
civilian
pillion
trillion
vermilion

gills
battle of wills
Beverly Hills
green about the gills

Mendip Hills
no-frills
old as the hills

You can add to this list by adding *-s* to some words that rhyme with *still*, as in *bills*

9.7

slim
acronym
Alastair Sim
antonym
brim
dim
Fatboy Slim
grim
gym
him
homonym
hymn
interim
Jim
Kim
limb
prim
pseudonym
rim
skim
swim
synonym
Tim
trim
whim

You can also make rhymes for these words by using words in section **9.8** that rhyme with *skin*

simmer
dimmer
glimmer
grimmer

'i'

primmer
shimmer
skimmer
slimmer
swimmer
trimmer
Zimmer®

women
persimmon

Jimmy
shimmy
Timmy

mimic
gimmick

image
scrimmage
spitting image

eliminate
discriminate (= to
    make a distinction)
incriminate

incriminating
discriminating
eliminating
undiscriminating

criminal
subliminal

slimming
brimming
dimming
rimming
skimming
slimming
swimming
trimming

limit
delimit
dim it
rim it

skim it
swim it
trim it

scimitar
perimeter

proximity
anonymity
equanimity
magnanimity
unanimity

timber
limber

nimble
cymbal
David Trimble
symbol
thimble

limbo
akimbo
bimbo
himbo

loose-limbed
brimmed
dimmed
hymned
limbed
rimmed
semi-skimmed
skimmed
slimmed
trimmed

nymph
lymph

dimly
grimly
primly

limp
blimp
chimp

crimp
imp
pimp
scrimp
shrimp
skimp
wimp

simper
crimper
scrimper
shrimper
whimper

simple
dimple
pimple
wimple

impish
wimpish

simply
limply
pimply

stimulate
simulate

9.8

skin
adrenalin(e)
akin
amphetamine
Anne Boleyn
aspirin
Bedouin
begin
Benjamin
Berlin
bin
built-in
bulletin
Catherine
chin
din

' **i** '

discipline
Errol Flynn
feminine
fin
Finn
genuine
get under someone's
  skin
gin
glycerin
Glyn
grin
Gwyn
heroin
heroine
Ho Chi Minh
Huckleberry Finn
in
indiscipline
inn
insulin
kaolin
kin
lanolin(e)
lie-in
Lohengrin
Lynn(e)
Madel(e)ine
mandolin
mannequin
masculine
medicine
melanin
moccasin
Nell Gwyn
next-of-kin
origin
paraffin
PIN
pin
rub it in
run-in
self-discipline
shin

sin
spin
stand-in
terrapin
thin
tin
Turin
twin
underpin
violin
vitamin
wafer-thin
win
within

➕
You can also make rhymes for
these words by using words in
section **9.7** that rhyme with
slim

dinner
beginner
Berliner
breadwinner
dog's dinner
Frank Skinner
grinner
inner
Michael Winner
moneyspinner
prizewinner
sinner
skinner
spinner
spin her
thinner
Yul Brynner
winner
win her

linear
Lavinia
non-linear
Sardinia
skinnier

tinnier
Virginia

aluminium
condominium

Sardinian
Argentinian
Palestinian
Virginian

skinny
cine
Albert Finney
Ginny
Guinea
guinea
Mini
mini
Minnie
Papua New Guinea
spinney
tinny
whinny
Winnie

clinic
cynic

clinical
cynical

winning
beginning
binning
chinning
disciplining
grinning
pinning
shinning
sinning
skinning
spinning
thinning
tinning
twinning
underpinning

'*i*'

sinister
administer
minister
prime minister

finish
diminish
Finnish

finishing
diminishing

finished
diminished
undiminished
unfinished

minute
begin it
bin it
discipline it
in it
Just a Minute
last-minute
pin it
skin it
spin it
thin it
twin it
underpin it
up-to-the-minute
win it
within it

Trinity
affinity
divinity
femininity
infinity
masculinity
vicinity
virginity

minnow
winnow

think
blink
brink
chink
clink
drink
hyperlink
Inc
ink
kink
link
mink
pink
rethink
rink
shrink
sink
slink
stink
sync(h)
wink
zinc

thinker
blinker
clinker
drinker
freethinker
Inca
inker
linker
shrinker
sinker
slinker
stinker
tinker
winker

drinkable
undrinkable
unsinkable
unthinkable

sprinkle
crinkle

Mrs Tiggy-Winkle
periwinkle
Rip Van Winkle
tinkle
twinkle
winkle
wrinkle

slinky
Helsinki
inky
kinky
minke
pinkie
stinky
Wee Willie Winkie

thinking
blinking
clinking
drinking
forward-thinking
hard-drinking
inking
kinking
linking
pinking
rethinking
right-thinking
rinking
shrinking
sinking
slinking
stinking
sync(h)ing
winking

crinkly
twinkly
wrinkly

inkling
sprinkling
tinkling
twinkling
wrinkling

jinx
lynx
sphinx
tiddlywinks

You can add to this list by adding **-s** to some words that rhyme with **think**, as in **links**

distinction
extinction

distinct
blinked
clinked
extinct
hyperlinked
index-linked
indistinct
inked
kinked
linked
pinked
rinked
succinct
sync(h)ed
winked

tinned
binned
chinned
close to the wind
dark-skinned
disciplined
finned
Gone With the Wind
grinned
indisciplined
pinned
rescind
Rosalind
self-disciplined
shinned
sinned
skinned

tamarind
thick-skinned
thinned
thin-skinned
twinned
underpinned
undisciplined
wind (= *a current of air*)

hinder
Belinda
cinder
Clarinda
Linda
Lucinda
tinder

swindle
dwindle
kindle
rekindle
spindle

linden
Swindon

windy
Cindy
Hindi
indie
Rawalpindi
shindy

India
windier

indicate
syndicate (= *to publish by means of a syndicate*)
vindicate

spindly
Myra Hindley

fringe
binge

cringe
hinge
impinge
infringe
singe
syringe
tinge
twinge
whinge

ginger
binger
injure
whinger

stringent
astringent
contingent

dingy
stingy (= *miserly*)

cringing
binging
singeing
swingeing
whingeing

ring
anything
B B King
Beijing
bring
cling
everything
fling
king
left-wing
Martin Luther King
Ming
Nanking
Peking
ping
right-wing
sing
sling

'i'

spring
Stephen King
Sting
sting
string
swing
The Ring
thing
ting-a-ling
wing
wring

clingy
dinghy
springy
stingy (= *stinging*)
stringy
thingy

singing
bringing
clinging
flinging
mudslinging
pinging
ringing
slinging
springing
stinging
stringing
swinging
upbringing
winging
wringing

finger
bell-ringer
bringer
bring her
clinger
flinger
fling her
forefinger
humdinger
left-winger

linger
malinger
right-winger
singer
slinger
springer
spring her
stinger
sting her
stringer
swinger
swing her
winger
wing her
wringer

single
intermingle
jingle
mingle
shingle
tingle

bingo
by jingo
dingo
flamingo
gringo
lingo

distinguish
extinguish

thinly
Finlay

since
convince
evince
mince
Port-au-Prince
prince
quince
rinse
wince

mincer
pincer
rinser

mincing
convincing
evincing
rinsing
unconvincing
wincing

spinster
minster
York Minster

Winston
Princeton

insular
peninsula
peninsular

print
bint
Clint
dint
fingerprint
flint
glint
hint
imprint
mint
Peer Gynt
peppermint
reprint
skint
spearmint
splint
sprint
squint
stint
tint

winter
Harold Pinter
midwinter
printer

sinter
splinter
sprinter
teleprinter

Quintin
Bill Clinton

printing
fingerprinting
glinting
hinting
imprinting
minting
reprinting
splinting
sprinting
squinting
stinting
tinting
unstinting

pinch
cinch
clinch
finch
flinch
half-inch
inch
lynch
the Grinch
winch

lynching
clinching
flinching
half-inching
inching
penny-pinching
pinching
unflinching
winching

plinth
hyacinth
labyrinth

pinion
dominion
minion
opinion

sinew
continue
discontinue

sinuous
continuous
discontinuous

ship
apprenticeship
battleship
blip
brinkmanship
censorship
chairmanship
championship
chip
citizenship
clip
companionship
comradeship
craftsmanship
dictatorship
dip
directorship
drip
equip
fellowship
felt-tip
fibre-tip
fingertip
flip
gamesmanship
governorship
grip
guardianship
gyp
hip

horsemanship
kip
ladyship
leadership
lip
membership
microchip
nip
one-upmanship
outstrip
ownership
paperclip
partisanship
partnership
Pip
pip
quip
receivership
relationship
rip
round-trip
salesmanship
scholarship
seamanship
showmanship
silicon chip
sip
skip
slip
snip
sponsorship
sportsmanship
strip
tip
trip
unhip
unzip
whip
workmanship
zip

flipper
big dipper
chipper

clip her
clipper
day-tripper
dipper
dripper
equip her
equipper
flip her
grip her
gripper
Jack the Ripper
kipper
nip her
nipper
outstrip her
Pippa
ripper
shipper
sipper
skipper
slipper
snipper
stripper
tipper
trip her
tripper
whipper
Yorkshire Ripper
zipper

ripple
cripple
nipple
tipple
triple

hippy
dippy
Mississippi
nippy
slippy
trippy
zippy

gripping
clipping
shipping
skipping

You can add to this list by adding *-ping* to some words that rhyme with **ship**, as in ***slipping***

snippet
Michael Tippett
whippet

You can also make rhymes for these words by using ***it*** after some words that rhyme with **ship**, as in **slip it**

rip-off
tip-off

slip-on
clip-on
get a grip on

clipboard
chipboard
flipboard
shipboard

crippling
rippling
Rudyard Kipling
stripling
tippling

shipment
equipment

eclipse
apocalypse
ellipse
Mr Chips

You can add to this list by adding *-s* to some words that rhyme with **ship**, as in ***trips***

tipsy
gipsy

lipstick
dipstick

description
conniption
conscription
decryption
Egyptian
encryption
inscription
prescription
subscription
transcription

script
conscript
crypt
decrypt
encrypt
manuscript
nondescript
transcript

You can add to this list by adding *-ped* to some words that rhyme with **ship**, as in ***tripped***

cryptic
apocalyptic
diptych
styptic
triptych

stipulate
manipulate

9.10

squirrel
Cyril

stirrup
chirrup
syrup

Miriam
delirium

lyrical
empirical
satirical

lyricism
empiricism

9.11

kiss
abyss
amiss
antithesis
armistice
avarice
Beatrice
bliss
cannabis
Chris
chrysalis
cowardice
dismiss
edifice
emphasis
genesis
hiss
hit-or-miss
hypothesis
Indianapolis
liquorice
metamorphosis
metropolis
Minneapolis
Miss
miss

near miss
orifice
parenthesis
photosynthesis
precipice
prejudice
reminisce
remiss
Swiss
synthesis
this

Melissa
Clarissa
dismiss her
kisser
kiss her
miss her

whistle
bristle
dismissal
epistle
gristle
missal
thistle

listen
christen
glisten

cissy
Chrissie
missy
prissy

permissible
admissible
inadmissible
kissable
missable
unmissable

participate
anticipate
dissipate

explicit
dismiss it
elicit
illicit
implicit
kiss it
licit
miss it
solicit

solicitous
duplicitous
felicitous

publicity
authenticity
complicity
duplicity
eccentricity
elasticity
electricity
Felicity
felicity
hydroelectricity
multiplicity
simplicity

Mrs
dismiss us
kiss us
misses
missus
miss us
prejudice us

risk
asterisk
brisk
compact disc
disc
disk
floppy disk
frisk
gold disc
hard disk
MiniDisc®

'i'

obelisk
platinum disc
silver disc
whisk

Biscay
risqué

discus
hibiscus
meniscus
viscous
whiskers

whisky
frisky
risky
whiskey

disco
Frisco
San Francisco

Christmas
isthmus

lisp
crisp
will-o'-the-wisp
wisp

mist
activist
amethyst
anarchist
arsonist
assist
atheist
bigamist
botanist
capitalist
catalyst
chauvinist
chiropodist
coexist
colonist
columnist

communist
conservationist
consist
conversationalist
cyst
desist
dismissed
dramatist
economist
ecoterrorist
egoist
egotist
enlist
essayist
Eucharist
evangelist
exhibitionist
exist
existentialist
exorcist
expressionist
federalist
feminist
fist
gist
grist
hedonist
herbalist
hissed
hypnotist
imperialist
impressionist
individualist
industrialist
insist
journalist
kissed
list
Liszt
lobbyist
lyricist
masochist
Methodist
misogynist

missed
monarchist
monetarist
motorist
naturalist
naturist
novelist
oboist
Oliver Twist
optimist
organist
pacifist
percussionist
persist
pessimist
pharmacist
philanthropist
physicist
physiotherapist
pianist
populist
pragmatist
prejudiced
psychiatrist
receptionist
reminisced
resist
round the twist
satirist
saxophonist
Schindler's List
scientist
separatist
socialist
soloist
strategist
subsist
symbolist
syndicalist
telephonist
televangelist
terrorist
The Exorcist
theorist

therapist
tobacconist
traditionalist
Trotskyist
tryst
twist
unionist
ventriloquist
vocalist
whist
wrist
Zionist

sister

assist her
blister
demister
enlist her
half-sister
kissed her
list her
missed her
Mister
Mr
resist her
resistor
stepsister
transistor
twister
twist her
vista

pistol

Bristol
Crystal
crystal

piston

cistern

distance

assistance
braking distance
coexistence
existence
insistence

long-distance
middle-distance
outdistance
persistence
resistance
subsistence

distant

assistant
consistent
equidistant
existent
inconsistent
insistent
nonexistent
persistent
resistant
water-resistant

distantly

consistently
inconsistently
insistently
persistently

history

mystery
prehistory

Christine

pristine

misty

Agatha Christie
Christy
twisty

mystic

altruistic
artistic
atavistic
autistic
ballistic
characteristic
chauvinistic
egotistic
euphemistic

fatalistic
futuristic
holistic
humanistic
idealistic
impressionistic
jingoistic
journalistic
linguistic
logistic
masochistic
materialistic
moralistic
nationalistic
naturalistic
nihilistic
optimistic
pessimistic
realistic
sadistic
simplistic
statistic
stylistic
uncharacteristic
unrealistic
voyeuristic

mystical

egotistical
logistical
statistical

linguistics

autistics
ballistics
characteristics
heuristics
logistics
mystics
statistics
stylistics

twisted

assisted
computer-assisted

coexisted
consisted
desisted
enlisted
existed
fisted
ham-fisted
insisted
listed
misted
persisted
resisted
subsisted
tight-fisted
unlisted

listing
assisting
consisting
coexisting
desisting
enlisting
existing
insisting
misting
persisting
resisting
subsist
twisting

wistful
fistful

9.12

vision
circumcision
collision
decision
derision
division
envision
Eurovision
imprecision
incision
indecision

precision
provision
revision
subdivision
supervision
television

9.13

wish
cuttlefish
dish
fish
jellyfish
Lillian Gish
kettle of fish
swish

fisher
fissure
kingfisher
Letitia
militia
Patricia
swisher
Trisha
wellwisher

official
artificial
beneficial
extrajudicial
initial
judicial
prejudicial
sacrificial
superficial
unofficial

officially
artificially
beneficially
initially
superficially
unofficially

fission
abolition
acquisition
addition
admission
ambition
ammunition
apparition
attrition
audition
beautician
coalition
cognition
commission
competition
composition
condition
contrition
decomposition
definition
demolition
deposition
dietician
disposition
edition
electrician
emission
erudition
exhibition
expedition
exposition
extradition
fruition
ignition
imposition
inhibition
inquisition
intermission
intuition
juxtaposition
magician
malnutrition
mathematician
Mauritian

'i'

mint condition
mission
mortician
musician
nutrition
obstetrician
omission
opposition
optician
paediatrician
partition
permission
petition
physician
politician
position
precondition
predisposition
premonition
preposition
presupposition
prohibition
proposition
recognition
remission
rendition
repetition
requisition
sedition
Spanish Inquisition
statistician
submission
superstition
supposition
suspicion
tactician
technician
theoretician
Titian
tradition
transition
transmission
tuition
volition

conditioner
audition her
condition her
parishioner
petitioner
petition her
position her
proposition her
requisition her

traditional
additional
conditional
nutritional
prepositional
transitional
unconditional

missionary
expeditionary

conditioning
air-conditioning
auditioning
commissioning
partitioning
petitioning
positioning
propositioning
requisitioning

reconditioned
air-conditioned
auditioned
commissioned
conditioned
partitioned
petitioned
positioned
propositioned
requisitioned

efficiency
deficiency
inefficiency
insufficiency

proficiency
sufficiency

efficient
coefficient
deficient
inefficient
insufficient
proficient
self-sufficient
sufficient

efficiently
deficiently
inefficiently
insufficiently
proficiently
sufficiently

vicious
ambitious
auspicious
capricious
delicious
fictitious
inauspicious
injudicious
judicious
malicious
Mauritius
nutritious
officious
pernicious
propitious
seditious
superstitious
surreptitious
suspicious
unambitious
wish us

viciously
ambitiously
auspiciously
capriciously
deliciously

inauspiciously
injudiciously
judiciously
maliciously
officiously
perniciously
propitiously
seditiously
superstitiously
surreptitiously
suspiciously
unambitiously

dishy
fishy
swishy

initiate
officiate
propitiate

fishing
dishing
fly-fishing
overfishing
swishing
wishing

issue
a-tishoo
Mogadishu
reissue
The Big Issue
tissue

sit
acquit
admit
alit
baby-sit
befit
benefit
bit
Brad Pitt

Brit
candlelit
chit
close-knit
commit
composite
deficit
emit
favourite
fit
flit
git
grit
hit
hypocrite
Identikit®
infinite
Inuit
it
Jesuit
keep-fit
kit
knit
lit
mitt
nit
omit
op cit
opposite
outwit
permit (= _to allow_)
pit
plebiscite
quit
readmit
refit
remit
resit
skit
slit
spit
Split
split
submit

tightknit
tit
transmit
twit
two-bit
unfit
unlit
Whit
whit
wit
writ
zit

bitter
acquit her
admit her
baby-sitter
bed-sitter
befit her
bit her
chitter
commit her
embitter
fit her
fitter
flitter
fritter
glitter
hit her
hitter
house-sitter
knitter
litter
omit her
outwit her
quitter
refitter
sitter
skitter
slitter
spitter
splitter
submitter
titter

transmitter
twitter
witter

hospitable
inhospitable
remittable

it'd
chittered
embittered
flittered
frittered
glittered
littered
skittered
tittered
twittered
wittered

little
acquittal
belittle
brittle
committal
it'll
noncommittal
remittal
skittle
spittle
whittle

bitterly
Italy

written
Benjamin Britten
bitten
Britain
Briton
flea-bitten
frostbitten
handwritten
hard-bitten
kitten
mitten

overwritten
rewritten
smitten
Tate Britain
underwritten
unwritten

Brittany
dittany
litany

pittance
admittance
remittance

obliterate
reiterate
transliterate

witty
bitty
city
committee
ditty
Forbidden City
gritty
Kansas City
Kitty
kitty
nitty-gritty
pity
pretty
self-pity
sitting pretty
subcommittee
Walter Mitty

critic
anti-Semitic
arthritic
bronchitic
paralytic
parasitic
Semitic

critical
analytical

apolitical
hypercritical
hypocritical
Jesuitical
parasitical
political
uncritical

fitted
committed
half-witted
hand-knitted
knitted
machine-knitted
quick-witted
slow-witted
uncommitted

You can add to this list by adding **-ted** to some words that rhyme with **sit**, as in **admitted**

mitigate
litigate

fitting
befitting
close-fitting
ear-splitting
hard-hitting
knitting
loose-fitting
side-splitting
sitting
splitting
tight-fitting
unremitting
unwitting

You can add to this list by adding **-ting** to some words that rhyme with **sit**, as in **admitting**

criticism
witticism

criticize
politicize

British
skittish

Britney
jitney
Whitney

witness
eyewitness
fitness

its
battle of wits
Biarritz
blitz
call it quits
double or quits
glitz
it's
quits
St Kitts
St Moritz
The Ritz

You can add to this list by adding -s to some words that rhyme with *sit*, as in *hits*

glitzy
ritzy

switch
bewitch
bitch
ditch
enrich
glitch
hitch
itch
kitsch
last-ditch
pitch
rich

Slobodan Milosevic
snitch
stitch
Switch®
ti(t)ch
twitch
which
witch

itchy
bitchy
kitschy
Richie
ti(t)chy
twitchy

situate
habituate

ritual
habitual

9.15

wither
dither
hither
slither
thither
whither
zither

withering
blithering
dithering
slithering

9.16

pith
Adam Smith
Bessie Smith
forthwith
Ian Smith
kith
myth
silversmith

smith
Will Smith

You can also make rhymes for these words by using words in section **9.4** that rhyme with *stiff*

neolithic
monolithic
mythic

You can also make rhymes for these words by using words in section **9.4** that rhyme with *terrific*

9.17

give
forgive
Liv
live (= *to exist*)
outlive
relive
sieve
spiv
Viv

*The following words
will also tend to rhyme
with these when they
come at the end of a
line:*
ablative
additive
adjective
administrative
affirmative
alternative
appreciative
authoritative
commemorative
competitive
conservative

contemplative
cumulative
decorative
definitive
derivative
diminutive
figurative
fugitive
genitive
imaginative
imitative
imperative
indicative
infinitive
initiative
innovative
intuitive
investigative
iterative
laxative
legislative
lucrative
manipulative
negative
nominative
operative
palliative
pejorative
positive
prerogative
preservative
primitive
prohibitive
punitive
putative
qualitative
quantitative
relative
remunerative
repetitive
secretive
sedative
sensitive
speculative

superlative
talkative
transitive
untalkative
vituperative

river
deliver
give her
forgive her
giver
liver
quiver
outlive her
shiver
sliver

livable
forgivable
relivable
unforgivable
unlivable

shrivel
civil
drivel
snivel
swivel
uncivil

equivalent
ambivalent

shrivelling
snivelling
swivelling

given
David Niven
driven
forgiven
striven

carnivorous
deliver us
herbivorous
omnivorous

shivery
delivery
livery
quivery

trivia
Bolivia
Olivia

trivial
convivial

Vivien
Bolivian
oblivion

oblivious
lascivious

privy
chiv(v)y
skivvy

vivid
livid

living
forgiving
giving
life-giving
misgiving
outliving
prizegiving
reliving
sieving
thanksgiving
unforgiving

rivet
forgive it
privet
trivet
live it
outlive it
relive it

activity
captivity

conductivity
festivity
inactivity
insensitivity
Nativity
negativity
objectivity
proclivity
productivity
radioactivity
relativity
subjectivity

9.18

whizz
Buck's fizz
Cádiz
fizz
his
is
Liz
Ms
quiz
swizz
Viz
viz

wizard
blizzard
gizzard
lizard

sizzle
chisel
drizzle
fizzle
grizzle

prism
alcoholism
altruism
Americanism
anachronism
Anglicanism
Anglicism

animism
antagonism
aphorism
atheism
barbarism
behaviourism
Bolshevism
botulism
Briticism
Calvinism
capitalism
cataclysm
catechism
Catholicism
chauvinism
classicism
colloquialism
colonialism
commercialism
communism
Constructivism
consumerism
despotism
dynamism
egotism
embolism
eroticism
euphemism
evangelism
existentialism
exorcism
expressionism
favouritism
federalism
feminism
feudalism
formalism
gradualism
hedonism
heroism
Hinduism
hooliganism
humanism
hypnotism

impressionism
jingoism
journalism
Judaism
liberalism
magnetism
mannerism
masochism
mechanism
metabolism
Methodism
militarism
modernism
monetarism
mysticism
naturalism
nepotism
opportunism
optimism
organism
ostracism
pacifism
paganism
paroxysm
patriotism
pessimism
plagiarism
pluralism
pointillism
post-modernism
pragmatism
professionalism
protectionism
Protestantism
radicalism
recidivism
regionalism
revisionism
rheumatism
romanticism
scepticism
schism
Scotticism
sensationalism

shamanism
Shintoism
socialism
spiritualism
stoicism
symbolism
syndicalism
terrorism
tribalism
Trotskyism
vandalism
ventriloquism
Vorticism
witticism
Zionism

prison
arisen
imprison
risen

Tunisia
busier
dizzier
fizzier

frizzier
Kirg(h)izia

Parisian
Tunisian

dizzy
busy
fizzy
frizzy
Lizzie
tizzy
whizzy

visible
divisible
indivisible
invisible
risible

physical
metaphysical
non-physical
quizzical

visit
exquisite
is it?

Lisbon
Brisbane

drizzly
busily
dizzily
grisly
grizzly

sizzling
drizzling
fizzling
grizzling
Quisling
quisling

dismal
abysmal
baptismal

gizmo
machismo

'ie'

pie, untied, fiery

All the words in this section use the sound '**ie**' in their main stressed syllable

10.1

try
abaci
AI (= *artificial insemination; Artificial Intelligence*)
alibi
alkali
ally (= *to join together*)
amplify
anno Domini
apple pie
apply
awry
beautify
belie
bone-dry
bring-and-buy
Brunei
BSI (= *British Standards Institute*)
butterfly
buy
by
bye
bye-bye
cacti
CAI (= *computer-aided instruction*)
Captain Bligh
CBI (= *Confederation of British Industry*)
CDI (= *compact disc interactive*)

certify
cherry pie
clarify
codify
comply
crucify
cry
Dai
decry
deep-fry
defy
deify
demystify
deny
descry
Di
die
diversify
DIY
dragonfly
drip-dry
dry
DTI (= *Department of Trade and Industry*)
Dubai
dye
edify
electrify
exemplify
eye
falsify
FBI
fly
foci

freeze-dry
fry
Gemini
GI
glorify
goodbye
Guy
guy
Hay-on-Wye
hereby
hi
hi-fi
high
HMI (= *Her Majesty's Inspector*)
horrify
hue and cry
I
identify
imply
indemnify
intensify
I-spy
July
justify
knee-high
let fly
lie
liquefy
London Eye
lullaby
lye
Madame Butterfly
magnify

160

'ie'

magpie
mince pie
modify
multiply
mummify
my
mystify
nearby
NI (= *National Insurance*)
nigh
notify
nullify
NY (= *New York*)
occupy
ossify
oversimplify
Paraguay
passer-by
personify
petrify
pi
pie
ply
preoccupy
Princess Di
Private Eye
private eye
prophesy
pry
purify
putrefy
qualify
quantify
rabbi
reapply
rely
reply
reunify
rhombi
River Kwai
RNLI (= *Royal National Lifeboat Institution*)

RPI (= *retail price index*)
RSI (= *repetitive strain injury*)
rye
sanctify
satisfy
shallow-fry
Shanghai
shy
sigh
simplify
sky
Skye
sly
solidify
specify
spin-dry
spry
spy
stand by
Stephen Fry
stir-fry
stupefy
stye
sun-dry
supply
testify
Thai
the apple of someone's eye
The Catcher in the Rye
thesauri
thigh
tie
tie-dye
tumble-dry
Tweety Pie
typify
UDI (= *Unilateral Declaration of Independence*)
underlie
unify

untie
Uruguay
vie
whereby
why
WI
wry
Y

fire
acquire
admire
aspire
attire
backfire
beautify her
Bedfordshire
Benjamin Zephaniah
Berwickshire
Billy Liar
briar
Buckinghamshire
buyer
buy her
Cambridgeshire
campfire
Carmarthenshire
Chariots of Fire
choir
Clackmannanshire
conspire
deep-fryer
defy her
dehumidifier
Denbighshire
denier
deny her
Derbyshire
desire
dire
Dunbartonshire
entire
expire
first-time buyer

friar
glorify her
Gloucestershire
hairdryer
Herefordshire
Hertfordshire
high-flier
hire
horrify her
humidifier
inquire
inspire
ire
Isaiah
Jeremiah
Kincardineshire
Kirkcudbrightshire
Lanarkshire
Lancashire
Leicestershire
liar
Lincolnshire
lyre
Messiah
mire
misfire
Monmouthshire
Morayshire
Northamptonshire
Nottinghamshire
owner-occupier
Oxfordshire
pariah
Peeblesshire
Pembrokeshire
perspire
petrify her
prior
pyre
quagmire
Renfrewshire
require
retire
rewire

Roxburghshire
sanctify her
sapphire
satire
satisfier
satisfy her
Selkirkshire
shire
sire
spare tyre
spin-drier
spire
squire
Staffordshire
Stirlingshire
tire
transpire
tumble-drier
Tyre
tyre
vampire
via
Warwickshire
washer-drier
Wigtownshire
wire
Worcestershire

You can add to this list by adding **-er** to some words that rhyme with **try**, as in **higher**

liable
deniable
justifiable
non-viable
pliable
reliable
undeniable
unjustifiable
unreliable
unverifiable
verifiable
viable

reliably
deniably
justifiably
undeniably
unjustifiably
unreliably
unverifiably
verifiably

tired
awe-inspired
dog-tired
hired
inspired
oil-fired
retired
uninspired
wired

You can add to this list by adding **-d** to some words that rhyme with **fire**, as in **attired**

trial
denial
dial
mistrial
phial
redial
retrial
self-denial

violate
annihilate

violet
inviolate
triolet
ultraviolet
Violet

tireless
wireless

requirement
retirement

lion
Brian
cast-iron
dandelion
grappling iron
gridiron
Hawaiian
ion
iron
Mayan
Paraguayan
Ryan
soldering iron
Uruguayan
wrought-iron
Zion

Briony
Hermione
irony (= *like iron*)

science
alliance
appliance
compliance
defiance
reliance
self-reliance

giant
client
compliant
defiant
reliant
self-reliant

hirer
admire her
admirer
desire her
direr
fire her
hire her
inquirer
inspire her
Ira

Myra
wire her

desirable
acquirable
undesirable

siren
Lord Byron

wiry
diary
enquiry
expiry
fiery
inquiry
priory

tiring
acquiring
admiring
aspiring
awe-inspiring
backfiring
conspiring
desiring
expiring
firing
hiring
inquiring
inspiring
misfiring
perspiring
requiring
retiring
rewiring
siring
squiring
uninspiring
untiring
wiring

bias
pious
Tobias

You can also make rhymes for
these words by using **us** after
some words that rhyme with **by**,
as in **spy us**

quiet
diet
disquiet
riot

rioter
dieter
proprietor
quieter

piety
anxiety
impropriety
notoriety
propriety
satiety
sobriety
society
variety

dietary
podiatry
proprietary
psychiatry

psychiatrist
podiatrist

dying
crying
edifying
electrifying
gratifying
high-flying
horrifying
low-flying
low-lying
lying
outlying
purifying
qualifying

quantifying
satisfying
stultifying
stupefying
terrifying
trying
underlying
unifying
unsatisfying

You can add to this list by adding **-ing** to some words that rhyme with **try**, as in **denying**

try-out
buyout
leveraged buyout

10.2

bribe
ascribe
circumscribe
describe
diatribe
gibe
imbibe
inscribe
prescribe
proscribe
scribe
subscribe
transcribe
tribe

fibre
bribe her
circumscribe her
describe her
imbiber
proscribe her
subscriber
Tiber

Bible
libel

tribal

eyebrow
highbrow

10.3

like
alike
bike
businesslike
dislike
dyke
Greg Dyke
hike
Ike
ladylike
lookalike
Mike
mike
motorbike
Offa's Dyke
pike
Private Pike
psych
share and share alike
soundalike
spike
sportsmanlike
statesmanlike
strike
trike
unalike
unbusinesslike
unlike
unsportsmanlike
workmanlike

striker
biker
dislike her
Formica®
hiker
hitchhiker
like her
mica

spike her
strike her
unlike her

cycle
cervical
Michael
motorcycle
recycle

spiky
crikey
Nike
psyche

striking
biking
disliking
hiking
liking
spiking
Viking

10.4

side
abide
allied
alongside
Ambleside
applied
aside
astride
backside
beady-eyed
beside
betide
bide
bleary-eyed
Bonnie and Clyde
bride
chide
classified
Clyde
coincide
collide

'ie'

confide
countryside
cried
cross-eyed
cyanide
decide
deep-fried
deride
dewy-eyed
dissatisfied
divide
doe-eyed
dried
eagle-eyed
fireside
fortified
fratricide
freeze-dried
fried
genocide
girl guide
glide
glorified
goggle-eyed
gratified
guide
herbicide
hide
homicide
horrified
Humberside
hydroxide
I'd
identified
implied
infanticide
insecticide
inside
Inverclyde
justified
matricide
Merseyside
Mr Hyde
nationwide

occupied
offside
outside
override
patricide
pesticide
Port Said
preoccupied
preside
pride
provide
rarefied
refried
reside
ride
riverside
satisfied
self-satisfied
shallow-fried
slide
sloe-eyed
snide
specified
spermicide
starry-eyed
stir-fried
Strathclyde
stride
subside
suicide
sun-dried
terrified
thorn in one's side
tide
tried
underside
unidentified
unjustified
unoccupied
unsatisfied
unspecified
untried
vied
waterside

wide

spider
abide her
alongside her
beside her
chide her
cider
collider
confider
decider
deride her
dried her
eider
Easy Rider
glider
glorified her
gratified her
guide her
hang-glider
hide her
horrified her
identified her
insider
inside her
joyrider
justified her
occupied her
outrider
outsider
outside her
preoccupied her
provider
rider
ride her
satisfied her
slider
spied her
tried her
wider

bridal
bridle
genocidal
homicidal

idle
idol
sidle
spermicidal
suicidal
tidal

widen
Leiden
Sidon

guidance
subsidence

strident
trident

tidy
bona fide
Friday
Heidi
Man Friday
untidy

guided
abided
bided
chided
coincided
collided
confided
decided
derided
divided
glided
lopsided
misguided
one-sided
presided
prided
provided
sided
subsided
tided
undecided

hiding
abiding
backsliding
biding
chiding
coinciding
colliding
confiding
deciding
deriding
dividing
gliding
guiding
hang-gliding
law-abiding
overriding
paragliding
presiding
providing
residing
riding
siding
sliding
striding
subsiding

guideline
sideline
tideline

10.5

life
afterlife
bane of one's life
Fife
for dear life
knife
long-life
Mack the Knife
paperknife
pocketknife
rife
strife
wife

cipher
decipher
Haifa
lifer

stifle
eyeful
rifle
trifle

hyphen
siphon

stifling
rifling
trifling

10.6

tiger
Eiger

10.7

smile
aisle
Anglophile
awhile
beguile
bibliophile
bile
Blue Nile
camomile
Carlisle
compile
crocodile
defile
domicile
Europhile
file
Francophile
guile
high-profile
I'll
infantile
isle

juvenile
Kyle
mercantile
mile
Nile
paedophile
pile
rank-and-file
reconcile
revile
rile
stile
style
tile
versatile
vile
volatile
while
worthwhile

Isla
beguile her
Delilah
compiler
filer
Islay
reconciler
reviler
revile her
rile her
rottweiler
smiler
tiler
Wat Tyler

nylon
pylon

island
Coney Island
Highland
Rhode Island
Thailand
Treasure Island

islander
Highlander

Highlands
islands

pilot
autopilot
copilot
eyelet
Pilate
twilit

shyly
drily
highly
Kylie
slyly
smiley
spryly
wily
wryly

mileage
silage

smiling
beguiling
compiling
defiling
filing
piling
profiling
reviling
riling
styling
tiling
whiling

styli
My Lai

skyline
by-line
try line

highlight
skylight

twilight

Lilo
Shiloh
silo

child
beguiled
compiled
defiled
domiciled
filed
great-grandchild
Madonna and Child
mild
Oscar Wilde
piled
reconciled
reviled
riled
smiled
styled
tiled
whiled
wild

wildly
mildly

wildness
mildness

wiles
Adrian Chiles
Giles
Nobby Stiles
piles

You can add to this list by adding -*s* to some words that rhyme with *smile*, as in *tiles*

10.8

time
all-time

chime
climb
crime
dime
extra-time
flex(i)time
full-time
Greenwich Mean Time
grime
Guggenheim
half-time
I'm
in one's prime
lime
maritime
mime
mistime
overtime
pantomime
paradigm
part-time
prime
rhyme
rime
slime
sublime
summertime
thyme
wintertime

You can also make rhymes for these words by using words in section **10.9** that rhyme with *line*

timer

chimer
climber
climb her
full-timer
Jemima
mimer
old-timer
part-timer

primer
prime her
rhymer
time her

slimy

blimey
grimy
limey
stymie

timing

chiming
climbing
miming
mistiming
non-rhyming
priming
rhyming

well-timed

ill-timed
unrhymed

You can add to this list by adding -(e)d to some words that rhyme with *time*, as in *climbed*

timely

sublimely
untimely

The Times

Peter Grimes
Radio Times
sign of the times

You can add to this list by adding -s to some words that rhyme with *time*, as in *rhymes*

line

align
alkaline

anodyne
aquiline
Argentine
asinine
assign
benign
borderline
brine
Calvin Klein
Caroline
Clementine
cloud nine
combine
concubine
confine
consign
Constantine
countersign
Courtney Pine
decline
define
design
dine
divine
endocrine
enshrine
entwine
fine
Frankenstein
incline
intertwine
Jeremy Vine
landmine
lay it on the line
Liechtenstein
Leonard Bernstein
malign
mine
mulled wine
nine
off-line
on-line
outshine
Palestine

pine
porcupine
realign
recline
refine
resign
Rhine
Rick Stein
shine
Shirley Valentine
shrine
sign
sine
spine
swine
tine
Torfaen
twine
Tyne
underline
undermine
valentine
vine
whine
wine

You can also make rhymes for these words by using words in section **10.8** that rhyme with *time*

liner

angina
Carolina
China
china
confine her
designer
Dinah
diner
diviner
enshrine her
eyeliner
finer

fine her
hardliner
Indochina
liner
maligner
malign her
miner
minor
mynah
Nixon in China
one-liner
outshine her
recliner
refiner
Regina
shiner
sign her
wine and dine her
whiner

definable

assignable
combinable
inclinable
indefinable
refinable

final

doctrinal
intestinal
quarterfinal
semifinal
spinal
urinal
vinyl

finery

binary
refinery

minus

confine us
define us
dryness
fine us
Highness

incline us
Linus
malign us
outshine us
shyness
sign us
sinus
undermine us
wine and dine us

tiny

briny
shiny
spiny
whiny

shining

assigning
combining
confining
consigning
declining
defining
designing
dining
divining
enshrining
entwining
inclining
intertwining
lining
mining
pining
reclining
refining
resigning
signing
underlining
undermining
whining
wining and dining

rhino

lino
wino

169

kind
behind
bind
blind
colour-blind
disinclined
find
grind
hind
humankind
lined
mankind
mastermind
mind
nonaligned
refined
remind
rewind
rind
unkind
unrefined
unsigned
unwind
wind (= *to twist*)

You can add to this list by adding -*(e)d* to some words that rhyme with **line**, as in **fined**

minder
baby-minder
behind her
binder
bind her
blinder
blind her
bookbinder
childminder
finder
find her
grinder
kinda
kinder
mind her

organ-grinder
rangefinder
reminder
remind her
viewfinder
winder

minded
absent-minded
blinded
bloody-minded
broad-minded
evil-minded
fair-minded
feeble-minded
high-minded
like-minded
narrow-minded
open-minded
reminded
right-minded
simple-minded
single-minded
small-minded
strong-minded

binding
blinding
bookbinding
fact-finding
finding
grinding
minding
reminding
rewinding
unwinding
winding

kindly
blindly
unkindly

kindness
blindness
unkindness

refinement
alignment
assignment
confinement
consignment

10.10

pipe
archetype
gripe
guttersnipe
hype
prototype
ripe
snipe
stereotype
stripe
swipe
tripe
type
unripe
wipe

viper
diaper
griper
hyper
hype her
piper
riper
sniper
stereotyper
swiper
swipe her
The Pied Piper
wiper
wipe her

disciple
archetypal

wiping
griping
hyping
piping

'ie'

sniping
swiping
typing

striped
griped
hyped
piped
sniped
stereotyped
swiped
typed
wiped

10.11

spiral
postviral
retiral
viral

virus
acquire us
admire us
attire us
Cyrus
desire us
desirous
fire us
hire us
Iris
inspire us
mire us
papyrus
require us
retire us
retrovirus
rewire us
sire us
tire us
wire us

Irene
polystyrene

giro
Biro®
Cairo
tyro

10.12

ice
advice
concise
cut-price
device
dice
entice
half-price
imprecise
lice
mice
nice
paradise
precise
price
rice
sacrifice
slice
spice
splice
suffice
thrice
trice
twice
vice

de-icer
dicer
entice her
icer
ISA
nicer
preciser
pricer
price her
ricer
sacrificer
sacrifice her

slicer
spicer
splicer

biceps
triceps

crises
Pisces

icy
dicey
pricey
spicy

bicycle
icicle
tricycle

icing
dicing
enticing
pricing
sacrificing
slicing
spicing
splicing
sufficing

crisis
Isis
midlife crisis

decisive
derisive
divisive
incisive
indecisive

nicely
concisely
imprecisely
precisely

iced
Antichrist
Christ
diced

'ie'

enticed
heist
overpriced
poltergeist
priced
sacrificed
sliced
spiced
spliced
sufficed

10.13

white
acolyte
alight
all right
anthracite
apartheid
appetite
bite
black-and-white
blight
Bonfire Night
bright
brownfield site
byte
candlelight
cellulite
cite
copyright
delight
despite
dynamite
erudite
excite
expedite
extradite
Fahrenheit
fight
flight
fly-by-night
Frank Lloyd Wright
fright
gelignite

gigabyte
goodnight
greenfield site
Guy Fawkes Night
height
hermaphrodite
ignite
impolite
incite
indict
in-flight
invite
Isle of Wight
Israelite
Jacobite
kilobyte
kite
knight
landfill site
light
megabyte
meteorite
might
mite
Muscovite
night
not a pretty sight
off-white
outright
overnight
oversight
overwrite
parasite
plight
polite
quite
recite
reunite
rewrite
right
rite
satellite
sight
site

sleight
slight
smite
Snow White
snow-white
socialite
spite
sprite
stalactite
stalagmite
tight
tonight
too right
trite
Twelfth Night
underwrite
unite
uptight
watertight
write

writer
bite her
biter
blighter
brighter
bullfighter
citer
copywriter
delight her
despite her
excite her
fighter
fight her
firefighter
firelighter
ghostwriter
highlighter
igniter
inciter
indicter
invite her
lighter
mitre

'ie'

overnighter
overwriter
politer
prizefighter
reciter
rewriter
righter
screenwriter
scriptwriter
sighter
slighter
smiter
songwriter
speechwriter
spite her
tighter
typewriter
underwriter
uniter
whiter
writer

excitable
indictable

vital
entitle
recital
subtitle
title

item
ad infinitum
despite 'em
fight 'em
smite 'em
spite 'em

frighten
brighten
Brighton
enlighten
heighten
lighten
tighten
whiten

frightened
brightened
enlightened
heightened
lightened
tightened
unenlightened
whitened

mighty
almighty
Aphrodite
blighty
flighty
nightie

sighted
alighted
blighted
cited
clear-sighted
copyrighted
delighted
dynamited
excited
expedited
extradited
far-sighted
flighted
ignited
incited
indicted
invited
knighted
lighted
long-sighted
near-sighted
overexcited
recited
requited
reunited
righted
sharp-sighted
short-sighted
sited

slighted
spited
uninvited
united
whited

writing
alighting
backbiting
biting
blighting
bullfighting
citing
copyrighting
delighting
dynamiting
exciting
expediting
extraditing
fighting
flighting
handwriting
igniting
inciting
indicting
infighting
inviting
knighting
lighting
moonlighting
nail-biting
overnighting
overwriting
reciting
reuniting
rewriting
righting
sighting
siting
slighting
smiting
spiting
underwriting
unexciting

uninviting
uniting
whiting

arthritis
appendicitis
bronchitis
conjunctivitis
cystitis
dermatitis
gastritis
gastroenteritis
gingivitis
hepatitis
laryngitis
mastitis
meningitis
osteoarthritis
peritonitis
rheumatoid arthritis
sinusitis
tonsillitis

frightful
delightful
insightful
rightful
spiteful

frightfully
delightfully
insightfully
rightfully
spitefully

sightless
flightless

slightly
brightly
fortnightly
lightly
nightly
politely
rightly
sprightly

tightly
unsightly

excitement
incitement
indictment

lightning
brightening
enlightening
frightening
heightening
lightening
tightening
whitening
unenlightening

brightness
impoliteness
lightness
politeness
tightness
whiteness

tights
Arabian Nights
Dolomites
human rights
see the sights
Wuthering Heights

You can add to this list by
adding **-s** to some words that
rhyme with **white**, as in **fights**

10.14

writhe
blithe
lithe
scythe

10.15

five
alive
arrive

Clive
connive
contrive
deprive
derive
dive
drive
hive
I've
jive
live (= *alive*)
MI5
overdrive
revive
skive
strive
survive
thrive

driver
conniver
deprive her
diver
drive her
fiver
Ivor
jiver
Lady Godiva
pile-driver
revive her
saliva
screwdriver
skiver
skydiver
striver
survivor
thriver
viva (= *an oral
   examination*)

rival
arrival
revival
survival

liven
enliven
Ivan

contrivance
connivance

driving
arriving
conniving
contriving
depriving
deriving
diving
drink-driving
reviving
skiving
skydiving
striving
surviving
thriving

thrived
arrived
connived
contrived
deprived
derived
dived
hived
jived
revived
skived
strived
survived

knives
chives
lives (= *existences*)
St Ives
wives

You can add to this list by
adding **-s** to some words that
rhyme with *five*, as in ***drives***

10.16

highway
byway
fly way
my way

10.17

prize
acclimatize
advertise
advise
agonize
anaesthetize
analyse
antagonize
apologize
appetize
arise
authorize
baptize
booby-prize
bowdlerize
breathalyse
brutalize
burglarize
cannibalize
canonize
capitalize
capsize
carbonize
categorize
cauterize
centralize
characterize
chastise
circumcise
civilize
collectivize
colonize
comprise
compromise
computerize
conceptualize

counter-clockwise
crystallize
customize
decentralize
dehumanize
demilitarize
demise
demobilize
demoralize
deputize
despise
destabilize
devise
dies
disenfranchise
disguise
dramatize
economize
empathize
emphasize
enfranchise
enterprise
epitomize
equalize
eulogize
evangelize
excise
exercise
exorcize
extemporize
familiarize
fantasize
fertilize
finalize
franchise
fraternize
fries
galvanize
generalize
glamorize
guise
half-size
harmonize
high-rise

'ie'

homogenize
hospitalize
humanize
hypnotize
hypothesize
idolize
immobilize
immunize
improvise
industrialize
institutionalize
internalize
ionize
itemize
jeopardize
king-size
legalize
liberalize
liquidize
Lord of the Flies
marginalize
maximize
mechanize
memorize
merchandise
mesmerize
miniaturize
minimize
mobilize
modernize
moisturize
monopolize
moralize
Morecambe and Wise
motorize
naturalize
neutralize
Nobel Prize
optimize
organize
ostracize
otherwise
overemphasize
oxidize

paralyse
pasteurize
patronize
pedestrianize
penalize
philosophize
photosynthesize
pixelize
plagiarize
polarize
popularize
pressurize
prioritize
prise
privatize
psychoanalyse
publicize
pulverize
queen-size
readvertise
recognize
reorganize
revise
revitalize
revolutionize
rhapsodize
rise
romanticize
sanitize
satirize
scrutinize
size
socialize
specialize
stabilize
standardize
sterilize
stigmatize
subsidize
summarize
supervise
surmise
surprise
symbolize

sympathize
synchronize
synthesize
systematize
tantalize
televise
terrorize
theorize
traumatize
trivialize
tyrannize
unionize
unwise
utilize
vaporize
verbalize
victimize
visualize
wise
worldly-wise

miser
advise her
adviser
antagonize her
appetizer
bowdlerizer
Breathalyser
centralizer
chastiser
civilizer
colonizer
compromise her
compromiser
despise her
despiser
deviser
disguise her
disguiser
economizer
Eliza
epitomizer
equalizer
exerciser

'ie'

fertilizer
franchiser
fraternizer
galvanizer
glamorize her
guiser
harmonizer
homogenizer
idolize her
idolizer
immobilizer
immunizer
improviser
incisor
ionizer
itemizer
liquidizer
Liza
maximizer
mesmerize her
mobilizer
modernizer
moisturizer
moralizer
neutralizer
optimizer
organizer
oxidizer
pasteurizer
polarizer
popularizer
privatizer
prizer
pulverizer
reviser
riser
sanitizer
sizer
socializer
stabilizer
standardizer
sterilizer
summarizer
supervisor

surmiser
surprise her
sympathizer
synchronizer
synthesizer
systematizer
tantalizer
terrorizer
tranquillizer
utilizer
vaporizer
victimizer
visor
visualizer
wiser
womanizer

siz(e)able
advisable
inadvisable
recognizable
unrecognizable

advisory
supervisory

rising
acclimatizing
advertising
advising
agonizing
anaesthetizing
analysing
apologizing
appetizing
arising
authorizing
baptizing
bowdlerizing
breathalysing
brutalizing
burglarizing
cannibalizing
canonizing
capitalizing

capsizing
carbonizing
categorizing
cauterizing
centralizing
characterizing
chastising
circumcising
civilizing
collectivizing
colonizing
comprising
compromising
computerizing
conceptualizing
crystallizing
customizing
decentralizing
dehumanizing
demilitarizing
demobilizing
demoralizing
deputizing
despising
destabilizing
devising
disenfranchising
disguising
downsizing
dramatizing
economizing
empathizing
emphasizing
enterprising
epitomizing
equalizing
eulogizing
evangelizing
excising
exercising
exorcizing
extemporizing
familiarizing
fantasizing

'ie'

fertilizing
finalizing
fraternizing
galvanizing
generalizing
glamorizing
harmonizing
homogenizing
hospitalizing
humanizing
hypnotizing
hypothesizing
idolizing
immobilizing
immunizing
improvising
industrializing
institutionalizing
internalizing
ionizing
itemizing
jeopardizing
legalizing
liberalizing
liquidizing
marginalizing
maximizing
mechanizing
memorizing
merchandising
mesmerizing
miniaturizing
minimizing
modernizing
moisturizing
monopolizing
moralizing
motorizing
nationalizing
naturalizing
neutralizing
optimizing
organizing
ostracizing

overemphasizing
oxidizing
paralysing
pasteurizing
patronizing
pedestrianizing
penalizing
philosophizing
photosynthesizing
pixelizing
plagiarizing
polarizing
popularizing
pressurizing
prioritizing
prising
privatizing
psychoanalysing
publicizing
pulverizing
readvertising
recognizing
reorganizing
revising
revitalizing
revolutionizing
rhapsodizing
romanticizing
sanitizing
satirizing
scrutinizing
sizing
socializing
specializing
stabilizing
standardizing
sterilizing
stigmatizing
subsidizing
summarizing
supervising
surmising
surprising
symbolizing

sympathizing
synchronizing
synthesizing
systematizing
tantalizing
televising
terrorizing
theorizing
traumatizing
trivializing
tyrannizing
unappetizing
uncompromising
unenterprising
unionizing
unsurprising
uprising
utilizing
vaporizing
verbalizing
victimizing
visualizing

proviso
Valparaíso

stylized
acclimatized
agonized
baptized
bowdlerized
brutalized
civilized
commercialized
compromised
computerized
disguised
disorganized
fossilized
galvanized
ill-advised
mechanized
middle-sized
motorized
organized

'ie'

oversized
paralysed
recognized
traumatized
unauthorized

uncivilized
unrecognized
unsupervised
well-advised
westernized

You can add to this list by adding **-d** to some words that rhyme with **prize**, as in **surprised**

'O'

dog, pocket, beyond

All the words in this section use the sound 'o' in their main stressed syllable

11.1

job
blob
Bob
bob
cob
corn on the cob
demob
fob
gob
hob
knob
lob
mob
rent-a-mob
Rob
rob
slob
snob
sob
swab
throb
yob

robber
clobber
cobber
demob her
fob her
jobber
lob her
mob her
robber
rob her

slobber
swabber
swab her

wobble
bobble
cobble
gobble
hobble
nobble
squabble

robbery
slobbery
snobbery

Robert
The Hobbit

hobby
blobby
Bobby
bobby
knobby
lobby
nobby
Robbie
slobby

robin
bobbin
dobbin
Robin

sobbing
blobbing
bobbing

demobbing
fobbing
gobbing
jobbing
lobbing
mobbing
robbing
slobbing
sobbing
swabbing
throbbing

wobbly
bobbly
knobbly
throw a wobbly

lobster
mobster

11.2

block
ad hoc
amok
Bangkok
baroque
bloc
chip off the old block
chock
chock-a-block
clock
cock
crock
culture shock
defrock

doc
dock
double-lock
electroshock
flock
frock
half-cock
hock
hollyhock
Jock
knock
loch
lock
mock
o'clock
Papa Doc
poppycock
rock
shock
shuttlecock
smock
sock
stock
unblock
unfrock
unlock
weathercock
wok

locker
blocker
block her
clocker
clock her
cocker
Davy Jones's locker
docker
knocker
knock her
lock her
mocker
mock her
rocker
rock her

shocker
shock her
soccer
sock her
stocker
unblock her
unlock her

mockery
crockery
rockery

vocative
evocative
locative
provocative

rocky
cocky
disc jockey
hockey
jockey
Milwaukee
Rocky
stocky

shocking
blocking
chocking
clocking
cocking
crocking
defrock
docking
flocking
hocking
interlocking
knocking
locking
mocking
rocking
socking
stocking
unblocking
unfrocking
unlocking

pocket
block it
clock it
cock it
crock it
dock it
hock it
knock it
locket
lock it
mock it
pickpocket
rocket
rock it
shock it
socket
sock it
sprocket
stock it
unblock it
unlock it

knockout
lock-out

mock-up
cock-up
lockup

Cockney
David Hockney
mockney

box
Brer Fox
Brian Cox
chatterbox
chickenpox
cox
equinox
Fort Knox
fox
Goldilocks
jack-in-the-box
mailbox
moneybox

orthodox
ox
paradox
tinderbox
unorthodox

You can add to this list by adding -s to some words that rhyme with **block**, as in **knocks**

oxen
coxswain
toxin

foxy
orthodoxy
poxy
proxy

shocked
blocked
chocked
clocked
cocked
concoct
crocked
defrocked
docked
flocked
hocked
knocked
locked
mocked
rocked
socked
stocked
unblocked
unfrocked
unlocked

11.3

God
arthropod
bod
clod

cod
demigod
god
iPod®
Ken Dodd
nod
odd
plod
pod
prod
quad
Rod
rod
shod
sod
squad
Sweeney Todd
Todd
trod
wad

fodder
dodder
nodder
odder
plodder
prodder

toddle
Chris Waddle
coddle
doddle
Glenn Hoddle
model
mollycoddle
supermodel
twaddle
waddle

sodden
downtrodden
modern
trodden
ultramodern

body
antibody
anybody
busybody
dogsbody
embody
everybody
Irrawaddy
nobody
Noddy
Roddy
shoddy
somebody
squaddie
wadi

melodic
periodic
rhapsodic
spasmodic

methodical
periodical

periodically
methodically
rhapsodically
spasmodically

full-bodied
able-bodied
disembodied
nodded
plodded
prodded

bodice
goddess

modest
immodest
oddest

oddity
commodity

oddly
godly

ungodly

lodge
bodge
dislodge
dodge
splodge
stodge

lodger
bodger
dislodge her
dodge her
dodger
Roger
The Artful Dodger

stodgy
dodgy
podgy
splodgy

logic
geologic
pedagogic

logical
anthropological
archaeological
astrological
bacteriological
biological
chronological
ecological
entomological
etymological
geological
gynaecological
ideological
illogical
meteorological
mythological
pathological
pedagogical
physiological
psychological

scatological
sociological
tautological
technological
terminological
theological
zoological

erogenous
androgynous
homogenous

module
nodule

11.4

off
browned-off
cough
doff
Gorbachev
hands-off
kalashnikov
knock it off
quaff
scoff
toff
trough
Vincent Van Gogh
well-off
whooping cough

You can also make rhymes for
these words by using words in
section **11.14** that rhyme with
froth

---

offer
coffer
cougher
doffer
proffer
quaffer
scoffer

oesophagus
sarcophagus

oesophagi
sarcophagi

waffle
offal

coffee
toffee

coffin
boffin

profit
cough it
doff it
prophet
quaff it
scoff it

soft
aloft
croft
Lara Croft
loft
waft

lofty
softy

softly
softly-softly

11.5

dog
agog
analogue
bog
catalogue
clog
cog
demagogue
dialogue
duologue
flog

fog
frog
grog
hog
jog
log
monologue
slog
smog
snog
synagogue
underdog

joggle
boggle
goggle
toggle
woggle

foggy
doggy
groggy
soggy

photographer
autobiographer
biographer
cartographer
choreographer
cinematographer
geographer
lexicographer
pornographer
radiographer
stenographer

geography
autobiography
bibliography
biography
cartography
choreography
cinematography
ethnography
hagiography
mammography

photography
pornography
radiography
topography
typography

togs
go to the dogs
pop one's clogs
Reservoir Dogs

You can add to this list by adding -s to some words that rhyme with *dog*, as in *frogs*

11.6

doll
aerosol
alcohol
cholesterol
Interpol
loll
paracetamol
parasol
protocol
Sebastopol
Sol

collar
ayatollah
bet one's bottom dollar
blue-collar
dollar
Eurodollar
Fats Waller
holler
hot under the collar
scholar
squalor
white-collar

apology
anthology
anthropology
archaeology

astrology
bacteriology
biology
biotechnology
cardiology
chronology
criminology
dermatology
ecology
endocrinology
entomology
ethnology
etymology
geology
graphology
gynaecology
ideology
meteorology
methodology
microbiology
mythology
nanotechnology
neurology
ophthalmology
ornithology
pathology
pharmacology
philology
phraseology
physiology
psychology
radiology
reflexology
seismology
sociology
tautology
technology
terminology
theology
urology
virology
zoology

'O'

psychologist
anthropologist
apologist
archaeologist
biologist
cardiologist
dermatologist
ecologist
endocrinologist
entomologist
escapologist
ethnologist
geologist
gynaecologist
musicologist
neurologist
ornithologist
pathologist
pharmacologist
philologist
radiologist
reflexologist
sociologist
zoologist

column
solemn

pollen
Colin

dollop
codswallop
lollop
scallop
trollop
wallop

jolly
brolly
collie
Dolly
dolly
folly
golly
Holly

holly
lolly
melancholy
Molly
Ollie
Polly
poly
trolley
volley
Wally
wally

frolic
alcoholic
apostolic
bucolic
carbolic
chocoholic
colic
metabolic
nonalcoholic
parabolic
shambolic
shopaholic
symbolic
vitriolic
workaholic

solid
squalid
stolid

college
acknowledge
knowledge
self-knowledge

qualify
disqualify
mollify

qualified
disqualified
mollified
overqualified
underqualified

unqualified

solace
Barnes Wallis
William Wallace

hydrolysis
electrolysis

polish
abolish
demolish

polished
abolished
demolished
unpolished

cosmopolitan
Cosmopolitan
metropolitan
Neapolitan

quality
equality
frivolity
inequality

follow
Apollo
hollow
Sleepy Hollow
swallow
wallow

golf
minigolf
Rolf

Volga
Olga

solve
absolve
devolve
dissolve
evolve
involve
resolve

revolve

involved
absolved
devolved
dissolved
evolved
involved
resolved
revolved
solved
unsolved

soluble
dissoluble
indissoluble
insoluble
voluble

11.7

prom
aplomb
bomb
CD-ROM
from
intercom
mom
Peeping Tom
pom
ROM
the Somme
Tom
tom
Uncle Tom

You can also make rhymes for
these words by using words in
section **11.8** that rhyme with
con

comma
bomber
bomb her
from her
prommer

commentary
promontory

promise
doubting Thomas
Thomas

commie
pommy
Tommy

comic
astronomic
atomic
economic
ergonomic
gastronomic
socioeconomic

comical
anatomical
astronomical
economical
gastronomical
uneconomical

economics
comics
ergonomics
macroeconomics
microeconomics

dominate
nominate
predominate

nominal
abdominal
phenomenal

nominally
phenomenally

prominence
dominance
predominance

prominent
dominant

predominant

vomit
comet
Wallace and Gromit

thermometer
barometer
gasometer
kilometre
micrometer
milometer
speedometer
tachometer

geometry
trigonometry

romp
aide-de-camp
clomp
pomp
stomp
swamp
yomp

11.8

con
anon
automaton
Babylon
Bonn
Canton
carry-on
Ceredigion
Ceylon
chiffon
COMECON (= *Council
for Mutual Economic
Assistance*)
Dionne
Don
don
echelon
Elton John

emoticon
Eva Perón
foregone
futon
Gabon
goings-on
gone
hands-on
hanger-on
hangers-on
head-on
Juan Perón
John
Lebanon
liaison
Little John
marathon
odds-on
on
outshone
polygon
roll-on
Ron
Saigon
scone
shone
spot-on
stick-on
swan
thereupon
Tucson
undergone
upon
wan
whereupon
woebegone
Yvonne

➕

You can also make rhymes for these words by using words in section **11.7** that rhyme with **prom**

honour
belladonna
Con(n)or
con her
Diego Maradona
dishonour
doner (= *kebab*)
Donna
goner
gonna
Honor
Madonna
madonna
on her
outshone her
upon her
wanna
wanner

Donald
Old MacDonald
Ronald

economy
agronomy
astronomy
autonomy
gastronomy
physiognomy
taxonomy

bonny
Bonnie
Connie
Donny
Johnny
Ronnie

tonic
bubonic
catatonic
chronic
demonic
electronic
embryonic
harmonic

histrionic
ironic
laconic
mnemonic
monophonic
moronic
Napoleonic
philharmonic
phonic
platonic
polyphonic
quadraphonic
sardonic
Slavonic
sonic
stereophonic
supersonic

Monica
harmonica
moni(c)ker
Veronica

conical
chronicle
ironical

electronics
harmonics
histrionics
mnemonics
phonics
quadraphonics
sonics
tonics

anonymous
eponymous
synonymous

astonish
admonish

astonishing
admonishing

astonished
admonished

bonnet
on it
outshone it
shone it
undergone it
upon it
sonnet

honk
bonk
conk
honky-tonk
Mont Blanc
plonk

conquer
conker
honker
reconquer

wonky
donkey

pond
abscond
beyond
blond(e)
bond
conned
correspond
donned
fond
frond
James Bond
respond
second (= to transfer)
swanned
vagabond
wand

ponder
absconder
anaconda
Bridget Fonda

beyond her
conned her
fonder
Henry Fonda
Honda
Jane Fonda
Peter Fonda
responder
Rhonda
Rhondda
second her
squander
Wanda
wander
yonder

despondent
co-respondent
correspondent
respondent

bonding
absconding
corresponding
responding
seconding

song
along
belong
bong
ding-dong
evensong
gong
Hong Kong
King Kong
long
Mekong
Neil Armstrong
overlong
Pete Tong
pong
prolong
prong
sarong

strong
thong
throng
wrong

Many English speakers
pronounce some words in
section **17.8** (eg *tongue*) in such
a way that they rhyme with
these words

longing
belonging
bonging
gonging
ponging
prolonging
pronging
thronging
wronging

conga
conger
longer
stronger
Tonga

strongly
wrongly

ponce
ambiance
bonce
ensconce
once
response

consul
tonsil

conscious
Pontius
self-conscious
semiconscious
subconscious
unconscious
unselfconscious

font
détente
Mary Quant
Nantes
Vermont
want

The Full Monty
Belo Horizonte
Brontë

pronto
Toronto

poncho
honcho

bronze
automatons
bonze
cons
dons
echelons
emoticons
futons
liaisons
marathons
mod cons
Mons
polygons
scones
swans
The Fonz

11.9

top
alcopop
barbershop
belly-flop
blow one's top
bop
chop
cop
crop
drag-and-drop

drop
escalope
flop
fop
glottal stop
hop
lollipop
mop
Mrs Malaprop
non-stop
op
over-the-top
plop
pop
prop
Robocop
shop
slop
sop
stop
strop
swap
turboprop
whistle-stop

stopper
bopper
chopper
copper
cropper
drop her
dropper
grasshopper
hopper
improper
knee-high to a
 grasshopper
mopper
name-dropper
popper
proper
prop her
shop her
shopper

stop her
swap her
teeny-bopper
top her
topper
whopper

properly
improperly
monopoly
oligopoly

copier
choppier
floppier
photocopier
sloppier
soppier
stroppier

copy
carbon copy
choppy
floppy
jalop(p)y
photocopy
poppy
sloppy
soppy
stroppy

topic
microscopic
misanthropic
myopic
philanthropic
stereoscopic
telescopic
tropic

tropical
semitropical
subtropical
topical

soppily
choppily

floppily
sloppily
stroppily

shopping
chopping
hopping
name-dropping
showstopping
teleshopping
topping
whopping
window-shopping

You can add to this list by adding *-ping* to some words that rhyme with **top**, as in **cropping**

dropout
cop-out
stop-out

hops
copse

You can add to this list by adding *-s* to some words that rhyme with **top**, as in **shops**

option
adoption

opt
adopt
close-cropped
co-opt

You can add to this list by adding *-ped* to some words that rhyme with **top**, as in **cropped**

populate
copulate
depopulate

11.10

horror
begorrah
Sodom and Gomorrah

moral
amoral
Balmoral
Coral
coral
immoral
Laurel
laurel
quarrel
sorrel
Stan Laurel

warren
foreign
Lauren
sporran
Warren

Florence
abhorrence

torrent
abhorrent
warrant

oratory
exploratory

sorry
articulated lorry
Hugh Laurie
John Laurie
Laurie
lorry
quarry

historic
meteoric
prehistoric
Warwick
Yorick

historical
categorical
metaphorical
rhetorical

horrid
florid
torrid

porridge
forage
Norwich

Doris
Boris
Horace
Maurice
morris
orris

forest
deforest
florist

forester
chorister

majority
authority
inferiority
minority
priority
seniority
superiority

borrow
morrow
sorrow
tomorrow

11.11

cross
across
albatross
Archbishop Makarios
Argos
boss

candyfloss
cos (= *lettuce*)
dental floss
DOS
doss
double-cross
dross
floss
gloss
Kate Moss
Joe Loss
Jonathan Ross
kudos
lacrosse
loss
Mikonos
moss
Ross
Stirling Moss
toss

dosser
across her
Barbarossa
boss her
crosser
cross her
double-crosser
double-cross her
flosser
gloss her

fossil
apostle
colossal
jostle

blossom
across 'em
boss 'em
cross 'em
double-cross 'em
opossum
possum
toss 'em

glossy
bossy
mossy
posse

atrocity
animosity
curiosity
ferocity
generosity
monstrosity
pomposity
precocity
velocity
verbosity

Tosca
Oscar

phosphorus
Bosphorus

cost
accost
bossed
crossed
defrost
dental floss
dossed
double-crossed
embossed
flossed
frost
glossed
Jack Frost
lost
mossed
Pentecoste
riposte
tossed

foster
accost her
bossed her
cost her
crossed her

double-crossed her
Gloucester
impostor
lost her
roster

agnostic
acrostic
diagnostic

frosting
accosting
costing
defrosting

rostrum
nostrum

gosh
awash
cosh
dosh
Hieronymus Bosch
josh
mac(k)intosh
nosh
Peter Tosh
posh
quash
slosh
squash
tosh
wash

washer
cosh her
dishwasher
josher
josh her
nosher
posher
quash her
squasher
squash her

'*O*'

washer
wash her

11.13

spot
Aldershot
allot
apricot
Argonaut
bergamot
blot
Camelot
Captain Scott
carrycot
chimneypot
clot
cot
Dot
dot
flowerpot
forget-me-not
forgot
garrotte
got
go to pot
guillemot
hot
James Watt
jot
kilowatt
knot
Lancelot
lot
mailshot
megawatt
not
ocelot
overshot
plot
Pol Pot
polyglot
pot
red-hot
Ridley Scott

rot
Scot
shallot
shot
slot
snot
squat
SWAT
swat
swot
tie the knot
tot
trot
watt
what
white-hot
yacht

plotter
blotter
cotter
garrotter
globetrotter
gotta
got her
Harry Potter
hotter
jotter
otter
plotter
potter
ricotta
rotter
spotter
spot her
squatter
swatter
terracotta
totter
trainspotter
trotter

bottle
Aristotle
throttle

mottled
bottled
throttled

bottom
allot 'em
forgot 'em
garrotte 'em
got 'em
rot 'em
spot 'em
swat 'em

lobotomy
dichotomy
laparotomy

rotten
cotton
forgotten
gotten
ill-gotten
long-forgotten

botany
monotony

lottery
pottery
tottery

dotty
grotty
knotty
Lanzarote
Luciano Pavarotti
potty
snotty
spotty
totty

neurotic
antibiotic
chaotic
despotic
erotic
exotic

hypnotic
idiotic
narcotic
patriotic
psychotic
quixotic
symbiotic
unpatriotic

robotics

antibiotics
exotics
macrobiotics
narcotics
neurotics
psychotics
probiotics

potted

besotted

You can add to this list by adding -*ted* to some words that rhyme with **spot**, as in *slotted*

cottage

pottage
wattage

yachting

cybersquatting
trainspotting

You can add to this list by adding -*ting* to some words that rhyme with **spot**, as in **trotting**

motto

blotto
Giotto
grotto
lotto
Otto
risotto

motley

hotly

Scots

call the shots
culottes
Mary Queen of Scots

You can add to this list by adding -*s* to some words that rhyme with **spot**, as in *pots*

Scotsman

yachtsman

Scotswoman

yachtswoman

notch

blotch
botch
butterscotch
crotch
Scotch
scotch
swatch
watch

11.14

froth

broth
cloth
Goth
moth
tablecloth
tiger moth
wrath

You can also make rhymes for these words by using words in section **11.4** that rhyme with **off**

11.15

novel

grovel
hovel

11.16

was

because
Cos
cos (= *because*)
Oz
Ros

closet

deposit
posit
was it?

'oe'

foe, Noel, mistletoe

All the words in this section use the sound 'oe' in their main stressed syllable

12.1

go
aglow
ago
although
archipelago
audio
below
bestow
blow
blow-by-blow
BO
Bordeaux
Borneo
bow (= *weapon*)
bravo
buffalo
bungalow
c/o
calico
cameo
CEO (= *chief executive officer*)
cheerio
CO (= *commanding officer*)
co (= *company*)
contraflow
crow
curio
doe
do(h)
domino
dough

dynamo
ebb and flow
Edgar Allan Poe
embryo
Eskimo
ex officio
Felixstowe
Flo
flow
FO (= *Foreign Office*)
foe
forego
fro
from top to toe
get-up-and-go
gigolo
glow
GMO (= *genetically modified organism*)
go-slow
GPO
grow
gung-ho
haricot
Hello!
hello
HMSO (= *Her Majesty's Stationery Office*)
hoe
Idaho
ILO (= *International Labour Organisation*)
indigo

Inspector Clouseau
ISO (= *International Standards Organization*)
Ivanhoe
Jacques Cousteau
Jean Cocteau
Jean Jacques Rousseau
Jericho
Jo
Joe
just so
know
KO
Kosovo
lo
low
Manon Lescaut
Marilyn Monroe
MBO (= *management buyout*)
Michelangelo
mistletoe
Mo
Monaco
mow
NCO (= *non-commissioned officer*)
need-to-know
NGO (= *Non-Governmental Organization*)
no

'oe'

no-show
O
oh
oho
ono (= or near(est)
    offer)
outgrow
overflow
overthrow
owe
patio
pedalo
piccolo
pistachio
PLO (= Palestine
    Liberation
    Organization)
PO (= Post Office)
pro
PTO
Punch and Judy show
radio
ratio
rodeo
roe
Romeo
row (= a line; to propel
    a boat)
Russell Crowe
San Antonio
Scorpio
sew
show
sloe
slow
snow
so
so-and-so
soh
sow (= to scatter seed)
status quo
stereo
stow
studio

the Alamo
though
throw
toe
tow
UFO
undergo
undertow
UNO (= United
    Nations
    Organization)
vertigo
video
VSO (= Voluntary
    Service Overseas)
WHO (= World Health
    Organization)
window
woe

mower
below her
bestow her
blower
blow her
boa
Boer
churchgoer
cinema-goer
flamethrower
Goa
goer
grower
grow her
knower
know her
lawnmower
lower (= further down)
moviegoer
Noah
outgrow her
overthrow her
owe her
Percy Thrower

pro her
radio her
rower
row her
Samoa
show her
slower
slow her
sower
stower
stow her
theatre-goer
thrower
throw her
tow her
video her

Joel
bestowal
Noel

stowaway
go away
throwaway

showy
blowy
Chloe
Joey
joey
snowy
Zoë

stoic
heroic

going
bestowing
blowing
crowing
easy-going
ebbing and flowing
flowing
foregoing
glass-blowing
glowing

growing
helloing
hoeing
ingrowing
knowing
lowing
mowing
ocean-going
ongoing
outgoing
outgrowing
overflowing
overthrowing
oweing
radioing
rowing (= *propelling a boat*)
seagoing
sewing
showing
slowing
snowing
sowing (= *scattering seed*)
stowing
thoroughgoing
throwing
towing
undergoing
videoing

12.2

globe
disrobe
earlobe
lobe
probe
robe
strobe

crowbar
towbar

sober
Manitoba

October

noble
Chernobyl
global
Grenoble
ignoble

Toby
adobe
Gobi
goby
Nairobi

aerobic
agoraphobic
anaerobic
aqua(e)robic
claustrophobic
phobic
xenophobic

aerobics
agoraphobics
aqua(e)robics
claustrophobics
phobics
xenophobics

12.3

smoke
artichoke
awoke
Basingstoke
bespoke
beyond a joke
bloke
broke
choke
cloak
Coke®
coke
croak
evoke
folk

invoke
joke
masterstroke
oak
poke
provoke
revoke
soak
spoke
stoke
stroke
woke
womenfolk
yoke
yolk

smoker
awoke her
Bram Stoker
broke her
broker
choke her
choker
cloak her
croaker
evoke her
invoke her
invoker
joker
mediocre
ochre
non-smoker
pawnbroker
poker
provoke her
soak her
stockbroker
stoker
stroke her
stroker
tapioca
woke her
yoke her

local
bifocal
focal
varifocal
vocal
yokel

broken
awoken
heartbroken
outspoken
plain-spoken
soft-spoken
spoken
token
unbroken
unspoken
well-spoken
woken

focus
awoke us
broke us
choke us
cloak us
crocus
evoke us
hocus-pocus
invoke us
poke us
provoke us
soak us
smoke us
stroke us
woke us
yoke us

smoky
hokey-cokey
joky
okey-dokey
poky

Tokyo
Pinocchio

smoking
broking
choking
cloaking
coking
croaking
evoking
invoking
joking
no-smoking
oaking
poking
provoking
revoking
soaking
stoking
stroking
thought-provoking
yoking

coax
hoax
Hollyoaks

You can add to this list by adding *-s* to some words that rhyme with **smoke**, as in **provokes**

soaked
smoked
unprovoked

You can add to this list by adding *-(e)d* to some words that rhyme with **smoke**, as in **provoked**

12.4

code
abode
bestowed
bode
commode

crowed
corrode
decode
discommode
download
encode
episode
erode
explode
flowed
glowed
goad
KO'd
load
lowed
middle-of-the-road
mode
mowed
node
ode
off-load
one for the road
overflowed
overload
overrode
owed
pigeon-toed
radioed
road
rode
rowed
sewed
showed
slowed
snowed
sowed
stowed
strode
The Da Vinci Code
toad
towed
unload
videoed

soda
bestowed her
coda
coder
decoder
downloader
encoder
exploder
freeloader
odour
owed her
pagoda
Rhoda
showed her
Skoda
slowed her

sodium
odium
podium
rhodium

custodian
Cambodian
melodeon
nickelodeon

odious
commodious
melodious
unmelodious

toady
Jodie
Miss Jean Brodie
roadie

loaded
coded
colour-coded
corroded
decoded
discommoded
downloaded
encoded
eroded

exploded
goaded
outmoded
overloaded
unloaded

loading
boding
coding
corroding
decoding
discommoding
downloading
encoding
eroding
exploding
foreboding
goading
off-loading
overloading
unloading

showdown
low-down
slow-down

Trojan
theologian

12.5

loaf
oaf

You can also make rhymes for these words by using words in section **12.16** that rhyme with *both*

loafer
chauffeur
gopher
sofa

trophy
Sophie

12.6

rogue
brogue
en vogue
Vogue
vogue

yoga
ogre
toga

ogle
mogul

fogey
bogey

pogo
logo
Togo

12.7

hole
Adrian Mole
bankroll
bowl
buttonhole
cajole
camisole
casserole
coal
console
control
cubbyhole
dole
droll
enrol
extol
foal
goal
mole
Nat King Cole
Nicole
Old King Cole
parole

patrol
pigeonhole
Pole
pole
poll
rigmarole
rock'n'roll
role
roll
scroll
self-control
Seoul
shoal
sole
soul
stole
stroll
Super Bowl®
toll
totem pole
troll
vole
watering hole
whole

polar
Angola
bankroll her
bowler
bowl her
buttonhole her
cajole her
cajoler
Coca-Cola®
cola
Francis Ford Coppola
console her
consoler
control her
controller
Emile Zola
enrol her
enroller
extol her

extoller
Hispaniola
Lola
molar
parole her
patroller
pigeonhole her
poll her
potholer
roller
roll her
solar
steamroller
stole her
stroller
toll her
viola
Zola

controllable
inconsolable
uncontrollable

stolen
Angolan
colon
semicolon
swollen

Poland
lowland
Roland

holier
lowlier
magnolia
Mongolia

linoleum
petroleum

Mongolian
Napoleon

holy
coley
goalie

guacamole
lowly
roly-poly
slowly
solely
Stromboli
unholy
wholly

polio
folio
portfolio

rolling
bankrolling
bowling
buttonholing
cajoling
casseroling
consoling
controlling
doling
enrolling
extolling
foaling
holing
J K Rowling
paroling
patrolling
pigeonholing
polling
potholing
scrolling
strolling
tenpin bowling
tolling

solo
Marco Polo
polo

cold
bankrolled
behold
bold
bowled

break the mould
buttonholed
cajoled
casseroled
centrefold
consoled
controlled
doled
enfold
enrolled
extolled
foaled
fold
foretold
gold
hold
holed
hundredfold
ice-cold
manifold
marigold
mould
old
outsold
paroled
patrolled
pigeonholed
polled
radio-controlled
remote-controlled
rolled
scold
scrolled
self-controlled
sold
stone-cold
stranglehold
strolled
told
tolled
uncontrolled
unfold
unsold
untold

uphold
withhold

shoulder
beholder
behold her
bolder
boulder
cajoled her
colder
cold-shoulder
consoled her
folder
freeholder
holder
hold her
householder
leaseholder
moulder
Noddy Holder
officeholder
older
paroled her
pigeonholed her
record-holder
scold her
shareholder
smallholder
smoulder
solder
sold her
stockholder
titleholder
told her
Tristan and Isolde

golden
beholden
embolden

mouldy
golden oldie
oldie

folding
holding

moulding
scolding
shareholding
smallholding

coldly
boldly

coldness
boldness

soulful
doleful

solely
wholly

soulless
goalless

coalman
patrolman

bolster
holster
upholster

bolt
colt
dolt
jolt
moult
revolt
smolt
thunderbolt
volt

molten
Bolton

12.8

home
aerodrome
chrome
chromosome
comb
dome
foam

gnome
honeycomb
Jerome
loam
metronome
Millennium Dome
monochrome
ohm
roam
Rome
tome

You can also make rhymes for these words by using words in section **12.9** that rhyme with *bone*

coma
aroma
beachcomber
carcinoma
diploma
glaucoma
Homer
homer
lymphoma
melanoma
misnomer
Oklahoma
Omagh
Paloma
roamer

Roman
omen
roman
showman

foamy
hom(e)y
loamy
Salome

roaming
chroming
combing

foaming
homing
honeycombing
loaming
roaming
Wyoming

slo-mo
Lake Como
major-domo
Perry Como

12.9

bone
accident-prone
Al Capone
alone
Anglophone
atone
baritone
bemoan
blown
bridging loan
chaperone
clone
collarbone
Cologne
cologne
condone
cone
cornerstone
cortisone
crone
dethrone
disown
drone
eau de Cologne
entryphone
Eurozone
flown
francophone
full-blown
full(y)-grown
gramophone

groan
grown
hailstone
heart of stone
Home Alone
home-grown
hone
hydrocortisone
intone
Joan
known
loan
lone
marrowbone
megaphone
microphone
moan
monotone
mown
nuclear-free zone
Oliver Stone
outgrown
overblown
overgrown
overthrown
overtone
own
phone
postpone
prone
Rhone
saxophone
semitone
sewn
shown
Sierra Leone
Simone
skin and bone
sown
stone
Sylvester Stallone
telephone
testosterone
throne

thrown
tone
trombone
Tyrone
undertone
unknown
well-known
xylophone
zone

You can also make rhymes for these words by using words in section **12.8** that rhyme with *home*

loner

Arizona
Barcelona
bemoaner
bemoan her
boner
chaperone her
clone her
condone her
co-owner
Desdemona
disown her
donor
Fiona
groaner
homeowner
Iona
Jonah
known her
krona
krone
kroner
landowner
loan her
moaner
Mona
outgrown her
overthrown her
owner

Pamplona
phone her
phoner
Rhona
shipowner
Shona
shown her
stone her
stoner
telephone her
telephoner
throne her
toner
Verona
Winona

bonus

chaperone us
disown us
lowness
no-claims bonus
onus
own us
phone us
slowness

bonier

ammonia
Antonia
begonia
Catalonia
catatonia
Cephalonia
Estonia
Macedonia
moanier
Patagonia
phonier
pneumonia
stonier

colonial

ceremonial
matrimonial
neocolonial

testimonial

plutonium

harmonium
pandemonium

Estonian

Caledonian
draconian
Ionian
Macedonian

harmonious

acrimonious
ceremonious
erroneous
parsimonious
sanctimonious

pony

baloney
bony
crony
Joanie
macaroni
Marconi
moany
phon(e)y
stony
Toni
Tony

phone-in

flown in
grown in
shown in
thrown in
serotonin

cloning

atoning
bemoaning
chaperoning
condoning
coning
dethroning
disowning

droning
groaning
honing
intoning
landowning
loaning
moaning
owning
phoning
postponing
stoning
telephoning
throning
toning
zoning

kimono
no-no

stoned
atoned
state-owned
unchaperoned

You can add to this list by adding -*(e)d* to some words that rhyme with **bone**, as in ***groaned***

only
lonely
read-only

atonement
postponement

don't
won't
wont

lazybones
Bridget Jones
bridging loans
feel it in one's bones
Indiana Jones
Inigo Jones

The Rolling Stones
Tom Jones
Vinnie Jones

You can add to this list by adding -*s* to some words that rhyme with **bone**, as in ***moans***

12.10

hope
antelope
Bob Hope
cope
docusoap
dope
elope
envelope
grope
gyroscope
Hope
horoscope
isotope
kaleidoscope
lope
microscope
misanthrope
mope
nope
periscope
pope
rope
scope
self-addressed
   envelope
slope
soap
stethoscope
telescope

no-hoper
doper
eloper
groper
hoper

interloper
loper
moper
roper

kopeck
OPEC (= *Organization
of Petroleum-
Exporting Countries*)

Utopia
Ethiopia
myopia

Utopian
Ethiopian

dop(e)y
rop(e)y
soapy

12.11

dose
bellicose
cellulose
close (= *near*)
comatose
grandiose
gross
lachrymose
morose
overdose
verbose

grocer
closer
greengrocer
grosser
samosa

neuroses
diagnoses
prognoses
psychoses

hypnosis
arteriosclerosis

arthrosis
asbestosis
cirrhosis
diagnosis
doses
halitosis
myxomatosis
narcosis
neurosis
osmosis
osteoporosis
process
prognosis
psychosis
sclerosis
thrombosis
tuberculosis

explosive
corrosive

closely
grossly

post
boast
bottommost
coast
engrossed
first-past-the-post
furthermost
ghost
give up the ghost
grossed
host
inmost
innermost
most
outermost
roast
toast
uppermost
uttermost

toaster
boaster

coaster
four-poster
poster
roaster
roller-coaster

postal
coastal

roasting
boasting
coasting
ghosting
hosting
posting
roasting
toasting

mostly
ghostly

12.12

closure
composure
disclosure
enclosure
exposure

explosion
corrosion
erosion
implosion

12.13

brochure
kosher
Nova Scotia

sociable
negotiable
non-negotiable
unsociable

notion
calamine lotion
cleansing lotion

commotion
demotion
devotion
emotion
hand lotion
locomotion
lotion
motion
ocean
potion
promotion

emotional
devotional
promotional
unemotional

ferocious
atrocious
precocious

12.14

note
afloat
anecdote
antidote
banknote
billy-goat
boat
coat
demote
denote
devote
dote
float
get someone's goat
gloat
goat
jump down someone's
    throat
misquote
moat
motorboat
nanny-goat
overcoat

overwrote
petticoat
promote
quote
remote
rewrote
rote
rowing boat
smote
stoat
throat
tote
undercoat
underwrote
unquote
vote
wrote

rota
boater
coat her
Dakota
demote her
floater
float her
gloater
iota
Minnesota
North Dakota
misquote her
motor
promote her
promoter
quota
quote her
rotor
smote her
South Dakota
voter
wrote her

total
anecdotal
subtotal
teetotal

rotary
notary
votary

notice
coat us
demote us
float us
lotus
misquote us
note us
promote us
quote us
smote us
wrote us

throaty
coyote
floaty

noted
bloated
coated
demoted
denoted
devoted
doted
floated
gloated
misquoted
noted
promoted
quoted
sugar-coated
unquoted
voted

coating
boating
demoting
denoting
devoting
doting
floating
gloating
misquoting

noting
promoting
quoting
toting
voting

motive
automotive
emotive
locomotive
votive

photo
Kyoto
telephoto

oats
Captain Oates
compare notes
John o'Groats

You can add to this list by adding -s to some words that rhyme with **note**, as in **votes**

coach
approach
broach
brooch
encroach
poach
reproach
roach

poachable
approachable
coachable
irreproachable
unapproachable

12.15

loathe
clothe

clothing
loathing

underclothing

betrothed
clothed
loathed
unclothed

clothes
loathes
underclothes

12.16

both
growth
loath
oath
sloth
undergrowth

You can also make rhymes for these words by using words in section **12.5** that rhyme with *loaf*

12.17

stove
clove
cove
drove
grove
hove
mauve
Primus® stove
rove
strove
throve
treasure-trove
wove

over
Anna Pavlova
Casanova
changeover
clover

Dover
drover
flyover
going-over
hangover
Jehovah
Land Rover
leftover
Maria Sharapova
Martina Navratilova
Moldova
moreover
once-over
ova
pavlova
pullover
pushover
Range Rover
rollover
rover
stopover
supernova
turnover
voice-over
walkover

woven
Beethoven
cloven
disproven
Eindhoven
Moldovan
proven

ovary
Madame Bovary

12.18

glow-worm
slow-worm

12.19

nose
arose

chose
close (= *to shut*)
come to blows
Comoros
compose
decompose
depose
diagnose
disclose
discompose
dispose
doze
enclose
expose
foreclose
foregoes
froze
get up someone's nose
goes
hose
impose
interpose
juxtapose
misdiagnose
oppose
overexpose
pantyhose
pose
predispose
presuppose
propose
prose
repose
Rose
rose
superimpose
suppose
those
throes
transpose
tread on someone's
    toes

You can add to this list by adding *-s* to some words that rhyme with **go**, as in **blows**

rosé
exposé

poser
bulldozer
close her
closer
composer
disposer
dozer
expose her
imposer
noser
oppose her
opposer
owes her
poser
proposer
Rosa
throws her
transposer

frozen
chosen
re-frozen

well-chosen

cosy
dozy
Nikolas Sarkozy
nosey
posy
Rosie
rosy

closing
composing
decomposing
deposing
diagnosing
disclosing
discomposing
disposing
dozing
enclosing
exposing
foreclosing
hosing
imposing
interposing
juxtaposing
misdiagnosing
nosing
opposing

overexposing
posing
predisposing
presupposing
proposing
reposing
superimposing
supposing
transposing

closed
composed
disposed
exposed
ill-disposed
indisposed
supposed
underexposed
undisclosed
unopposed
well-disposed

You can add to this list by adding *-d* to some words that rhyme with **nose**, as in **proposed**

'OW'

town, power, allow

All the words in this section use the sound '**ow**' in their main stressed syllable

13.1

now
allow
anyhow
bough
bow (= *to bend the body in respect*)
brow
cow
disallow
endow
Guinea-Bissau
how
kowtow
miaow
middlebrow
ow
plough
prow
row (= *an argument*)
sow (= *a female pig*)
vow
wow

power
bell-tower
Blackpool Tower
bower
brainpower
cauliflower
cornflour
cornflower
cower
devour

Eisenhower
empower
flour
flower
glower
horsepower
hour
lower (= *to scowl*)
man-hour
manpower
Mayflower
our
overpower
plain flour
Post Office Tower
scour
self-raising flour
shower
sour
staying power
sunflower
superpower
sweet-and-sour
tower
wallflower
watchtower
willpower

coward
cowered
devoured
empowered
flowered
glowered
high-powered

Howard
jet-powered
lowered (= *scowled*)
Noël Coward
overpowered
powered
scoured
showered
solar-powered
soured

towel
avowal
bowel
dowel
Enoch Powell
Hywel
Simon Cowell
trowel
vowel

hourly
half-hourly
sourly

towering
cowering
devouring
empowering
flowering
glowering
lowering (= *being overcast*)
overpowering
powering
scouring

showering
souring

Maui
David Bowie

prowess
Powys

13.2

proud
allowed
aloud
avowed
bowed
cloud
cowed
crowd
disallowed
endowed
Girls Allowed
kowtowed
loud
miaowed
ploughed
rowed (= *argued*)
shroud
Stroud
thundercloud
Turin Shroud
vowed
wowed

powder
allowed her
bowed her
chowder
cloud her
cowed her
crowd her
disallowed her
endowed her
gunpowder
louder
prouder

shroud her
talcum powder
wowed her

rowdy
Audi
cloudy
dowdy
Saudi

proudly
loudly

13.3

owl
cheek by jowl
cowl
foul
fowl
growl
howl
jowl
prowl
scowl
waterfowl
yowl

Many English speakers
pronounce some words in
section **13.1** (eg *towel*) in such a
way that they rhyme with these
words

prowler
foul her
fowler
growler
howler
scowler

howling
cowling
fouling
fowling
growling

prowling
scowling
yowling

13.4

town
bogged down
brown
clown
crown
Down
down
downtown
dressing down
dressing gown
drown
dumbing down
eiderdown
frown
Gordon Brown
gown
James Brown
lie down
noun
one-horse town
on the town
Portadown
put down
renown
run-down
tumbledown
upside down
uptown

brownie
Brownie
downy
towny

pound
abound
aground
all-round
around
astound

battleground
bound
browned
clowned
compound (= *to add to*)
confound
crowned
downed
drowned
expound
frowned
found
ground
hound
impound
leather-bound
merry-go-round
mound
profound
propound
rebound
renowned
resound
rewound
round
run-around
sound
stamping ground
surround
turnaround
ultrasound
underground
unsound
unwound
wound (= *past tense of wind*)

bounder
all-rounder
around her
astound her
bound her
confound her

crowned her
expounder
flounder
founder
found her
grounder
ground her
hound her
impound her
pounder
quarter-pounder
rebounder
rounder
sounder
surround her

dumbfounded
abounded
astounded
bounded
compounded (= *added to*)
confounded
expounded
founded
grounded
hounded
ill-founded
impounded
mounded
pounded
propounded
rebounded
rounded
sounded
surrounded
unbounded
unfounded
well-founded

grounding
abounding
astounding
bounding
compounding

confounding
expounding
founding
hounding
impounding
mounding
pounding
propounding
rebounding
resounding
rounding
sounding
surrounding

soundings
surroundings

soundly
profoundly
roundly

boundless
groundless
soundless

foundry
boundary

lounge
scrounge

crowning
browning
clowning
downing
drowning
frowning
Robert Browning

bounce
announce
denounce
flounce
mispronounce
ounce
pounce
pronounce

renounce
trounce

bouncer
announce her
announcer
denounce her
denouncer
pronounce her
renounce her
trounce her

announcement
pronouncement

pronounced
announced
bounced
denounced
flounced
mispronounced
pounced
renounced
trounced
unannounced

count
account
amount
discount
dismount
fount
mount
paramount
recount
surmount
tantamount

counter
Brief Encounter
discounter
discount her
encounter
Geiger counter
surmount her

countable
accountable
insurmountable
surmountable
unaccountable
uncountable

county
bounty

mounted
accounted
amounted
counted
discounted
dismounted
recounted
surmounted
unaccounted

mounting
accounting
amounting
counting
discounting
dismounting
recounting
surmounting

mountain
fountain
soda fountain
Table Mountain

13.5
dowry
Lowry
Maori

13.6
mouse
clearing house
douse
fieldmouse
grouse

house (= *a home*)
house-to-house
in-house
jailhouse
Laos
louse
Mickey Mouse
nous
powerhouse
slaughterhouse
souse
spouse
Strauss
summerhouse

oust
groused
Faust
joust
loused
moused
soused

13.7

out
about
all-out
bout
boy scout
Brussels sprout
burnt-out
carry-out
clapped-out
clout
devout
doubt
down-and-out
drought
flout
gout
grout
hand out
hang-out
layabout

211

lout
out-and-out
pout
roundabout
rout
sauerkraut
scout
self-doubt
shout
snout
spaced out
spout
sprout
stout
thought-out
throughout
tout
trout
turnabout
walkabout
way-out
well-thought-out
without
zonked out

outing

clouting
doubting
flouting
grouting
pouting
routing
scouting

shouting
spouting
sprouting
touting

whereabouts

have one's doubts
hereabouts
thereabouts

You can add to this list by adding **-s** to some words that rhyme with **out**, as in **sprouts**

pouch

couch
crouch
grouch
ouch
slouch
vouch

13.8

mouth

foot and mouth
hand-to-mouth
Louth
south

13.9

drowse

arouse

browse
carouse
espouse
house (= *to provide accommodation for*)
rehouse
rouse

You can add to this list by adding **-s** to some words that rhyme with **now**, as in **cows**

tousle

arousal
carousal
espousal
spousal

drowsy

blowzy
lousy

rousing

arousing
browsing
carousing
drowsing
espousing
housing
rehousing

'or'

sort, corner, afford

All the words in this section use the sound 'or' in their main stressed syllable

14.1

draw
abhor
adore
ambassador
Arkansas
ashore
at death's door
Aviemore
awe
Baltimore
before
boar
bore
brother-in-law
carnivore
caw
chore
claw
commodore
common-law
core
corps (= a military
    body)
corridor
daughter-in-law
Demi Moore
deplore
dinosaur
door
door-to-door
drawer
Ecuador
evermore

explore
father-in-law
flaw
floor
for
forbore
fore
foresaw
forswore
four
furthermore
galore
George Bernard Shaw
gnaw
gore
guarantor
guffaw
hard-core
herbivore
ignore
implore
inshore
jackdaw
jaw
Jude Law
labrador
Lahore
law
lore
louvre door
macaw
matador
metaphor
more

mother-in-law
Mysore
Nassau
next-door
Nineteen Eighty-Four
nor
oar
offshore
omnivore
or
ore
overawe
oversaw
paw
pinafore
pore
postwar
pour
prewar
rapport
raw
restore
roar
San Salvador
saw
score
semaphore
shore
Singapore
Sir Thomas More
sister-in-law
snore
soar
son-in-law

sophomore
sore
spore
squaw
stevedore
store
straw
superstore
swore
sycamore
thaw
Theodore
tore
toreador
tug-of-war
war
Wichita
withdraw
wore
you're
your

➡️

Many English speakers pronounce some words in section **19.1** (eg *poor*) in such a way that they rhyme with these words

14.2

orb
absorb
daub

bauble
warble

floorboard
scoreboard

lawbreaker
jawbreaker

14.3

talk
Bob Hawke
chalk
Cork
cork
gawk
hawk
New York
pork
sparrowhawk
squawk
stalk
stork
tomahawk
tuning fork
uncork
walk
York

walker
baby-walker
corker
deerstalker
gawker
hawker
hillwalker
jaywalker
Majorca
Minorca
New Yorker
porker
sleepwalker
squawker
stalker
stalk her
streetwalker
talker
walk her
yorker
york her

Majorcan
Minorcan

raucous
caucus
stalk us
walk us
york us

chalky
gawky
Gorky
porky
walkie-talkie

walking
chalking
corking
gawking
hawking
hillwalking
jaywalking
smooth-talking
squawking
Stephen Hawking
stalking
talking
uncorking
yorking

mawkish
hawkish

lawcourt
forecourt

forked
chalked
corked
gawked
hawked
squawked
stalked
talked
uncorked
walked

14.4

board
aboard
abroad
accord
across-the-board
afford
Anna Ford
applaud
award
baud
broad
chord
Claud(e)
cord
defraud
fjord
ford
fraud
harpsichord
Harrison Ford
Henry Ford
hoard
horde
laud
lord
Maud(e)
motherboard
noticeboard
overboard
plasterboard
record (= *to register*)
reward
skirting board
sounding board
sword
tape-record
toward
umbilical cord
untoward
ward

You can add to this list by adding **-ed** to some words that rhyme with **draw**, as in **explored**

Many English speakers pronounce some words in section **19.2** (eg *insured*) in such a way that they rhyme with these words

order
boarder
border
bored her
broader
camcorder
defrauder
disorder
hoarder
ignored her
implored her
keyboarder
marauder
recorder
reorder
tape-recorder
toward her
video recorder
warder

laudable
affordable
unaffordable

ordered
bordered
disordered
reordered

warden
broaden
cordon
Gordon

Jordan
Lizzie Borden
Michael Jordan
traffic warden

mordant
discordant

Borders
boarders
borders
camcorders
hoarders
keyboarders
marauders
marching orders
orders
recorders
reorders
tape recorders
under starter's orders
video recorders
warders

cordial
primordial

accordion
Edwardian

gaudy
bawdy
Geordie

sordid
accorded
afforded
applauded
awarded
boarded
defrauded
forded
hoarded
lauded
lorded
prerecorded
recorded

rewarded
tape-recorded
unrecorded
warded

inordinate
coordinate
insubordinate
subordinate

boarding
according
affording
applauding
awarding
defrauding
fording
hoarding
lauding
lording
marauding
recording
rewarding
snowboarding
unrewarding
warding

broadly
lordly

tawdry
Audrey

gorge
David Lloyd-George
forge
George

14.5

dwarf
Düsseldorf
swarf
wharf

✚
You can also make rhymes for these words by using words in section **14.16** that rhyme with **north**

awful
drawerful
lawful
unlawful

14.6

organ
Glamorgan
Gorgon

14.7

forehand
beforehand

warhead
forehead

storehouse
poorhouse

14.8

small
Alan Ball
all
Annie Hall
appal
awl
ball
basketball
bawl
befall
belle of the ball
Bengal
brawl
call
cannonball
Charles de Gaulle
crawl

Donegal
drawl
enthral
fall
firewall
forestall
free-for-all
gall
Gaul
Hadrian's Wall
hall
handball
haul
install
Kirsty MacColl
know-it-all
Lauren Bacall
long-haul
mall
market stall
maul
Montreal
Nepal
off-the-wall
overall
overhaul
pall
Paul
recall
Royal Albert Hall
Saul
scrawl
Senegal
shawl
short-haul
sprawl
squall
stall
tall
trawl
volleyball
Wailing Wall
wall
wall-to-wall

warts and all
waterfall
wherewithal
withal
Zoë Ball

caller
appal her
befall her
brawler
call her
crawler
drawler
enthral her
faller
footballer
gall her
hauler
Paula
recall her
scrawler
smaller
sprawler
stall her
taller
trawler
what-d'ye-call-her

sorely
Bengali
creepy-crawly
Nepali
Sir Walter Raleigh
squally

Many English speakers pronounce some words in section **19.3** (eg *poorly*) in such a way that they rhyme with these words

all-in
call in
crawl in
tarpaulin

wall in

calling
appalling
enthralling
galling
hauling
name-calling
sprawling

You can add to this list by adding *-ing* to some words that rhyme with **small**, as in *falling*

flawless
lawless

falcon
Balkan
peregrine falcon

bald
appalled
balled
bawled
brawled
called
crawled
drawled
enthralled
forestalled
galled
hauled
installed
mauled
overhauled
palled
recalled
scald
scrawled
so-called
sprawled
squalled
stalled
trawled

walled

scalding
balding

false
waltz

fault
assault
default
exalt
malt
salt
somersault
vault
Walt

alter
altar
assault her
defaulter
exalt her
falter
fault her
Gibraltar
halter
halt her
Malta
pole-vaulter
salter
vaulter
Walter

faulty
Basil Fawlty
salty

vaulted
assaulted
defaulted
faulted
exalted
malted
salted
somersaulted
unsalted

hallway
Galway

14.9

form
Benidorm
chloroform
conform
deform
dorm
inform
Norm
norm
perform
re-form
reform
storm
swarm
thunderstorm
transform
underperform
uniform
warm

You can also make rhymes for these words by using words in section **14.10** that rhyme with *born*

format
doormat
re-format

former
chloroform her
conformer
dormer
form her
informer
inform her
Norma
performer
reformer
reform her

storm her
swarmer
transformer
transform her
trauma
underperformer
warmer
warm her

normal
abnormal
formal
informal
paranormal
subnormal

normally
abnormally
formally
formerly
informally

formalize
normalize

foreman
doorman
longshoreman
Mormon
Norman
storeman

dormant
informant

enormous
chloroform us
ginormous
inform us
reform us
storm us
transform us
warm us

formative
informative
normative

performing
barnstorming
brainstorming
heart-warming
housewarming

You can add to this list by adding *-ing* to some words that rhyme with *form*, as in *swarming*

deformity
conformity
enormity
uniformity

reformed
chloroformed
conformed
deformed
formed
ill-informed
informed
malformed
performed
re-formed
stormed
swarmed
transformed
underperformed
uniformed
warmed
well-informed

warmly
uniformly

14.10

born
adorn
at daggers drawn
borne
brawn
Capricorn
corn

Dawn
dawn
drawn
faun
fawn
forborne
forewarn
forlorn
forsworn
Goldie Hawn
horn
Jason Bourne
lawn
leprechaun
Matterhorn
Mountains of Mourne
mourn
outworn
overdrawn
pawn
peppercorn
prawn
Quorn®
reborn
sawn
scorn
Sean
Shane Warne
shorn
Siobhán
spawn
sworn
thorn
torn
unicorn
warn
waterborne
well-worn
withdrawn
worn
yawn

You can also make rhymes for these words by using words in section **14.9** that rhyme with **form**

corner
adorn her
borne her
fauna
fawner
fight one's corner
forewarn her
forsworn her
Lorna
mourner
mourn her
sauna
sawn her
scorn her
shorn her
torn her
warn her
withdrawn her
yawner

scrawnier
brawnier
California
cornea
cornier
hornier
thornier

corny
brawny
horny
scrawny
tawny
thorny

morning
adorning
awning
corning
dawning

fawning
forewarning
midmorning
mourning
pawning
scorning
spawning
warning
yawning

hornet
adorn it
borne it
cornet
drawn it
mourn it
outworn it
pawn it
sawn it
scorn it
spawn it
sworn it
torn it
warn it
withdrawn it
worn it

mournful
scornful

haunt
daunt
flaunt
gaunt
jaunt
taunt
vaunt

haunted
daunted
flaunted
jaunted
taunted
vaunted
undaunted

daunting
flaunting
haunting
jaunting
taunting
vaunting

launch
haunch
paunch
staunch

14.11

warp
gawp

pauper
torpor

14.12

flora
adorer
Andorra
angora
aura
Aurora
borer
Cora
corer
Dora
explorer
floorer
Flora
gnawer
ignorer
implorer
Laura
Leonora
Nora(h)
Pandora
pourer
restorer
roarer
scorer

snorer
soarer
storer
Thora
withdrawer

Many English speakers pronounce some words in section **19.4** (eg *juror*) in such a way that they rhyme with these words

adorable
deplorable

oral
aural
choral
floral

forum
decorum
quorum

chorus
abhor us
adore us
before us
bore us
ignore us
implore us
overawe us
oversaw us
paw us
porous
restore us
saw us
Taurus
thesaurus
tore us
withdraw us

Maureen
chlorine
Noreen

Gloria
crematoria
euphoria
moratoria
Pretoria
sanatoria
Victoria

memorial
conspiratorial
dictatorial
editorial
equatorial
immemorial
pictorial
sartorial
territorial
tutorial

auditorium
crematorium
moratorium
sanatorium

historian
Dorian
Singaporean
Victorian

glorious
censorious
inglorious
laborious
meritorious
notorious
uproarious
victorious

Many English speakers pronounce some words in section **19.4** (eg *furious*) in such a way that they rhyme with these words

gloriously
laboriously
notoriously
uproariously
victoriously

story
Frankie Dettori
furore
glory
gory
hoary
knickerbocker glory
Lake Maggiore
multistorey
Rory
storey
Tory
West Side Story

boring
abhorring
adoring
boring
cawing
clawing
coring
deploring
exploring
flooring
gnawing
goring
guffawing
ignoring
imploring
jawing
pawing
pouring
restoring
roaring
sawing
scoring
snoring
soaring
storing

thawing
warring
withdrawing

Many English speakers pronounce
some words in section **19.4**
(eg *during*) in such a way that
they rhyme with these words

moron
boron
draw on
gnaw on
oxymoron
pour on
wore on
you're on

14.13

horse
coarse
course
discourse
divorce
endorse
enforce
force
gorse
hoarse
hobbyhorse
Inspector Morse
intercourse
Morse
recourse
reinforce
remorse
resource
rocking horse
sauce
source
soy sauce
tartar(e) sauce
tour de force
vaulting horse

watercourse

saucer
Chaucer
coarser
divorce her
endorse her
endorser
enforcer
force her
hoarser
reinforce her

morsel
dorsal

awesome
divorce 'em
endorse 'em
force 'em
foursome

saucy
hors(e)y

corset
Dorset
endorse it
enforce it
faucet
force it
reinforce it
resource it
source it

forceful
remorseful
resourceful
unremorseful

enforcement
endorsement
reinforcement

forced
coursed
discoursed
divorced

endorsed
enforced
exhaust
holocaust
outsourced
recoursed
reinforced
resourced
sauced
sourced
unforced

14.14

portion
abortion
apportion
caution
contortion
distortion
extortion
precaution
proportion

extortionate
proportionate

14.15

sort
abort
afterthought
Agincourt
alphasort
astronaut
besought
bought
brought
caught
cavort
consort
contort
cosmonaut
court
deport
distort

distraught
escort (= to accompany)
exhort
export
extort
fort
fought
fraught
Hampton Court
hard-fought
heliport
import
juggernaut
life-support
naught
nought
ought
overwrought
port
purport
quart
report
resort (= holiday destination)
rethought
retort
self-taught
short
snort
sought
sport
support
taught
taut
thought
thwart
transport (= to move)
wart

water
aorta
backwater
bought her

breakwater
brought her
caught her
Cole Porter
court her
daughter
deport her
dishwater
distort her
escort her
exhort her
exporter
export her
fought her
freshwater
goddaughter
granddaughter
great-granddaughter
hot-water
importer
manslaughter
mortar
porter
quarter
rainwater
reporter
report her
saltwater
shorter
slaughter
snorter
sorter
sort her
sought her
stepdaughter
supporter
support her
taught her
thwart her
transporter
transport her
underwater

mortal
chortle
immortal
portal

mortally
quarterly

autumn
bought 'em
brought 'em
caught 'em
fought 'em
report 'em
support 'em
taught 'em
thwart 'em

shorten
tauten

important
all-important
oughtn't
unimportant

watering
mouthwatering
quartering

headquarters
hindquarters
Muddy Waters

You can add to this list by
adding **-s** to some words that
rhyme with **water**, as in
supporters

vortex
cortex

courtier
consortia

forty
forte
haughty

naughty
sporty
UB40

nautical
aeronautical
cortical

sorted
assorted
distorted
unreported
unsupported

You can add to this list by
adding **-ed** to some words that
rhyme with **sort**, as in **distorted**

mortify
fortify

sorting
aborting
cavorting
consorting
contorting
courting
deporting
distorting
escorting
exhorting
exporting
extorting
importing
purporting
reporting
resorting
retorting
shorting
snorting
sporting
supporting
thwarting
transporting
unsporting

vortices
cortices

supportive
abortive
sportive
unsupportive

auto
Oporto
quarto

shortly
portly

assortment
deportment

sports
Hogwarts
quartz
shorts

You can add to this list by
adding **-s** to some words that
rhyme with **sort**, as in **thoughts**

scorch
porch
torch

scorcher
torture

14.16

north
back and forth
forth
fourth
henceforth

You can also make rhymes for
these words by using words in
section **14.5** that rhyme with
dwarf

14.17

dwarves
wharves

14.18

doorway
Norway

14.19

lawyer
Tom Sawyer

14.20

pause
applause
Azores
because
cause
clause
drawers
gauze
menopause
outdoors
out-of-doors
Rebel Without a
   Cause
Santa Claus

[+]

You can add to this list by
adding **-s** to some words
that rhyme with **draw**, as
in **paws**

'*oi*'

co*i*n, po*i*nted, av*oi*d

All the words in this section use the sound '**oi**' in their main stressed syllable

15.1

boy
ahoy
alloy
annoy
blue-eyed boy
buoy
choirboy
corduroy
coy
deploy
destroy
employ
enjoy
Hanoi
Helen of Troy
Illinois
Joy
joy
Little Lord Fauntleroy
oi
Old Man of Hoy
ploy
pride and joy
redeploy
Rob Roy
Roy
Siegfried and Roy
toy
Troy

soya
annoy her
buoy her

coyer
deploy her
destroyer
destroy her
employer
employ her
enjoyer
enjoy her
Goya
paranoia
redeploy her
sequoia

enjoyable
deployable
employable
unemployable
unenjoyable

loyal
disloyal
royal

loyally
disloyally
royally

royalist
loyalist

loyalty
disloyalty
royalty

buoyant
clairvoyant
flamboyant

cloying
alloying
annoying
buoying
deploying
destroying
employing
enjoying
redeploying
soul-destroying
toying

15.2

void
alloyed
annoyed
asteroid
avoid
buoyed
Celluloid®
Clive Lloyd
deployed
destroyed
devoid
employed
enjoyed
Floyd
haemorrhoid
Harold Lloyd
humanoid
Lloyd
Lucian Freud
overjoyed
paranoid

Pink Floyd
Polaroid®
self-employed
Sigmund Freud
toyed
unemployed

15.3

oil
boil
broil
castor oil
coil
counterfoil
embroil
foil
hydrofoil
olive oil
Olive Oyl
parboil
recoil
soil
spoil
toil
uncoil

oily
doily

15.4

enjoyment
deployment
employment
redeployment
unemployment

15.5

join
adjoin
Battle of the Boyne
Boulogne
coin
enjoin

groin
loin
purloin
rejoin

point
anoint
appoint
ball-and-socket joint
boiling point
break-even point
clip joint
counterpoint
disappoint
freezing point
joint
jumping-off point
power point
sore point
strip joint
vantage point

pointed
anointed
appointed
disappointed
disjointed
jointed
self-appointed
well-appointed

ointment
appointment
disappointment

15.6

voice
choice
James Joyce
Joyce
multiple-choice
rejoice
Rolls-Royce

foist
Ally McCoist
hoist
joist
moist
rejoiced
unvoiced
voiced

oyster
cloister
foist her
hoist her
moister

15.7

exploit
adroit
Detroit
maladroit
quoit

loiter
exploiter
goitre

15.8

noise
alloys
annoys
blue-eyed boys
boys
buoys
choirboys
corduroys
deploys
destroys
employs
enjoys
joys
ploys
poise
redeploys
toys

'oo'

book, cooker, mistook

All the words in this section use the sound 'oo' in their main stressed syllable

16.1

book
brook
Captain Cook
Chinook
cook
copybook
crook
fishing hook
forsook
grappling hook
hook
look
mistook
nook
Osnabrück
overbook
overcook
overlook
overtook
partook
Peter Cook
pocketbook
rook
shook
storybook
Tobruk
took
undercook
undertook

cooker
book her
brook her

hooker
hook her
looker
mistook her
onlooker
overbook her
overlook her
overtook her
shook her
took her

cookery
rookery

cookie
bookie
fortune cookie
hook(e)y
rookie

cooking
bad-looking
booking
brooking
evil-looking
forward-looking
good-looking
hooking
inward-looking
looking
nice-looking
overbooking
overcooking
overlooking
undercooking

hooked
booked
brooked
cooked
double-booked
looked
overbooked
overcooked
overlooked
precooked
uncooked
undercooked

16.2

good
adulthood
babyhood
brotherhood
could
fatherhood
Hollywood
hood
likelihood
livelihood
misunderstood
motherhood
neighbourhood
parenthood
Robin Hood
should
sisterhood
stood
understood
up to no good

withstood
wood
would

Buddha
do-gooder
hood her
misunderstood her
Pablo Neruda
understood her
withstood her

couldn't
shouldn't
wouldn't

woody
goody
goody-goody

16.3

full
Abdul
bull
dyed-in-the-wool
Istanbul
John Bull
like a red rag to a bull
pull
wool

*The following words
will also tend to rhyme
with these when they
come at the end of a
line:*
abominable
acceptable
accessible
adaptable
adjustable
admirable
admiral
affable
allowable

all-powerful
amenable
amiable
amicable
animal
apocryphal
appreciable
arguable
arsenal
audible
barnacle
basketful
bellyful
biblical
bicameral
bookable
bountiful
cannibal
capital
cardinal
carnival
cerebral
certifiable
charitable
classical
clavicle
cockerel
collapsible
colourful
combustible
comfortable
communal
communicable
companionable
compatible
conjugal
considerable
constable
contemptible
contestable
convertible
corpuscle
creditable
cubicle

culpable
cultural
cylindrical
demonstrable
detachable
digestible
digital
dispensable
disposable
disreputable
doggerel
ecumenical
electrical
elliptical
encyclical
enviable
ephemeral
episcopal
equable
evangelical
exceptional
execrable
fallible
fanciful
farcical
fathomable
feasible
federal
festival
fictional
flappable
forcible
formidable
fractional
funeral
general
gullible
guttural
habitable
hierarchical
horrible
hospital
identical
imaginable

'oo'

impeccable
impenetrable
imperceptible
imperturbable
implacable
implausible
imponderable
impregnable
impressionable
inalienable
inapplicable
inaudible
inaugural
incompatible
incontestable
incontrovertible
incorrigible
incorruptible
indecipherable
indefatigable
indelible
indescribable
indigestible
indispensable
indistinguishable
indomitable
ineffable
inestimable
inevitable
inexhaustible
inexorable
inimical
inimitable
innumerable
insatiable
insufferable
insuperable
integral
interminable
interval
invincible
inviolable
invulnerable
irascible

irreconcilable
irredeemable
irremediable
irreplaceable
irresistible
irreversible
irrevocable
irritable
Ivan the Terrible
justifiable
knowledgeable
lackadaisical
lamentable
lateral
latitudinal
laughable
legible
lexical
liberal
likeable
Lionel
literal
longitudinal
lovable
magical
malleable
manageable
mandible
marginal
marital
marketable
marriageable
masterful
meaningful
medical
medicinal
memorable
merciful
mineral
minimal
miracle
miserable
monocle
multiple

municipal
musical
mythical
natural
nautical
navigable
negligible
negotiable
Newcastle
non-negotiable
nonsensical
notable
noticeable
numeral
objectionable
observable
obstacle
occasional
Oedipal
optical
optional
oracle
ordinal
original
palatable
palpable
paradoxical
participle
pastoral
peaceable
pedestal
perceptible
Percival
peripheral
perishable
personable
personal
pineapple
pinnacle
pitiable
pitiful
pivotal
plausible
plentiful

portable
Portugal
powerful
practicable
preferable
prodigal
proportional
provisional
purposeful
questionable
radical
reachable
receptacle
rechargeable
reciprocal
recoverable
regional
remarkable
renewable
reputable
reversible
sceptical
seasonal
seminal
serviceable
several
shovelful
skeletal
sorrowful
spectacle
stoical
structural
suggestible
surgical
susceptible
symmetrical
tangible
technical
temporal
tentacle

terminal
terrible
testicle
theatrical
unacceptable
unbeatable
uncomfortable
understandable
unfathomable
unflappable
ungovernable
unimaginable
unlovable
unnatural
unprintable
unpronounceable
unquestionable
unspeakable
untouchable
unverifiable
valuable
variable
vegetable
vehicle
venerable
verifiable
veritable
vertical
visceral
vulnerable
whimsical
wonderful

fully
bully
pulley
woolly

bullet
pullet

pull it

16.4

push
bush
George W Bush
Hindu Kush
Kate Bush
shush

pushy
bushy
cushy

bushed
hard-pushed
pushed
shushed

16.5

foot
afoot
barefoot
hotfoot
kaput
Lilliput
pussyfoot
put
soot
stay put
underfoot

footing
off-putting
pussyfooting
putting
sooting

butch
putsch

'*u*'

club, butter, begun

All the words in this section use the sound '**u**' in their main stressed syllable

17.1

club
Beelzebub
blub
cub
dub
grub
hub
nub
pub
rub
scrub
shrub
snub
stub
sub
tub

rubber
blubber
clubber
club her
dub her
grubber
rub her
scrubber
scrub her
snub her
Tony Gubba

blubbered
cupboard
walk-in cupboard

bubble
double
Edwin Hubble
rubble
stubble
trouble

troubled
bubbled
doubled
stubbled
untroubled

shrubbery
rubbery

You can make rhymes for these
words by using words in section
17.15 that rhyme with
discovery

chubby
grubby
hubby
scrubby
stubby
tubby

doubly
bubbly
grubbily
stubbly

publican
Republican
republican

17.2

luck
amuck
buck
Chuck
chuck
cluck
Donald Duck
duck
fork-lift truck
Friar Tuck
lame duck
muck
pluck
potluck
Puck
ruck
snuck
struck
stuck
suck
thunderstruck
truck
tuck
unstuck
yu(c)k

pucker
bloodsucker
buck her
chucker
chuck her
chukka
ducker

duck her
mucker
plucker
pluck her
pukka
struck her
sucker
suck her
trucker
tucker
yucca

chuckle

buckle
honeysuckle
knuckle
suckle

lucky

happy-go-lucky
Kentucky
mucky
plucky
unlucky
yucky

luckily

pluckily
unluckily

bucket

buck it
chuck it
duck it
kick the bucket
Nantucket
pluck it
snuck it
struck it
stuck it
suck it

duckling

buckling
chuckling
knuckling

suckling
swashbuckling
ugly duckling

flux

Benelux
bucks
chucks
clucks
crux
de luxe
ducks
fork-lift trucks
lame ducks
mucks
plucks
rucks
shucks
sucks
trucks
tucks
tux

suction

abduction
conduction
construction
coproduction
deduction
destruction
induction
instruction
introduction
liposuction
obstruction
overproduction
production
reconstruction
reduction
reintroduction
reproduction
seduction
self-destruction
underproduction

duct

abduct
aqueduct
bucked
chucked
clucked
conduct (= to lead)
construct
deduct
ducked
induct
instruct
misconduct
mucked
obstruct
plucked
reconstruct
rucked
self-destruct
sucked
trucked
tucked
viaduct

instructor

abduct her
abductor
bucked her
chucked her
conduct her
conductor
construct her
instruct her
obstruct her
plucked her
reconstruct her
semiconductor
superconductor
trucked her

deductible

conductible
indestructible
ineluctable
tax-deductible

constructive
counterproductive
destructive
inductive
instructive
obstructive
productive
reproductive
seductive
unproductive

succulent
truculent

17.3

mud
bad blood
blood
bud
cud
dud
Elmer Fudd
flood
spud
stick-in-the-mud
stud
thud
Zola Budd

shudder
judder
rudder
udder

cuddle
huddle
muddle
puddle

muddy
bloody
buddy
fuddy-duddy
ruddy
study

understudy

studied
blooded
budded
cold-blooded
flooded
hot-blooded
muddied
red-blooded
studded
thudded
warm-blooded

budding
blooding
flooding
studding
thudding

cuddly
Dudley

judge
adjudge
begrudge
budge
drudge
fudge
grudge
misjudge
nudge
prejudge
sludge
smudge
trudge

budgie
pudgy

grudging
adjudging
begrudging
budging
drudging
fudging
judging

misjudging
nudging
prejudging
smudging
trudging
ungrudging

budget
adjudge it
begrudge it
budge it
fudge it
judge it
low-budget
misjudge it
nudge it
prejudge it
smudge it

17.4

stuff
bluff
Brian Clough
buff
Call My Bluff
cuff
duff
enough
fluff
gruff
guff
huff
muff
off-the-cuff
powder puff
puff
rebuff
rough
ruff
scruff
scuff
slough
snuff
tough

suffer
bluffer
bluff her
buffer
buff her
duffer
gruffer
puffer
rebuff her
rougher
snuffer
stuffer
stuff her
tougher

shuffle
duffle
kerfuffle
muffle
reshuffle
ruffle
scuffle
snuffle
truffle

muffled
kerfuffled
muffled
reshuffled
ruffled
scuffled
shuffled
snuffled
truffled
unruffled

puffy
fluffy
huffy
scruffy
stuffy
toughie

muffin
puffin
ragamuffin

puff in
stuff in

gruffly
roughly
toughly

gruffness
roughness
toughness

tuft
bluffed
buffed
chuffed
cuffed
duffed
fluffed
huffed
muffed
puffed
rebuffed
roughed
scuffed
sloughed
snuffed
stuffed
toughed

17.5

drug
bug
chug
debug
Doug
dug
fug
hug
jitterbug
jug
litterbug
lug
mug
plug
pug

rug
shrug
slug
smug
snug
thug
trug
tug
unplug

mugger
bug her
debug her
drugger
drug her
dug her
hugger
hug her
lug her
mug her
plug her
plugger
rugger
slugger
smugger
snugger
tugger
tug her
unplug her

struggle
juggle
smuggle
snuggle

buggy
druggie
Duggie
muggy

plughole
lughole

smuggler
juggler
struggler

ugly
smugly
snugly

17.6

dull
annul
cull
gull
Hull
hull
Jethro Tull
lull
Mull
mull
null
Rod Hull
scull
skull
Solihull

duller
annul her
colour
cull her
discolour
gull her
lull her
null her
off-colour
sculler
watercolour

coloured
dullard
many-coloured
multicoloured
rose-coloured
self-coloured

gully
sully

gullet
annul it

cull it
mullet
mull it

bulk
hulk
Incredible Hulk
skulk
sulk

bulky
sulky

bulge
divulge
indulge
overindulge

culminate
fulminate

gulp
pulp

pulse
convulse
dulse
repulse

ulcer
convulse her
repulse her
Tulsa

repulsive
compulsive
convulsive
impulsive

compulsion
emulsion
expulsion
propulsion
repulsion
revulsion

cult
adult
catapult

consult
exult
insult
occult
result

consultant
exultant
resultant

mulch
gulch

culture
agriculture
horticulture
subculture
vulture

17.7

drum
become
bothersome
bum
burdensome
capsicum
cerebrum
chewing gum
chrysanthemum
chum
come
crumb
cumbersome
curriculum
dumb
glum
gum
hum
humdrum
kettledrum
laudanum
maximum
meddlesome
minimum
modicum

mum
numb
optimum
overcome
pendulum
platinum
plum
plumb
quarrelsome
Red Rum
rum
scrum
scum
slum
some
strum
succumb
sum
swum
thumb
tiresome
Tom Thumb
troublesome
tum
Tweedledum
wearisome

You can also make rhymes for these words by using words in section **17.8** that rhyme with *run*

summer

become her
bummer
comer
drummer
dumber
glummer
hummer
latecomer
midsummer
mummer
newcomer

numb her
overcome her
plumber
rummer
strum her
strummer

summon

cumin

summery

Colin Montgomerie
Field Marshal
  Montgomery
flummery
Montgomery
mummery
summary

hummus

pumice

mummy

Brummie
chummy
dummy
gummy
plummy
scrummy
tummy
yummy

coming

becoming
bumming
crumbing
drumming
dumbing
forthcoming
gumming
have another think
  coming
homecoming
humming
incoming
mind-numbing

mumming
numbing
oncoming
overcoming
plumbing
scrumming
slumming
strumming
succumbing
summing
thumbing
unbecoming
unforthcoming
up-and-coming

summit

become it
drum it
hum it
numb it
overcome it
plummet
slum it
strum it
swum it

number

St Columba
cucumber
encumber
lumbar
lumber
outnumber
slumber

stumble

crumble
fumble
grumble
humble
jumble
mumble
rough-and-tumble
rumble
tumble

tumbling
bumbling
crumbling
fumbling
grumbling
humbling
jumbling
mumbling
rumbling
stumbling

jumbo
Colombo
Dumbo
mumbo jumbo

tumbler
fumbler
grumbler
humbler
mumbler

crumbly
humbly

lump
bump
chump
clump
Donald Trump
dump
Forrest Gump
frump
gazump
grump
hump
jump
plump
pump
rump
slump
stump
sugar lump
sump
thump
trump

jumper
bumper
bump her
dumper
dump her
gazumper
gazump her
humper
plumper
pumper
stumper
stump her
thumper
thump her
trump her

crumple
rumple

rumpus
compass
encompass

bumpy
dumpy
frumpy
grumpy
jumpy
lumpy
stumpy

thumping
bumping
bungee jumping
clumping
dumping
gazumping
grumping
humping
jumping
lumping
plumping
pumping
slumping
stumping
thumping

trumping

trumpet
bump it
crumpet
dump it
jump it
lump it
pump it
thump it
trump it

pumpkin
bumpkin

mumps
dumps

You can add to this list by
adding -s to some words that
rhyme with **lump**, as in **bumps**

jump-start
bump-start

assumption
consumption
gumption
presumption
resumption

scrumptious
bumptious

sumptuous
presumptuous

17.8

run
aftersun
Attila the Hun
begun
bun
Clive Dunn
close-run
done

fun
great-grandson
gun
hard-won
hit-and-run
machine gun
megaton(ne)
none
nun
one
one-to-one
outdone
outrun
overdone
overrun
Peter Gunn
pun
redone
rerun
sawn-off shotgun
shotgun
shun
son
spun
stun
sub-machine gun
sun
The Sun
tommy gun
ton(ne)
Trevor Nunn
twenty-one
undone
won

The following words will also tend to rhyme with these when they come at the end of a line:
abdomen
acumen
Alison
Amazon

Amundsen
Anglican
anyone
badminton
cardigan
chairwoman
charlatan
charwoman
cinnamon
citizen
Congressman
Corsican
cyclamen
David Livingstone
Dominican
Edison
Englishman
Englishwoman
everyone
Frenchman
Frenchwoman
Galveston
gentleman
Gilbert and Sullivan
heptagon
hexagon
highwayman
hooligan
hurricane
hydrogen
Imogen
Irishman
jettison
John Betjeman
Jonathan
Kosovan
Leif Eriksson
Lexington
Mendelssohn
Mexican
Michigan
Moldavian
Monaghan
nitrogen

octagon
ombudsman
Oregon
Oscar Peterson
oxygen
Pamela Anderson
pelican
pentagon
phenomenon
ptarmigan
puritan
quieten
sacristan
Samaritan
Scandinavian
silicon
simpleton
Shackleton
skeleton
Solomon
subaltern
talisman
UNISON
unison
Vatican
veteran
Welshman
Welshwoman
Wimbledon
Zimbabwean

You can also make rhymes for these words by using words in section **17.7** that rhyme with **drum**

runner
forerunner
frontrunner
gunner
gunrunner
outdone her
outrun her
overrun her

roadrunner
run her
shun her
stun her
stunner
undone her
won her

tunnel

Channel Tunnel
funnel
gunwale
Sally Gunnell

funny

Bugs Bunny
bunny
honey
money
runny
sonny
sunny
unfunny

stunning

cunning
gunning
gunrunning
outrunning
overrunning
punning
rerunning
running
shunning
stunning
sunning

punnet

begun it
done it
gun it
outdone it
outrun it
overdone it
overrun it
redone it

rerun it
run it
shun it
spun it
stun it
undone it
whodun(n)it
won it

chunk

bunk
debunk
drunk
dunk
flunk
funk
gunk
hunk
junk
monk
preshrunk
punk
shrunk
skunk
slunk
spunk
stunk
sunk
trunk

uncle

carbuncle
great-uncle

drunken

Duncan
shrunken
sunken

chunky

clunky
flunkey
funky
hunky
junkie
monkey

punky

function

compunction
conjunction
dysfunction
injunction
junction
malfunction
T-junction
unction

functional

conjunctional
dysfunctional
multi-functional

puncture

acupuncture
juncture

fund

gunned
moribund
punned
refund
Rosamund
rotund
shunned
stunned
sunned

Sunday

Burundi
Lundy
Monday
sundae

thunder

asunder
blunder
down under
plunder
Stevie Wonder
under
wonder

bundle
trundle

abundant
overabundant
redundant

rundown
sundown

plunge
expunge
grunge
gunge
lunge
sponge

plunger
conjure
sponger

lung
among
Brigham Young
bung
clung
dung
far-flung
flung
hamstrung
highly strung
hung
Jimmy Young
Kirsty Young
Mao Zedong
overhung
rung
slung
sprung
strung
stung
sung
swung
tongue
wrung
young

hunger
fishmonger
gossipmonger
ironmonger
not getting any
  younger
warmonger
younger

jungle
bungle
fungal

dunce
experience
influence
once

hunt
affront
blunt
brunt
confront
front
grunt
James Blunt
James Hunt
punt
runt
shunt
stunt
upfront
waterfront

hunter
Billy Bunter
blunter
blunt her
confront her
grunter
hunt her
junta
punter
shunter
shunt her
stunt her

stunted
affronted
blunted
confronted
fronted
grunted
hunted
punted
shunted

hunting
blunting
bunting
confronting
fox-hunting
fronting
grunting
punting
shunting
stunting

bunch
brunch
crunch
hunch
lunch
munch
Punch
punch
scrunch

luncheon
truncheon

crunchy
punchy
scrunchie

munchies
bunches
brunches
crunches
hunches
lunches
munches
punches

scrunches
scrunchies

runway
one-way

bunion
Damon Runyon
onion

17.9

up
built-up
buttercup
cover-up
cup
FA Cup
follow-up
grown-up
jumped-up
made-up
mixed-up
pent-up
pick-me-up
pup
runner-up
Ryder Cup
stand up
stuck-up
summing-up
sup
UEFA Cup
washing-up
World Cup

supper
cuppa
scupper
upper

supple
couple

comeuppance
twopence

puppy
guppy
yuppie

corruption
disruption
eruption
interruption

corrupt
abrupt
cupped
disrupt
erupt
interrupt
pupped
supped
upped

17.10

thorough
borough
kookaburra

hurry
Andy Murray
curry
Edwina Curry
flurry
Murray
scurry
Surrey
worry

hurried
curried
scurried
worried

flourish
nourish

nourishing
flourishing

furrow
burrow

17.11

fuss
abacus
adulterous
analogous
anomalous
asparagus
autonomous
barbarous
bigamous
blasphemous
blunderbuss
bus
cacophonous
cadaverous
calculus
cancerous
cantankerous
Caucasus
chivalrous
covetous
dangerous
diaphanous
discuss
Ephesus
exodus
fabulous
frivolous
gangrenous
garrulous
gelatinous
genius
gluttonous
Gus
hazardous
hippopotamus
Icarus
impetus
indigenous
infamous
ingenious
languorous
Lazarus
ludicrous

'u'

marvellous
minibus
miraculous
mischievous
monogamous
monotonous
mountainous
nebulous
Nic(h)olas
obstreperous
octopus
Oedipus
ominous
omnibus
onerous
Pegasus
perilous
plus
poisonous
ponderous
populace
populous
posthumous
precipitous
preposterous
pretentious
prosperous
pus
querulous
rapturous
rhinoceros
riotous
Romulus
ruinous
sarcophagus
scandalous
scrupulous
scurrilous
slanderous
sonorous
Spartacus
stimulus
suss
syllabus

terminus
tetanus
thunderous
thus
timorous
tinnitus
tremulous
truss
unscrupulous
us
uterus
venomous
villainous
Vilnius
Wenceslas

rustle
Bertrand Russell
bustle
Darcey Bussell
hustle
muscle
mussel
Russell
tussle

muscles
Brussels
bustles
hustles
mussels
rustles
tussles

fussy
hussy
pussy (= *full of pus*)

russet
discuss it
gusset
suss it
truss it

dusk
busk

husk
musk
rusk
tusk

Tuscan
Etruscan

hustler
bustler
rustler

just
adjust
august
bite the dust
bussed
bust
concussed
crust
discussed
disgust
distrust
dry as dust
dust
entrust
fussed
gust
lust
mistrust
must
nonplussed
readjust
robust
rust
sussed
thrust
trussed
trust
unjust
upper-crust
wanderlust

cluster
adjuster
adjust her

Augusta
bussed her
bluster
buster
bust her
concussed her
discussed her
disgust her
distrust her
duster
dust her
entrust her
fluster
General Custer
knuckle-duster
loss adjuster
lustre
mistrust her
muster
nonplussed her
readjust her
sussed her
thrust her
trussed her
trust her

custard
blustered
clustered
flustered
lustred
mustard
mustered

custom
accustom
bust 'em
concussed 'em
disgust 'em
distrust 'em
nonplussed 'em
rust 'em
sussed 'em

dusty
crusty
gusty
lusty
musty
rusty
trusty

trusted
adjusted
busted
crusted
disgusted
distrusted
dusted
encrusted
entrusted
gusted
lusted
maladjusted
mistrusted
readjusted
rusted
well-adjusted

Justin
Dustin
just in
trust in

trusting
adjusting
busting
disgusting
distrusting
dusting
entrusting
gusting
lusting
mistrusting
rusting
thrusting

bust-up
dust-up

lustful
distrustful
mistrustful
trustful

adjustment
entrustment
readjustment

industrious
illustrious

rush
blush
brush
crush
flush
gush
hush
lush
mush
plush
Portrush
scrubbing brush
slush
sweeping brush
tarred with the same
  brush
thrush

blusher
brusher
Byelorussia
crusher
flusher
gusher
husher
lusher
musher
plusher
Prussia
rusher
Russia
usher

Russian
Byelorussian
concussion
discussion
percussion
Prussian
repercussion

slushy
gushy
mushy

crushing
blushing
brushing
flushing
gushing
hushing
lushing
mushing
rushing
slushing

hushed
blushed
brushed
crushed
flushed
gushed
lushed
mushed
rushed
slushed

17.13

nut
Brazil nut
but
butt
clean-cut
clear-cut
coconut
cut
do one's nut
glut

gut
halibut
hazelnut
hut
jut
low-cut
monkey nut
mutt
putt
rebut
rut
shut
slut
smut
strut
uncut
undercut

The following words will also tend to rhyme with these when they come at the end of a line:
accurate
adequate
advocate (= a legal representative)
affectionate
aggregate
animate (= living)
approximate (= rough)
articulate (= fluent)
aspirate
barbiturate
celibate
certificate
commensurate
compatriot
confederate
conglomerate
Connecticut
considerate
consulate
corporate

degenerate (= degraded)
delegate (= a representative)
deliberate (= intentional)
desolate
desperate
devil's advocate
disconsolate
disproportionate
doctorate
duplicate (= a copy)
effeminate
elaborate (= ornate)
electorate
estimate (= a guess)
expatriate
fortunate
graduate (= a person with a degree)
Harrogate
illiterate
immaculate
immoderate
inanimate
indeterminate
intimate (= close)
intricate
inveterate
moderate (= not extreme)
numerate
obstinate
passionate
patriot
precipitate
predicate (= part of a sentence)
profligate
separate (= apart)
surrogate
syndicate (= a group of businesses)

triplicate
ultimate

mutter
bread-and-butter
butter
Calcutta
clutter
cut her
cutter
flutter
gut her
gutter
nutter
putter
shut her
shutter
splutter
sputter
stutter
undercut her
utter
woodcutter

scuttle
rebuttal
shuttle
subtle

utterly
subtly

button
belly-button
glutton
Jensen Button
Lord Hutton
mutton
push-button
unbutton

nutty
putty
slutty
smutty

cutting
gutting
jutting
nutting
price-cutting
putting
rebutting
rutting
shutting
strutting
undercutting

nuts
misery-guts

You can add to this list by adding -*s* to some words that rhyme with **nut**, as in **cuts**

clutch
crutch
Dutch
hutch
much
overmuch
such
touch

touchy
duchy

touched
clutched
untouched

other
another
Big Brother
brother
godmother
grandmother
great-grandmother
half-brother
mother

smother
stepbrother
stepmother

brotherhood
motherhood

mother-in-law
brother-in-law

love
above
cupboard love
dove
glove
shove
tug-of-love

lover
above her
cover
Danny Glover
discover
Lady Chatterley's
  Lover
love her
plover
recover
rediscover
shove her
uncover
undercover

oven
govern
misgovern

discovery
recovery

You can make rhymes for these words by using words in section **17.1** that rhyme with **shrubbery**

loving
fun-loving
peace-loving
shoving

unloved
beloved
gloved
loved
shoved

well-loved

17.16

buzz
does
fuzz

puzzle
guzzle
muzzle

nuzzle

cousin
dozen

fuzzy
buzzy
does he?
muzzy
scuzzy

'ue'

blue, cruel, avenue

All the words in this section use the sound '**ue**' in their main stressed syllable

---

18.1

zoo

accrue
ado
anew
askew
Autocue®
avenue
ballyhoo
bamboo
barbecue
bill and coo
bird's-eye view
black and blue
blew
blue
boo
brand-new
brew
can-do
canoe
caribou
cashew
Catch-22
chew
clue
cock-a-doodle-doo
cockatoo
construe
coo
Corfu
coup
CPU (= *central
    processing unit*)

crew
Crewe
cue
dew
do (= *to perform*)
Doctor Who
Drew
drew
due
Duncan Goodhew
EMU (= *European
    Monetary Union*)
ensue
eschew
EU
ewe
FAQ (= *frequently
    asked question*)
few
flew
flu
flue
GCHQ (= *Government
    Communications
    Headquarters*)
GHQ (= *general
    headquarters*)
glue
gnu
goo
grew
hew
hitherto
HQ

hue
Hugh
hullabaloo
imbue
in lieu
interview
IOU
IQ
Jew
Jimmy Choo
K2
kangaroo
Kat(h)mandu
knew
lasso
loo
Lou
mew
Michel Roux
misconstrue
moo
navy-blue
nearly-new
new
NVQ (= *national
    vocational
    qualification*)
outdo
outgrew
overdo
overdue
overshoe
overthrew
overview

'ue'

pay-per-view
Pepe le Pew
Peru
pew
phew
pooh-pooh
POW
Pru(e)
pursue
Q
QE2
queue
redo
rendezvous
renew
residue
retinue
revenue
review
revue
RFU (= *Rugby Football Union*)
Rhapsody in Blue
royal-blue
rue
Scooby Doo
screw
set-to
shampoo
shoe
shoo
shrew
skew
sky-blue
slew
spew
stew
strew
subdue
Sue
sue
taboo
talking-to
tattoo

thank you
The Taming of the Shrew
The Who
threw
through
Timbuktu
to
to-do
too
true
Tuvalu
two
U
undo
undue
unscrew
untrue
Vanuatu
VDU
view
W
Waterloo
well-to-do
WEU (= *Western European Union*)
whew
who
Winnie the Pooh
withdrew
woo
Xanadu
yew
you
you-know-who

fewer
bluer
brewer
Dudley Moore
drew her
evildoer
interviewer
interview her

knew her
newer
pursuer
pursue her
reviewer
sewer (= a *drain*)
skewer
tattoo her
threw her
truer
viewer
view her
wrongdoer

cruel
dual
duel
fuel
gruel
jewel
refuel
renewal

jeweller
crueller

gruelling
fuelling
refuelling

fluency
truancy

fluent
truant

chewy
gooey
GUI (= *graphical user interface*)
Hughie
Louis

fluid
Clwyd
druid

doing
canoeing
ensuing
undoing
wrongdoing

You can add to this list by adding *-ing* to some words that rhyme with **zoo**, as in **viewing**

Lewis
Jewess
St Louis

fewest
bluest
canoeist
newest
tattooist
truest
Uist

suet
cruet

You can also make rhymes for these words by using *it* after some words that rhyme with **zoo**, as in **view it**

gratuitous
circuitous
fortuitous

gratuity
ambiguity
continuity
incongruity
ingenuity
perpetuity
promiscuity

18.2

tube
boob

cube
Eustachian tube
Fallopian tube
YouTube

Cuba
scuba
tuba
tuber

Cuban
Reuben

exuberance
protuberance

ruby
booby
newbie
Ruby

cubic
pubic

lugubrious
insalubrious
salubrious

18.3

duke
archduke
Faruq
fluke
gobbledygook
Luke
nuke
puke
rebuke
spook

snooker
bazooka
lucre
nuke her
puker
rebuke her
spook her

verruca

Lord Lucan
toucan

mucus
Lucas
Matt Lucas
mucous
nuke us
rebuke us
spook us

spooky
fluk(e)y
Newquay

18.4

rude
allude
altitude
amplitude
aptitude
attitude
Babes in the Wood
brood
certitude
collude
conclude
crude
delude
denude
dude
elude
exactitude
exclude
exude
feud
food
fortitude
gratitude
include
ineptitude
interlude
intrude

Jude
lassitude
latitude
lewd
longitude
magnitude
mood
multitude
nude
preclude
protrude
prude
pseud
rectitude
servitude
shrewd
solitude
who'd
verisimilitude
you'd

You can add to this list by adding *-ed* to some words that rhyme with **zoo**, as in **viewed**

Tudor

Antigua and Barbuda
barracuda
Bermuda
booed her
colluder
cruder
excluder
intruder
include her
interviewed her
ruder
shrewder

doodle

caboodle
canoodle
feudal
poodle

noodles
canoodles
oodles
poodles

student

imprudent
prudent

moody

broody
Judy
Trudi(e)

including

alluding
brooding
colluding
concluding
deluding
denuding
eluding
excluding
exuding
feuding
intruding
precluding
protruding

judo

Cluedo®
escudo
Pierre Trudeau
pseudo

huge

centrifuge
Scrooge
stooge
subterfuge

18.5

proof

aloof
bulletproof
burglar-proof

El-Hadj Diouf
fireproof
goof
hoof
oven-proof
pouf(fe)
reproof
roof
shatterproof
shower-proof
spoof
waterproof
weatherproof

You can also make rhymes for these words by using words in section **18.16** that rhyme with **truth**

18.6

frugal

bugle
centrifugal
Dougal

18.7

pool

birthing pool
Blackpool
cagoule
cool
drool
fool
ghoul
joule
Liverpool
minuscule
misrule
molecule
mule
overrule
paddling pool
Pontypool

preschool
ridicule
rule
school
spool
stool
swimming pool
tool
Ullapool
uncool
vestibule
work-to-rule
you'll

ruler
cooler
cool her
fool her
misrule her
overrule her
Petula
preschooler
ridicule her
rule her
school her
spooler
tooler

Julia
peculiar
unrulier

truly
duly
Julie
newly
unduly
unruly

schooling
cooling
drooling
fooling
misruling
overruling
pooling

ridiculing
ruling
spooling
tooling

foolish
coolish
ghoulish

Zulu
Honolulu
Lulu
lulu

room
Alec Douglas-Home
anteroom
assume
bloom
boom
broom
changing room
consume
David Hume
doom
exhume
fume
gloom
groom
Khartoum
loom
perfume
plume
presume
resume
subsume
tomb
whom
womb
zoom

You can also make rhymes for
these words by using words in
section **18.9** that rhyme with
moon

bloomer
baby-boomer
consume her
consumer
doom her
exhume her
groom her
humour
Montezuma
Nkrumah
perfume her
perfumer
puma
subsume her
tumour

human
Harry S Truman
inhuman
Paul Newman
subhuman
superhuman

numerous
humerus
humorous
humour us

gloomy
roomy

ruminate
illuminate

luminous
voluminous

booming
assuming
blooming
brooming

consuming
dooming
exhuming
fuming
grooming
looming
perfuming
pluming
presuming
resuming
rooming
subsuming
time-consuming
tombing
unassuming
zooming

18.9

moon
afternoon
baboon
balloon
bassoon
boon
Brigadoon
buffoon
Cameroon
cartoon
change one's tune
cocoon
commune
croon
dragoon
dune
festoon
goon
Haroun
harpoon
hewn
High Noon
honeymoon
hot-air balloon
immune
impugn

inopportune
June
lagoon
lampoon
macaroon
maroon
monsoon
noon
opportune
platoon
pontoon
prune
rac(c)oon
Rangoon
saloon
soon
spoon
strewn
swoon
tablespoon
Troon
tune
Tutankhamun
tycoon
typhoon
Walloon

You can also make rhymes for
these words by using words in
section **18.8** that rhyme with
room

tuna
cocoon her
crooner
dragoon her
festoon her
harpoon her
honeymooner
impugner
impugn her
lampooner
lampoon her
lacuna

lunar
maroon her
mooner
moon her
pruner
schooner
sooner
Reverend W.A.
  Spooner
tune her
tuner
Una

loony
George Clooney
moony
puny
Wayne Rooney

tunic
Munich

newness
Eunice
Tunis

cartoonist
balloonist
bassoonist
harpoonist
opportunist

unity
community
disunity
immunity
impunity
opportunity

attuned
ballooned
cocooned
communed
crooned
dragooned
festooned
harpooned

honeymooned
impugned
lampooned
marooned
mooned
pruned
spooned
swooned
tuned
wound (= *to injure*)

tuneful
spoonful

junior
Tristan da Cunha

union
communion
reunion
Soviet Union

18.10

loop
cantaloup(e)
cock-a-hoop
coop
droop
drupe
dupe
group
Guadeloupe
hoop
nincompoop
recoup
regroup
scoop
sloop
snoop
soup
stoop
swoop
troop
troupe
whoop

snooper
cooper
dupe her
group her
hooper
looper
Mini Cooper
paratrooper
pea-souper
pooper-scooper
scooper
scoop her
stooper
stupor
super
super-duper
Tommy Cooper
trooper
whooper

scruple
pupil

loopy
droopy
groupie
Snoopy

stupid
Cupid

two-pin
lupin

oops
whoops

You can add to this list by
adding -s to some words that
rhyme with **loop**, as in **hoops**

18.11

truce
abstruse
abuse (= *maltreatment*)

Belarus
Bruce
deduce
deuce
diffuse (= *spread out*)
disuse
excuse (= *a
   justification*)
goose
ill-use (= *harsh
   treatment*)
induce
introduce
juice
Ken Bruce
loose (= *slack*)
mass-produce
misuse (= *improper
   use*)
moose
Mother Goose
mousse
noose
obtuse
overuse (= *excessive
   use*)
produce
profuse
recluse
reduce
reproduce
Robert the Bruce
seduce
sluice
spruce
Spruce Goose
stew in one's own
   juice
use (= *the act of using*)

producer
induce her
introduce her
juicer

253

'ue'

looser
Medusa
produce her
reduce her
reproduce her
seduce her
seducer

gruesome

twosome
introduce 'em
juice 'em
produce 'em
seduce 'em
sluice 'em

juicy

Lucy

exclusive

abusive
conclusive
conducive
effusive
elusive
inclusive
inconclusive
intrusive
obtrusive
unobtrusive

exclusively

abusively
conclusively
effusively
intrusively
obtrusively
unobtrusively

trousseau

do so
Robinson Crusoe

loosely

abstrusely
profusely

roost

boost
Proust
reduced
unused (=
    unaccustomed to
    something)
used (= accustomed to
    something)

You can add to this list by
adding -**d** to some words that
rhyme with **truce**, as in
produced

rooster

booster
boost her
reduced her
used to

acoustics

Pooh sticks

18.12

rouge

Bruges
luge

fusion

allusion
collusion
conclusion
confusion
contusion
delusion
disillusion
exclusion
illusion
infusion
intrusion
profusion
seclusion
transfusion

18.13

solution

absolution
circumlocution
constitution
contribution
counter-revolution
devolution
dilution
distribution
electrocution
elocution
evolution
execution
high-resolution
institution
locution
persecution
pollution
prosecution
prostitution
resolution
retribution
revolution
substitution

constitutional

institutional
unconstitutional

revolutionary

counter-revolutionary
evolutionary

18.14

shoot

absolute
acute
arrowroot
astute
attribute (= a
    characteristic)
bald as a coot
beaut

Beirut
birthday suit
boot
brute
Canute
chute
commute
compute
cute
depute
destitute
dilute
dispute
disrepute
dissolute
electrocute
execute
flute
fruit
hoot
impute
institute
irresolute
jute
loot
lute
minute (= *tiny*)
moot
mute
newt
overshoot
parachute
persecute
pollute
prosecute
prostitute
pursuit
recruit
refute
repute
resolute
root
route
salute

scoot
substitute
suit
toot
uproot

scooter
boot her
commuter
computer
cuter
disputer
electrocute her
execute her
fruiter
hooter
hoot her
imputer
looter
microcomputer
neuter
parachute her
peashooter
persecute her
persecutor
pewter
polluter
prosecute her
prosecutor
recruiter
recruit her
refuter
refute her
router
salute her
sharpshooter
shooter
shoot her
six-shooter
substitute her
suit her
suitor
troubleshooter
tutor

uproot her

suitable
disputable
executable
immutable
indisputable
inscrutable
irrefutable
substitutable
unsuitable

Luton
gluten
Isaac Newton

mutant
pollutant

duty
beauty
booty
Djibouti
fruity
heavy-duty
off-duty
snooty
Sooty

cuticle
pharmaceutical

muted
booted
commuted
computed
convoluted
deep-rooted
deputed
diluted
disputed
electrocuted
executed
fluted
hooted
ill-suited
imputed

instituted
looted
mooted
parachuted
persecuted
polluted
prosecuted
prostituted
recruited
refuted
reputed
rooted
routed
saluted
scooted
substituted
suited
tooted
undiluted
undisputed
unpolluted
unsuited
uprooted

beautiful
dutiful

mutinous
glutinous

mutiny
scrutiny

shooting
booting
commuting
computing
deputing
diluting
disputing
electrocuting
executing
fluting
hooting
imputing
instituting

looting
microcomputing
mooting
muting
overshooting
parachuting
persecuting
polluting
prosecuting
prostituting
recruiting
refuting
reputing
rooting
routing
saluting
scooting
substitute
suiting
telecommuting
tooting
uprooting

Pluto
Benazir Bhutto

acutely
absolutely
astutely
dissolutely
minutely
resolutely

smooch
Graham Gooch
hooch
mooch

future
moocher
smoocher
suture

18.15

smooth
booth
soothe

18.16

truth
forsooth
half-truth
long in the tooth
Ruth
sleuth
sooth
tooth
uncouth
untruth
youth

You can also make rhymes for these words by using words in section **18.5** that rhyme with *proof*

truthful
untruthful
youthful

ruthless
toothless

18.17

move
approve
Catherine Deneuve
disapprove
disprove
groove
improve
prove
remove
reprove
you've

mover
approve her
groover
Hoover®
improve her
manoeuvre
remove her
remover
reprove her
Vancouver

movable
approvable
disprovable
immovable
removable

approval
disapproval
removal

movie
groovy

moving
approving
disapproving
disproving
improving
proving
removing
reproving

improved
approved
disapproved
disproved
grooved
moved
proved
removed
reproved
unmoved

movement
improvement

18.18

two-way
thruway

18.19

ooze
abuse (= *to maltreat*)
accuse
amuse
blow a fuse
booze
bruise
choose
confuse
cruise
defuse
diffuse (= *to spread*)
disabuse
enthuse
excuse (= *to forgive*)
fuse
hypotenuse
ill-use (= *to treat
 harshly*)
infuse
lose (= *to misplace; to
 be beaten*)
misuse (= *to use
 wrongly*)
Muse
muse
overuse (= *to use
 excessively*)
peruse
refuse (= *not to accept*)
rendezvous
reuse (= *to use again*)
ruse
snooze
suffuse
Syracuse
Ted Hughes
Tom Cruise

Toulouse
use (= *to utilize*)
whose

You can add to this list by
adding *-s* to some words that
rhyme with **zoo**, as in **blues**

user
accuse her
accuser
amuse her
boozer
bruiser
choose her
chooser
cruiser
infuser
interviews her
loser
pursues her
snoozer
woos her

usable
excusable
inexcusable
reusable
unusable

refusal
bamboozle
perusal

choosy
boozy
floozy
Jacuzzi®
oozy
snoozy
Susie
woozy

oozing
abusing
accusing

'ue'

amusing
boozing
bruising
choosing
confusing
cruising
defusing
diffusing
disabusing
enthusing
excusing
fusing

ill-using
infusing
losing
misusing
musing
overusing
perusing
refusing
reusing
snoozing
suffusing
using

fused

accused
bemused
confused
unused (= *not used*)
used (= *utilized*)

You can add to this list by adding **-d** to some words that rhyme with **ooze**, as in **amused**

'ur'

sure, fury, secure

All the words in this section use the sound 'ur' in their main stressed syllable

19.1

sure
allure
aperture
assure
boor
candidature
caricature
coiffure
cure
curvature
demure
discomfiture
dour
endure
ensure
expenditure
furniture
immature
impure
insecure
insure
legislature
liqueur
literature
lure
manicure
manure
mature
miniature
Moor
moor
nomenclature
obscure

overture
Patrick Moore
pedicure
poor
premature
procure
pure
reassure
reinsure
secure
signature
sinecure
temperature
tour
unsure

19.2

gourd
allured
assured
caricatured
cured
endured
ensured
insured
lured
manicured
manured
matured
moored
obscured
pedicured
procured
reassured

reinsured
secured
self-assured
sinecured
toured
uninsured

19.3

surely
demurely
immaturely
insecurely
maturely
obscurely
poorly
prematurely
purely
securely
slowly but surely

19.4

juror
allure her
assure her
coiffure her
cure her
curer
endure her
ensure her
ensurer
insure her
insurer
lure her

'ur'

manicure her
mature her
obscure her
poorer
procure her
procurer
purer
reassure her
reinsure her
secure her
surer
tourer
tour her

curable
durable
endurable
incurable
insurable
procurable
unendurable
uninsurable

plural
extramural
mural
neural
rural

insurance
assurance
endurance
reassurance

reinsurance

Muriel
mercurial

prurient
luxuriant

furious
curious
incurious
luxurious
spurious

fury
brewery
Jewry
jury
Missouri
potpourri

Zurich
sulphuric

during
alluring
assuring
caricaturing
curing
enduring
ensuring
insuring
luring
manicuring

maturing
mooring
obscuring
procuring
reassuring
securing
touring

tourist
caricaturist
impurest
jurist
maturest
poorest
purist
surest

boorish
Moorish

purity
immaturity
impurity
insecurity
maturity
obscurity
security
surety

Euro
bureau
euro
Truro

Index

A

A 3.1
a 3.1
AA 3.1
AAA 3.1
AB 6.1
abaci 10.1
aback 1.2
abacus 17.11
abaft 2.5
abandon 1.8
abase 3.11
abashed 1.12
abasing 3.11
abate 3.14
abatement 3.14
abator 3.14
abattoir 2.1
Abba 1.1
abbey 1.1
abbreviate 3.14, 6.17
abbreviation 3.13
abbreviator 3.14
Abby 1.1
ABC 6.1
abdicate 3.14
abdication 3.13
abdicator 3.14
abdomen 17.8
abdominal 11.7
abduct 17.2
abduction 17.2
abductor 17.2
Abdul 16.3
Abel 3.2
Abelard 2.4
Aberdare 4.1
Aberdeen 6.9
Aberfan 1.8
aberration 3.13
abet 5.14
abetted 5.14
abetting 5.14
abeyance 3.1
abhor 14.1
abhorrence 11.10
abhorrent 11.10
abhorring 14.12

abide 10.4
abided 10.4
abiding 10.4
Abie 3.2
Abigail 3.7
ability 9.6
ablative 9.17
ablaze 3.18
able 3.2
able-bodied 11.3
abnormal 14.9
abnormality 1.6
abnormally 14.9
aboard 14.4
abode 12.4
abolish 11.6
abolished 11.6
abolition 9.13
abominable 16.3
abomination 3.13
aborigine 6.1
abort 14.15
aborting 14.15
abortion 14.14
abortive 14.15
abound 13.4
abounded 13.4
abounding 13.4
about 13.7
about-face 3.11
about-turn 8.9
about-turned 8.9
above 17.15
above-mentioned 5.8
above-named 3.8
Abraham 1.7
abrasion 3.12
abrasive 3.11
abreast 5.11
abridge 9.3
abridged 9.3
abroad 14.4
abrupt 17.9
abscond 11.8
absconder 11.8
absconding 11.8
abseil 3.7
abseiled 3.7

abseiler 3.7
abseiling 3.7
absentee 6.1
absent-minded 10.9
absent-mindedness 5.11
absolute 18.14
absolutely 18.14
absolution 18.13
absolve 11.6
absolved 11.6
absorb 14.2
abstain 3.9
abstention 5.8
abstract 1.2
abstracted 1.2
abstracting 1.2
abstraction 1.2
abstruse 18.11
abstrusely 18.11
absurd 8.4
absurdity 6.1
Abu Dhabi 2.2
abundant 17.8
abundantly 6.1
abuse 18.11, 18.19
abusing 18.19
abusive 18.11
abusively 18.11
abysmal 9.18
abyss 9.11
academic 5.7
academy 6.1
accede 6.4
accelerate 3.14
acceleration 3.13
accelerator 3.14
accent 5.8
accentuate 3.14
accept 5.9
acceptable 16.3
accessibility 9.6
accessible 5.11, 16.3
accession 5.13
accessory 5.11
accident 5.8
accidental 5.8
accidentally 5.8
accident-prone 12.9

acclaim   3.8
acclaimed   3.8
acclaims   3.8
acclamation   3.13
acclimatize   10.17
acclimatized   10.17
acclimatizing   10.17
accolade   3.4
accommodate   3.14
accommodating   3.14
accommodation   3.13
accompaniment   5.8
accompany   6.1
accord   14.4
accorded   14.4
according   14.4
accordingly   6.1
accordion   14.4
accost   11.11
accosting   11.11
account   13.4
accountability   6.1
accountable   13.4
accountancy   6.1
accounted   13.4
accounting   13.4
Accra   2.1
accrue   18.1
accumulate   3.14
accumulation   3.13
accumulator   3.14
accuracy   6.1
accurate   17.13
accurately   6.1
accusation   3.13
accuse   18.19
accused   18.19
accuser   18.19
accusing   18.19
accustom   17.11
ace   3.11
acetate   1.11
ache   3.3
ached   3.3
achievable   6.17
achieve   6.17
achieved   6.17
achievement   6.17
achiever   6.17
achieves   6.17
aching   3.3
achy   3.3
acid   1.11
acidity   9.3
acknowledge   11.6
acknowledg(e)ment   5.8

acne   1.2
acolyte   10.13
acoustics   18.11
acquaint   3.9
acquainted   3.9
acquiesce   5.11
acquiesced   5.11
acquiescence   5.11
acquiescent   5.11
acquirable   10.1
acquire   10.1
acquiring   10.1
acquisition   9.13
acquit   9.14
acquittal   9.14
acre   3.3
acrimonious   12.9
acrimony   6.1
acrobat   1.13
acrobatic   1.13
acrobatics   1.13
acronym   9.7
across   11.11
across-the-board   14.4
acrostic   11.11
acrylic   9.6
act   1.2
acting   1.2
action   1.2
activate   3.14
activator   3.14
active   1.2
actively   6.1
activist   9.11
activity   9.17
actor   1.2
actress   1.2
actual   1.2
actually   6.1
actuary   6.1
acumen   17.8
acupuncture   17.8
acute   18.14
acutely   18.14
AD   6.1
ad   1.3
ADA   2.4
Ada   3.4
Adam   1.3
adapt   1.9
adaptable   16.3
adaptation   3.13
adapter   1.9
ADC   6.1
add   1.3
adder   1.3

addict   9.2
addicted   9.2
addiction   9.2
addictive   9.2
addition   9.13
additional   9.13
additive   9.17
addle   1.3
address   5.11
addressed   5.11
Adelaide   3.4
Adele   5.6
Aden   3.4
adept   5.9
adequacy   6.1
adequate   17.13
adequately   6.1
adhere   7.1
adherence   7.5
adherer   7.5
adhering   7.5
adhesion   6.12
ad hoc   11.2
ad infinitum   10.13
adjacent   3.11
adjective   9.17
adjoin   15.5
adjourn   8.9
adjourned   8.9
adjourning   8.9
adjournment   8.9
adjudge   17.3
adjudging   17.3
adjudicate   3.14
adjudication   3.13
adjudicator   3.14
adjust   17.11
adjustable   16.3
adjusted   17.11
adjuster   17.11
adjusting   17.11
adjustment   17.11
ad-lib   9.1
ad-libber   9.1
ad-man   1.3
administer   9.8
administration   3.13
administrative   9.17
administrator   3.14
admirable   16.3
admiral   16.3
Admiralty   6.1
admiration   3.13
admire   10.1
admirer   10.1
admiring   10.1

admissible   9.11
admission   9.13
admit   9.14
admittance   9.14
admittedly   6.1
admonish   11.8
admonished   11.8
admonishing   11.8
ad nauseam   1.7
ado   18.1
adobe   12.2
adolescence   5.11
adolescent   5.11
adopt   11.9
adoption   11.9
adorable   14.12
adoration   3.13
adore   14.1
adorer   14.12
adoring   14.12
adorn   14.10
adorning   14.10
adrenalin(e)   9.8
Adrian   3.4
Adriatic   1.13
Adrienne   3.4
adrift   9.4
adroit   15.7
adulation   3.13
adult   17.6
adulterate   3.14
adulteration   3.13
adulterator   3.14
adulterous   17.11
adultery   6.1
adulthood   16.2
advance   2.10
advancer   2.10
advancing   2.10
advantageous   3.4
advantageously   3.4
adventure   5.8
adversary   6.1
adverse   8.12
adversely   8.12
adversity   6.1
advert   8.14
advertise   10.17
advertisement   5.8
advertising   10.17
adverts   8.14
advice   10.12
advisable   10.17
advise   10.17
adviser   10.17
advising   10.17

advisory   10.17
advocate   3.14, 17.13
advocator   3.14
AEA   3.1
Aegean   6.1
aegis   6.4
aerial   4.6
aerobic   12.2
aerobics   12.2
aerodrome   12.8
aerodynamic   1.7
aerodynamics   1.7
aerogram(me)   1.7
aeronautical   14.15
aeroplane   3.9
aerosol   11.6
aesthetic   5.14
aesthetics   5.14
afar   2.1
affable   16.3
affair   4.1
affect   5.2
affectation   3.13
affected   5.2
affecting   5.2
affection   5.2
affectionate   17.13
affiliate   3.14, 9.6
affiliation   3.13
affinity   9.8
affirm   8.8
affirmation   3.13
affirmative   9.17
affirmed   8.8
affirmer   8.8
affix   1.4, 9.2
affixed   9.2
afflict   9.2
afflicted   9.2
affliction   9.2
afford   14.4
affordable   14.4
afforded   14.4
affording   14.4
afforestation   3.13
affray   3.1
affront   17.8
affronted   17.8
Afghani   1.8
Afghanistan   2.10
afield   6.7
afloat   12.14
afoot   16.5
aforementioned   5.8
afraid   3.4
afresh   5.13

Afrikaans   2.10
aft   2.5
after   2.5
afterbirth   8.16
aftercare   4.1
after-effect   5.2
afterlife   10.5
aftermath   2.18
afternoon   18.9
aftershave   3.17
aftersun   17.8
aftertaste   3.11
afterthought   14.15
Aga®   2.6
again   5.8
age   3.4
aged   3.4
ageing   3.4
agency   6.1
agenda   5.8
aggravate   3.14
aggravating   3.14
aggravation   3.13
aggregate   17.13
aggression   5.13
aggressive   5.11
aggressively   5.11
aggressor   5.11
aggrieved   6.17
aghast   2.13
agile   1.3
agility   9.6
Agincourt   14.15
agitate   3.14
agitated   3.14
agitation   3.13
agitator   3.14
aglow   12.1
AGM   5.7
Agnes   1.5
agnostic   11.11
ago   12.1
agog   11.5
agonize   10.17
agonized   10.17
agonizing   10.17
agony   6.1
agoraphobic   12.2
agoraphobics   12.2
agrarian   4.6
agrarianism   4.6
agree   6.1
agreeable   6.1
agreed   6.4
agreeing   6.1
agriculture   17.6

agronomy 11.8
aground 13.4
ahead 5.3
ahoy 15.1
AI 10.1
aid 3.4
Aida 6.4
Aidan 3.4
aide 3.4
aided 3.4
aide-de-camp 11.7
aiding 3.4
AIDS 3.4
ail 3.7
ailed 3.7
Aileen 6.9
ailing 3.7
ailment 3.7
aim 3.8
aimed 3.8
aimer 3.8
aimless 3.8
aims 3.8
ain't 3.9
air 4.1
air-conditioned 9.13
air-conditioning 9.13
aired 4.2
airing 4.6
airless 4.3
airlift 4.3
airline 4.3
airsickness 9.2
airway 4.7
airworthy 8.15
airy 4.6
airy-fairy 4.6
Aisha 6.13
aisle 10.7
ajar 2.1
aka 3.1
akimbo 9.7
akin 9.8
Al 1.6
Alabama 1.7
alabaster 1.11
alacrity 6.1
Aladdin 1.3
Alamo 12.1
alarm 2.9
alarmed 2.9
alarmer 2.9
alarming 2.9
alarms 2.9
alas 1.11
Alaska 1.11

Albania 3.9
Albanian 3.9
Albany 6.1
albatross 11.11
Alberta 8.14
albino 6.9
Albuquerque 8.3
alchemy 6.1
alcohol 11.6
alcoholic 11.6
alcoholism 9.18
alcopop 11.9
Aldershot 11.13
ale 3.7
Alec 1.6
Alexander 2.10
Alexandria 1.8
alexia 5.2
Alf 1.6
alfresco 5.11
Algeria 7.5
Algerian 7.5
Algiers 7.7
Ali 2.8
alibi 10.1
Alicante 1.8
Alice 1.6
Alien 3.7
alien 3.7
alienate 3.14
Ali G 6.1
alight 10.13
alighted 10.13
alighting 10.13
align 10.9
alignment 10.9
alike 10.3
alimony 6.1
Alison 17.8
alit 9.14
alive 10.15
alkali 10.1
alkaline 10.9
all 14.8
Allah 1.6
Al(l)an 1.6
allay 3.1
allaying 3.1
all-clear 7.1
allegation 3.13
allege 5.3
alleged 5.3
allegedly 6.1
allegory 6.1
all-embracing 3.11
Allen 1.6

allergenic 5.8
allergy 1.6
alleviate 6.17
alley 1.6
alleyway 3.1
alliance 10.1
allied 10.4
alligator 3.14
all-important 14.15
all-in 14.8
alliteration 3.13
allocate 3.14
allocation 3.13
allot 11.13
all-out 13.7
allow 13.1
allowable 16.3
allowed 13.2
alloy 15.1
alloyed 15.2
alloying 15.1
alloys 15.8
all-powerful 16.3
all-round 13.4
all-rounder 13.4
all-time 10.8
allude 18.4
alluding 18.4
allure 19.1
allured 19.2
alluring 19.4
allusion 18.12
Ally 1.6
ally 10.1
Alma 1.6
almanac 1.2
almanacs 1.2
almighty 10.13
alms 2.9
aloft 11.4
alone 12.9
along 11.8
alongside 10.4
aloof 18.5
aloud 13.2
alpaca 1.2
alpacas 1.2
alphabet 5.14
alphabetical 5.14
alphabetically 5.14
alphasort 14.15
already 5.3
Alsatian 3.13
also-ran 1.8
altar 14.8
alter 14.8

alteration 3.13
altercation 3.13
alternate 3.14
alternately 6.1
alternating 3.14
alternative 9.17
alternatively 6.1
alternator 3.14
although 12.1
altitude 18.4
alto 1.6
altogether 5.15
altruism 9.18
altruistic 9.11
aluminium 9.8
AM 5.7
am 1.7, 5.7
amalgamate 3.14
Amanda 1.8
Amarillo 9.6
amass 1.11
amassed 1.11
amatory 1.7
amaze 3.18
amazed 3.18
amazing 3.18
Amazon 17.8
ambassador 14.1
Amber 1.7
amber 1.7
ambiance 11.8
ambiguity 18.1
ambition 9.13
ambitious 9.13
ambitiously 9.13
ambivalent 9.17
amble 1.7
Ambleside 10.4
Amelia 6.7
amen 5.8
amenable 16.3
amend 5.8
amendable 5.8
amender 5.8
amending 5.8
America 5.10
Americanism 9.18
amethyst 9.11
amiable 16.3
amicable 16.3
amid 9.3
Amin 6.9
amiss 9.11
ammeter 1.7
ammonia 12.9
ammunition 9.13

amnesia 6.19
amnesty 6.1
amniocentesis 6.11
amoeba 6.2
amok 11.2
among 17.8
amoral 11.10
amorous 1.7
amount 13.4
amounted 13.4
amounting 13.4
amp 1.7
ampersand 1.8
amphetamine 9.8
amphibian 9.1
ample 1.7
amplify 10.1
amplitude 18.4
amputate 3.14
amputation 3.13
amputator 3.14
Amsterdam 1.7
amuck 17.2
Amundsen 17.8
amuse 18.19
amusing 18.19
Amy 3.8
an 1.8
anachronism 9.18
anaconda 11.8
anaemia 6.8
anaerobic 12.2
anaesthetic 5.14
anaesthetics 5.14
anaesthetize 10.17
anaesthetizing 10.17
anagram 1.7
analogous 17.11
analogue 11.5
analogy 1.6
analyse 10.17
analysing 10.17
analysis 1.6
analyst 1.8
analytical 9.14
anarchist 9.11
anarchy 6.1
Anastasia 3.18
anatomical 11.7
anatomy 6.1
ANC 6.1
ancestral 5.11
ancestry 6.1
anchor 1.8
anchorage 9.3
anchorman 1.8

anchovy 6.1
ancillary 9.6
and 1.8
Anderson 17.8
Andorra 14.12
Andrea 1.8
androgynous 11.3
Andy 1.8
anecdotal 12.14
anecdote 12.14
anemone 5.7
anew 18.1
Angeleno 6.9
angelic 5.6
Angelina 6.9
anger 1.8
angina 10.9
angle 1.8
Anglesey 6.1
Anglican 17.8
Anglicanism 9.18
Anglicism 9.18
angling 1.8
Anglophile 10.7
Anglophone 12.9
Anglo-Saxon 1.2
Angola 12.7
Angolan 12.7
angora 14.12
angrily 6.1
anguish 1.8
angular 1.8
Anil 6.7
animal 16.3
animate 3.14, 17.13
animated 3.14
animation 3.13
animator 3.14
animism 9.18
animosity 11.11
aniseed 6.4
Anita 6.14
ankle 1.8
Anna 1.8
Annabel(l)e 5.6
Ann(e) 1.8
Anne 1.8
Anne of Cleves 6.17
Annette 5.14
annex 5.2
annexation 3.13
annexed 5.2
Annie 1.8
annihilate 3.14, 10.1
annihilation 3.13
annihilator 3.14

anniversary 8.12
anno Domini 10.1
annotate 3.14
annotator 3.14
announce 13.4
announced 13.4
announcement 13.4
announcer 13.4
annoy 15.1
annoyed 15.2
annoying 15.1
annoys 15.8
annual 1.8
annually 1.8
annul 17.6
anodyne 10.9
anoint 15.5
anointed 15.5
anomalous 17.11
anomaly 6.1
anon 11.8
anonymity 9.7
anonymous 11.8
anorak 1.2
anoraks 1.2
anorexia 5.2
anorexic 5.2
another 17.14
answer 2.10
ant 1.8
antagonism 9.18
antagonist 1.5
antagonize 10.17
Ant and Dec 5.2
ante 1.8
antebellum 5.6
antelope 12.10
antenatal 3.14
antenna 5.8
anterior 7.5
anteroom 18.8
anthology 11.6
Ant(h)ony 6.1
anthracite 10.13
anthropological 11.3
anthropologist 11.6
anthropology 11.6
anti 1.8
antibiotic 11.13
antibiotics 11.13
antibody 11.3
Antichrist 10.12
anticipate 3.14, 9.11
anticipation 3.13
anticipator 3.14
antics 1.8

antidepressant 5.11
antidote 12.14
antifreeze 6.19
antipathy 6.1
Antipodes 6.19
antiquarian 4.6
antiquarianism 4.6
antiquated 3.14
antique 6.3
antiquity 9.2
antiracist 3.11
anti-Semitic 9.14
antiseptic 5.9
antithesis 9.11
antivivisection 5.2
antivivisectionist 5.2
Antoinette 5.14
Antonia 12.9
antonym 9.7
Antrim 1.8
ants 1.8
anxiety 10.1
anxiously 6.1
any 5.8
anybody 11.3
anyhow 13.1
anyone 17.8
anyplace 3.11
anything 9.8
anyway 3.1
anywhere 4.1
aorta 14.15
apart 2.16
apartheid 10.13
apartment 2.16
apathetic 5.14
apathetically 5.14
apathy 6.1
ape 3.10
aperitif 6.5
aperture 19.1
aphasia 3.18
aphorism 9.18
aphrodisiac 1.2
aphrodisiacs 1.2
Aphrodite 10.13
apiece 6.11
aplenty 5.8
aplomb 11.7
apocalypse 9.9
apocalyptic 9.9
apocryphal 16.3
apolitical 9.14
Apollo 11.6
apologetic 5.14
apologetically 5.14

apologist 11.6
apologize 10.17
apologizing 10.17
apology 11.6
apoplectic 5.2
apoplexy 5.2
apostle 11.11
apostolic 11.6
apostrophe 6.1
appal 14.8
appalled 14.8
appalling 14.8
apparatus 3.14
apparel 1.10
apparent 1.10
apparently 6.1
apparition 9.13
appeal 6.7
appealed 6.7
appealing 6.7
appear 7.1
appearance 7.5
appearing 7.5
appeased 6.19
appeaser 6.19
appeasing 6.19
append 5.8
appendicitis 10.13
appending 5.8
apperception 5.9
appetite 10.13
appetize 10.17
appetizer 10.17
appetizing 10.17
applaud 14.4
applauded 14.4
applauding 14.4
applause 14.20
apple 1.9
applecart 2.16
appliance 10.1
applicable 9.2
application 3.13
applied 10.4
apply 10.1
appoint 15.5
appointed 15.5
appointment 15.5
apportion 14.14
appraisal 3.18
appraise 3.18
appraised 3.18
appraising 3.18
appreciable 16.3
appreciate 3.14
appreciating 3.14

appreciation 3.13
appreciative 9.17
appreciator 3.14
apprehend 5.8
apprehending 5.8
apprehension 5.8
apprehensive 5.8
apprehensively 5.8
apprenticeship 9.9
approach 12.14
approachable 12.14
appropriate 3.14
appropriately 6.1
appropriation 3.13
appropriator 3.14
approvable 18.17
approval 18.17
approve 18.17
approved 18.17
approving 18.17
approximate 3.14, 17.13
approximately 6.1
approximation 3.13
APR 2.1
apricot 11.13
apt 1.9
aptitude 18.4
aqua(e)robic 12.2
aqua(e)robics 12.2
aquamarine 6.9
aquarium 4.6
Aquarius 4.6
aquatic 1.13
aqueduct 17.2
aquiline 10.9
Arab 1.10
Arabella 5.6
Arabian Nights 10.13
Arabic 9.2
arable 1.10
arachnid 1.2
Ararat 1.13
arbitrage 2.14
arbitrary 6.1
arbitrate 3.14
arbitration 3.13
arbitrator 3.14
arc 2.3
arcade 3.4
arced 2.3
arch 2.16
archaeological 11.3
archaeologist 11.6
archaeology 11.6
archaic 3.1

archdeacon 6.3
archduke 18.3
Archer 2.16
archer 2.16
archery 6.1
archetypal 10.10
archetype 10.10
Archie 2.16
archipelago 12.1
architect 5.2
architecture 5.2
arcing 2.3
ardour 2.4
are 2.1
area 4.6
arena 6.9
aren't 2.10
Aretha 6.16
Argentina 6.9
Argentine 10.9
Argentinian 9.8
Argonaut 11.13
Argos 11.11
arguable 16.3
arguably 6.1
argument 5.8
argumentative 5.8
aria 2.12
arid 1.10
Aries 4.6
arise 10.17
arisen 9.18
arising 10.17
aristocracy 6.1
aristocrat 1.13
aristocratic 1.13
Aristotle 11.13
arithmetic 9.2
arithmetical 5.14
Arizona 12.9
ark 2.3
Arkansas 14.1
Arles 2.8
Arlott 2.8
arm 2.9
armadillo 9.6
Armageddon 5.3
Armagh 2.1
Armani 2.10
armed 2.9
Armenia 6.9
Armenian 6.9
armer 2.9
armers 2.9
arming 2.9
armistice 9.11

armour 2.9
armoury 6.1
arms 2.9
Armstrong 11.8
army 2.9
aroma 12.8
aromatic 1.13
aromatics 1.13
arose 12.19
around 13.4
arousal 13.9
arouse 13.9
arousing 13.9
arraign 3.9
arraignment 3.9
Arran 1.10
arrange 3.9
arrangeable 3.9
arranged 3.9
arranger 3.9
arranging 3.9
array 3.1
arrears 7.7
arrest 5.11
arrested 5.11
arresting 5.11
arrival 10.15
arrive 10.15
arrived 10.15
arriving 10.15
arrow 1.10
arrowhead 5.3
arrowroot 18.14
arsenal 16.3
arsenic 9.2
arson 2.13
arsonist 9.11
art 2.16
artefact 1.2
arteriosclerosis 12.11
artery 6.1
arthritic 9.14
arthritis 10.13
arthropod 11.3
arthrosis 12.11
Arthur 2.18
artichoke 12.3
article 2.16
articulate 3.14, 9.2, 17.13
articulation 3.13
articulator 3.14
artificial 9.13
artificially 9.13
artillery 9.6
artisan 1.8

artistic 9.11
artistry 6.1
artless 2.16
arty 2.16
Aryan 4.6
as 1.17
asap 6.1
asbestosis 12.11
ascend 5.8
ascendancy 5.8
ascendant 5.8
ascender 5.8
ascending 5.8
Ascension 5.8
ascent 5.8
ascertain 3.9
ascertainment 3.9
ascetic 5.14
ascribe 10.2
ASEAN 1.8
aseptic 5.9
ash 1.12
ashamed 3.8
ashen 1.12
Ashley 1.12
ashore 14.1
ashy 1.12
Asia 3.12
Asian 3.12
Asiatic 1.13
aside 10.4
asinine 10.9
ask 2.13
askance 1.8
askew 18.1
ASL 5.6
asleep 6.10
asparagus 17.11
aspect 5.2
asperity 5.10
asphyxiate 3.14
asphyxiation 3.13
asphyxiator 3.14
aspirate 17.13
aspiration 3.13
aspire 10.1
aspirin 9.8
aspiring 10.1
ass 1.11
assail 3.7
assailable 3.7
assailed 3.7
assailer 3.7
assailing 3.7
assassinate 1.11
assassination 3.13

assault 14.8
assaulted 14.8
assemble 5.7
assent 5.8
assert 8.14
asserted 8.14
asserter 8.14
assertion 8.13
assertive 8.14
assertiveness 5.11
asserts 8.14
assess 5.11
assessed 5.11
assessor 5.11
asset 1.11
assign 10.9
assignable 10.9
assignation 3.13
assigning 10.9
assignment 10.9
assimilate 3.14
assimilation 3.13
assimilator 3.14
Assisi 6.11
assist 9.11
assistance 9.11
assistant 9.11
assisted 9.11
assisting 9.11
associate 3.14
associated 3.14
association 3.13
assorted 14.15
assortment 14.15
assuage 3.4
assuaged 3.4
assuaging 3.4
assume 18.8
assuming 18.8
assumption 17.7
assurance 19.4
assure 19.1
assured 19.2
assuredly 6.1
assuring 19.4
Astaire 4.1
aster 1.11
asterisk 9.11
asteroid 15.2
asthmatic 1.13
astonish 11.8
astonished 11.8
astonishing 11.8
astonishment 5.8
astound 13.4
astounded 13.4

astounding 13.4
astray 3.1
astride 10.4
astringent 9.8
astrological 11.3
astrology 11.6
astronaut 14.15
astronomic 11.7
astronomical 11.7
astronomy 11.8
Astroturf® 8.5
astute 18.14
astutely 18.14
asunder 17.8
Aswan 2.10
asylum-seeker 6.3
at 1.13
atavistic 9.11
ate 3.14
atheism 9.18
atheist 9.11
athletic 5.14
athletically 5.14
athletics 5.14
a-tishoo 9.13
Atlanta 1.8
Atlantic 1.8
atlas 1.13
ATM 5.7
atmosphere 7.1
atmospheric 5.10
atom 1.13
atomic 11.7
atone 12.9
atoned 12.9
atonement 12.9
atoning 12.9
atrocious 12.13
atrocity 11.11
atrophy 6.1
attach 1.13
attached 1.13
attaching 1.13
attachment 1.13
attack 1.2
attacked 1.2
attacker 1.2
attackers 1.2
attacking 1.2
attacks 1.2
attain 3.9
attainable 3.9
attained 3.9
attainment 3.9
attempt 5.7
attend 5.8

attendance   5.8
attendant   5.8
attender   5.8
attending   5.8
attention   5.8
attentive   5.8
attentively   6.1
attest   5.11
attested   5.11
attesting   5.11
attic   1.13
attics   1.13
Attila   9.6
attire   10.1
attitude   1.13, 18.4
Attlee   1.13
attorney   8.9
attract   1.2
attracted   1.2
attracting   1.2
attraction   1.2
attractive   1.2
attribute   18.14
attrition   9.13
attuned   18.9
aubergine   6.9
Auchterarder   2.4
auctioneer   7.1
audacious   3.13
audacity   1.11
Audi   13.2
audible   16.3
audio   12.1
audition   9.13
auditioned   9.13
auditioning   9.13
auditorium   14.12
auditory   6.1
Audrey   14.4
augment   5.8
augmentable   5.8
august   17.11
Augusta   17.11
aunt   2.10
auntie   2.10
au pair   4.1
aura   14.12
aural   14.12
au revoir   2.1
Aurora   14.12
aurora borealis   1.6
auspicious   9.13
auspiciously   9.13
austere   7.1
austerely   7.4
austerity   5.10

Australasia   3.12
Australasian   3.12
Australia   3.7
Australian   3.7
authenticate   3.14
authenticated   3.14
authenticator   3.14
authenticity   9.11
authoritarian   4.6
authoritarianism   4.6
authoritative   9.17
authority   11.10
authorization   3.13
authorize   10.17
authorizing   10.17
autistic   9.11
autistics   9.11
auto   14.15
autobiographer   11.5
autobiographical   1.4
autobiography   11.5
autocrat   1.13
autocratic   1.13
Autocue®   18.1
autograph   2.5
autographed   2.5
autographing   2.5
automat   1.13
automate   3.14
automatic   1.13
automatically   1.13
automatics   1.13
automation   3.13
automaton   11.8
automatons   11.8
automobile   6.7
automotive   12.14
autonomous   17.11
autonomy   11.8
autopilot   10.7
autopsy   6.1
autumn   14.15
auxiliary   6.1
avail   3.7
availability   9.6
available   3.7
availed   3.7
availing   3.7
avalanche   2.10
avant-garde   2.4
avarice   9.11
avenge   5.8
avenue   18.1
aver   8.1
average   9.3
averaged   9.3

averred   8.4
averring   8.11
avers   8.18
averse   8.12
aversion   8.13
avert   8.14
averted   8.14
averts   8.14
aviary   6.1
aviation   3.13
avidly   6.1
Aviemore   14.1
avocado   2.4
avoid   15.2
Avon   3.17
avowal   13.1
avowed   13.2
await   3.14
awake   3.3
awaken   3.3
awaking   3.3
award   14.4
awarded   14.4
awarding   14.4
aware   4.1
awareness   4.5
awash   11.12
away   3.1
awe   14.1
awe-inspired   10.1
awe-inspiring   10.1
awesome   14.13
awful   14.5
awhile   10.7
awl   14.8
awning   14.10
awoke   12.3
awoken   12.3
awry   10.1
axe   1.2
axed   1.2
axing   1.2
axiomatic   1.13
axis   1.2
ayatollah   11.6
Ayia Napa   1.9
Aylesbury   6.1
Ayr   4.1
azalea   3.7
Azerbaijan   2.10
Azerbaijani   2.10
Azeri   4.6
Azores   14.20

B
B   6.1

BA   3.1
baa   2.1
baaed   2.4
baaing   2.12
babble   1.1
Babel   3.2
baboon   18.9
baby   3.2
baby-boomer   18.8
baby-faced   3.11
babyhood   16.2
Babylon   11.8
baby-minder   10.9
baby-sit   9.14
baby-sitter   9.14
baby-walker   14.3
Bacall   14.8
Bacardi®   2.4
baccy   1.2
Bach   2.3
bacillus   9.6
back   1.2
backbencher   5.8
backbiting   10.13
backbreaking   3.3
backdate   3.14
backer   1.2
backers   1.2
backfire   10.1
backfiring   10.1
backgammon   1.7
backhanded   1.8
backhander   1.8
backing   1.2
backpacker   1.2
backpackers   1.2
back-pedal   5.3
backside   10.4
backsliding   10.4
backstage   3.4
back-to-back   1.2
backwardness   5.11
backwater   14.15
bacon   3.3
bacteria   7.5
bacterial   7.5
bacteriological   11.3
bacteriology   11.6
bad   1.3
baddie   1.3
bade   3.4
Bader   2.4
badge   1.3
bad-looking   16.1
badly   1.3
badminton   17.8

badness   1.3
BAF   5.4
baffle   1.4
BAFTA   1.4
bag   1.5
bagel   3.6
baggy   1.5
Baghdad   1.3
bah   2.1
Bahamas   2.9
Bahrain   3.9
Bahraini   3.9
bail   3.7
bailed   3.7
bailing   3.7
Baird   4.2
bairn   4.5
bait   3.14
baiter   3.14
baize   3.18
bake   3.3
baked   3.3
baked beans   6.9
baker   3.3
baking   3.3
balaclava   2.19
balance   1.6
balanced   1.6
balcony   6.1
bald   14.8
bald as a coot   18.14
balderdash   1.12
balding   14.8
bale   3.7
Balearic   1.10
baled   3.7
baler   3.7
Bali   2.8
Balinese   6.19
baling   3.7
Balkan   14.8
Ball   14.8
ball   14.8
ballad   1.6
balled   14.8
ballerina   6.9
ballet   1.6
ballistic   9.11
ballistics   9.11
balloon   18.9
ballooned   18.9
balloonist   18.9
ballot   1.6
Ballyclare   4.1
ballyhoo   18.1
balm   2.9

balmed   2.9
balmer   2.9
balming   2.9
Balmoral   11.10
balms   2.9
balmy   2.9
baloney   12.9
Baltimore   14.1
balustrade   3.4
Bambi   1.7
bamboo   18.1
bamboozle   18.19
ban   1.8
banal   2.8
banality   1.6
banana   2.10
band   1.8
bandan(n)a   1.8
banded   1.8
banding   1.8
bandmaster   2.13
bandstand   1.8
bandy   1.8
bane   3.9
bang   1.8
banger   1.8
Bangkok   11.2
Bangladesh   5.13
Bangladeshi   5.13
bangle   1.8
Bangor   1.8
banish   1.8
banishment   5.8
bank   1.8
banker   1.8
banknote   12.14
bankroll   12.7
bankrolled   12.7
bankrolling   12.7
bankruptcy   6.1
banned   1.8
banner   1.8
banning   1.8
ban(n)ister   1.8
Bannockburn   8.9
bantam   1.8
bantamweight   3.14
banter   1.8
bap   1.9
baptismal   9.18
baptize   10.17
baptized   10.17
baptizing   10.17
bar   2.1
barb   2.2
Barbadian   3.4

Barbara 2.2
barbarian 4.6
barbaric 1.10
barbarism 9.18
barbarity 1.10
Barbarossa 11.11
barbarous 17.11
barbecue 18.1
barber 2.2
barbershop 11.9
Barbie 2.2
barbiturate 17.13
Barbuda 18.4
Barcelona 12.9
bard 2.4
bare 4.1
bared 4.2
barefoot 16.5
bareheaded 5.3
barely 4.3
bareness 4.5
barer 4.6
barf 2.5
barfed 2.5
barfing 2.5
bargain 2.6
barge 2.4
barger 2.4
baring 4.6
barista 6.11
baritone 12.9
barium 4.6
bark 2.3
barked 2.3
barkeeper 6.10
barker 2.3
barking 2.3
barley 2.8
barman 2.9
barmy 2.9
barn 2.10
barnacle 16.3
Barnet 2.10
Barney 2.10
barnstorming 14.9
barometer 11.7
baron 1.10
baroness 5.11
baronet 5.14
baroque 11.2
Barra 1.10
barracuda 18.4
barrage 2.14
barred 2.4
barrel 1.10
barrelled 1.10

barren 1.10
barrenness 5.11
barrette 5.14
barricade 3.4
barricaded 3.4
barricading 3.4
barrier 1.10
barring 2.12
barrow 1.10
Barry 1.10
Bart 2.16
bartender 5.8
barter 2.16
base 3.11
baseless 3.11
basement 3.11
bases 3.11
bash 1.12
bashed 1.12
basher 1.12
bashfulness 5.11
bashing 1.12
basically 6.1
Basie 3.11
Basil 1.17
basil 1.17
basilica 9.6
basin 3.11
Basingstoke 12.3
basis 3.11
bask 2.13
basket 2.13
basketball 14.8
basketful 16.3
Basle 2.8
Basque 2.13
bas-relief 6.5
bass 1.11, 3.11
basset 1.11
bassist 3.11
bassoon 18.9
bassoonist 18.9
baste 3.11
Bastille 6.7
basting 3.11
bat 1.13
batch 1.13
batched 1.13
batching 1.13
bated 3.14
Bath 2.18
bath 2.18
bathe 3.15
bathing 3.15
bathos 3.16
batik 6.3

Batista 6.11
Batmobile 6.7
baton 1.13
battalion 1.6
batten 1.13
batter 1.13
battered 1.13
battering 1.13
battery 1.13
battle 1.13
battleaxe 1.2
battledress 5.11
battlefield 6.7
battleground 13.4
battle-hardened 2.4
battle of wills 9.6
battle of wits 9.14
battle-scarred 2.4
battleship 9.9
batty 1.13
bauble 14.2
baud 14.4
Bavaria 4.6
Bavarian 4.6
bawdy 14.4
bawl 14.8
bawled 14.8
bay 3.1
baying 3.1
bazaar 2.1
bazooka 18.3
BBC 6.1
BC 6.1
be 6.1
Bea 6.1
beach 6.14
beachcomber 12.8
beaching 6.14
beacon 6.3
bead 6.4
beady 6.4
beady-eyed 10.4
beagle 6.6
beak 6.3
beaker 6.3
beam 6.8
beamer 6.8
beaming 6.8
Bean 6.9
bean 6.9
Beano 6.9
beano 6.9
bear 4.1
bearable 4.6
beard 7.2
bearer 4.6

bearing 4.6
beast 6.11
beat 6.14
beaten 6.14
beater 6.14
beatification 3.13
beating 6.14
Beatle 6.14
Beatrice 9.11
Beatrix 9.2
beats 6.14
beaut 18.14
beautician 9.13
beautiful 18.14
beautifully 6.1
beautify 10.1
beauty 18.14
beaver 6.17
becalmed 2.9
became 3.8
because 11.16, 14.20
beck 5.2
Becker 5.2
beckon 5.2
beckoned 5.2
Becks 5.2
become 17.7
becoming 17.7
BEd 5.3
bed 5.3
bedded 5.3
bedder 5.3
bedding 5.3
Bede 6.4
bedeck 5.2
bedecked 5.2
bedecks 5.2
bedevil 5.17
bedfellow 5.6
Bedfordshire 10.1
Bedouin 9.8
bedpan 5.3
bedridden 9.3
bedroom 5.3
bed-sitter 9.14
bee 6.1
beech 6.14
beef 6.5
beefy 6.5
beekeeper 6.10
beeline 6.7
Beelzebub 17.1
been 6.9
beep 6.10
beeper 6.10
beeping 6.10

beer 7.1
beery 7.5
beet 6.14
Beethoven 12.17
Beetle 6.14
beetle 6.14
beets 6.14
befall 14.8
befell 5.6
befit 9.14
befitting 9.14
before 14.1
beforehand 14.7
befriend 5.8
befriending 5.8
beg 5.5
began 1.8
beggar 5.5
Begin 3.6
begin 9.8
beginner 9.8
beginning 9.8
begonia 12.9
begorrah 11.10
begrudge 17.3
begrudging 17.3
begs 5.5
beguile 10.7
beguiled 10.7
beguiling 10.7
beguine 6.9
begun 17.8
behalf 2.5
behave 3.17
behaved 3.17
behaviour 3.17
behaviourism 9.18
behead 5.3
beheaded 5.3
beheading 5.3
beheld 5.6
behest 5.11
behind 10.9
behold 12.7
beholden 12.7
beholder 12.7
beige 3.12
Beijing 9.8
being 6.1
Beirut 18.14
Belarus 18.11
belated 3.14
belch 5.6
Belfast 2.13
Belgrade 3.4
belie 10.1

belief 6.5
believable 6.17
believe 6.17
believed 6.17
believer 6.17
believes 6.17
Belinda 9.8
belittle 9.14
Belize 6.19
Bell 5.6
bell 5.6
Bella 5.6
belladonna 11.8
Belle 5.6
belle 5.6
belled 5.6
bellicose 12.11
belligerent 5.8
belling 5.6
bellow 5.6
bell-ringer 9.8
bell-tower 13.1
belly 5.6
bellyache 3.3
bellyached 3.3
bellyacher 3.3
bellyaching 3.3
belly-button 17.13
belly-flop 11.9
bellyful 16.3
Belo Horizonte 11.8
belong 11.8
belonging 11.8
beloved 17.15
below 12.1
belt 5.6
belter 5.6
bemoan 12.9
bemoaner 12.9
bemoaning 12.9
bemused 18.19
Ben 5.8
Benazir 7.1
bench 5.8
bend 5.8
bender 5.8
bending 5.8
bendy 5.8
beneath 6.16
Benedict 9.2
benediction 9.2
benefactor 1.2
benefactress 1.2
beneficent 5.8
beneficial 9.13
beneficially 9.13

beneficiary 6.1
benefit 9.14
Benelux 17.2
benevolence 5.17
benevolent 5.17
Bengal 14.8
Bengali 14.8
Benghazi 2.21
Benidorm 14.9
benign 10.9
Benin 6.9
Benjamin 9.8
Benn 5.8
Bennet 5.8
Bennett 5.8
Ben Nevis 5.17
Benny 5.8
bent 5.8
Bentley 5.8
bequeath 6.15
bequeather 6.15
bequeathing 6.15
bequest 5.11
bequested 5.11
bequesting 5.11
berate 3.14
bereaved 6.17
bereavement 6.17
bereft 5.4
bergamot 11.13
berk 8.3
Berlin 9.8
Berliner 9.8
Bermuda 18.4
Bernadette 5.14
Bern(e) 8.9
Bernice 6.11
Bernie 8.9
Bernstein 10.9
Berry 5.10
berry 5.10
berserk 8.3
berserker 8.3
Bert 8.14
berth 8.16
Bertha 8.16
Berwickshire 10.1
Beryl 5.10
beseech 6.14
beseeching 6.14
beset 5.14
besetting 5.14
beside 10.4
besiege 6.4
besmirch 8.14
besmirching 8.14

besotted 11.13
besought 14.15
bespatter 1.13
bespattered 1.13
bespattering 1.13
bespoke 12.3
Bess 5.11
Bessie 5.11
Best 5.11
best 5.11
bested 5.11
bestial 5.11
besting 5.11
bestow 12.1
bestowal 12.1
bestowed 12.4
bestowing 12.1
bestseller 5.6
bestsellers 5.6
best-selling 5.6
bet 5.14
betel 6.14
Beth 5.16
Bethany 6.1
Bethlehem 5.7
betide 10.4
Betjeman 17.8
betray 3.1
betrayal 3.1
betraying 3.1
betrothed 12.15
Betsy 5.14
betted 5.14
better 5.14
betterment 5.8
betting 5.14
bettor 5.14
Betty 5.14
between 6.9
Bevan 5.17
bevel 5.17
beverage 9.3
Beverley 5.17
Beverley Hills 9.6
bevvy 5.17
bevy 5.17
bewail 3.7
bewailed 3.7
bewailing 3.7
beware 4.1
bewilder 9.6
bewilderment 5.8
bewitch 9.14
beyond 11.8
bezique 6.3
Bhopal 2.8

Bhutan 2.10
Bhutto 18.14
Bianca 1.8
Biarritz 9.14
bias 10.1
bib 9.1
bibber 9.1
Bible 10.2
biblical 16.3
bibliography 11.5
bibliophile 10.7
bicameral 16.3
bicarbonate 3.14
bicentenary 6.9
bicentennial 5.8
biceps 10.12
bicker 9.2
bicycle 10.12
bid 9.3
bidden 9.3
bidder 9.3
bidding 9.3
bide 10.4
bided 10.4
biding 10.4
biennial 5.8
bier 7.1
biff 9.4
bifocal 12.3
big 9.5
bigamist 9.11
bigamous 17.11
bigamy 6.1
bigger 9.5
biggie 9.5
Biggs 9.5
biggy 9.5
bigheaded 5.3
big-hearted 2.16
bigot 9.5
bigotry 6.1
bike 10.3
biker 10.3
biking 10.3
Bikini 6.9
bikini 6.9
Bilbao 2.1
bilberry 9.6
bile 10.7
bilious 9.6
Bill 9.6
bill 9.6
billed 9.6
Billericay 9.2
billet 9.6
billing 9.6

billion 9.6
billionaire 4.1
billow 9.6
billowy 9.6
Billy 9.6
billy-can 1.8
billy-goat 12.14
bimbo 9.7
bin 9.8
binary 10.9
bind 10.9
binder 10.9
binding 10.9
binge 9.8
binger 9.8
binging 9.8
bingo 9.8
binned 9.8
binning 9.8
bint 9.8
biochemical 5.7
biodegradable 3.4
biodiversity 6.1
bioengineer 7.1
biographer 11.5
biographical 1.4
biography 11.5
biological 11.3
biologist 11.6
biology 6.1, 11.6
biopsy 6.1
biosphere 7.1
biotechnology 11.6
bipartisan 1.8
birch 8.14
birching 8.14
Bird 8.4
bird 8.4
birdie 8.4
Biro® 10.11
birth 8.16
Biscay 9.11
bisect 5.2
bisected 5.2
bisecting 5.2
bishopric 9.2
bishoprics 9.2
bit 9.14
bitch 9.14
bitchy 9.14
bite 10.13
biter 10.13
biting 10.13
bitten 9.14
bitter 9.14
bitterly 9.14

bitterness 5.11
bittersweet 6.14
bitty 9.14
bivouac 1.2
bivouacs 1.2
bi-weekly 6.3
bizarre 2.1
blab 1.1
blabber 1.1
Black 1.2
black 1.2
black-and-white 10.13
blackberry 6.1
blacked 1.2
blacken 1.2
blacker 1.2
black-haired 4.2
black marketeer 7.1
blackness 1.2
Blackpool 18.7
blacks 1.2
bladder 1.3
blade 3.4
Blair 4.1
blame 3.8
blamed 3.8
blameless 3.8
blames 3.8
blameworthy 8.15
blanch 2.10
Blanche 2.10
bland 1.8
blander 1.8
blandly 1.8
blank 1.8
Blankety Blank 1.8
blanking 1.8
blankly 1.8
blare 4.1
blared 4.2
blaring 4.6
blarney 2.10
blasé 3.1
blaspheme 6.8
blasphemer 6.8
blaspheming 6.8
blasphemous 17.11
blasphemy 6.1
blast 2.13
blaster 2.13
blasting 2.13
blast-off 2.13
blatant 3.14
blatantly 3.14
blather 1.14
blaze 3.18

blazed 3.18
blazer 3.18
blazing 3.18
bleach 6.14
bleaching 6.14
bleak 6.3
bleaker 6.3
bleakly 6.3
blear 7.1
bleary 7.5
bleary-eyed 10.4
bleat 6.14
bleated 6.14
bleating 6.14
bleats 6.14
bled 5.3
bleed 6.4
bleeder 6.4
bleep 6.10
bleeper 6.10
bleeping 6.10
blemish 5.7
blench 5.8
blend 5.8
blender 5.8
blending 5.8
bless 5.11
blessed 5.11
blessing 5.11
blest 5.11
blether 5.15
blew 18.1
Bligh 10.1
blight 10.13
blighted 10.13
blighter 10.13
blighting 10.13
blighty 10.13
blimey 10.8
blimp 9.7
blind 10.9
blinded 10.9
blinder 10.9
blinding 10.9
blindly 10.9
blindness 10.9
blink 9.8
blinked 9.8
blinker 9.8
blinking 9.8
blip 9.9
bliss 9.11
blissfully 6.1
blister 9.11
blithe 10.14
blithering 9.15

blitz 9.14
blizzard 9.18
bloated 12.14
blob 11.1
blobbing 11.1
blobby 11.1
bloc 11.2
block 11.2
blockade 3.4
blocked 11.2
blocker 11.2
blocking 11.2
bloke 12.3
blond(e) 11.8
blood 17.3
blooded 17.3
blooding 17.3
bloodletting 5.14
bloodsucker 17.2
bloodthirsty 6.1
bloody 17.3
bloody-minded 10.9
bloom 18.8
bloomer 18.8
blooming 18.8
blossom 11.11
blot 11.13
blotch 11.13
blotter 11.13
blotto 11.13
blow 12.1
blow-by-blow 12.1
blower 12.1
blowing 12.1
blown 12.9
blowy 12.1
blowzy 13.9
blub 17.1
blubber 17.1
blubbered 17.1
Blue 18.1
blue 18.1
blue-collar 11.6
bluer 18.1
bluest 18.1
Bluff 17.4
bluff 17.4
bluffed 17.4
bluffer 17.4
blunder 17.8
blunderbuss 17.11
Blunt 17.8
blunt 17.8
blunted 17.8
blunter 17.8
blunting 17.8

blur 8.1
blurb 8.2
blurred 8.4
blurring 8.11
blurs 8.18
blurt 8.14
blurted 8.14
blurts 8.14
blush 17.12
blushed 17.12
blusher 17.12
blushing 17.12
bluster 17.11
blustered 17.11
blustery 6.1
BMA 3.1
BO 12.1
boa 12.1
boa constrictor 9.2
Boadicea 7.1
boar 14.1
board 14.4
boarded 14.4
boarder 14.4
boarders 14.4
boarding 14.4
boast 12.11
boaster 12.11
boasting 12.11
boat 12.14
boater 12.14
boating 12.14
Bob 11.1
bob 11.1
bobbin 11.1
bobbing 11.1
bobble 11.1
bobbly 11.1
Bobby 11.1
bobby 11.1
bod 11.3
bode 12.4
bodge 11.3
bodger 11.3
bodice 11.3
bodily 6.1
boding 12.4
body 11.3
bodyguard 2.4
bodywork 8.3
bodyworker 8.3
Boer 12.1
boffin 11.4
bog 11.5
bogey 12.6
bogeyman 1.8

boggle 11.5
Bognor Regis 6.4
Bogotá 2.1
boil 15.3
bold 12.7
bolder 12.7
boldly 12.7
boldness 12.7
bolero 4.6
Boleyn 9.8
Bolivia 9.17
Bolivian 9.17
bolognese 3.18
Bolshevik 9.2
Bolsheviks 9.2
Bolshevism 9.18
bolster 12.7
bolt 12.7
Bolton 12.7
bomb 11.7
bombard 2.4
bombarded 2.4
bombastic 1.11
Bombay 3.1
bomber 11.7
bona fide 10.4
bonanza 1.8
bonce 11.8
Bond 11.8
bond 11.8
bonding 11.8
bone 12.9
bone-dry 10.1
boner 12.9
bong 11.8
bonging 11.8
bonhomie 6.1
bonier 12.9
bonk 11.8
Bonn 11.8
bonnet 11.8
Bonnie 11.8
bonny 11.8
bonus 12.9
bony 12.9
bonze 11.8
boo 18.1
boob 18.2
booby 18.2
booby-prize 10.17
booby-trap 1.9
booby-trapping 1.9
book 16.1
bookable 16.3
bookbinder 10.9
bookbinding 10.9

Index

booked 16.1
bookie 16.1
booking 16.1
bookkeeping 6.10
bookmaker 3.3
bookmarker 2.3
Book of Kells 5.6
bookseller 5.6
booksellers 5.6
boom 18.8
boomerang 1.8
booming 18.8
boon 18.9
boor 19.1
boorish 19.4
boost 18.11
booster 18.11
boot 18.14
booted 18.14
bootee 6.1
booth 18.15
booting 18.14
booty 18.14
booze 18.19
boozer 18.19
boozing 18.19
boozy 18.19
bop 11.9
bopper 11.9
boracic 1.11
Bordeaux 12.1
Borden 14.4
border 14.4
bordered 14.4
borderland 1.8
borderline 10.9
Borders 14.4
borders 14.4
bore 14.1
borer 14.12
boring 14.12
Boris 11.10
born 14.10
born-again 5.8
borne 14.10
Borneo 12.1
boron 14.12
borough 17.10
borrow 11.10
Bosch 11.12
Bosnia-Herzegovina 6.9
Bosphorus 11.11
boss 11.11
bossed 11.11
bossy 11.11
botanical 1.8

botanist 9.11
botany 11.13
botch 11.13
both 12.16
bothersome 17.7
Botswana 2.10
Botticelli 5.6
bottle 11.13
bottled 11.13
bottle-fed 5.3
bottle-feed 6.4
bottle-green 6.9
bottleneck 5.2
bottlenecks 5.2
bottom 11.13
bottommost 12.11
botulism 9.18
bough 13.1
bought 14.15
boulder 12.7
boulevard 2.4
Boulogne 15.5
bounce 13.4
bounced 13.4
bouncer 13.4
bound 13.4
boundary 13.4
bounded 13.4
bounder 13.4
bounding 13.4
boundless 13.4
bountiful 16.3
bounty 13.4
bouquet 3.1
bourbon 8.2
bourgeoisie 6.1
Bourne 14.10
bout 13.7
boutique 6.3
Boutros-Boutros Ghali 2.8
Bovary 12.17
bow 12.1, 13.1
bowdlerize 10.17
bowdlerized 10.17
bowdlerizer 10.17
bowdlerizing 10.17
bowed 13.2
bowel 13.1
bower 13.1
Bowie 13.1
bowl 12.7
bowled 12.7
bowler 12.7
bowling 12.7
box 11.2

boy 15.1
Boyne 15.5
boys 15.8
bra 2.1
brace 3.11
bracing 3.11
bracken 1.2
bracket 1.2
Brad 1.3
Bradley 1.3
Bradman 1.3
brag 1.5
braggart 1.5
bragger 1.5
bragging 1.5
Brahms 2.9
braid 3.4
Braille 3.7
brain 3.9
brainiac 3.9
brainless 3.9
brainpower 13.1
brains 3.9
brainstorm 3.9
brainstorming 14.9
brainy 3.9
braise 3.18
braised 3.18
braising 3.18
brake 3.3
braking 3.3
bramble 1.7
bran 1.8
branch 2.10
brand 1.8
branded 1.8
Brandenburg 8.6
brander 1.8
branding 1.8
brandish 1.8
brand-new 18.1
brandy 1.8
brash 1.12
brasher 1.12
Brasília 9.6
brass 2.13
brassy 2.13
brat 1.13
Bratislava 2.19
bravado 2.4
brave 3.17
braved 3.17
bravely 3.17
braver 3.17
bravery 3.17
bravo 12.1

brawl 14.8
brawled 14.8
brawler 14.8
brawn 14.10
brawnier 14.10
brawny 14.10
bray 3.1
brayed 3.4
braying 3.1
brazen 3.18
brazier 3.18
Brazil 9.6
brazil 9.6
Brazilian 9.6
breach 6.14
breaching 6.14
bread 5.3
bread-and-butter 17.13
breadbasket 2.13
breadboard 5.3
breaded 5.3
breading 5.3
breadline 5.3
breadwinner 9.8
break 3.3
breakable 3.3
breakaway 3.3
breaker 3.3
breaking 3.3
breakout 3.3
break-up 3.3
breakwater 14.15
Bream 6.8
bream 6.8
breast 5.11
breast-feed 6.4
breath 5.16
breathalyse 10.17
Breathalyser 10.17
breathalysing 10.17
breathe 6.15
breather 6.15
breathing 6.15
breathtaking 3.3
Brecon 5.2
bred 5.3
breech 6.14
breed 6.4
breeder 6.4
breeding 6.4
breeze 6.19
breezed 6.19
breezier 6.19
breezily 6.19
breezy 6.19
Bremen 3.8

Brenda 5.8
Brendan 5.8
Breton 5.14
Brett 5.14
breviary 6.1
brevity 5.17
brew 18.1
brewer 18.1
brewery 19.4
Brian 10.1
briar 10.1
bribe 10.2
bric-à-brac 1.2
brick 9.2
bricked 9.2
brickie 9.2
bricking 9.2
bricklayer 3.1
bricks 9.2
bridal 10.4
bride 10.4
bridge 9.3
bridged 9.3
Bridgend 5.8
Bridget 9.3
bridging loans 12.9
bridle 10.4
brief 6.5
briefing 6.5
briefly 6.5
brigade 3.4
brigadier 7.1
Brigadoon 18.9
bright 10.13
brighten 10.13
brightened 10.13
brightening 10.13
brighter 10.13
brightly 10.13
brightness 10.13
Brighton 10.13
brilliantly 6.1
brim 9.7
brimmed 9.7
brimming 9.7
brine 10.9
bring 9.8
bring-and-buy 10.1
bringer 9.8
bringing 9.8
brink 9.8
brinkmanship 9.9
briny 10.9
Briony 10.1
Brisbane 9.18
brisk 9.11

bristle 9.11
Bristol 9.11
Brit 9.14
Britain 9.14
Britannia 1.8
Briticism 9.18
British 9.14
Britney 9.14
Briton 9.14
Brittany 9.14
Britten 9.14
brittle 9.14
broach 12.14
broad 14.4
broadcaster 2.13
broadcasting 2.13
broaden 14.4
broader 14.4
broadly 14.4
broad-minded 10.9
brocade 3.4
broccoli 6.1
brochure 12.13
Brodie 12.4
brogue 12.6
broil 15.3
broke 12.3
broken 12.3
brokenhearted 2.16
broker 12.3
broking 12.3
brolly 11.6
bronchitic 9.14
bronchitis 10.13
Brontë 11.8
bronze 11.8
brooch 12.14
brood 18.4
brooding 18.4
broody 18.4
brook 16.1
brooked 16.1
brooking 16.1
broom 18.8
brooming 18.8
broth 11.14
Brother 17.14
brother 17.14
brotherhood 16.2,
  17.14
brother-in-law 14.1,
  17.14
brotherly 6.1
brought 14.15
brow 13.1
Brown 13.4

brown 13.4
browned 13.4
browned-off 11.4
brown-haired 4.2
Brownie 13.4
brownie 13.4
Browning 13.4
browning 13.4
browse 13.9
browsing 13.9
Bruce 18.11
Bruges 18.12
bruise 18.19
bruiser 18.19
bruising 18.19
Brummie 17.7
brunch 17.8
brunches 17.8
Brunei 10.1
Brunel 5.6
brunette 5.14
brunt 17.8
brush 17.12
brushed 17.12
brusher 17.12
brushing 17.12
Brussels 17.11
brutality 1.6
brutalization 3.13
brutalize 10.17
brutalized 10.17
brutalizing 10.17
brute 18.14
Brynner 9.8
BSc 6.1
BSE 6.1
BSI 10.1
BST 6.1
bubble 17.1
bubbled 17.1
bubbly 17.1
bubonic 11.8
buccaneer 7.1
buccaneering 7.5
Bucharest 5.11
buck 17.2
bucked 17.2
Bucket 3.1
bucket 17.2
Buckinghamshire 10.1
buckle 17.2
buckling 17.2
bucks 17.2
buckteeth 6.16
bucolic 11.6
bud 17.3

Budapest 5.11
Budd 17.3
budded 17.3
Buddha 16.2
budding 17.3
buddy 17.3
budge 17.3
budgerigar 2.1
budget 17.3
budgetary 6.1
budgie 17.3
budging 17.3
buff 17.4
buffalo 12.1
buffed 17.4
buffer 17.4
buffoon 18.9
bug 17.5
Bugatti 1.13
bug-free 6.1
buggy 17.5
bugle 18.6
build 9.6
builder 9.6
building 9.6
built 9.6
built-in 9.8
built-up 17.9
Bulgaria 4.6
Bulgarian 4.6
bulge 17.6
bulk 17.6
bulky 17.6
Bull 16.3
bull 16.3
bulldozer 12.19
bullet 16.3
bulletin 9.8
bulletproof 18.5
bullfighter 10.13
bullfighting 10.13
bully 16.3
bum 17.7
bumblebee 6.1
bumbling 17.7
bummer 17.7
bumming 17.7
bump 17.7
bumper 17.7
bumping 17.7
bumpkin 17.7
bump-start 17.7
bumptious 17.7
bumpy 17.7
bun 17.8
bunch 17.8

bunches 17.8
bundle 17.8
bung 17.8
bungalow 12.1
bungle 17.8
bunion 17.8
bunk 17.8
Bunny 17.8
bunny 17.8
Bunter 17.8
bunting 17.8
buoy 15.1
buoyancy 6.1
buoyant 15.1
buoyed 15.2
buoying 15.1
buoys 15.8
burble 8.2
burdensome 17.7
bureau 19.4
bureaucracy 6.1
bureaucrat 1.13
bureaucratic 1.13
burgeon 8.4
burglarize 10.17
burglarizing 10.17
burglar-proof 18.5
burglary 6.1
burgle 8.6
Burkina-Faso 1.11
burlesque 5.11
burly 8.7
Burma 8.8
Burmese 6.19
burn 8.9
burned 8.9
burner 8.9
burning 8.9
burnish 8.9
burnt 8.9
burnt-out 13.7
burp 8.10
burr 8.1
burrito 6.14
burrow 17.10
burrs 8.18
bursar 8.12
bursary 8.12
burst 8.12
Burundi 17.8
bury 5.10
bus 17.11
Bush 16.4
bush 16.4
bushed 16.4
bushy 16.4

busier 9.18
busily 6.1, 9.18
businesslike 10.3
businessman 1.8
busk 17.11
bussed 17.11
Bussell 17.11
bust 17.11
busted 17.11
buster 17.11
busting 17.11
bustle 17.11
bustler 17.11
bustles 17.11
bust-up 17.11
busy 9.18
busybody 11.3
but 17.13
butch 16.5
butchery 6.1
butt 17.13
butter 17.13
buttercup 17.9
butterfly 10.1
buttermilk 9.6
butterscotch 11.13
Button 17.13
button 17.13
buttonhole 12.7
buttonholed 12.7
buttonholing 12.7
buy 10.1
buyer 10.1
buyout 10.1
buzz 17.16
buzzy 17.16
by 10.1
bye 10.1
bye-bye 10.1
by-election 5.2
Byelorussia 17.12
Byelorussian 17.12
by jingo 9.8
by-line 10.7
Byron 10.1
bystander 1.8
byte 10.13
byway 10.16
Byzantine 1.8

C

C 6.1
CAB 6.1
cab 1.1
cabal 1.6

Cabaret 3.1
cabaret 3.1
cabby 1.1
caber 3.2
cabinet-maker 3.3
Cable 3.2
cable 3.2
cabled 3.2
caboodle 18.4
cacao 2.1
cache 1.12
cack-handed 1.8
cackle 1.2
cacophonous 17.11
cacti 10.1
CAD 6.1
cad 1.3
cadaver 1.16
cadaverous 17.11
caddie 1.3
caddy 1.3
cadenza 5.8
cadet 5.14
cadge 1.3
Cadillac 1.2
Cadillacs 1.2
Cádiz 9.18
Caerphilly 9.6
Caesar 6.19
Caesarean 4.6
café 1.4
cafeteria 7.5
caff 1.4
caffeine 6.9
cage 3.4
caged 3.4
caging 3.4
cagoule 18.7
CAI 10.1
Cain 3.9
Caine 3.9
cairn 4.5
Cairo 10.11
Caithness 5.11
cajole 12.7
cajoled 12.7
cajoler 12.7
cajoling 12.7
cake 3.3
caked 3.3
caking 3.3
Cal 1.6
Calais 1.6
calamity 6.1
calculate 3.14
calculated 3.14

calculating 3.14
calculation 3.13
calculator 3.14
calculus 17.11
Calcutta 17.13
Caledonian 12.9
calf 2.5
Calgary 6.1
Caliban 1.8
calibrate 3.14
calibrator 3.14
calico 12.1
California 14.10
call 14.8
Callas 1.6
called 14.8
caller 14.8
calligraphy 6.1
calling 14.8
callous 1.6
callow 1.6
call the shots 11.13
callus 1.6
calm 2.9
calmed 2.9
calmer 2.9
calming 2.9
Calor Gas® 1.11
calorie 1.6
calumny 6.1
calve 2.19
calves 2.19
calving 2.19
Calvinism 9.18
CAM 5.7
cam 1.7
Cambodian 12.4
Cambridgeshire 10.1
camcorder 14.4
camcorders 14.4
came 3.8
camel 1.7
camelhair 4.1
camellia 6.7
Camelot 11.13
cameo 12.1
cameraman 1.8
Cameroon 18.9
Camilla 9.6
camisole 12.7
camomile 10.7
camouflage 2.14
camp 1.7
campaign 3.9
campaigner 3.9
Campari 2.12

camper 1.7
campfire 10.1
campion 1.7
can 1.8
Canadian 3.4
canal 1.6, 2.8
Canary 4.6
canary 4.6
cancellation 3.13
Cancer 1.8
cancer 1.8
cancerous 17.11
candelabra 2.2
candid 1.8
candidacy 6.1
candidate 3.14
candidature 19.1
candidly 1.8
candied 1.8
candle 1.8
candlelight 10.13
candlelit 9.14
candlestick 9.2
candlesticks 9.2
can-do 18.1
candour 1.8
Candy 1.8
candy 1.8
candyfloss 11.11
cane 3.9
canister 1.8
canker 1.8
cannabis 9.11
canned 1.8
cannery 1.8
Cannes 1.8
cannibal 16.3
cannibalize 10.17
cannibalizing 10.17
cannier 1.8
canning 1.8
cannon 1.8
cannonball 14.8
canny 1.8
canoe 18.1
canoeing 18.1
canoeist 18.1
canon 1.8
canonize 10.17
canonizing 10.17
canoodle 18.4
canoodles 18.4
canopy 6.1
cant 1.8
can't 2.10
cantaloup(e) 18.10

cantankerous 17.11
canteen 6.9
canter 1.8
Canterbury 6.1
cantilever 6.17
Canton 11.8
Cantonese 6.19
Canute 18.14
canyon 1.8
CAP 6.1
cap 1.9
capability 9.6
capable 3.10
capably 6.1
capacious 3.13
capacity 1.11
cape 3.10
caper 3.10
capercaillie 3.7
Cape Verde 8.4
capillary 9.6
capital 16.3
capitalism 9.18
capitalist 9.11
capitalization 3.13
capitalize 10.17
capitalizing 10.17
capitulate 3.14
capon 3.10
Capone 12.9
cappuccino 6.9
Capri 6.1
caprice 6.11
capricious 9.13
capriciously 9.13
Capricorn 14.10
capsicum 17.7
capsize 10.17
capsizing 10.17
captaincy 6.1
caption 1.9
captivate 3.14
captivating 3.14
captivity 9.17
captor 1.9
capture 1.9
car 2.1
Caracas 1.2
carafe 1.4
caramel 5.6
carat 1.10
caravan 1.8
caravaned 1.8
caravanning 1.8
caravel 5.6
caraway 3.1

carbolic 11.6
carbonate 3.14
carbonated 3.14
carbonize 10.17
carbonizing 10.17
carbuncle 17.8
carburettor 5.14
carcass 2.3
carcinogenic 5.8
carcinoma 12.8
card 2.4
cardboard 2.4
cardiac 1.2
cardigan 17.8
cardinal 16.3
cardiograph 2.5
cardiologist 11.6
cardiology 11.6
care 4.1
cared 4.2
career 7.1
careering 7.5
carefully 6.1
careless 4.3
carelessly 6.1
carelessness 5.11
carer 4.6
caress 5.11
caressed 5.11
caretaker 3.3
Carey 4.6
cargo 2.6
Caribbean 6.1
caribou 18.1
caricature 19.1
caricatured 19.2
caricaturing 19.4
caricaturist 19.4
caries 4.6
caring 4.6
Carla 2.8
Carling 2.8
Carlisle 10.7
Carlow 2.8
Carly 2.8
Carmarthenshire 10.1
Carmen 2.9
carnation 3.13
carnival 16.3
carnivore 14.1
carnivorous 9.17
carob 1.10
carol 1.10
Carol(e) 1.10
Carolina 10.9
Caroline 10.9

carolled 1.10
Carolyn 1.10
carousal 13.9
carouse 13.9
carousel 5.6
carousing 13.9
carp 2.11
carpentry 6.1
carpet-sweeper 6.10
Carr 2.1
carriage 1.10
carriageway 3.1
Carrie 1.10
carried 1.10
carrier 1.10
carrion 1.10
Carroll 1.10
carrot 1.10
carry 1.10
carrycot 11.13
carry-on 11.8
carry-out 13.7
carsickness 9.2
cart 2.16
carte blanche 2.10
carted 2.16
cartel 5.6
Carter 2.16
carter 2.16
carting 2.16
cartographer 11.5
cartography 11.5
carton 2.16
cartoon 18.9
cartoonist 18.9
cartridge 2.16
carve 2.19
carving 2.19
Casablanca 1.8
Casanova 12.17
cascade 3.4
cascaded 3.4
cascading 3.4
case 3.11
caseful 3.11
casement 3.11
Cash 1.12
cash 1.12
cashback 1.12
cashed 1.12
cashew 18.1
cashier 7.1
cashiering 7.5
cashing 1.12
cashmere 7.1
casing 3.11

casino 6.9
cask 2.13
casket 2.13
Cassandra 1.8
cassava 2.19
casserole 12.7
casseroled 12.7
casseroling 12.7
cassette 5.14
Cassie 1.11
cast 2.13
castaway 3.1
caste 2.13
castigate 3.14
castigator 3.14
casting 2.13
cast-iron 10.1
castle 2.13
cast-off 2.13
castor 2.13
castrate 3.14
castration 3.13
casualization 3.13
casually 6.1
casualty 6.1
cat 1.13
cataclysm 9.18
Catalan 1.8
catalogue 11.5
Catalonia 12.9
catalyst 9.11
catamaran 1.8
catapult 17.6
cataract 1.2
catarrh 2.1
catastrophe 6.1
catatonia 12.9
catatonic 11.8
catch 1.13
Catch-22 18.1
catcher 1.13
catching 1.13
catchment 1.13
catchy 1.13
catechism 9.18
categorical 11.10
categorize 10.17
categorizing 10.17
category 6.1
cater 3.14
caterpillar 9.6
catfish 1.13
Catherine 9.8
Catholicism 9.18
Catriona 6.9
cattery 1.13

cattle 1.13
catty 1.13
Caucasian 3.12
Caucasus 17.11
caucus 14.3
caught 14.15
cauliflower 13.1
cause 14.20
cauterize 10.17
cauterizing 10.17
caution 14.14
cautiously 6.1
cautiousness 5.11
Cava 2.19
cavalcade 3.4
cavalcaded 3.4
cavalcading 3.4
cavalier 7.1
cavalry 6.1
Cavan 1.16
cave 3.17
cavern 1.16
cavernous 1.16
caviar(e) 2.1
cavity 1.16
cavort 14.15
cavorting 14.15
caw 14.1
cawing 14.12
cayenne 5.8
CB 6.1
CBE 6.1
CBI 10.1
cc 6.1
CD 6.1
CDI 10.1
CD-ROM 11.7
cease 6.11
ceased 6.11
ceaselessly 6.1
ceasing 6.11
Cecil 5.11
Cecilia 6.7
cedar 6.4
cede 6.4
cedilla 9.6
Cedric 5.3
ceilidh 3.7
ceiling 6.7
ceilings 6.7
Celebes 6.19
celebrate 3.14
celebrated 3.14
celebration 3.13
celebrations 3.13
celebrator 3.14

celebrity 6.1
celery 6.1
Celeste 5.11
celestial 5.11
Celia 6.7
celibacy 6.1
celibate 17.13
cell 5.6
cellar 5.6
cellars 5.6
cello 5.6
Cellophane® 3.9
cellulite 10.13
Celluloid® 15.2
cellulose 12.11
Celt 5.6
cement 5.8
cemetery 6.1
cenotaph 2.5
censor 5.8
censorious 14.12
censorship 9.9
census 5.8
cent 5.8
centenarian 4.6
centenary 6.9
centennial 5.8
centigrade 3.4
centigram(me) 1.7
centilitre 6.14
centimetre 6.14
centipede 6.4
centralize 10.17
centralizer 10.17
centralizing 10.17
centrally 6.1
centre 5.8
centrefold 12.7
centrepiece 6.11
centrifugal 18.6
centrifuge 18.4
century 6.1
CEO 12.1
Cephalonia 12.9
ceramic 1.7
ceramics 1.7
cereal 7.5
cerebellum 5.6
cerebral 16.3
cerebrum 17.7
Ceredigion 11.8
ceremonial 12.9
ceremonious 12.9
ceremony 6.1
cert 8.14
certain 8.14

certainly 6.1
certifiable 16.3
certificate 17.13
certify 10.1
certitude 18.4
certs 8.14
cervical 10.3
cessation 3.13
Ceylon 11.8
cf 5.4
CFC 6.1
Chad 1.3
chafe 3.5
chafer 3.5
chaff 2.5
chaffed 2.5
chaffing 2.5
chain 3.9
chair 4.1
chaired 4.2
chairing 4.6
chairlift 4.3
chairman 4.4
chairmanship 9.9
chairperson 8.12
chairwoman 17.8
chalet 1.6
chalice 1.6
chalk 14.3
chalked 14.3
chalking 14.3
chalky 14.3
chambermaid 3.4
chamois 1.7
champ 1.7
champagne 3.9
champion 1.7
championship 9.9
chance 2.10
chancer 2.10
chancing 2.10
chancy 1.8
chandelier 7.1
change 3.9
changeable 3.9
changed 3.9
changeover 12.17
changer 3.9
changing 3.9
channel 1.8
channelling 1.8
chant 2.10
Chantal 1.6
chanting 2.10
chaotic 11.13
chap 1.9

chapati 2.16
chapel 1.9
chaperone 12.9
chaperoning 12.9
chaplaincy 6.1
chapped 1.9
chappie 1.9
chapter 1.9
char 2.1
characteristic 9.11
characteristics 9.11
characterization 3.13
characterize 10.17
characterizing 10.17
charade 2.4
charge 2.4
charger 2.4
chariot 1.10
charismatic 1.13
charitable 16.3
Charity 1.10
charity 1.10
charlatan 17.8
Charlemagne 3.9
Charlene 6.9
Charles 2.8
Charlie 2.8
Charlotte 2.8
charm 2.9
Charmaine 3.9
charmed 2.9
charmer 2.9
charmers 2.9
Charming 2.9
charming 2.9
charms 2.9
charred 2.4
charring 2.12
chart 2.16
charted 2.16
charter 2.16
charting 2.16
charwoman 17.8
chary 4.6
chase 3.11
chaser 3.11
chasing 3.11
chasm 1.17
chassis 1.11
chaste 3.11
chasten 3.11
chastise 10.17
chastiser 10.17
chastising 10.17
chastity 6.1
chat 1.13

château 1.13
châteaux 1.13
chattel 1.13
chatter 1.13
chatterbox 11.2
chattered 1.13
chattering 1.13
chatty 1.13
Chaucer 14.13
chauffeur 12.5
chauvinism 9.18
chauvinist 9.11
chauvinistic 9.11
cheap 6.10
cheapen 6.10
cheaper 6.10
cheat 6.14
cheated 6.14
cheater 6.14
cheating 6.14
cheats 6.14
check 5.2
checked 5.2
Checker 5.2
checks 5.2
Cheddar 5.3
cheek 6.3
cheeking 6.3
cheeky 6.3
cheep 6.10
cheeper 6.10
cheer 7.1
cheerer 7.5
cheerful 7.3
cheerfully 6.1
cheerier 7.5
cheerily 7.5
cheering 7.5
cheerio 12.1
cheerleader 6.4
cheerless 7.4
cheery 7.5
cheese 6.19
cheesed 6.19
cheetah 6.14
chef 5.4
Che Guevara 2.12
Chelsea 5.6
chemical 5.7
chemistry 6.1
cheque 5.2
cheques 5.2
Cher 4.1
Cherie 6.1
cherish 5.10
Chernobyl 12.2

cherry 5.10
Cheryl 5.10
chess 5.11
chessman 5.11
chest 5.11
chested 5.11
Chester 5.11
chesting 5.11
Chevrolet 3.1
chew 18.1
chewy 18.1
chic 6.3
Chicago 2.6
chick 9.2
chicken 9.2
chickenpox 11.2
chicks 9.2
chicory 9.2
chid 9.3
chidden 9.3
chide 10.4
chided 10.4
chiding 10.4
chief 6.5
chiefly 6.5
chiffon 11.8
child 10.7
child-bearing 4.6
childminder 10.9
Chile 9.6
Chilean 9.6
Chiles 10.7
chill 9.6
chilled 9.6
chiller 9.6
chilli 9.6
chilling 9.6
chilly 9.6
chime 10.8
chimer 10.8
chiming 10.8
chimneypot 11.13
chimp 9.7
chimpanzee 6.1
chin 9.8
China 10.9
china 10.9
Chinese 6.19
chink 9.8
chinned 9.8
chinning 9.8
Chinook 16.1
chip 9.9
chipboard 9.9
chipper 9.9
Chips 9.9

Chirac 1.2
chiropodist 9.11
chiropody 6.1
chirp 8.10
chirrup 9.10
chisel 9.18
chit 9.14
chitter 9.14
chittered 9.14
chivalrous 17.11
chivalry 6.1
chives 10.15
chiv(v)y 9.17
Chloe 12.1
chlorinate 3.14
chlorine 14.12
chloroform 14.9
chloroformed 14.9
chlorophyl(l) 9.6
chock 11.2
chock-a-block 11.2
chocked 11.2
chocking 11.2
chocoholic 11.6
choice 15.6
choir 10.1
choirboy 15.1
choirboys 15.8
choke 12.3
choker 12.3
choking 12.3
cholesterol 11.6
Choo 18.1
choose 18.19
chooser 18.19
choosing 18.19
choosy 18.19
chop 11.9
chopper 11.9
choppier 11.9
choppily 11.9
chopping 11.9
choppy 11.9
choral 14.12
chord 14.4
chore 14.1
choreograph 2.5
choreographed 2.5
choreographer 11.5
choreographing 2.5
choreography 11.5
chorister 11.10
chortle 14.15
chorus 14.12
chose 12.19
chosen 12.19

chowder 13.2
Chris 9.11
Chrissie 9.11
Christ 10.12
christen 9.11
Christianity 1.8
Christie 9.11
Christina 6.9
Christine 9.11
Christmas 9.11
Christy 9.11
chrome 12.8
chroming 12.8
chromosome 12.8
chronic 11.8
chronicle 11.8
chronological 11.3
chronology 11.6
chrysalis 9.11
chrysanthemum 17.7
chubby 17.1
Chuck 17.2
chuck 17.2
chucked 17.2
chucker 17.2
chuckle 17.2
chuckling 17.2
chucks 17.2
chuffed 17.4
chug 17.5
chukka 17.2
chum 17.7
chummy 17.7
chump 17.7
chunk 17.8
chunky 17.8
church 8.14
churchgoer 12.1
churlish 8.7
churn 8.9
churned 8.9
churner 8.9
churning 8.9
chute 18.14
CIA 3.1
cicada 2.4, 3.4
Cicely 6.1
CID 6.1
cider 10.4
cigar 2.1
cigarette 5.14
C-in-C 6.1
cinch 9.8
Cincinnati 1.13
cinder 9.8
Cinderella 5.6

Cindy 9.8
cine 9.8
cinema-goer 12.1
cinematographer 11.5
cinematography 11.5
cinnamon 17.8
cipher 10.5
circa 8.3
circuit 8.3
circuitous 18.1
circulate 3.14
circulation 3.13
circulator 3.14
circumcise 10.17
circumcising 10.17
circumcision 9.12
circumflex 5.2
circumflexed 5.2
circumlocution 18.13
circumnavigate 3.14
circumscribe 10.2
circumspect 5.2
circumstantial 1.8
circumvent 5.8
Cirencester 5.11
cirrhosis 12.11
cissy 9.11
cistern 9.11
citadel 5.6
citation 3.13
cite 10.13
cited 10.13
citer 10.13
citing 10.13
citizen 17.8
citizenship 9.9
city 9.14
civil 9.17
civilian 9.6
civility 9.6
civilization 3.13
civilize 10.17
civilized 10.17
civilizer 10.17
civilizing 10.17
CJD 6.1
Clackmannanshire 10.1
clad 1.3
claim 3.8
claimant 3.8
claimed 3.8
claimer 3.8
claims 3.8
Cla(i)re 4.1
clairvoyant 15.1
clam 1.7

clamber 1.7
clamming 1.7
clammy 1.7
clamorous 1.7
clamour 1.7
clamoured 1.7
clamp 1.7
clamper 1.7
clan 1.8
Clancy 1.8
clandestine 5.11
clang 1.8
clanger 1.8
clank 1.8
clanking 1.8
clap 1.9
clapped-out 13.7
clapper 1.9
clapping 1.9
Clara 2.12
Clare 4.1
claret 1.10
clarification 3.13
clarify 10.1
Clarinda 9.8
clarinet 5.14
Clarissa 9.11
clarity 1.10
clash 1.12
clashed 1.12
clashing 1.12
clasp 2.13
class 2.13
classable 2.13
classed 2.13
classes 2.13
classic 1.11
classical 16.3
classicism 9.18
classification 3.13
classified 10.4
classify 1.11
classy 2.13
clatter 1.13
clattered 1.13
clattering 1.13
Claud(e) 14.4
Claudette 5.14
clause 14.20
claustrophobic 12.2
claustrophobics 12.2
clavicle 16.3
claw 14.1
clawing 14.12
Clay 3.1
clay 3.1

clean 6.9
clean-cut 17.13
cleaner 6.9
cleaning 6.9
cleanliness 5.11
cleanly 6.9
cleanse 5.8
cleanser 5.8
clean-shaven 3.17
clear 7.1
clearance 7.5
clear-cut 17.13
clearer 7.5
clear-headed 5.3
clearing 7.5
clearly 7.4
clear-sighted 10.13
cleave 6.17
cleaved 6.17
cleaver 6.17
cleaves 6.17
Cleese 6.19
clef 5.4
cleft 5.4
clemency 6.1
Clementine 10.9
clementine 6.9
clench 5.8
Cleo 6.1
cleric 5.10
clerical 5.10
clerk 2.3
clever 5.17
cleverly 5.17
cleverness 5.11
click 9.2
clicked 9.2
clicker 9.2
clicking 9.2
clicks 9.2
client 10.1
clientele 5.6
Cliff 9.4
cliff 9.4
cliffhanger 1.8
Clifford 9.4
climactic 1.2
climatic 1.13
climb 10.8
climber 10.8
climbing 10.8
clinch 9.8
clinching 9.8
cling 9.8
clinger 9.8
clinging 9.8

clingy 9.8
clinic 9.8
clinical 9.8
clink 9.8
clinked 9.8
clinker 9.8
clinking 9.8
Clint 9.8
Clinton 9.8
clip 9.9
clipboard 9.9
clip-on 9.9
clipper 9.9
clipping 9.9
clique 6.3
Clive 10.15
cloak 12.3
cloak-and-dagger 1.5
cloaking 12.3
clobber 11.1
clock 11.2
clocked 11.2
clocker 11.2
clocking 11.2
clockmaker 3.3
clod 11.3
clog 11.5
cloister 15.6
clomp 11.7
clone 12.9
cloning 12.9
Clooney 18.9
close 12.11, 12.19
close-cropped 11.9
closed 12.19
close-fitting 9.14
close-knit 9.14
closely 12.11
closer 12.11, 12.19
close-run 17.8
close-set 5.14
closet 11.16
closing 12.19
closure 12.12
clot 11.13
cloth 11.14
clothe 12.15
clothed 12.15
clothes 12.15
clothing 12.15
cloud 13.2
cloudy 13.2
Clough 17.4
Clouseau 12.1
clout 13.7
clouting 13.7

clove 12.17
cloven 12.17
clover 12.17
clown 13.4
clowned 13.4
clowning 13.4
cloying 15.1
club 17.1
clubber 17.1
cluck 17.2
clucked 17.2
clucks 17.2
clue 18.1
Cluedo® 18.4
clump 17.7
clumping 17.7
clumsiness 5.11
clung 17.8
clunky 17.8
cluster 17.11
clustered 17.11
clutch 17.13
clutched 17.13
clutter 17.13
Clwyd 18.1
Clyde 10.4
CNAA 3.1
CND 6.1
CO 12.1
c/o 12.1
co 12.1
coach 12.14
coachable 12.14
coagulate 3.14
coal 12.7
coalesce 5.11
coalesced 5.11
coalition 9.13
coalman 12.7
coarse 14.13
coarser 14.13
coast 12.11
coastal 12.11
coaster 12.11
coasting 12.11
coat 12.14
coated 12.14
coating 12.14
coax 12.3
cob 11.1
cobber 11.1
cobble 11.1
Coca-Cola® 12.7
cocaine 3.9
cock 11.2
cockade 3.4

cock-a-doodle-doo 18.1
cock-a-hoop 18.10
cockamamie 3.8
cockatoo 18.1
cocked 11.2
cocker 11.2
cockerel 16.3
cocking 11.2
Cockney 11.2
cock-up 11.2
cocky 11.2
coconut 17.13
cocoon 18.9
cocooned 18.9
Cocteau 12.1
COD 6.1
cod 11.3
coda 12.4
coddle 11.3
code 12.4
coded 12.4
coder 12.4
codify 10.1
coding 12.4
codswallop 11.6
coeducational 3.13
coefficient 9.13
coerce 8.12
coerced 8.12
coercion 8.13
coexist 9.11
coexisted 9.11
coexistence 9.11
coexisting 9.11
coffee 11.4
coffer 11.4
coffin 11.4
cog 11.5
cogitate 3.14
cognition 9.13
cohabit 1.1
cohabitation 3.13
coherence 7.5
cohesion 6.12
coiffure 19.1
coil 15.3
coin 15.5
coincide 10.4
coincided 10.4
coincidence 5.8
coincidental 5.8
coincidentally 5.8
coinciding 10.4
coin-operated 3.14
Coke® 12.3
coke 12.3

coking 12.3
cola 12.7
cold 12.7
cold-blooded 17.3
colder 12.7
cold-hearted 2.16
coldly 12.7
coldness 12.7
cold-shoulder 12.7
Cole 12.7
Colette 5.14
coley 12.7
colic 11.6
Colin 11.6
collaborate 1.1
collaboration 3.13
collaborator 3.14
collapse 1.9
collapsible 16.3
collar 11.6
collarbone 12.9
collate 3.14
collator 3.14
collect 5.2
collectable 5.2
collected 5.2
collecting 5.2
collection 5.2
collective 5.2
collectively 5.2
collectivize 10.17
collectivizing 10.17
collector 5.2
Colleen 6.9
college 11.6
collide 10.4
collided 10.4
collider 10.4
colliding 10.4
collie 11.6
colliery 6.1
collision 9.12
colloquialism 9.18
collude 18.4
colluder 18.4
colluding 18.4
collusion 18.12
Cologne 12.9
cologne 12.9
Colombo 17.7
colon 12.7
colonel 8.9
colonial 12.9
colonialism 9.18
colonist 9.11
colonize 10.17

colonizer 10.17
colonizing 10.17
colonnade 3.4
colony 6.1
Colorado 2.4
colossal 11.11
colour 17.6
colour-blind 10.9
colour-coded 12.4
coloured 17.6
colourful 16.3
colourless 5.11
colt 12.7
Columba 17.7
column 11.6
columnist 9.11
coma 12.8
comatose 12.11
comb 12.8
combinable 10.9
combination 3.13
combine 10.9
combing 12.8
combining 10.9
combustible 16.3
come 17.7
COMECON 11.8
comedian 6.4
comedienne 5.8
comediennes 5.8
comedy 6.1
comer 17.7
comet 11.7
come to blows 12.19
comeuppance 17.9
comfortable 16.3
comfortably 6.1
comic 11.7
comical 11.7
comics 11.7
coming 17.7
comma 11.7
command 2.10
commandant 1.8
commandants 1.8
commandeer 7.1
commandeering 7.5
commander 2.10
commanding 2.10
commemorate 3.14
commemoration 3.13
commemorative 9.17
commemorator 3.14
commence 5.8
commend 5.8
commendable 5.8

commendation 3.13
commending 5.8
commensurate 17.13
commentary 11.7
commentate 3.14
commentator 3.14
commercial 8.13
commercialism 9.18
commercialized 10.17
commercially 6.1
commie 11.7
commiserate 3.14
commiseration 3.13
commission 9.13
commissionaire 4.1
commissioned 9.13
commissioning 9.13
commit 9.14
committal 9.14
committed 9.14
committee 9.14
commode 12.4
commodious 12.4
commodity 11.3
commodore 14.1
common-law 14.1
commonly 6.1
commonplace 3.11
Commonwealth 5.6
commotion 12.13
communal 16.3
commune 18.9
communed 18.9
communicable 16.3
communicate 3.14
communication 3.13
communicator 3.14
communion 18.9
communism 9.18
communist 9.11
community 18.9
commute 18.14
commuted 18.14
commuter 18.14
commuting 18.14
Como 12.8
Comoros 12.19
compact 1.2
compacted 1.2
compacting 1.2
companion 1.8
companionable 16.3
companionship 9.9
company 6.1
comparative 1.10
compare 4.1

compared 4.2
compare notes 12.14
comparing 4.6
comparison 1.10
compartment 2.16
compass 17.7
compassion 1.12
compassionate 1.12
compatibility 9.6
compatible 16.3
compatriot 17.13
compel 5.6
compelled 5.6
compelling 5.6
compensate 3.14
compensation 3.13
compensator 3.14
compensatory 3.14
compete 6.14
competed 6.14
competes 6.14
competing 6.14
competition 9.13
competitive 9.17
compilation 3.13
compile 10.7
compiled 10.7
compiler 10.7
compiling 10.7
complacency 6.1
complacent 3.11
complain 3.9
complained 3.9
complainer 3.9
complaint 3.9
complement 5.8
complementary 5.8
complete 6.14
completed 6.14
completely 6.14
completes 6.14
completing 6.14
completion 6.13
complexion 5.2
complexity 5.2
compliance 10.1
compliant 10.1
complicate 3.14
complicated 3.14
complication 3.13
complicity 9.11
compliment 5.8
complimentary 5.8
comply 10.1
compose 12.19
composed 12.19

composer 12.19
composing 12.19
composite 9.14
composition 9.13
composure 12.12
compound 13.4
compounded 13.4
compounding 13.4
comprehend 5.8
comprehending 5.8
comprehensible 5.8
comprehensibly 5.8
comprehension 5.8
comprehensive 5.8
comprehensively 5.8
compress 5.11
compressed 5.11
compression 5.13
compressor 5.11
comprise 10.17
comprising 10.17
compromise 10.17
compromised 10.17
compromiser 10.17
compromising 10.17
compulsion 17.6
compulsive 17.6
compulsory 6.1
compunction 17.8
computation 3.13
compute 18.14
computed 18.14
computer 18.14
computer-aided 3.4
computer-assisted 9.11
computerization 3.13
computerize 10.17
computerized 10.17
computerizing 10.17
computing 18.14
comradeship 9.9
con 11.8
concave 3.17
conceal 6.7
concealed 6.7
concealer 6.7
concealing 6.7
concede 6.4
conceit 6.14
conceited 6.14
conceits 6.14
conceivable 6.17
conceivably 6.1
conceive 6.17
conceived 6.17
conceives 6.17

consequence 5.8
consequent 5.8
consequential 5.8
consequentially 5.8
consequently 6.1
conservation 3.13
conservationist 9.11
conservative 9.17
conservatory 6.1
conserve 8.17
conserved 8.17
conserver 8.17
conserving 8.17
consider 9.3
considerable 16.3
considerate 17.13
consideration 3.13
consign 10.9
consigning 10.9
consignment 10.9
consist 9.11
consisted 9.11
consistent 9.11
consistently 9.11
consisting 9.11
consolation 3.13
console 12.7
consoled 12.7
consoler 12.7
consolidate 3.14
consolidation 3.13
consolidator 3.14
consoling 12.7
consort 14.15
consortia 14.15
consorting 14.15
conspiracy 6.1
conspiratorial 14.12
conspire 10.1
conspiring 10.1
constable 16.3
constabulary 1.1
Constantine 10.9
constellation 3.13
consternation 3.13
constipated 3.14
constipation 3.13
constituency 6.1
constitution 18.13
constitutional 18.13
constrain 3.9
constraint 3.9
constrict 9.2
constricted 9.2
constriction 9.2
construct 17.2

construction 17.2
constructive 17.2
Constructivism 9.18
construe 18.1
consul 11.8
consulate 17.13
consult 17.6
consultancy 6.1
consultant 17.6
consultation 3.13
consume 18.8
consumer 18.8
consumerism 9.18
consuming 18.8
consummate 3.14
consummator 3.14
consumption 17.7
contagious 3.4
contagiously 3.4
contain 3.9
containable 3.9
container 3.9
containment 3.9
contaminate 1.7
contamination 3.13
contemplate 3.14
contemplation 3.13
contemplative 9.17
contemplator 3.14
contemporary 6.1
contempt 5.7
contemptible 16.3
contend 5.8
contender 5.8
contending 5.8
content 5.8
contented 5.8
contention 5.8
contentious 5.8
contently 5.8
contentment 5.8
contest 5.11
contestable 16.3
contestant 5.11
contested 5.11
contesting 5.11
continent 5.8
continental 5.8
contingency 6.1
contingent 9.8
continuation 3.13
continue 9.8
continuity 18.1
continuous 9.8
contort 14.15
contorting 14.15

contortion 14.14
contraband 1.8
contraception 5.9
contract 1.2
contracted 1.2
contracting 1.2
contraction 1.2
contractor 1.2
contractual 1.2
contradict 9.2
contradictable 9.2
contradicted 9.2
contradiction 9.2
contradictory 9.2
contraflow 12.1
contralto 1.6
contraption 1.9
contrary 4.6, 6.1
contrast 2.13
contrasting 2.13
contrasty 2.13
contravene 6.9
contravener 6.9
contravening 6.9
contravention 5.8
contribution 18.13
contrition 9.13
contrivance 10.15
contrive 10.15
contrived 10.15
contriving 10.15
control 12.7
controllable 12.7
controlled 12.7
controller 12.7
controlling 12.7
controversial 8.13
controversy 6.1
contusion 18.12
conurbation 3.13
convalesce 5.11
convalesced 5.11
convalescence 5.11
convalescent 5.11
convection 5.2
convene 6.9
convener 6.9
convenient 6.9
convening 6.9
convention 5.8
conventional 5.8
converge 8.4
convergence 8.4
conversation 3.13
conversational 3.13
conversationalist 9.11

converse 8.12
conversely 8.12
converser 8.12
conversion 8.13
convert 8.14
converted 8.14
converter 8.14
convertible 16.3
converts 8.14
convex 5.2
convexed 5.2
convexity 5.2
convey 3.1
conveyable 3.1
conveyance 3.1
convict 9.2
convictable 9.2
convicted 9.2
conviction 9.2
convince 9.8
convincing 9.8
convivial 9.17
convoluted 18.14
convulse 17.6
convulsive 17.6
coo 18.1
Cook 16.1
cook 16.1
cooked 16.1
cooker 16.1
cookery 16.1
cookie 16.1
cooking 16.1
cool 18.7
cooler 18.7
cool-headed 5.3
cooling 18.7
coolish 18.7
coop 18.10
Cooper 18.10
cooper 18.10
cooperate 3.14
cooperation 3.13
co-opt 11.9
coordinate 3.14, 14.4
coordination 3.13
coordinator 3.14
co-owner 12.9
cop 11.9
cope 12.10
Copenhagen 3.6
copier 11.9
copilot 10.7
cop-out 11.9
copper 11.9
copperplate 3.14

Coppola 12.7
coproduction 17.2
copse 11.9
copulate 11.9
copulation 3.13
copy 11.9
copybook 16.1
copycat 1.13
copyright 10.13
copyrighted 10.13
copyrighting 10.13
copywriter 10.13
coquette 5.14
Cora 14.12
Coral 11.10
coral 11.10
cord 14.4
Cordelia 6.7
cordial 14.4
cordon 14.4
corduroy 15.1
corduroys 15.8
core 14.1
Corea 7.1
corer 14.12
co-respondent 11.8
Corfu 18.1
coriander 1.8
coring 14.12
Cork 14.3
cork 14.3
corked 14.3
corker 14.3
corking 14.3
corn 14.10
cornea 14.10
corner 14.10
cornerstone 12.9
cornet 14.10
cornflour 13.1
cornflower 13.1
cornier 14.10
corning 14.10
corny 14.10
corollary 6.1
coronary 6.1
coronation 3.13
corporate 17.13
corporation 3.13
corps 14.1
corpulent 5.8
corpuscle 16.3
corral 1.6, 2.8
corralling 2.8
corrals 2.8
correct 5.2

correctable 5.2
corrected 5.2
correcting 5.2
correction 5.2
corrective 5.2
correctly 5.2
correlate 3.14
correlation 3.13
correspond 11.8
correspondent 11.8
corresponding 11.8
corridor 14.1
corroborate 3.14
corroboration 3.13
corroborator 3.14
corrode 12.4
corroded 12.4
corroding 12.4
corrosion 12.12
corrosive 12.11
corrugated 3.14
corrupt 17.9
corruption 17.9
corsage 2.14
corset 14.13
Corsican 17.8
cortex 14.15
cortical 14.15
cortices 14.15
Cortina 6.9
cortisone 12.9
Corvette 5.14
Cos 11.16
cos 11.11, 11.16
cosh 11.12
cosmetic 5.14
cosmetically 5.14
cosmetics 5.14
cosmonaut 14.15
Cosmopolitan 11.6
cosmopolitan 11.6
cost 11.11
Costa Rica 6.3
Costello 5.6
costing 11.11
cosy 12.19
cot 11.13
cottage 11.13
cotter 11.13
cotton 11.13
couch 13.7
cough 11.4
cougher 11.4
could 16.2
couldn't 16.2
couldn't-care-less 5.11

count   13.4
countable   13.4
counted   13.4
counter   13.4
counteract   1.2
counteracted   1.2
counteracting   1.2
counterattack   1.2
counterattacker   1.2
counterattackers   1.2
counterattacking   1.2
counterattacks   1.2
counter-clockwise   10.17
counterfoil   15.3
countermand   2.10
countermander   2.10
countermanding   2.10
countermeasure   5.12
counteroffensive   5.8
counterpane   3.9
counterpart   2.16
counterpoint   15.5
counterproductive   17.2
counter-revolution   18.13
counter-revolutionary   18.13
countersign   10.9
counterweight   3.14
counting   13.4
countryside   10.4
county   13.4
coup   18.1
couple   17.9
courageous   3.4
courageously   3.4
courgette   5.14
course   14.13
coursed   14.13
Court   14.15
court   14.15
courtier   14.15
courting   14.15
court-martial   2.15
cousin   17.16
Cousteau   12.1
cove   12.17
Coventry   6.1
cover   17.15
cover-up   17.9
covetous   17.11
cow   13.1
Coward   13.1
coward   13.1

cowardice   9.11
cowardly   6.1
cowed   13.2
Cowell   13.1
cower   13.1
cowered   13.1
cowering   13.1
cowl   13.3
cowling   13.3
coworker   8.3
Cox   11.2
cox   11.2
coxswain   11.2
coy   15.1
coyer   15.1
coyote   12.14
CPU   18.1
crab   1.1
crabbed   1.1
crabby   1.1
crack   1.2
cracked   1.2
cracker   1.2
crackers   1.2
cracking   1.2
crackle   1.2
crackpot   1.2
cracks   1.2
cradle   3.4
Cradock   1.3
craft   2.5
craftsman   2.5
craftsmanship   9.9
crafty   2.5
crag   1.5
craggy   1.5
Craig   3.6
cram   1.7
crammer   1.7
cramp   1.7
crampon   1.7
cranberry   6.1
crane   3.9
crania   3.9
cranium   3.9
crank   1.8
cranky   1.8
cranny   1.8
crash   1.12
crashed   1.12
crasher   1.12
crashing   1.12
crash-land   1.8
crash-landed   1.8
crash-landing   1.8
crass   1.11

Cratchit   1.13
crate   3.14
crater   3.14
cravat   1.13
crave   3.17
craved   3.17
craving   3.17
crawl   14.8
crawled   14.8
crawler   14.8
crayon   3.1
craze   3.18
crazed   3.18
crazier   3.18
crazing   3.18
crazy   3.18
creak   6.3
creaking   6.3
creaky   6.3
cream   6.8
creamer   6.8
creamier   6.8
creaming   6.8
creamy   6.8
crease   6.11
creased   6.11
creasing   6.11
create   3.14
creation   3.13
creative   3.14
creator   3.14
creature   6.14
crèche   5.13
credibility   9.6
credible   5.3
credit   5.3
creditable   16.3
creditor   5.3
credulity   6.1
creed   6.4
creek   6.3
creep   6.10
creeper   6.10
creeping   6.10
creepy   6.10
creepy-crawly   14.8
cremate   3.14
cremation   3.13
cremator   3.14
crematoria   14.12
crematorium   14.12
crêpe   3.10, 5.9
crept   5.9
crescendo   5.8
crescent   5.11
cress   5.11

crest   5.11
crested   5.11
cresting   5.11
Cretan   6.14
Crete   6.14
cretin   5.14
crevice   5.17
crew   18.1
Crewe   18.1
crib   9.1
cribber   9.1
crick   9.2
cricked   9.2
cricket   9.2
cricking   9.2
cricks   9.2
cried   10.4
crikey   10.3
crime   10.8
Crimea   7.1
Crimean   6.1
criminal   9.7
criminology   11.6
crimp   9.7
crimper   9.7
cringe   9.8
cringing   9.8
crinkle   9.8
crinkly   9.8
cripple   9.9
crippling   9.9
crises   10.12
crisis   10.12
crisp   9.11
criteria   7.5
criterion   7.5
critic   9.14
critical   9.14
criticism   9.14
criticize   9.14
critique   6.3
croak   12.3
croaker   12.3
croaking   12.3
Croatian   3.13
crock   11.2
crocked   11.2
crockery   11.2
crocking   11.2
crocodile   10.7
crocus   12.3
Croesus   6.11
Croft   11.4
croft   11.4
Cromarty   6.1
crone   12.9

crony   12.9
crook   16.1
croon   18.9
crooned   18.9
crooner   18.9
crop   11.9
cropper   11.9
croquette   5.14
cross   11.11
cross-Channel   1.8
crossed   11.11
crosser   11.11
cross-examination   3.13
cross-examine   1.7
cross-eyed   10.4
cross-reference   5.4
cross-section   5.2
crotch   11.13
crotchety   6.1
crouch   13.7
crow   12.1
crowbar   12.2
crowd   13.2
crowd pleaser   6.19
Crowe   12.1
crowed   12.4
crowing   12.1
crown   13.4
crowned   13.4
crowning   13.4
crucifix   9.2
crucifixion   9.2
crucify   10.1
crude   18.4
cruder   18.4
cruel   18.1
Cruella De Vil   9.6
crueller   18.1
cruet   18.1
Cruise   18.19
cruise   18.19
cruiser   18.19
cruising   18.19
crumb   17.7
crumbing   17.7
crumble   17.7
crumbling   17.7
crumbly   17.7
crumpet   17.7
crumple   17.7
crunch   17.8
crunches   17.8
crunchy   17.8
crusade   3.4
crusaded   3.4
crusader   3.4

Crusades   3.4
crusading   3.4
crush   17.12
crushed   17.12
crusher   17.12
crushing   17.12
Crusoe   18.11
crust   17.11
crustacean   3.13
crusted   17.11
crusty   17.11
crutch   17.13
crux   17.2
cruzado   2.4
cry   10.1
crybaby   3.2
crying   10.1
crypt   9.9
cryptic   9.9
Crystal   9.11
crystal   9.11
crystal-clear   7.1
crystallize   10.17
crystallizing   10.17
CSA   3.1
CSE   6.1
cub   17.1
Cuba   18.2
Cuban   18.2
cubbyhole   12.7
cube   18.2
cubic   18.2
cubicle   16.3
cucumber   17.7
cud   17.3
cuddle   17.3
cuddly   17.3
cue   18.1
cuff   17.4
cuffed   17.4
cuisine   6.9
cul-de-sac   1.2
cul-de-sacs   1.2
culinary   6.1
cull   17.6
culminate   17.6
culmination   3.13
culottes   11.13
culpable   16.3
cult   17.6
cultivate   3.14
cultivated   3.14
cultivater   3.14
cultivation   3.13
cultural   16.3
culture   17.6

cumbersome 17.7
cumin 17.7
cumulative 9.17
cunning 17.8
cup 17.9
cupboard 17.1
Cupid 18.10
cuppa 17.9
cupped 17.9
curable 19.4
curb 8.2
curbed 8.2
curd 8.4
curdle 8.4
cure 19.1
cured 19.2
curer 19.4
curing 19.4
curio 12.1
curiosity 11.11
curious 19.4
curl 8.7
curled 8.7
curling 8.7
curly 8.7
curly-haired 4.2
curly-wurly 8.7
currency 6.1
currently 6.1
curricular 9.2
curriculum 17.7
curried 17.10
Curry 17.10
curry 17.10
curse 8.12
cursed 8.12
cursor 8.12
cursory 8.12
curt 8.14
curtail 3.7
curtailed 3.7
curtailer 3.7
curtailing 3.7
curtain 8.14
curvaceous 3.13
curvature 19.1
curve 8.17
curved 8.17
curving 8.17
cushy 16.4
custard 17.11
Custer 17.11
custodian 12.4
custody 6.1
custom 17.11
customary 6.1

custom-built 9.6
customize 10.17
customizing 10.17
custom-made 3.4
cut 17.13
cut-and-paste 3.11
cute 18.14
cuter 18.14
cuticle 18.14
cutlery 6.1
cut-price 10.12
cutter 17.13
cutting 17.13
cuttlefish 9.13
Cutty Sark 2.3
CV 6.1
cyanide 10.4
cybercafé 1.4
cybernetics 5.14
cyberspace 3.11
cybersquatting 11.13
cyclamen 17.8
cycle 10.3
cylindrical 16.3
cymbal 9.7
cynic 9.8
cynical 9.8
Cyril 9.10
Cyrus 10.11
cyst 9.11
cystitis 10.13
czar 2.1
Czech 5.2
Czechoslovakia 1.2
Czechs 5.2

D
D 6.1
DA 3.1
dab 1.1
dabble 1.1
dad 1.3
daddy 1.3
daffier 1.4
daffodil 9.6
daffy 1.4
daft 2.5
dagger 1.5
Dahl 2.8
dahlia 3.7
Dai 10.1
daily 3.7
dairy 4.6
Daisy 3.18
daisy 3.18

daisywheel 6.7
Dakar 1.2
Dakota 12.14
Dalai Lama 2.9
dale 3.7
Dalglish 6.13
Dali 2.8
Dallas 1.6
dallied 1.6
dally 1.6
Dalmatian 3.13
dam 1.7
dame 3.8
dames 3.8
damming 1.7
damn 1.7
damnation 3.13
damning 1.7
Damon 3.8
damp 1.7
damper 1.7
Dan 1.8
Dana 2.10
dance 2.10
dancer 2.10
dancing 2.10
dandelion 10.1
dander 1.8
dandle 1.8
dandy 1.8
Dane 3.9
danger 3.9
dangerous 17.11
dangerously 6.1
dangle 1.8
dangled 1.8
dangling 1.8
Daniel 1.8
Daniella 5.6
Danielle 5.6
dank 1.8
dankly 1.8
Danny 1.8
Dante 1.8
dapper 1.9
dapple 1.9
Dare 4.1
dare 4.1
dared 4.2
daredevil 5.17
Dar es Salaam 2.9
daring 4.6
Darjeeling 6.7
dark 2.3
darker 2.3
dark-haired 4.2

dark-skinned 9.8
darling 2.8
darn 2.10
darned 2.10
Darren 1.10
Darryl 1.10
dart 2.16
darted 2.16
darter 2.16
Darth Vader 3.4
darting 2.16
dash 1.12
dashed 1.12
dasher 1.12
dashing 1.12
data 3.14
database 3.11
date 3.14
dateless 3.14
dative 3.14
daub 14.2
daughter 14.15
daughter-in-law 14.1
daunt 14.10
daunted 14.10
daunting 14.10
Dave 3.17
Davina 6.9
Davis 3.17
Davy 3.17
Dawn 14.10
dawn 14.10
dawning 14.10
Day 3.1
day 3.1
Dayan 2.10
daytime 3.14
day-to-day 3.1
day-tripper 9.9
daze 3.18
dazed 3.18
dazing 3.18
dazzle 1.17
DC 6.1
deacon 6.3
deaconess 5.11
dead 5.3
deaden 5.3
deadline 5.3
deadlock 5.3
deadly 5.3
deadpan 5.3
deaf 5.4
deal 6.7
dealer 6.7
dealing 6.7

dealings 6.7
dealt 5.6
Dean 6.9
dean 6.9
Deanna 1.8
dear 7.1
dearly 7.4
dearth 8.16
death 5.16
debacle 2.3
debar 2.1
debarred 2.4
debarring 2.12
debase 3.11
debasement 3.11
debasing 3.11
debatable 3.14
debate 3.14
debater 3.14
debauchery 6.1
Debbie 5.1
debilitate 3.14, 9.6
debilitating 3.14
debility 9.6
debonair 4.1
debonairly 4.3
Deborah 5.1
debrief 6.5
debriefing 6.5
debt 5.14
debtor 5.14
debug 17.5
debunk 17.8
débutant(e) 2.10
decadence 5.8
decadent 5.8
decaf(f) 1.4
decaffeinated 3.14
decant 1.8
decanter 1.8
decapitate 3.14
decay 3.1
decayable 3.1
decaying 3.1
decease 6.11
deceased 6.11
deceit 6.14
deceits 6.14
deceive 6.17
deceived 6.17
deceiver 6.17
deceives 6.17
decelerate 3.14
decelerator 3.14
December 5.7
decent 6.11

decently 6.11
decentralization 3.13
decentralize 10.17
decentralizing 10.17
deception 5.9
deceptively 6.1
decibel 5.6
decide 10.4
decided 10.4
decidedly 6.1
decider 10.4
deciding 10.4
decimal 5.11
decimalization 3.13
decimate 3.14
decimator 3.14
decipher 10.5
decision 9.12
decision-making 3.3
decisive 10.12
deck 5.2
decked 5.2
decks 5.2
declaim 3.8
declaimed 3.8
declaimer 3.8
declaims 3.8
declamatory 1.7
declaration 3.13
declare 4.1
declared 4.2
declaring 4.6
declassify 1.11
declension 5.8
decline 10.9
declining 10.9
decode 12.4
decoded 12.4
decoder 12.4
decoding 12.4
decompose 12.19
decomposing 12.19
decomposition 9.13
decompression 5.13
decongestant 5.11
decontaminate 1.7
decorate 3.14
decoration 3.13
decorative 9.17
decorator 3.14
decorum 14.12
decrease 6.11
decreased 6.11
decreasing 6.11
decree 6.1
decreed 6.4

decreeing 6.1
decrescendo 5.8
decretal 6.14
decry 10.1
decrypt 9.9
decryption 9.9
dedicate 5.3
dedicated 5.3
dedication 3.13
deduce 18.11
deduct 17.2
deductible 17.2
deduction 17.2
Dee 6.1
deed 6.4
deem 6.8
deeming 6.8
deep 6.10
deepen 6.10
deeper 6.10
deep-freeze 6.19
deep-fried 10.4
deep-fry 10.1
deep-fryer 10.1
deep-rooted 18.14
deep-sea 6.1
deep-seated 6.14
deer 7.1
deerstalker 14.3
Deeside 6.11
deface 3.11
defacing 3.11
defamation 3.13
defamatory 1.7
defame 3.8
defamed 3.8
defames 3.8
default 14.8
defaulted 14.8
defaulter 14.8
defeat 6.14
defeated 6.14
defeating 6.14
defeatism 6.14
defeatist 6.14
defeats 6.14
defecate 3.14
defect 5.2, 6.5
defected 5.2
defecting 5.2
defection 5.2
defective 5.2
defector 5.2
defence 5.8
defenceless 5.8
defend 5.8

defendant 5.8
defender 5.8
defending 5.8
defensible 5.8
defensibly 5.8
defensive 5.8
defensively 5.8
defer 8.1
deference 5.4
deferential 5.8
deferentially 5.8
deferred 8.4
deferring 8.11
defers 8.18
defiance 10.1
defiant 10.1
deficiency 9.13
deficient 9.13
deficiently 9.13
deficit 9.14
defile 10.7
defiled 10.7
defiling 10.7
definable 10.9
define 10.9
defining 10.9
definition 9.13
definitive 9.17
deflate 3.14
deflated 3.14
deflation 3.13
deflationary 3.13
deflect 5.2
deflected 5.2
deflecting 5.2
deflection 5.2
deflector 5.2
deforest 11.10
deforestation 3.13
deform 14.9
deformation 3.13
deformed 14.9
deformity 14.9
defraud 14.4
defrauded 14.4
defrauder 14.4
defrauding 14.4
defray 3.1
defrayable 3.1
defraying 3.1
defrock 11.2
defrocked 11.2
defrost 11.11
defrosting 11.11
deft 5.4
defuse 18.19

defusing 18.19
defy 10.1
de Gaulle 14.8
degenerate 5.8, 17.13
degeneration 3.13
degradable 3.4
degradation 3.13
degrade 3.4
degraded 3.4
degrading 3.4
degree 6.1
dehumanize 10.17
dehumanizing 10.17
dehumidifier 10.1
dehydrated 3.14
dehydration 3.13
de-icer 10.12
deify 10.1
Deighton 3.14
deign 3.9
deindustrialization 3.13
deity 3.1
dejected 5.2
dejection 5.2
Dekker 5.2
Del 5.6
de la Mare 4.1
Delaware 4.1
delay 3.1
delayed-action 1.2
delaying 3.1
delectable 5.2
delegate 5.6, 17.13
delegation 3.13
delete 6.14
deleted 6.14
deleterious 7.5
deletes 6.14
deleting 6.14
deletion 6.13
Delhi 5.6
deli 5.6
Delia 6.7
deliberate 3.14, 17.13
deliberately 6.1
deliberation 3.13
delicacy 6.1
delicately 6.1
delicatessen 5.11
delicious 9.13
deliciously 9.13
delight 10.13
delighted 10.13
delightful 10.13
delightfully 10.13
delighting 10.13

Delilah 10.7
delimit 9.7
delineate 3.14
delineator 3.14
delinquency 6.1
deliriously 6.1
delirium 9.10
deliver 9.17
delivery 9.17
Della 5.6
delta 5.6
delude 18.4
deluding 18.4
delusion 18.12
de luxe 17.2
delve 5.6
demagogue 11.5
demand 2.10
demanding 2.10
demarcation 3.13
demean 6.9
demeaning 6.9
demeanour 6.9
demented 5.8
demerit 5.10
demigod 11.3
demilitarize 10.17
demilitarizing 10.17
demise 10.17
demisemiquaver 3.17
demister 9.11
demo 5.7
demob 11.1
demobbing 11.1
demobilization 3.13
demobilize 10.17
demobilizing 10.17
democracy 6.1
Democrat 1.13
democrat 1.13
democratic 1.13
democratically 1.13
demographic 1.4
demolish 11.6
demolished 11.6
demolition 9.13
demon 6.8
demonic 11.8
demonstrable 16.3
demonstrate 5.7
demonstration 3.13
demonstrator 3.14
demoralize 10.17
demoralizing 10.17
demote 12.14
demoted 12.14

demoting 12.14
demotion 12.13
demur 8.1
demure 19.1
demurely 19.3
demurred 8.4
demurring 8.11
demurs 8.18
demystify 10.1
den 5.8
denationalization 3.13
denationalize 1.12
Denbighshire 10.1
Dench 5.8
Deneuve 18.17
deniable 10.1
deniably 10.1
denial 10.1
denier 10.1
denigrate 3.14
denigrator 3.14
De Niro 7.5
Denise 6.19
Den(n)is 5.8
denomination 3.13
denominational 3.13
denominator 3.14
denote 12.14
denoted 12.14
denoting 12.14
denounce 13.4
denounced 13.4
denouncer 13.4
dens 5.8
dense 5.8
densely 5.8
denser 5.8
density 5.8
Dent 5.8
dent 5.8
dental 5.8
dentistry 6.1
denude 18.4
denuding 18.4
denunciation 3.13
deny 10.1
depart 2.16
departed 2.16
departer 2.16
departing 2.16
department 2.16
departmental 5.8
departmentally 5.8
departure 2.16
depend 5.8
dependable 5.8

dependant 5.8
dependence 5.8
dependency 5.8
dependent 5.8
depending 5.8
depict 9.2
depicted 9.2
depicter 9.2
depiction 9.2
depilatory 9.6
deplete 6.14
depleted 6.14
depletes 6.14
depleting 6.14
depletion 6.13
deplorable 14.12
deplore 14.1
deploring 14.12
deploy 15.1
deployable 15.1
deployed 15.2
deploying 15.1
deployment 15.4
deploys 15.8
depopulate 11.9
depopulation 3.13
deport 14.15
deportation 3.13
deporting 14.15
deportment 14.15
depose 12.19
deposing 12.19
deposit 11.16
deposition 9.13
Depp 5.9
depravation 3.13
depraved 3.17
depravity 1.16
deprecate 3.14
deprecating 3.14
deprecation 3.13
deprecator 3.14
depreciate 3.14
depreciating 3.14
depreciation 3.13
depreciator 3.14
depress 5.11
depressed 5.11
depressing 5.11
depression 5.13
depressive 5.11
depressively 5.11
deprivation 3.13
deprive 10.15
deprived 10.15
depriving 10.15

deputation 3.13
depute 18.14
deputed 18.14
deputing 18.14
deputize 10.17
deputizing 10.17
deputy 6.1
derail 3.7
derailed 3.7
derailer 3.7
derailing 3.7
derailment 3.7
deranged 3.9
Derby 2.2
derby 2.2
Derbyshire 10.1
deregulate 3.14
deregulation 3.13
deregulator 3.14
Derek 5.10
derelict 9.2
dereliction 9.2
deride 10.4
derided 10.4
deriding 10.4
derision 9.12
derisive 10.12
derivation 3.13
derivative 9.17
derive 10.15
derived 10.15
deriving 10.15
dermatitis 10.13
dermatologist 11.6
dermatology 11.6
derogatory 6.1
derrick 5.10
Derry 5.10
derv 8.17
desalination 3.13
descend 5.8
descender 5.8
descending 5.8
descent 5.8
describe 10.2
description 9.9
descry 10.1
Desdemona 12.9
desecrate 3.14
desecrater 3.14
desecration 3.13
desegregation 3.13
desert 8.14
deserted 8.14
deserter 8.14
desertion 8.13

deserts 8.14
deserve 8.17
deserved 8.17
deserving 8.17
design 10.9
designate 3.14
designation 3.13
designator 3.14
designer 10.9
designing 10.9
desirable 10.1
desire 10.1
desiring 10.1
desirous 10.11
desist 9.11
desisted 9.11
desisting 9.11
desk 5.11
desolate 17.13
desolation 3.13
despair 4.1
despaired 4.2
despairing 4.6
despairingly 4.6
desperate 17.13
desperately 6.1
desperation 3.13
despicable 9.2
despise 10.17
despiser 10.17
despising 10.17
despite 10.13
despondency 6.1
despondent 11.8
despotic 11.13
despotism 9.18
dessert 8.14
desserts 8.14
destabilize 10.17
destabilizing 10.17
destination 3.13
destine 5.11
destiny 6.1
destitute 18.14
destroy 15.1
destroyed 15.2
destroyer 15.1
destroying 15.1
destroys 15.8
destruction 17.2
destructive 17.2
desultory 6.1
detach 1.13
detachable 16.3
detached 1.13
detaching 1.13

detachment 1.13
detail 6.14
detain 3.9
detainee 6.1
detainment 3.9
detect 5.2
detectable 5.2
detected 5.2
detecting 5.2
detection 5.2
detective 5.2
detector 5.2
détente 11.8
detention 5.8
deter 8.1
detergent 8.4
deteriorate 3.14
deterioration 3.13
determination 3.13
determine 8.8
deterred 8.4
deterrent 5.10
deterring 8.11
deters 8.18
detest 5.11
detested 5.11
detesting 5.11
dethrone 12.9
dethroning 12.9
detonate 3.14
detonation 3.13
detonator 3.14
detoxification 3.13
detract 1.2
detracted 1.2
detracting 1.2
detractor 1.2
detriment 5.8
detrimental 5.8
detrimentally 5.8
Detroit 15.7
Dettol® 5.14
Dettori 14.12
deuce 18.11
de Valera 4.6
devaluation 3.13
devastate 3.14
devastating 3.14
devastation 3.13
devastator 3.14
development 5.8
deviate 6.17
deviation 3.13
device 10.12
devil 5.17
devil-may-care 4.1

devious   6.17
devise   10.17
deviser   10.17
devising   10.17
devoid   15.2
devolution   18.13
devolve   11.6
devolved   11.6
Devon   5.17
devote   12.14
devoted   12.14
devotee   6.1
devoting   12.14
devotion   12.13
devotional   12.13
devour   13.1
devoured   13.1
devouring   13.1
devout   13.7
dew   18.1
dewy-eyed   10.4
dexterity   5.10
Dhaka   1.2
Di   10.1
diabetic   5.14
diabetics   5.14
diadem   5.7
diagnose   12.19
diagnoses   12.11
diagnosing   12.19
diagnosis   12.11
diagnostic   11.11
diagonal   1.5
diagram   1.7
dial   10.1
dialect   5.2
dialectic   5.2
dialogue   11.5
dialysis   1.6
diameter   1.7
diametrically   6.1
Diana   1.8
Dian(n)e   1.8
diaper   10.10
diaphanous   17.11
diaphragm   1.7
diarrhoea   7.1
diary   10.1
diatribe   10.2
dice   10.12
diced   10.12
dicer   10.12
dicey   10.12
dichotomy   11.13
dicing   10.12
Dick   9.2

dicky   9.2
dictate   3.14
dictation   3.13
dictator   3.14
dictatorial   14.12
dictatorship   9.9
diction   9.2
dictionary   6.1
did   9.3
didactic   1.2
diddle   9.3
die   10.1
Dieppe   5.9
dies   10.17
diesel   6.19
diet   10.1
dietary   10.1
dieter   10.1
dietician   9.13
differ   9.4
differed   9.4
differential   5.8
differentiate   3.14
differentiator   3.14
differently   6.1
difficulty   6.1
diffidence   5.8
diffident   5.8
diffuse   18.11, 18.19
diffusing   18.19
dig   9.5
digest   5.11
digested   5.11
digestible   16.3
digesting   5.11
digestion   5.11
digestive   5.11
digger   9.5
digit   9.3
digital   16.3
digitally   6.1
dignified   9.5
dignify   9.5
dignitary   6.1
digress   5.11
digressed   5.11
digression   5.13
digs   9.5
dilapidated   3.14
dilapidation   3.13
dilate   3.14
dilation   3.13
dilator   3.14
dilatory   9.6
dilemma   5.7
dilettante   1.8

diligence   5.8
diligent   5.8
dill   9.6
dilly-dallied   1.6
dilly-dally   1.6
dilute   18.14
diluted   18.14
diluting   18.14
dilution   18.13
dim   9.7
dime   10.8
dimension   5.8
dimensioned   5.8
diminish   9.8
diminished   9.8
diminishing   9.8
diminuendo   5.8
diminutive   9.17
dimly   9.7
dimmed   9.7
dimmer   9.7
dimming   9.7
dimple   9.7
din   9.8
Dinah   10.9
dine   10.9
diner   10.9
ding-dong   11.8
dinghy   9.8
dingo   9.8
dingy   9.8
dining   10.9
dinner   9.8
dinosaur   14.1
dint   9.8
Dionne   11.8
Diouf   18.5
dip   9.9
DipEd   5.3
diphtheria   7.5
diploma   12.8
diplomacy   6.1
diplomat   1.13
diplomatic   1.13
dipper   9.9
dippy   9.9
dipsomaniac   3.9
dipstick   9.9
diptych   9.9
dire   10.1
direct   5.2
directed   5.2
directing   5.2
direction   5.2
directive   5.2
directly   5.2

director 5.2
directorate 3.14
directorship 9.9
directory 5.2
direr 10.1
dirge 8.4
Dirk 8.3
dirk 8.3
dirking 8.3
dirt 8.14
dirt-cheap 6.10
dirty 8.14
disability 9.6
disable 3.2
disabled 3.2
disabuse 18.19
disabusing 18.19
disaffected 5.2
disaffection 5.2
disagree 6.1
disagreeable 6.1
disagreed 6.4
disallow 13.1
disallowed 13.2
disappear 7.1
disappearance 7.5
disappearing 7.5
disappoint 15.5
disappointed 15.5
disappointment 15.5
disapproval 18.17
disapprove 18.17
disapproved 18.17
disapproving 18.17
disarm 2.9
disarmed 2.9
disarmer 2.9
disarmers 2.9
disarming 2.9
disarms 2.9
disarray 3.1
disaster 2.13
disband 1.8
disbanded 1.8
disbander 1.8
disbanding 1.8
disbelief 6.5
disbelieve 6.17
disbelieved 6.17
disbeliever 6.17
disbelieves 6.17
disburse 8.12
disbursed 8.12
disburser 8.12
disc 9.11
discard 2.4

discarded 2.4
discarder 2.4
discern 8.9
discerned 8.9
discernible 8.9
discerning 8.9
discernment 8.9
discharge 2.4
discharger 2.4
disciple 10.10
disciplinarian 4.6
disciplinary 6.1
discipline 9.8
disciplined 9.8
disciplining 9.8
disclaim 3.8
disclaimed 3.8
disclaimer 3.8
disclaims 3.8
disclose 12.19
disclosing 12.19
disclosure 12.12
disco 9.11
discolour 17.6
discomfiture 19.1
discommode 12.4
discommoded 12.4
discommoding 12.4
discompose 12.19
discomposing 12.19
disconcert 8.14
disconcerted 8.14
disconcerts 8.14
disconnect 5.2
disconnected 5.2
disconnecting 5.2
disconsolate 17.13
discontent 5.8
discontented 5.8
discontinue 9.8
discontinuous 9.8
discordant 14.4
discotheque 5.2
discotheques 5.2
discount 13.4
discounted 13.4
discounter 13.4
discounting 13.4
discourse 14.13
discoursed 14.13
discover 17.15
discovery 17.15
discredit 5.3
discreet 6.14
discreetly 6.14
discrepancy 6.1

discrete 6.14
discretion 5.13
discretionary 5.13
discriminate 9.7
discriminating 9.7
discrimination 3.13
discriminatory 6.1
discursive 8.12
discus 9.11
discuss 17.11
discussed 17.11
discussion 17.12
disdain 3.9
disdained 3.9
disdainful 3.9
disdainfully 3.9
diseased 6.19
disembark 2.3
disembarker 2.3
disembarking 2.3
disembodied 11.3
disenfranchise 10.17
disenfranchising 10.17
disengage 3.4
disengaged 3.4
disengaging 3.4
disentangle 1.8
disentangled 1.8
disfavour 3.17
disfavouring 3.17
disfigure 9.5
disfigurement 9.5
disgrace 3.11
disgraceful 3.11
disgracefully 3.11
disgracing 3.11
disguise 10.17
disguised 10.17
disguiser 10.17
disguising 10.17
disgust 17.11
disgusted 17.11
disgusting 17.11
dish 9.13
disheartening 2.16
dishing 9.13
dishonour 11.8
dishwasher 11.12
dishwater 14.15
dishy 9.13
disillusion 18.12
disincentive 5.8
disinclination 3.13
disinclined 10.9
disinfect 5.2
disinfectant 5.2

disinfected 5.2
disinfecting 5.2
disinformation 3.13
disingenuous 5.8
disinherit 5.10
disintegrate 3.14
disintegration 3.13
disintegrator 3.14
disjointed 15.5
disk 9.11
diskette 5.14
dislike 10.3
disliking 10.3
dislocate 3.14
dislocation 3.13
dislodge 11.3
disloyal 15.1
disloyally 15.1
disloyalty 15.1
dismal 9.18
dismay 3.1
dismaying 3.1
dismember 5.7
dismiss 9.11
dismissal 9.11
dismissed 9.11
dismount 13.4
dismounted 13.4
dismounting 13.4
disobedience 5.8
disobedient 6.4
disobey 3.1
disobeying 3.1
disorder 14.4
disordered 14.4
disorderly 6.1
disorganization 3.13
disorganized 10.17
disorient 5.8
disorientate 3.14
disorientation 3.13
disown 12.9
disowning 12.9
disparage 1.10
disparity 1.10
dispassionate 1.12
dispatch 1.13
dispatched 1.13
dispatcher 1.13
dispatching 1.13
dispel 5.6
dispelled 5.6
dispelling 5.6
dispensable 16.3
dispensary 5.8
dispensation 3.13

dispense 5.8
dispenser 5.8
dispersal 8.12
disperse 8.12
dispersed 8.12
disperser 8.12
displace 3.11
displacement 3.11
displacing 3.11
display 3.1
displaying 3.1
displeased 6.19
displeasing 6.19
displeasure 5.12
disposable 16.3
dispose 12.19
disposed 12.19
disposer 12.19
disposing 12.19
disposition 9.13
dispossess 5.11
dispossessed 5.11
disproportionate 17.13
disprovable 18.17
disprove 18.17
disproved 18.17
disproven 12.17
disproving 18.17
disputable 18.14
dispute 18.14
disputed 18.14
disputer 18.14
disputing 18.14
disqualification 3.13
disqualified 11.6
disqualify 11.6
disquiet 10.1
Disraeli 3.7
disregard 2.4
disregarded 2.4
disregarder 2.4
disrepair 4.1
disrepairing 4.6
disreputable 16.3
disrepute 18.14
disrespect 5.2
disrespectable 5.2
disrespected 5.2
disrespectful 5.2
disrespecting 5.2
disrobe 12.2
disrupt 17.9
disruption 17.9
dissatisfaction 1.2
dissatisfied 10.4
dissect 5.2

dissected 5.2
dissecting 5.2
dissemble 5.7
disseminate 3.14
disseminator 3.14
dissension 5.8
dissent 5.8
dissenter 5.8
dissenting 5.8
dissertation 3.13
dissident 5.8
dissimilarity 1.10
dissipate 9.11
dissipation 3.13
dissociate 3.14
dissoluble 11.6
dissolute 18.14
dissolutely 18.14
dissolve 11.6
dissolved 11.6
dissuade 3.4
dissuaded 3.4
dissuading 3.4
distance 9.11
distant 9.11
distantly 9.11
distaste 3.11
distasteful 3.11
distastefully 6.1
distend 5.8
distending 5.8
distil 9.6
distilled 9.6
distiller 9.6
distillery 9.6
distilling 9.6
distinct 9.8
distinction 9.8
distinguish 9.8
distort 14.15
distorted 14.15
distorting 14.15
distortion 14.14
distract 1.2
distracted 1.2
distracting 1.2
distraction 1.2
distraught 14.15
distress 5.11
distressed 5.11
distressing 5.11
distribution 18.13
distrust 17.11
distrusted 17.11
distrustful 17.11
distrusting 17.11

disturb 8.2
disturbed 8.2
disunity 18.9
disuse 18.11
ditch 9.14
dither 9.15
dithering 9.15
dittany 9.14
ditty 9.14
divan 1.8
dive 10.15
dived 10.15
diver 10.15
diverge 8.4
divergence 8.4
divergent 8.4
diverse 8.12
diversification 3.13
diversify 10.1
diversion 8.13
diversity 6.1
divert 8.14
diverted 8.14
diverts 8.14
divest 5.11
divested 5.11
divesting 5.11
divide 10.4
divided 10.4
dividend 5.8
dividing 10.4
divine 10.9
diviner 10.9
diving 10.15
divining 10.9
divinity 9.8
divisible 9.18
division 9.12
divisive 10.12
divorce 14.13
divorced 14.13
divorcee 6.1
divulge 17.6
DIY 10.1
dizzier 9.18
dizzily 9.18
dizzy 9.18
DJ 6.4
Djakarta 2.16
Djibouti 18.14
DNA 3.1
do 18.1
dobbin 11.1
doc 11.2
dock 11.2
docked 11.2

docker 11.2
docking 11.2
doctorate 17.13
doctrinaire 4.1
doctrinal 10.9
document 5.8
documentary 5.8
documentation 3.13
docusoap 12.10
Dodd 11.3
dodder 11.3
doddle 11.3
dodge 11.3
Dodger 11.3
dodger 11.3
dodgy 11.3
DOE 6.1
doe 12.1
doe-eyed 10.4
does 17.16
doff 11.4
doffer 11.4
dog 11.5
dogs 11.5
doggerel 16.3
doggy 11.5
dogmatic 1.13
do-gooder 16.2
dogsbody 11.3
dog-tired 10.1
do(h) 12.1
doily 15.3
doing 18.1
do-it-yourself 5.6
dole 12.7
doled 12.7
doleful 12.7
doling 12.7
doll 11.6
dollar 11.6
dollop 11.6
Dolly 11.6
dolly 11.6
Dolomites 10.13
dolt 12.7
domain 3.9
dome 12.8
domestic 5.11
domesticate 3.14
domesticator 3.14
domicile 10.7
domiciled 10.7
dominance 11.7
dominant 11.7
dominate 3.14, 11.7
domination 3.13

dominator 3.14
Dominic 9.2
Dominican 17.8
dominion 9.8
domino 12.1
Don 11.8
don 11.8
Donald 11.8
donate 3.14
Donatello 5.6
donation 3.13
Doncaster 2.13
done 17.8
Donegal 14.8
doner 11.8
donkey 11.8
Donna 11.8
donned 11.8
Donny 11.8
donor 12.9
dons 11.8
don't 12.9
doodle 18.4
doom 18.8
dooming 18.8
doom-laden 3.4
door 14.1
doorkeeper 6.10
doorman 14.9
doormat 14.9
door-to-door 14.1
doorway 14.18
dopamine 6.9
dope 12.10
doper 12.10
dop(e)y 12.10
Dora 14.12
Dorian 14.12
Doris 11.10
dorm 14.9
dormant 14.9
dormer 14.9
Dorothea 7.1
Dorothy 6.1
dorsal 14.13
Dorset 14.13
DOS 11.11
dose 12.11
doses 12.11
dosh 11.12
doss 11.11
dossed 11.11
dosser 11.11
dossier 3.1
Dot 11.13
dot 11.13

dote 12.14
doted 12.14
doting 12.14
dotty 11.13
double 17.1
double-barrelled 1.10
double-booked 16.1
double-breasted 5.11
double-check 5.2
double-checked 5.2
double-checks 5.2
double-cross 11.11
double-crossed 11.11
double-crosser 11.11
doubled 17.1
double-dealing 6.7
double-decker 5.2
double-edged 5.3
double-glazing 3.18
double-lock 11.2
double-park 2.3
double-parked 2.3
double-parking 2.3
double-quick 9.2
double whammy 1.7
doubly 17.1
doubt 13.7
doubting 13.7
doubts 13.7
Doug 17.5
Dougal 18.6
dough 12.1
Douglas-Home 18.8
dour 19.1
douse 13.6
dove 17.15
Dover 12.17
dowdy 13.2
dowel 13.1
Down 13.4
down 13.4
down-and-out 13.7
downbeat 6.14
downed 13.4
downgrade 3.4
downgraded 3.4
downgrading 3.4
downhearted 2.16
downhill 9.6
downing 13.4
download 12.4
downloaded 12.4
downloader 12.4
downloading 12.4
downsizing 10.17
downstairs 4.8

downstream 6.8
down-to-earth 8.16
downtown 13.4
downtrodden 11.3
downy 13.4
dowry 13.5
doze 12.19
dozen 17.16
dozer 12.19
dozing 12.19
dozy 12.19
drab 1.1
Drabble 1.1
draconian 12.9
Dracula 1.2
draft 2.5
drag 1.5
drag-and-drop 11.9
dragger 1.5
dragging 1.5
dragon 1.5
dragonfly 10.1
dragoon 18.9
dragooned 18.9
drain 3.9
Drake 3.3
drake 3.3
dram 1.7
drama 2.9
dramas 2.9
dramatic 1.13
dramatically 1.13
dramatist 9.11
dramatize 10.17
dramatizing 10.17
drank 1.8
drape 3.10
draper 3.10
drastic 1.11
drastically 1.11
drat 1.13
draught 2.5
draughtsman 2.5
draughty 2.5
draw 14.1
drawer 14.1
drawerful 14.5
drawers 14.20
drawl 14.8
drawled 14.8
drawler 14.8
drawn 14.10
dread 5.3
dreaded 5.3
dreadfully 6.1
dreading 5.3

dreadlock 5.3
dream 6.8
dreamer 6.8
dreamier 6.8
dreaming 6.8
dreamy 6.8
drearier 7.5
drearily 7.5
dreary 7.5
Dredd 5.3
dredge 5.3
dredged 5.3
dredger 5.3
dregs 5.5
drench 5.8
dress 5.11
dressed 5.11
dresser 5.11
dressing 5.11
dressmaker 3.3
dressmaking 3.3
dressy 5.11
Drew 18.1
drew 18.1
drib 9.1
dribble 9.1
dried 10.4
drift 9.4
drifter 9.4
drifting 9.4
drill 9.6
drilled 9.6
driller 9.6
drilling 9.6
drily 10.7
drink 9.8
drinkable 9.8
drink-driving 10.15
drinker 9.8
drinking 9.8
drip 9.9
drip-dry 10.1
dripper 9.9
drive 10.15
drivel 9.17
driven 9.17
driver 10.15
driving 10.15
drizzle 9.18
drizzling 9.18
drizzly 9.18
droll 12.7
dromedary 6.1
drone 12.9
droning 12.9
drool 18.7

drooling 18.7
droop 18.10
droopy 18.10
drop 11.9
dropout 11.9
dropper 11.9
dross 11.11
drought 13.7
drove 12.17
drover 12.17
drown 13.4
drowned 13.4
drowning 13.4
drowse 13.9
drowsiness 5.11
drowsing 13.9
drowsy 13.9
drudge 17.3
drudgery 6.1
drudging 17.3
drug 17.5
drugger 17.5
druggie 17.5
druid 18.1
drum 17.7
drummer 17.7
drumming 17.7
drunk 17.8
drunken 17.8
drupe 18.10
dry 10.1
dry-clean 6.9
dry-cleaner 6.9
dry-cleaning 6.9
dryness 10.9
DSS 5.11
DTI 10.1
DTP 6.1
DTs 6.19
dual 18.1
Duane 3.9
dub 17.1
Dubai 10.1
duchy 17.13
Duck 17.2
duck 17.2
ducked 17.2
ducker 17.2
duckling 17.2
ducks 17.2
duct 17.2
dud 17.3
dude 18.4
Dudley 17.3
due 18.1
duel 18.1

duet 5.14
duetted 5.14
duetting 5.14
duff 17.4
duffed 17.4
duffer 17.4
duffle 17.4
dug 17.5
Duggie 17.5
duke 18.3
dull 17.6
dullard 17.6
duller 17.6
dulse 17.6
duly 18.7
dumb 17.7
dumber 17.7
dumbfounded 13.4
dumbing 17.7
Dumbo 17.7
Dumfries 6.11
dummy 17.7
dump 17.7
dumper 17.7
dumping 17.7
dumps 17.7
dumpy 17.7
Dunbartonshire 10.1
Dunblane 3.9
Duncan 17.8
dunce 17.8
Dundee 6.1
dune 18.9
Dunedin 6.4
dung 17.8
dungarees 6.19
dunk 17.8
Dunkirk 8.3
Dunn 17.8
duodenal 6.9
duologue 11.5
dupe 18.10
duplicate 3.14, 17.13
duplication 3.13
duplicator 3.14
duplicitous 9.11
duplicity 9.11
du Pré 3.1
durability 9.6
durable 19.4
duration 3.13
Durban 8.2
duress 5.11
during 19.4
dusk 17.11
Düsseldorf 14.5

dust 17.11
dusted 17.11
duster 17.11
Dustin 17.11
dusting 17.11
dust-up 17.11
dusty 17.11
Dutch 17.13
dutiful 18.14
duty 18.14
duty-free 6.1
DVD 6.1
dwarf 14.5
dwarves 14.17
dwell 5.6
dwelled 5.6
dweller 5.6
dwellers 5.6
dwelling 5.6
dwelt 5.6
dwindle 9.8
dye 10.1
dyed-in-the-wool 16.3
dying 10.1
dyke 10.3
Dylan 9.6
dynamic 1.7
dynamics 1.7
dynamism 9.18
dynamite 10.13
dynamited 10.13
dynamiting 10.13
dynamo 12.1
dynastic 1.11
dynasty 6.1
dysentery 6.1
dysfunction 17.8
dysfunctional 17.8
dyslexia 5.2
dyslexic 5.2
dystrophy 6.1

E
E 6.1
each 6.14
eager 6.6
eagerly 6.6
eagerness 5.11
eagle 6.6
eagle-eyed 10.4
Eamonn 3.8
ear 7.1
earful 7.3
earl 8.7
earlobe 12.2

early 8.7
earn 8.9
earned 8.9
earner 8.9
earnest 8.9
earnestly 6.1
earning 8.9
earring 7.5
ear-splitting 9.14
earth 8.16
Eartha 8.16
earthenware 4.1
earth-shattering 1.13
ease 6.19
eased 6.19
easel 6.19
easier 6.19
easily 6.19
easiness 5.11
easing 6.19
east 6.11
Easter 6.11
easterly 6.1
easy 6.19
easy-going 12.1
eat 6.14
eaten 6.14
eater 6.14
eatery 6.1
eating 6.14
eats 6.14
eau de Cologne 12.9
eaves 6.17
ebb 5.1
ebony 6.1
e-card 6.3
eccentricity 9.11
ecclesiastic 1.11
ECG 6.1
echelon 11.8
echelons 11.8
eclair 4.1
eclectic 5.2
eclipse 9.9
ecological 11.3
ecologist 11.6
ecology 11.6
economic 11.7
economical 11.7
economically 6.1
economics 11.7
economist 9.11
economize 10.17
economizer 10.17
economizing 10.17
economy 11.8

ecoterrorist 9.11
ecstasy 6.1
ecstatic 1.13
ECT 6.1
Ecuador 14.1
ecumenical 16.3
Ed 5.3
ed 5.3
Eddie 5.3
eddy 5.3
Eden 6.4
edge 5.3
edged 5.3
edgy 5.3
edible 5.3
edification 3.13
edifice 9.11
edify 10.1
edifying 10.1
Edison 17.8
edit 5.3
edition 9.13
editor 5.3
editorial 14.12
EDP 6.1
educate 3.14
educated 3.14
education 3.13
educational 3.13
educator 3.14
Edwardian 14.4
Edwina 6.9
EEC 6.1
eel 6.7
eerie 7.5
eerier 7.5
eerily 7.5
eff 5.4
efface 3.11
effacement 3.11
effacing 3.11
effect 5.2
effected 5.2
effecting 5.2
effective 5.2
effectively 5.2
effectiveness 5.11
effectual 5.2
effeminate 17.13
effervescence 5.11
effervescent 5.11
effete 6.14
efficacious 3.13
efficacy 6.1
efficiency 6.1, 9.13
efficient 9.13

efficiently 9.13
effortless 5.11
effortlessly 6.1
effrontery 6.1
effusive 18.11
effusively 18.11
EFL 5.6
EFT 6.1
eg 6.1
egalitarian 4.6
egalitarianism 4.6
egg 5.5
eggs 5.5
egoist 9.11
egotism 9.18
egotist 9.11
egotistic 9.11
egotistical 9.11
Egyptian 9.9
eider 10.4
eiderdown 13.4
Eiger 10.6
Eigg 5.5
eight 3.14
eighteen 6.9
eighty 3.14
Eileen 6.9
Eilidh 3.7
Eindhoven 12.17
Eire 4.6
Eisenhower 13.1
either 6.15
ejaculation 3.13
eject 5.2
ejected 5.2
ejecting 5.2
ejection 5.2
ejector 5.2
eke 6.3
elaborate 1.1, 17.13
Elaine 3.9
El Alamein 3.9
elan 2.10
elapse 1.9
elastic 1.11
elasticated 3.14
elasticity 9.11
Elastoplast® 2.13
elated 3.14
elation 3.13
El Cid 9.3
elder 5.6
elderly 6.1
elect 5.2
electable 5.2
elected 5.2

electing 5.2
election 5.2
electioneering 7.5
elective 5.2
elector 5.2
electoral 5.2
electorate 17.13
Electra 5.2
electrical 16.3
electrically 6.1
electrician 9.13
electricity 9.11
electrification 3.13
electrify 10.1
electrifying 10.1
electrocardiogram 1.7
electrocardiograph 2.5
electrocute 18.14
electrocuted 18.14
electrocuting 18.14
electrocution 18.13
electrolysis 11.6
electronic 11.8
electronically 6.1
electronics 11.8
electroplated 3.14
electroshock 11.2
elegantly 6.1
elegy 6.1
element 5.8
elemental 5.8
elementally 5.8
elementary 5.8
elephantine 1.8
elevate 3.14
elevated 3.14
elevation 3.13
elevator 3.14
eleven 5.17
eleventh 5.17
elf 5.6
elfish 5.6
elicit 9.11
eligibility 9.6
eligible 5.6
eliminate 9.7
eliminating 9.7
elimination 3.13
elite 6.14
elites 6.14
elitism 6.14
elitist 6.14
elixir 9.2
Eliza 10.17
Elizabeth 5.16
elk 5.6

Ella 5.6
Ellen 5.6
Ellie 5.6
Ellington 5.6
ellipse 9.9
elliptical 16.3
Ellis 5.6
elm 5.6
elocution 18.13
elongate 3.14
elope 12.10
eloper 12.10
eloquence 5.8
eloquent 5.8
El Paso 1.11
Elsie 5.6
ELT 6.1
elucidate 3.14
elucidator 3.14
elude 18.4
eluding 18.4
elusive 18.11
elves 5.6
Elvira 7.5
Elvis 5.6
emaciated 3.14
e-mail 6.8
emanate 3.14
emanator 3.14
emancipate 3.14
emancipated 3.14
emancipation 3.13
emancipator 3.14
emasculate 3.14
emasculator 3.14
embalm 2.9
embalmed 2.9
embalmer 2.9
embalmers 2.9
embalming 2.9
embalms 2.9
embargo 2.6
embark 2.3
embarked 2.3
embarker 2.3
embarking 2.3
embarrass 1.10
embarrassed 1.10
embarrassment 5.8
embassy 6.1
embattle 1.13
embed 5.3
embedded 5.3
embedding 5.3
embellish 5.6
embezzlement 5.8

embitter 9.14
embittered 9.14
emblazon 3.18
embodiment 5.8
embody 11.3
embolden 12.7
embolism 9.18
embossed 11.11
embrace 3.11
embracing 3.11
embroidery 6.1
embroil 15.3
embryo 12.1
embryonic 11.8
emend 5.8
emendable 5.8
emendation 3.13
emending 5.8
emerald-green 6.9
emerge 8.4
emergence 8.4
emergency 8.4
emergent 8.4
emery 5.7
emetic 5.14
emetics 5.14
emigrate 3.14
emigration 3.13
émigré 3.1
émigrés 3.18
Emily 6.1
Eminem 5.7
eminence 5.8
eminently 6.1
emirate 3.14
emissary 6.1
emission 9.13
emit 9.14
Emma 5.7
Emmanuel 1.8
emoticon 11.8
emoticons 11.8
emotion 12.13
emotional 12.13
emotionally 6.1
emotive 12.14
empathize 10.17
empathizing 10.17
empathy 6.1
emphasis 9.11
emphasize 10.17
emphasizing 10.17
emphatic 1.13
emphatically 1.13, 6.1
empirical 9.10
empiricism 9.10

entertaining 3.9
entertainment 3.9
enthral 14.8
enthralled 14.8
enthralling 14.8
enthuse 18.19
enthusiasm 1.17
enthusiast 1.11
enthusiastic 1.11
enthusiastically 1.11
enthusing 18.19
entice 10.12
enticed 10.12
enticing 10.12
entire 10.1
entirely 6.1
entirety 6.1
entitle 10.13
entitlement 5.8
entity 5.8
entomological 11.3
entomologist 11.6
entomology 11.6
entourage 2.14
entrance 2.10
entrancer 2.10
entrancing 2.10
entreat 6.14
entreated 6.14
entreating 6.14
entreats 6.14
entreaty 6.14
entrepreneur 8.1
entrepreneurs 8.18
entrust 17.11
entrusted 17.11
entrusting 17.11
entrustment 17.11
entry 5.8
entryphone 12.9
entwine 10.9
entwining 10.9
enumerate 3.14
enumerator 3.14
enunciate 3.14
enunciator 3.14
envelope 12.10
enviable 16.3
enviously 6.1
environment 5.8
environmental 5.8
environmentalist 5.8
environmentally 5.8
envision 9.12
EOC 6.1
epaulette 5.14

ephemeral 16.3
Ephesus 17.11
epicentre 5.8
epicurean 6.1
epidemic 5.7
epigram 1.7
epileptic 5.9
Epiphany 9.4
episcopal 16.3
episcopalian 3.7
episode 12.4
epistle 9.11
epitaph 2.5
epitaphed 2.5
epitaphing 2.5
epithet 5.14
epitome 6.1
epitomize 10.17
epitomizer 10.17
epitomizing 10.17
epoch-making 3.3
eponymous 11.8
equable 16.3
equal 6.3
equality 11.6
equalize 10.17
equalizer 10.17
equalizing 10.17
equally 6.1
equanimity 9.7
equate 3.14
equation 3.12
equator 3.14
equatorial 14.12
equestrian 5.11
equidistant 9.11
equinox 11.2
equip 9.9
equipment 9.9
equipper 9.9
equivalent 9.17
equivocate 3.14
equivocation 3.13
equivocator 3.14
ER 2.1
era 7.5
eradicate 3.14
eradicator 3.14
erase 3.18
erased 3.18
eraser 3.18
erasing 3.18
erect 5.2
erectable 5.2
erected 5.2
erecting 5.2

erection 5.2
erg 8.6
ergonomic 11.7
ergonomics 11.7
Eric 5.10
Erica 5.10
Erie 7.5
Eriksson 17.8
Eritrea 3.1
Eritrean 3.1
ERM 5.7
ermine 8.8
Ernest 8.9
Ernie 8.9
erode 12.4
eroded 12.4
eroding 12.4
erogenous 11.3
erosion 12.12
erotic 11.13
eroticism 9.18
err 8.1
errand 5.10
errata 2.16
erratic 1.13
erred 8.4
erring 8.11
Errol 5.10
erroneous 12.9
error 5.10
errs 8.18
erudite 10.13
erudition 9.13
erupt 17.9
eruption 17.9
escalate 3.14
escalation 3.13
escalator 3.14
escalope 11.9
escapable 3.10
escapade 3.4
escape 3.10
escapee 6.1
escapologist 11.6
eschew 18.1
escort 14.15
escorting 14.15
escudo 18.4
Esher 6.13
Eskimo 12.1
esoteric 5.10
ESP 6.1
espionage 2.14
esplanade 3.4
espousal 13.9
espouse 13.9

espousing   13.9
essayist   9.11
essence   5.11
essential   5.8
essentially   5.8
EST   6.1
establishment   5.8
estate   3.14
esteem   6.8
esteeming   6.8
Estelle   5.6
Esther   5.11
estimate   3.14, 17.13
estimation   3.13
estimator   3.14
Estonia   12.9
Estonian   12.9
estranged   3.9
estuary   6.1
ET   6.1
ETA   3.1
et al   1.6
et cetera   5.14
etch   5.14
etcher   5.14
etching   5.14
eternal   8.9
eternally   8.9
eternity   8.9
ether   6.16
ethereal   7.5
ethically   6.1
Ethiopia   12.10
Ethiopian   12.10
ethnically   6.1
ethnography   11.5
ethnologist   11.6
ethnology   11.6
etiquette   5.14
Eton   6.14
Etruscan   17.11
etymological   11.3
etymology   11.6
EU   18.1
Eucharist   9.11
Eugenie   3.9
eulogize   10.17
eulogizing   10.17
eulogy   6.1
Eunice   18.9
euphemism   9.18
euphemistic   9.11
euphoria   14.12
Eurasia   3.12
Eurasian   3.12
EURATOM   1.13

eureka   6.3
Euro   19.4
euro   19.4
Eurodollar   11.6
Euroland   1.8
Euro-MP   6.1
European   6.1
Europhile   10.7
Eurosceptic   5.9
Eurostar®   2.1
Eurovision   9.12
Eurozone   12.9
euthanasia   3.18
Eva   6.17
evacuate   3.14
evacuation   3.13
evacuator   3.14
evacuee   6.1
evadable   3.4
evade   3.4
evaded   3.4
evading   3.4
evaluate   3.14
evaluation   3.13
evaluator   3.14
Evan   5.17
evangelical   16.3
evangelism   9.18
evangelist   9.11
evangelize   10.17
evangelizing   10.17
evaporate   3.14
evaporation   3.13
evaporator   3.14
evasion   3.12
evasive   3.11
Eve   6.17
eve   6.17
even   6.17
even-handed   1.8
evenly   6.1
evensong   11.8
event   5.8
eventful   5.8
eventuality   1.6
eventually   6.1
ever   5.17
Everglades   3.4
evergreen   6.9
everlasting   2.13
evermore   14.1
everybody   11.3
everyday   3.1
everyone   17.8
everything   9.8
everywhere   4.1

evict   9.2
evicted   9.2
eviction   9.2
evidence   5.8
evidently   6.1
evil   6.17
evildoer   18.1
evil-looking   16.1
evil-minded   10.9
evil-smelling   5.6
evince   9.8
evincing   9.8
Evita   6.14
evocation   3.13
evocative   11.2
evoke   12.3
evoking   12.3
evolution   18.13
evolutionary   18.13
evolve   11.6
evolved   11.6
ewe   18.1
ex   5.2
exacerbate   3.14
exact   1.2
exacted   1.2
exacting   1.2
exactitude   18.4
exaggerate   3.14
exaggerated   3.14
exaggeration   3.13
exaggerator   3.14
exalt   14.8
exalted   14.8
exam   1.7
examination   3.13
examine   1.7
examinee   6.1
examiner   1.7
example   2.9
exasperate   3.14
exasperating   3.14
exasperation   3.13
exasperator   3.14
excavate   3.14
excavation   3.13
excavator   3.14
exceed   6.4
exceedingly   6.1
excel   5.6
excelled   5.6
excellence   5.8
excellency   6.1
excellent   5.8
excelling   5.6
except   5.9

exception   5.9
exceptional   16.3
exceptionally   6.1
excess   5.11
excessive   5.11
excessively   5.11
exchange   3.9
exchangeable   3.9
exchanged   3.9
exchanger   3.9
exchanging   3.9
exchequer   5.2
excise   10.17
excising   10.17
excitable   10.13
excite   10.13
excited   10.13
excitedly   6.1
excitement   10.13
exciting   10.13
exclaim   3.8
exclaimed   3.8
exclaims   3.8
exclamation   3.13
exclamatory   1.7
exclude   18.4
excluder   18.4
excluding   18.4
exclusion   18.12
exclusive   18.11
exclusively   18.11
excommunicate   3.14
excommunication   3.13
excommunicator   3.14
excrement   5.8
excrescence   5.11
excrete   6.14
excreted   6.14
excretes   6.14
excreting   6.14
excruciating   3.14
excursion   8.13
excusable   18.19
excuse   18.11, 18.19
excusing   18.19
ex-directory   5.2
execrable   16.3
executable   18.14
execute   18.14
executed   18.14
executing   18.14
execution   18.13
executive   5.2
exemplary   6.1
exemplify   10.1
exempt   5.7

exemption   5.7
exercise   10.17
exerciser   10.17
exercising   10.17
exert   8.14
exerted   8.14
exertion   8.13
exerts   8.14
exhalation   3.13
exhale   3.7
exhaled   3.7
exhaler   3.7
exhaling   3.7
exhaust   14.13
exhibit   9.1
exhibition   9.13
exhibitionist   9.11
exhilarated   3.14
exhilarating   3.14
exhort   14.15
exhortation   3.13
exhorting   14.15
exhume   18.8
exhuming   18.8
exigent   5.8
exist   9.11
existed   9.11
existence   9.11
existent   9.11
existential   5.8
existentialism   9.18
existentialist   9.11
existing   9.11
exodus   17.11
ex officio   12.1
exonerate   3.14
exonerator   3.14
exorcism   9.18
exorcist   9.11
exorcize   10.17
exorcizing   10.17
exotic   11.13
exotics   11.13
expand   1.8
expanded   1.8
expander   1.8
expanding   1.8
expanse   1.8
expansion   1.8
expat   1.13
expatriate   17.13
expect   5.2
expectancy   6.1
expectant   5.2
expectation   3.13
expected   5.2

expecting   5.2
expediency   6.1
expedient   6.4
expedite   10.13
expedited   10.13
expediting   10.13
expedition   9.13
expeditionary   9.13
expel   5.6
expelled   5.6
expelling   5.6
expendable   5.8
expenditure   19.1
expense   5.8
expensive   5.8
expensively   5.8
experience   17.8
experiment   5.10
experimental   5.8
experimentally   5.8
expertise   6.19
expertly   6.1
expiate   3.14
expiator   3.14
expire   10.1
expiring   10.1
expiry   10.1
explain   3.9
explainer   3.9
explaining   3.9
explanation   3.13
explanatory   6.1
explicable   9.2
explicit   9.11
explicitly   6.1
explode   12.4
exploded   12.4
exploder   12.4
exploding   12.4
exploit   15.7
exploitation   3.13
exploiter   15.7
exploration   3.13
exploratory   11.10
explore   14.1
explorer   14.12
exploring   14.12
explosion   12.12
explosive   12.11
exponential   5.8
export   14.15
exportation   3.13
exporter   14.15
exporting   14.15
expose   12.19
exposé   12.19

exposed 12.19
exposing 12.19
exposition 9.13
expostulate 3.14
expostulator 3.14
exposure 12.12
expound 13.4
expounded 13.4
expounder 13.4
expounding 13.4
express 5.11
expressed 5.11
expressible 5.11
expression 5.13
expressionism 9.18
expressionist 9.11
expressionless 5.11
expressive 5.11
expressively 5.11
expropriate 3.14
expropriation 3.13
expropriator 3.14
expulsion 17.6
expunge 17.8
expurgate 3.14
expurgator 3.14
exquisite 9.18
exquisitely 6.1
extant 1.8
extemporize 10.17
extemporizing 10.17
extend 5.8
extendable 5.8
extender 5.8
extending 5.8
extension 5.8
extensive 5.8
extensively 5.8
extent 5.8
exterior 7.5
exterminate 8.8
extermination 3.13
external 8.9
externally 8.9
extinct 9.8
extinction 9.8
extinguish 9.8
extirpate 3.14
extirpator 3.14
extol 12.7
extolled 12.7
extoller 12.7
extolling 12.7
extort 14.15
extorting 14.15
extortion 14.14

extortionate 14.14
extract 1.2
extracted 1.2
extracting 1.2
extraction 1.2
extracurricular 9.2
extradite 10.13
extradited 10.13
extraditing 10.13
extradition 9.13
extrajudicial 9.13
extramural 19.4
extraneous 3.9
extraordinarily 6.1
extraordinary 6.1
extrapolate 3.14
extrapolation 3.13
extrasensory 5.8
extra-time 10.8
extravaganza 1.8
extravaganzas 1.8
extreme 6.8
extremely 6.8
extricate 3.14
extrovert 8.14
extroverted 8.14
extroverts 8.14
exuberance 18.2
exude 18.4
exuding 18.4
exult 17.6
exultant 17.6
eye 10.1
eyebrow 10.2
eye-catching 1.13
eyeful 10.5
eyeglasses 2.13
eyelet 10.7
eyeliner 10.9
eyewitness 9.14
Eyre 4.1
eyrie 7.5

F
F 5.4
FA 3.1
fab 1.1
fable 3.2
fabled 3.2
fabricate 3.14
fabricator 3.14
fabulous 17.11
fabulously 6.1
façade 2.4
face 3.11

faceless 3.11
face-saving 3.17
facet 1.11
facetious 6.13
face-to-face 3.11
facial 3.13
facilitate 9.6
facility 9.6
facing 3.11
facsimile 6.1
fact 1.2
fact-finding 10.9
faction 1.2
factor 1.2
factory 1.2
factual 1.2
faculty 6.1
fad 1.3
fade 3.4
faded 3.4
fading 3.4
faeces 6.11
faff 1.4
fag 1.5
faggot 1.5
Fagin 3.6
fa(h) 2.1
Fahrenheit 10.13
fail 3.7
failed 3.7
failer 3.7
failing 3.7
failings 3.7
faint 3.9
fainted 3.9
faint-hearted 2.16
faintly 3.9
fair 4.1
fairer 4.6
fair-haired 4.2
fairly 4.3
fair-minded 10.9
fairness 4.5
fairway 4.7
fairy 4.6
fairytale 3.7
fait accompli 6.1
Faith 3.16
faith 3.16
faithfully 6.1
fake 3.3
faked 3.3
faker 3.3
faking 3.3
falcon 14.8
falconry 6.1

fall 14.8
fallacious 3.13
fallacy 6.1
faller 14.8
fallibility 9.6
fallible 16.3
fallow 1.6
false 14.8
falsetto 5.14
falsify 10.1
falter 14.8
fame 3.8
famed 3.8
familiar 9.6
familiarity 1.10
familiarize 10.17
familiarizing 10.17
family 1.7
famine 1.7
famous 3.8
famously 6.1
fan 1.8
fanatic 1.13
fanatical 1.13
fanatics 1.13
fanciful 16.3
fancy 1.8
fanfare 4.1
fanfared 4.2
fanfaring 4.6
fang 1.8
fanned 1.8
fanning 1.8
Fanny 1.8
Fantasia 3.18
fantasize 10.17
fantasizing 10.17
fantastic 1.11
fantastically 1.11
fantasy 6.1
FAQ 18.1
far 2.1
Faraday 3.1
faraway 3.1
farce 2.13
farces 2.13
farcical 16.3
fare 4.1
fared 4.2
farewell 5.6
far-flung 17.8
faring 4.6
Farm 2.9
farm 2.9
farmed 2.9
farmer 2.9

farmers 2.9
farming 2.9
farms 2.9
Faro 2.12
Far(r)ah 1.10
far-reaching 6.14
farrier 1.10
Farrow 1.10
far-sighted 10.13
farther 2.17
Faruq 18.3
fascinate 1.11
fascinating 3.14
fascination 3.13
fashion 1.12
fashionable 1.12
fashioned 1.12
fashionista 6.11
fast 2.13
fasten 2.13
faster 2.13
fastidious 9.3
fasting 2.13
fat 1.13
fatal 3.14
fatalistic 9.11
fatality 1.6
fatally 6.1
fate 3.14
fated 3.14
fateful 3.14
father 2.17
fatherhood 16.2
father-in-law 14.1
fatherly 6.1
fathomable 16.3
fatigue 6.6
fatten 1.13
fatter 1.13
fatty 1.13
faucet 14.13
fault 14.8
faulted 14.8
faulty 14.8
faun 14.10
fauna 14.10
Fauntleroy 15.1
Faust 13.6
favour 3.17
favouring 3.17
favourite 9.14
favouritism 9.18
Fawlty 14.8
fawn 14.10
fawner 14.10
fawning 14.10

fax 1.2
faxed 1.2
faxing 1.2
Fay(e) 3.1
faze 3.18
fazed 3.18
fazing 3.18
FBI 10.1
fear 7.1
fearful 7.3
fearing 7.5
fearless 7.4
fearlessly 6.1
feasibility 9.6
feasible 16.3
feast 6.11
feat 6.14
feather 5.15
featherweight 3.14
feathery 5.15
feats 6.14
feature 6.14
featureless 5.11
February 6.1
feckless 5.2
Fed 5.3
fed 5.3
federal 16.3
federalism 9.18
federalist 9.11
federation 3.13
fee 6.1
feeble 6.2
feeble-minded 10.9
feed 6.4
feeder 6.4
feel 6.7
feeler 6.7
feeling 6.7
feelings 6.7
feet 6.14
feign 3.9
feint 3.9
feinted 3.9
felicitous 9.11
Felicity 9.11
felicity 9.11
feline 6.7
Felixstowe 12.1
fell 5.6
felled 5.6
felling 5.6
fellow 5.6
fellowship 9.9
felon 5.6
felony 5.6

florist 11.10
floss 11.11
flossed 11.11
flosser 11.11
flotation 3.13
flounce 13.4
flounced 13.4
flounder 13.4
flour 13.1
flourish 17.10
flourishing 17.10
flout 13.7
flouting 13.7
flow 12.1
flowed 12.4
flower 13.1
flowerbed 5.3
flowered 13.1
flowering 13.1
flowerpot 11.13
flowing 12.1
flown 12.9
Floyd 15.2
flu 18.1
fluctuate 3.14
fluctuation 3.13
flue 18.1
fluency 18.1
fluent 18.1
fluently 6.1
fluff 17.4
fluffed 17.4
fluffy 17.4
fluid 18.1
fluidity 9.3
fluke 18.3
fluk(e)y 18.3
flummery 17.7
flung 17.8
flunk 17.8
flunkey 17.8
fluorescence 5.11
fluorescent 5.11
flurry 17.10
flush 17.12
flushed 17.12
flusher 17.12
flushing 17.12
fluster 17.11
flustered 17.11
flute 18.14
fluted 18.14
fluting 18.14
flutter 17.13
flux 17.2
fly 10.1

fly-by-night 10.13
fly-fishing 9.13
Flynn 9.8
flyover 12.17
flypaper 3.10
flyweight 3.14
FM 5.7
FO 12.1
foal 12.7
foaled 12.7
foaling 12.7
foam 12.8
foaming 12.8
foamy 12.8
fob 11.1
fobbing 11.1
focal 12.3
foci 10.1
focus 12.3
fodder 11.3
foe 12.1
f(o)etal 6.14
fog 11.5
fogey 12.6
foggy 11.5
foil 15.3
foist 15.6
fold 12.7
foldaway 3.1
folder 12.7
folding 12.7
foliage 9.3
folio 12.7
folk 12.3
follow 11.6
follow-up 17.9
folly 11.6
foment 5.8
fomenter 5.8
fond 11.8
Fonda 11.8
fonder 11.8
font 11.8
Fontaine 3.9
Fonteyn 3.9
Fonz 11.8
food 18.4
fool 18.7
foolhardy 2.4
fooling 18.7
foolish 18.7
foolishly 6.1
foot 16.5
footballer 14.8
footing 16.5
fop 11.9

for 14.1
forage 11.10
forbade 3.4
forbear 4.1
forbearing 4.6
forbid 9.3
forbidden 9.3
forbidding 9.3
forbore 14.1
forborne 14.10
force 14.13
forced 14.13
force-fed 5.3
force-feed 6.4
forceful 14.13
forcible 16.3
forcibly 6.1
Ford 14.4
ford 14.4
forded 14.4
fording 14.4
fore 14.1
foreboding 12.4
foreclose 12.19
foreclosing 12.19
forecourt 14.3
forefinger 9.8
forego 12.1
foregoes 12.19
foregoing 12.1
foregone 11.8
forehand 14.7
forehead 14.7
foreign 11.10
foreman 14.9
forerunner 17.8
foresaw 14.1
foresee 6.1
foreseeable 6.1
foreseeing 6.1
foreseen 6.9
foreshadow 1.3
forest 11.10
forestall 14.8
forestalled 14.8
forester 11.10
forestry 6.1
foretaste 3.11
foretell 5.6
foretelling 5.6
foretold 12.7
forever 5.17
forewarn 14.10
forewarning 14.10
forewent 5.8
forgave 3.17

forge 14.4
forgery 6.1
forget 5.14
forgetful 5.14
forget-me-not 11.13
forgettable 5.14
forgetting 5.14
forgivable 9.17
forgive 9.17
forgiven 9.17
forgiving 9.17
forgot 11.13
forgotten 11.13
fork 14.3
forked 14.3
forlorn 14.10
form 14.9
formal 14.9
formalism 9.18
formality 1.6
formalize 14.9
formally 14.9
format 14.9
formation 3.13
formative 14.9
formed 14.9
former 14.9
formerly 14.9
Formica® 10.3
formidable 16.3
formulae 6.1
formulate 3.14
formulator 3.14
fornication 3.13
forsake 3.3
forsaken 3.3
forsaking 3.3
forsook 16.1
forsooth 18.16
forswear 4.1
forswearing 4.6
forswore 14.1
forsworn 14.10
fort 14.15
forte 14.15
forth 14.16
forthcoming 17.7
forthwith 9.16
fortification 3.13
fortified 10.4
fortify 14.15
fortitude 18.4
Fort Knox 11.2
fortnightly 10.13
fortuitous 18.1
fortunate 17.13

fortunately 6.1
fortune-teller 5.6
fortune-tellers 5.6
Fort Worth 8.16
forty 14.15
forum 14.12
forward-looking 16.1
forward-thinking 9.8
fossil 11.11
fossilized 10.17
foster 11.11
fought 14.15
foul 13.3
fouling 13.3
found 13.4
foundation 3.13
founded 13.4
founder 13.4
founding 13.4
foundry 13.4
fount 13.4
fountain 13.4
four 14.1
four-figure 9.5
four-poster 12.11
foursome 14.13
fourteen 6.9
fourth 14.16
four-wheeled 6.7
fowl 13.3
fowler 13.3
fowling 13.3
Fox 11.2
fox 11.2
fox-hunting 17.8
foxy 11.2
fraction 1.2
fractional 16.3
fracture 1.2
fragile 1.3
fragility 9.6
fragment 5.8
fragrant 3.6
frail 3.7
frailer 3.7
frame 3.8
framed 3.8
framer 3.8
frames 3.8
franc 1.8
France 2.10
franchise 10.17
franchiser 10.17
Francophile 10.7
francophone 12.9
Frank 1.8

frank 1.8
Frankenstein 10.9
franker 1.8
Frankie 1.8
frankincense 5.8
franking 1.8
frankly 1.8
frantic 1.8
frantically 6.1
Fraser 3.18
fraternal 8.9
fraternally 8.9
fraternity 8.9
fraternize 10.17
fraternizer 10.17
fraternizing 10.17
fratricide 10.4
fraud 14.4
fraudulent 5.8
fraught 14.15
fray 3.1
frazzle 1.17
freak 6.3
freaking 6.3
freaky 6.3
freckle 5.2
Fred 5.3
Freda 6.4
Freddie 5.3
Frederic(k) 5.3
free 6.1
freed 6.4
free-for-all 14.8
freeholder 12.7
freeing 6.1
freeloader 12.4
freely 6.7
freemason 3.11
freer 6.1
free-range 3.9
freesia 6.12
freethinker 9.8
freeway 6.18
free-wheeling 6.7
freeze 6.19
freeze-dried 10.4
freeze-dry 10.1
freezer 6.19
freezing 6.19
freight 3.14
freighter 3.14
French 5.8
Frenchman 17.8
French-speaking 6.3
Frenchwoman 17.8
frenetic 5.14

frenetically   5.14
frequency   6.1
frequent   5.8
frequenter   5.8
frequently   6.1
fresco   5.11
fresh   5.13
freshen   5.13
fresher   5.13
freshwater   14.15
fret   5.14
fretful   5.14
fretted   5.14
fretting   5.14
Freud   15.2
friar   10.1
fricassee   6.1
friction   9.2
Friday   10.4
fridge   9.3
fridge-freezer   6.19
fried   10.4
friend   5.8
friendless   5.8
fries   10.17
Fri(e)sian   6.12
frieze   6.19
frigate   9.5
fright   10.13
frighten   10.13
frightened   10.13
frightening   10.13
frightful   10.13
frightfully   10.13
frigid   9.3
frill   9.6
frilled   9.6
frilly   9.6
fringe   9.8
Frisco   9.11
frisk   9.11
frisky   9.11
fritter   9.14
frittered   9.14
frivolity   11.6
frivolous   17.11
frizzier   9.18
frizzy   9.18
fro   12.1
frock   11.2
frog   11.5
frolic   11.6
from   11.7
frond   11.8
front   17.8
fronted   17.8

fronting   17.8
frontispiece   6.11
frontrunner   17.8
Frost   11.11
frost   11.11
frostbitten   9.14
frosting   11.11
froth   11.14
frown   13.4
frowned   13.4
frowning   13.4
froze   12.19
frozen   12.19
frugal   18.6
fruit   18.14
fruiter   18.14
fruition   9.13
fruity   18.14
frump   17.7
frumpy   17.7
frustrate   3.14
frustrated   3.14
frustrating   3.14
frustration   3.13
Fry   10.1
fry   10.1
FTP   6.1
Fudd   17.3
fuddy-duddy   17.3
fudge   17.3
fudging   17.3
fuel   18.1
fuelling   18.1
fug   17.5
fugitive   9.17
fulfil   9.6
fulfilled   9.6
fulfilling   9.6
fulfilment   9.6
full   16.3
full-blown   12.9
full-bodied   11.3
full-length   5.8
full-scale   3.7
full-term   8.8
full-time   10.8
full-timer   10.8
fully   16.3
fully-fledged   5.3
full(y)-grown   12.9
fulminate   17.6
fumble   17.7
fumbler   17.7
fumbling   17.7
fume   18.8
fumigate   3.14

fumigator   3.14
fuming   18.8
fun   17.8
function   17.8
functional   17.8
functionary   6.1
fund   17.8
fundamental   5.8
fundamentalist   5.8
fundamentally   5.8
funeral   16.3
fungal   17.8
funk   17.8
funky   17.8
fun-loving   17.15
funnel   17.8
funnily   6.1
funny   17.8
fur   8.1
furious   19.4
furiously   6.1
furl   8.7
furled   8.7
furling   8.7
furnish   8.9
furniture   19.1
furore   14.12
furred   8.4
furring   8.11
furrow   17.10
furs   8.18
furthermore   14.1
furthermost   12.11
furtive   8.14
fury   19.4
fuse   18.19
fused   18.19
fuselage   2.14
fusillade   3.4
fusing   18.19
fusion   18.12
fuss   17.11
fussed   17.11
fussy   17.11
futility   9.6
futon   11.8
futons   11.8
future   18.14
futuristic   9.11
fuzz   17.16
fuzzy   17.16
F W de Klerk   8.3

G
G   6.1
gab   1.1

gabardine 6.9
gabble 1.1
Gab(b)y 1.1
Gable 3.2
gable 3.2
gabled 3.2
Gabon 11.8
Gabonese 6.19
Gabrielle 5.6
gad 1.3
Gaels 3.7
gaff 1.4
gaffe 1.4
gaffer 1.4
gag 1.5
gaggle 1.5
gaiety 6.1
Gail 3.7
gaily 3.7
gain 3.9
gainful 3.9
gainfully 3.9
gainsaid 5.3
gainsay 3.1
gainsaying 3.1
gait 3.14
gaiter 3.14
gal 1.6
gala 2.8
galactic 1.2
galaxy 6.1
gale 3.7
Galilee 6.1
Galileo 3.1
gall 14.8
gallant 1.6
gallantry 6.1
galled 14.8
galleon 1.6
gallery 1.6
galley 1.6
Gallic 1.6
galling 14.8
gallivant 1.8
gallivanter 1.8
gallon 1.6
Galloway 3.1
galore 14.1
Galtieri 4.6
galvanize 10.17
galvanized 10.17
galvanizer 10.17
galvanizing 10.17
Galveston 17.8
Galway 14.8
Gambia 1.7

gamble 1.7
gambler 1.7
gambling 1.7
gambol 1.7
game 3.8
gamed 3.8
gamekeeper 6.10
gamely 3.8
gamer 3.8
games 3.8
gamesmanship 9.9
gamma 1.7
gammon 1.7
gammy 1.7
gamy 3.8
gander 1.8
Gandhi 1.8
gang 1.8
gangling 1.8
gangrenous 17.11
gannet 1.8
gantry 1.8
Ganymede 6.4
gap 1.9
gape 3.10
gappy 1.9
garage 1.10
garb 2.2
garble 2.2
garbled 2.2
Garda 2.4
garden 2.4
garnet 2.10
Garnett 2.10
garnish 2.10
garret 1.10
garrison 1.10
garrotte 11.13
garrotter 11.13
garrulous 17.11
Gar(r)y 1.10
garter 2.16
gas 1.11
gash 1.12
gashed 1.12
gasket 1.11
gasoline 1.11
gasometer 11.7
gasp 2.13
gassed 1.11
gassy 1.11
gastritis 10.13
gastroenteritis 10.13
gastronomic 11.7
gastronomical 11.7
gastronomy 11.8

gate 3.14
gâteau 1.13
gâteaux 1.13
gatekeeper 6.10
gather 1.14
GATT 1.13
gaudily 6.1
gaudy 14.4
gauge 3.4
gauged 3.4
gauging 3.4
Gaul 14.8
gaunt 14.10
gauze 14.20
gave 3.17
gavel 1.16
Gavin 1.16
gawk 14.3
gawked 14.3
gawker 14.3
gawking 14.3
gawky 14.3
gawp 14.11
gay 3.1
Gay(e) 3.1
Gaynor 3.9
Gaz 1.17
Gaza 2.21
gaze 3.18
gazed 3.18
gazelle 5.6
gazer 3.18
gazette 5.14
gazetteer 7.1
gazing 3.18
gazump 17.7
gazumper 17.7
gazumping 17.7
GB 6.1
GCE 6.1
GCHQ 18.1
GCSE 6.1
GDP 6.1
GDR 2.1
gear 7.1
gearing 7.5
gee 6.1
geed 6.4
gee-gee 6.4
geek 6.3
geese 6.11
geezer 6.19
gel 5.6
gelatine 6.9
gelatinous 17.11
gelding 5.6

gelignite   10.13
gelled   5.6
gelling   5.6
gem   5.7
Gemini   10.1
Gemma   5.7
gen   5.8
gender   5.8
Gene   6.9
gene   6.9
genealogy   1.6
general   16.3
generality   1.6
generalization   3.13
generalize   10.17
generalizing   10.17
generally   6.1
generate   5.8
generation   3.13
generator   3.14
generic   5.10
generosity   11.11
generously   6.1
genesis   9.11
genetic   5.14
genetically   5.14
genetics   5.14
Geneva   6.17
Genevieve   6.17
genial   6.9
geniality   1.6
genially   6.1
genie   6.9
genitive   9.17
genius   17.11
genocidal   10.4
genocide   10.4
gent   5.8
genteel   6.7
gentle   5.8
gentleman   17.8
gentlemanly   6.1
gentleness   5.11
gently   5.8
gentrification   3.13
gentry   5.8
genuflect   5.2
genuflected   5.2
genuflecting   5.2
genuine   9.8
genuinely   6.1
genus   6.9
Geoff   5.4
geographer   11.5
geographic   1.4
geographical   1.4

geography   11.5
geologic   11.3
geological   11.3
geologist   11.6
geology   11.6
geometry   11.7
geopolitics   9.2
Geordie   14.4
George   14.4
Georgette   5.14
Georgina   6.9
geothermal   8.8
Gerald   5.10
Geraldine   6.9
geranium   3.9
Gerard   5.10
gerbil   8.2
Gerda   8.4
Gere   7.1
geriatric   1.13
geriatrics   1.13
germ   8.8
Germaine   3.9
German   8.8
germane   3.9
Germanic   1.8
Germany   6.1
germinate   3.14, 8.8
germination   3.13
Gerry   5.10
Gertie   8.14
gerund   5.10
gestation   3.13
gesticulate   9.2
get   5.14
getaway   3.1
get-rich-quick   9.2
getting   5.14
get-together   5.15
Getty   5.14
Gettysburg   8.6
get-up   5.14
get-up-and-go   12.1
geyser   6.19
Ghana   2.10
Ghanaian   3.1
ghastly   2.13
Ghent   5.8
ghetto   5.14
ghost   12.11
ghosting   12.11
ghostly   12.11
ghostwriter   10.13
ghoul   18.7
ghoulish   18.7
GHQ   18.1

GI   10.1
giant   10.1
gibber   9.1
gibbet   9.1
gibbon   9.1
gibe   10.2
Gibraltar   14.8
giddiness   5.11
GIFT   9.4
gift   9.4
gifting   9.4
gig   9.5
gigabyte   10.13
gigantic   1.8
giggle   9.5
Giggs   9.5
gigolo   12.1
gigs   9.5
Gil   9.6
gild   9.6
gilding   9.6
Giles   10.7
gill   9.6
Gillian   9.6
gills   9.6
gilt   9.6
gimmick   9.7
gimmicky   6.1
gin   9.8
Gina   6.9
ginger   9.8
gingerbread   5.3
gingerly   6.1
gingivitis   10.13
Ginny   9.8
ginormous   14.9
Giotto   11.13
gipsy   9.9
giraffe   2.5
gird   8.4
girder   8.4
girdle   8.4
girl   8.7
girlie   8.7
girlish   8.7
Girls Allowed   13.2
giro   10.11
Girobank   1.8
girt   8.14
girth   8.16
Gisèle   5.6
Gish   9.13
gist   9.11
git   9.14
Gita   6.14
give   9.17

give-and-take   3.3
giveaway   3.1
given   9.17
giver   9.17
giving   9.17
gizmo   9.18
gizzard   9.18
glad   1.3
gladden   1.3
gladder   1.3
glade   3.4
gladiator   3.14
gladly   1.3
gladness   1.3
Glamis   2.9
Glamorgan   14.6
glamorize   10.17
glamorizing   10.17
glamorous   1.7
glamour   1.7
glance   2.10
glancer   2.10
glancing   2.10
gland   1.8
glare   4.1
glared   4.2
glaring   4.6
glaringly   4.6
glass   2.13
glass-blowing   12.1
glassed   2.13
glasses   2.13
glasspaper   3.10
glassy   2.13
Glastonbury   6.1
Glaswegian   6.4
glaucoma   12.8
glaze   3.18
glazed   3.18
glazer   3.18
glazier   3.18
glazing   3.18
gleam   6.8
gleaming   6.8
glean   6.9
gleaner   6.9
gleaning   6.9
glee   6.1
glen   5.8
Glenda   5.8
Glen(n)   5.8
glens   5.8
Glenys   5.8
glib   9.1
glibber   9.1
glide   10.4

glided   10.4
glider   10.4
gliding   10.4
glimmer   9.7
glint   9.8
glinting   9.8
glisten   9.11
glitch   9.14
glitter   9.14
glittered   9.14
glitz   9.14
glitzy   9.14
gloat   12.14
gloated   12.14
gloater   12.14
gloating   12.14
global   12.2
globalization   3.13
globalizations   3.13
globe   12.2
globetrotter   11.13
gloom   18.8
gloomy   18.8
Gloria   14.12
glorified   10.4
glorify   10.1
glorious   14.12
gloriously   14.12
glory   14.12
gloss   11.11
glossary   6.1
glossed   11.11
glossy   11.11
Gloucester   11.11
Gloucestershire   10.1
glove   17.15
gloved   17.15
Glover   17.15
glow   12.1
glowed   12.4
glower   13.1
glowered   13.1
glowering   13.1
glowing   12.1
glow-worm   12.18
glue   18.1
glum   17.7
glummer   17.7
glut   17.13
gluten   18.14
glutinous   18.14
glutton   17.13
gluttonous   17.11
gluttony   6.1
glycerin   9.8
glycerine   6.9

Glyn   9.8
GM   5.7
GMO   12.1
GMT   6.1
gnarled   2.8
gnash   1.12
gnashed   1.12
Gnasher   1.12
gnasher   1.12
gnashing   1.12
gnat   1.13
gnaw   14.1
gnawer   14.12
gnawing   14.12
gnome   12.8
GNP   6.1
gnu   18.1
go   12.1
Goa   12.1
goad   12.4
goaded   12.4
goading   12.4
go-ahead   5.3
goal   12.7
goalie   12.7
goalkeeper   6.10
goalkeeping   6.10
goalless   12.7
goat   12.14
gob   11.1
gobbing   11.1
gobble   11.1
gobbledygook   18.3
go-between   6.9
Gobi   12.2
goby   12.2
God   11.3
god   11.3
goddaughter   14.15
goddess   11.3
God-fearing   7.5
godforsaken   3.3
Godiva   10.15
godly   11.3
godmother   17.14
goer   12.1
goes   12.19
go-getter   5.14
goggle   11.5
goggle-eyed   10.4
going   12.1
going-away   3.1
going-over   12.17
goings-on   11.8
goitre   15.7
gold   12.7

gold-digger 9.5
golden 12.7
Goldilocks 11.2
gold-plated 3.14
golf 11.6
golly 11.6
Gomorrah 11.10
gondolier 7.1
gone 11.8
goner 11.8
gong 11.8
gonging 11.8
gonna 11.8
goo 18.1
Gooch 18.14
good 16.2
goodbye 10.1
Goodhew 18.1
good-looking 16.1
goodnight 10.13
Good Vibrations 3.13
goodwill 9.6
goody 16.2
goody-goody 16.2
gooey 18.1
goof 18.5
goon 18.9
goose 18.11
gooseberry 6.1
gopher 12.5
Gorbachev 11.4
Gordon 14.4
gore 14.1
gorge 14.4
Gorgon 14.6
gorilla 9.6
goring 14.12
Gorky 14.3
Gormenghast 2.13
gorse 14.13
gory 14.12
gosh 11.12
go-slow 12.1
gossipmonger 17.8
gossipy 6.1
got 11.13
Goth 11.14
Gothenburg 8.6
gotta 11.13
gotten 11.13
gourd 19.2
gout 13.7
govern 17.15
governess 5.11
governmental 5.8
governmentally 5.8

governorship 9.9
gown 13.4
Goya 15.1
GP 6.1
GPO 12.1
grab 1.1
Grable 3.2
Grace 3.11
grace 3.11
graceful 3.11
gracefully 3.11
graceless 3.11
gracing 3.11
gracious 3.13
graciously 6.1
gradation 3.13
grade 3.4
graded 3.4
gradient 3.4
grading 3.4
gradualism 9.18
gradually 6.1
graduate 3.14, 17.13
graduated 3.14
graduation 3.13
graft 2.5
grafter 2.5
grain 3.9
grainy 3.9
grammar 1.7
grammarian 4.6
grammatical 1.13
grammatically 1.13
gram(me) 1.7
gramophone 12.9
Grampian 1.7
gran 1.8
Granada 2.4
granary 1.8
Gran Canaria 2.12
grand 1.8
grandaddy 1.3
granddaughter 14.15
grander 1.8
grandiloquent 5.8
grandiose 12.11
grandly 1.8
grandmother 17.14
Grand Prix 6.1
Grange Hill 9.6
grandstand 1.8
granite 1.8
granny 1.8
Grant 2.10
grant 2.10
granting 2.10

grape 3.10
graph 2.5
graphed 2.5
graphic 1.4
graphically 6.1
graphics 1.4
graphing 2.5
graphology 11.6
grapnel 1.9
grapple 1.9
grasp 2.13
grass 2.13
grassed 2.13
grasses 2.13
grasshopper 11.9
grassy 2.13
grate 3.14
grateful 3.14
gratefully 6.1
grater 3.14
gratification 3.13
gratified 10.4
gratify 1.13
gratifying 10.1
grating 3.14
gratitude 1.13, 18.4
gratuitous 18.1
gratuitously 6.1
gratuity 18.1
grave 3.17
gravedigger 9.5
gravel 1.16
gravelly 6.1
gravely 3.17
graven 3.17
gravitate 3.14
gravitational 3.13
gravity 1.16
gravy 3.17
Gray 3.1
graze 3.18
grazed 3.18
grazer 3.18
grazing 3.18
Grease 6.11
grease 6.11
greased 6.11
greasing 6.11
greasy 6.11
great 3.14
Great Expectations 3.13
great-grandchild 10.7
great-granddaughter 14.15
great-grandmother 17.14

great-grandson   17.8
greatly   3.14
greatness   3.14
great-uncle   17.8
Greaves   6.17
Grecian   6.13
Greece   6.11
greed   6.4
greedier   6.4
greedily   6.4
greediness   5.11
greedy   6.4
Greek   6.3
Green   6.9
green   6.9
greener   6.9
greenery   6.9
greengrocer   12.11
greet   6.14
greeted   6.14
greeter   6.14
greeting   6.14
greets   6.14
gregarious   4.6
gremlin   5.7
Grenada   3.4
grenade   3.4
grenadier   7.1
grenadine   6.9
Grenoble   12.2
Greta   5.14
grew   18.1
Grey   3.1
grey   3.1
grey-haired   4.2
greying   3.1
grid   9.3
griddle   9.3
gridiron   10.1
grief   6.5
grief-stricken   9.2
grieve   6.17
grieved   6.17
grieves   6.17
grieving   6.17
grievously   6.1
griffin   9.4
grifter   9.4
grill   9.6
grille   9.6
grilled   9.6
griller   9.6
grilling   9.6
grim   9.7
grime   10.8
Grimes   10.8

grimly   9.7
grimmer   9.7
grimy   10.8
grin   9.8
Grinch   9.8
grind   10.9
grinder   10.9
grinding   10.9
gringo   9.8
grinned   9.8
grinner   9.8
grinning   9.8
grip   9.9
gripe   10.10
griped   10.10
griper   10.10
griping   10.10
gripper   9.9
gripping   9.9
grisly   9.18
grist   9.11
gristle   9.11
grit   9.14
gritty   9.14
grizzle   9.18
grizzling   9.18
grizzly   9.18
groan   12.9
groaner   12.9
groaning   12.9
grocer   12.11
grocery   6.1
grog   11.5
groggy   11.5
groin   15.5
Gromit   11.7
groom   18.8
grooming   18.8
groove   18.17
grooved   18.17
groover   18.17
groovy   18.17
grope   12.10
groper   12.10
gross   12.11
grossed   12.11
grosser   12.11
grossly   12.11
grotesque   5.11
grotto   11.13
grotty   11.13
grouch   13.7
ground   13.4
ground-breaking   3.3
grounded   13.4
grounder   13.4

grounding   13.4
groundless   13.4
group   18.10
groupie   18.10
grouse   13.6
groused   13.6
grout   13.7
grouting   13.7
grove   12.17
grovel   11.15
grow   12.1
grower   12.1
growing   12.1
growl   13.3
growler   13.3
growling   13.3
grown   12.9
grown-up   17.9
growth   12.16
grub   17.1
grubber   17.1
grubbily   17.1
grubby   17.1
grudge   17.3
grudging   17.3
grudgingly   6.1
gruel   18.1
gruelling   18.1
gruesome   18.11
gruesomely   6.1
gruff   17.4
gruffer   17.4
gruffly   17.4
gruffness   17.4
grumble   17.7
grumbler   17.7
grumbling   17.7
grump   17.7
grumpily   6.1
grumping   17.7
grumpy   17.7
grunge   17.8
grunt   17.8
grunted   17.8
grunter   17.8
grunting   17.8
gryphon   9.4
guacamole   12.7
Guadalajara   2.12
Guadalcanal   2.8
Guadeloupe   18.10
Guam   2.9
guarantee   6.1
guaranteed   6.4
guaranteeing   6.1
guarantor   14.1

guard 2.4
guarded 2.4
guardedly 6.1
guardianship 9.9
Guatemala 2.8
Guatemalan 2.8
guava 2.19
Gubba 17.1
guer(r)illa 9.6
guess 5.11
guessed 5.11
guest 5.11
guested 5.11
guesting 5.11
guff 17.4
guffaw 14.1
guffawing 14.12
Guggenheim 10.8
GUI 18.1
guidance 10.4
guide 10.4
guided 10.4
guideline 10.4
guiding 10.4
guild 9.6
guilder 9.6
guile 10.7
guillemot 11.13
guillotine 6.9
guillotining 6.9
guilt 9.6
guiltily 6.1
Guinea 9.8
guinea 9.8
Guinea-Bissau 13.1
Guinean 3.1
Guinevere 7.1
guise 10.17
guiser 10.17
guitar 2.1
guitarist 2.12
Gujarat 1.13
gulch 17.6
gull 17.6
gullet 17.6
gullibility 9.6
gullible 16.3
gully 17.6
gulp 17.6
gum 17.7
gumming 17.7
gummy 17.7
Gump 17.7
gumption 17.7
gun 17.8
gunge 17.8

gung-ho 12.1
gunk 17.8
Gunn 17.8
gunned 17.8
Gunnell 17.8
gunner 17.8
gunning 17.8
gunpowder 13.2
gunrunner 17.8
gunrunning 17.8
gunwale 17.8
guppy 17.9
gurgle 8.6
Gurkha 8.3
Gus 17.11
gush 17.12
gushed 17.12
gusher 17.12
gushing 17.12
gushy 17.12
gusset 17.11
gust 17.11
gusted 17.11
gusting 17.11
gusty 17.11
gut 17.13
gutter 17.13
guttersnipe 10.10
gutting 17.13
guttural 16.3
Guy 10.1
guy 10.1
Guyana 2.10
Guyanese 6.19
guzzle 17.16
Gwen 5.8
Gwenda 5.8
Gwent 5.8
Gwyn 9.8
gym 9.7
gymkhana 2.10
gymnastic 1.11
gynaecological 11.3
gynaecologist 11.6
gynaecology 11.6
gyp 9.9
gyrate 3.14
gyration 3.13
gyroscope 12.10

H
haberdashery 6.1
habit 1.1
habitable 16.3
habitat 1.13

habitation 3.13
habitual 9.14
habitually 6.1
habituate 9.14
hacienda 5.8
hack 1.2
hacked 1.2
hacker 1.2
hackers 1.2
hacking 1.2
Hackney 1.2
hackneyed 1.2
hacks 1.2
had 1.3
haddock 1.3
hadj 1.3
Hadrian 3.4
haemophilia 9.6
haemophiliac 1.2
haemophiliacs 1.2
haemorrhage 9.3
haemorrhaged 9.3
haemorrhoid 15.2
hag 1.5
haggard 1.5
haggle 1.5
hagiography 11.5
Hague 3.6
Haifa 10.5
Haig 3.6
hail 3.7
hailed 3.7
hailer 3.7
Haile Selassie 1.11
hailing 3.7
hailstone 12.9
Hair 4.1
hair 4.1
hairdryer 10.1
hairless 4.3
hairline 4.3
hairy 4.6
Haiti 3.14
Haitian 3.13
hake 3.3
Hal 1.6
halcyon days 3.18
hale 3.7
half 2.5
half-baked 3.3
half-brother 17.14
half-cock 11.2
halfed 2.5
half-hearted 2.16
half-heartedly 6.1
half-hourly 13.1

half-inch 9.8
half-inching 9.8
halfing 2.5
half-mast 2.13
half-price 10.12
half-sister 9.11
half-size 10.17
half-term 8.8
half-time 10.8
half-truth 18.16
halfway 3.1
half-witted 9.14
half-yearly 7.4
halibut 17.13
Halifax 1.2
halitosis 12.11
Hall 14.8
hall 14.8
hallow 1.6
Hallowe(')en 6.9
hallucinate 3.14
hallucination 3.13
hallucinatory 6.1
hallucinogenic 5.8
hallway 14.8
halma 1.6
halter 14.8
halterneck 5.2
halternecks 5.2
halve 2.19
halves 2.19
halving 2.19
ham 1.7
ham-fisted 9.11
hammer 1.7
hammered 1.7
hammily 1.7
hamming 1.7
hammy 1.7
hamper 1.7
hamstrung 17.8
hand 1.8
handbag 1.8
handball 14.8
Handel 1.8
handicap 1.9
handicapped 1.9
handicapper 1.9
handicapping 1.9
handicraft 2.5
handiwork 8.3
handkerchief 6.5
hand-knitted 9.14
handle 1.8
handlebars 2.21
handmade 3.4

hands-off 11.4
handsome 1.8
handsomely 6.1
hands-on 11.8
handstand 1.8
hand-to-hand 1.8
hand-to-mouth 13.8
handwriting 10.13
handwritten 9.14
handy 1.8
handyman 1.8
hang 1.8
hangar 1.8
hanger 1.8
hanger-on 11.8
hangers-on 11.8
hang-glider 10.4
hang-gliding 10.4
hang-out 13.7
hangover 12.17
Hank 1.8
hanker 1.8
hanky 1.8
hanky-panky 1.8
Hannah 1.8
Hanoi 15.1
Hants 1.8
haphazardly 6.1
hapless 1.9
happily 1.9
happiness 1.9
happy 1.9
happy-clappy 1.9
happy-go-lucky 17.2
harangue 1.8
Harare 2.12
harass 1.10
harassed 1.10
harbour 2.2
hard 2.4
hard-and-fast 2.13
hard-bitten 9.14
hardboard 2.4
hard-core 14.1
hard-drinking 9.8
hard-earned 8.9
harden 2.4
hardenable 2.4
hardened 2.4
harder 2.4
hard-faced 3.11
hard-fought 14.15
hard-headed 5.3
hard-hearted 2.16
hard-hitting 9.14
Hardie 2.4

hardliner 10.9
hard-pressed 5.11
hard-pushed 16.4
hard-wearing 4.6
hard-won 17.8
hard-working 8.3
Hardy 2.4
hardy 2.4
Hare 4.1
hare 4.1
harem 6.8
haricot 12.1
haring 4.6
hark 2.3
harked 2.3
harker 2.3
harking 2.3
Harlem 2.8
Harlow 2.8
harm 2.9
harmed 2.9
harmer 2.9
harming 2.9
harmonic 11.8
harmonica 11.8
harmonics 11.8
harmonious 12.9
harmonium 12.9
harmonization 3.13
harmonize 10.17
harmonizer 10.17
harmonizing 10.17
harmony 6.1
harms 2.9
Harold 1.10
Haroun 18.9
harp 2.11
harpoon 18.9
harpooned 18.9
harpoonist 18.9
harpsichord 14.4
harried 1.10
harrier 1.10
Harriet 1.10
Harris 1.10
Harrogate 17.13
harrow 1.10
Harry 1.10
harry 1.10
harsh 2.15
Harvey 2.19
Harvey Nicks 9.2
has 1.17
has-been 6.9
hash 1.12
hashed 1.12

hashing 1.12
hashish 6.13
Has(s)an 1.8
hassle 1.11
haste 3.11
hasten 3.11
hastily 6.1
Hastings 3.11
hasty 3.11
hat 1.13
hatch 1.13
hatched 1.13
hatcher 1.13
hatchet 1.13
hatching 1.13
hate 3.14
hateful 3.14
hater 3.14
hatless 1.13
hatter 1.13
Hattie 1.13
haughty 14.15
haul 14.8
hauled 14.8
hauler 14.8
hauling 14.8
haunch 14.10
haunt 14.16
haunted 14.10
haunting 14.10
Havana 1.8
haven 3.17
haversack 1.2
haversacks 1.2
Hawaiian 10.1
hawk 14.3
Hawke 14.3
hawked 14.3
hawker 14.3
Hawking 14.3
hawking 14.3
hawkish 14.3
Hawn 14.10
hay 3.1
hayfever 6.17
Hayley 3.7
Hay-on-Wye 10.1
hazardous 17.11
haze 3.18
hazed 3.18
Hazel 3.18
hazel 3.18
hazelnut 17.13
hazier 3.18
hazily 6.1
hazy 3.18

he 6.1
head 5.3
headboard 5.3
headed 5.3
header 5.3
headfirst 8.12
headily 5.3
heading 5.3
headline 5.3
headmaster 2.13
head-on 11.8
headquarters 14.15
headroom 5.3
heady 5.3
heal 6.7
healed 6.7
healer 6.7
healing 6.7
health 5.6
healthy 5.6
heap 6.10
heaping 6.10
hear 7.1
heard 8.4
hearer 7.5
hearing 7.5
hearse 8.12
heart 2.16
heartbreaking 3.3
heartbroken 12.3
hearten 2.16
heartening 2.16
heartfelt 5.6
hearth 2.18
heartily 6.1
heartless 2.16
heartrending 5.8
heart-to-heart 2.16
heart-warming 14.9
hearty 2.16
heat 6.14
heated 6.14
heater 6.14
Heath 6.16
heath 6.16
Heather 5.15
heather 5.15
heathery 5.15
heating 6.14
heats 6.14
heave 6.17
heaved 6.17
heaven 5.17
heavenly 6.1
heaven-sent 5.8
heaves 6.17

heavily 6.1
heaving 6.17
heavy 5.17
heavy-duty 18.14
heavy-handed 1.8
heavyweight 3.14
Hebridean 6.1
Hebrides 6.19
heck 5.2
heckle 5.2
hectic 5.2
Hector 5.2
hector 5.2
he'd 6.4
hedge 5.3
hedged 5.3
hedonism 9.18
hedonist 9.11
heed 6.4
heedless 6.4
heel 6.7
heeled 6.7
heeler 6.7
heeling 6.7
Hegel 3.6
Heidelberg 8.6
Heidi 10.4
heifer 5.4
height 10.13
heighten 10.13
heightened 10.13
heightening 10.13
heinous 3.9
heir 4.1
heiress 4.6
heist 10.12
held 5.6
Helen 5.6
heliport 14.15
hell 5.6
he'll 6.7
hellish 5.6
Hello! 12.1
hello 12.1
helloing 12.1
helm 5.6
helmet 5.6
Heloise 6.19
help 5.6
helpfully 6.1
helplessly 6.1
Helsinki 9.8
helter-skelter 5.6
hem 5.7
Hemingway 3.1
hemisphere 7.1

hemp 5.7
hen 5.8
hence 5.8
henceforth 14.16
Hendrix 9.2
henna 5.8
Henrietta 5.14
hens 5.8
hepatitis 10.13
heptagon 17.8
her 8.1
herald 5.10
heraldry 6.1
herb 8.2
herbal 8.2
herbalist 9.11
herbed 8.2
Herbert 8.2
herbicide 10.4
herbivore 14.1
herbivorous 9.17
Hercules 6.19
herd 8.4
herder 8.4
here 7.1
hereabouts 13.7
hereafter 2.5
hereby 10.1
hereditary 6.1
heredity 6.1
Herefordshire 10.1
heresy 6.1
heretic 9.2
heretical 5.14
heretics 9.2
heritage 9.3
Herman 8.8
hermaphrodite 10.13
hermetic 5.14
hermetically 5.14
hermetics 5.14
Hermione 10.1
hermit 8.8
hero 7.5
Herod 5.10
heroic 12.1
heroically 6.1
heroin 9.8
heroine 9.8
heroism 9.18
hers 8.18
herself 5.6
Hertfordshire 10.1
hertz 8.14
he's 6.19
hesitancy 6.1

hesitate 3.14
hesitation 3.13
hesitator 3.14
Hess 5.11
Hester 5.11
Heston 5.11
Hetty 5.14
heuristics 9.11
hew 18.1
hewn 18.9
hexagon 17.8
hexagonal 1.5
hey 3.1
heyday 3.4
Heyerdahl 2.8
HGV 6.1
hi 10.1
hiatus 3.14
hibernate 3.14
hibernation 3.13
hibiscus 9.11
hiccup 9.2
hick 9.2
hickory 9.2
hicks 9.2
hid 9.3
hidden 9.3
hide 10.4
hide-and-seek 6.3
hideous 9.3
hideously 6.1
hiding 10.4
hierarchical 16.3
hierarchy 2.3
hi-fi 10.1
high 10.1
highbrow 10.2
high-calorie 1.6
high-flier 10.1
high-flying 10.1
high-handed 1.8
high-heeled 6.7
Highland 10.7
Highlander 10.7
Highlands 10.7
high-level 5.17
highlight 10.7
highlighter 10.13
highly 10.7
high-minded 10.9
Highness 10.9
high-powered 13.1
high-pressure 5.13
high-profile 10.7
high-resolution 18.13
high-rise 10.17

high-speed 6.4
high-stepper 5.9
high-tech 5.2
highway 10.16
highwayman 17.8
hike 10.3
hiker 10.3
hiking 10.3
hilarious 4.6
hilariously 4.6
hilarity 1.10
Hilary 9.6
Hilda 9.6
Hill 9.6
hill 9.6
Hillary 9.6
hillbilly 9.6
hillwalker 14.3
hillwalking 14.3
hilly 9.6
hilt 9.6
him 9.7
Himalayan 3.1
himbo 9.7
himself 5.6
hind 10.9
hinder 9.8
Hindi 9.8
Hindley 9.8
hindquarters 14.15
Hinduism 9.18
Hindu Kush 16.4
Hindustani 2.10
hinge 9.8
hint 9.8
hinterland 1.8
hinting 9.8
hip 9.9
hippopotamus 17.11
hippy 9.9
Hird 8.4
hire 10.1
hired 10.1
hirer 10.1
hiring 10.1
Hirohito 6.14
Hiroshima 6.8
Hirst 8.12
his 9.18
Hispanic 1.8
Hispaniola 12.7
hiss 9.11
hissed 9.11
histogram 1.7
historian 14.12
historic 11.10

historical   11.10
historically   6.1
history   9.11
histrionic   11.8
histrionics   11.8
hit   9.14
hit-and-run   17.8
hitch   9.14
hitchhiker   10.3
hither   9.15
hitherto   18.1
hit-or-miss   9.11
hitter   9.14
HIV   6.1
hive   10.15
hived   10.15
HMG   6.1
HMI   10.1
HMS   5.11
HMSO   12.1
HNC   6.1
HND   6.1
hoard   14.4
hoarded   14.4
hoarder   14.4
hoarders   14.4
hoarding   14.4
hoarse   14.13
hoarser   14.13
hoary   14.12
hoax   12.3
hob   11.1
Hobbit   11.1
hobble   11.1
hobby   11.1
hobbyhorse   14.13
Ho Chi Minh   9.8
hock   11.2
hocked   11.2
hockey   11.2
hocking   11.2
Hockney   11.2
hocus-pocus   12.3
Hoddle   11.3
hoe   12.1
hoeing   12.1
hog   11.5
Hogmanay   3.1
Hogwarts   14.15
hoist   15.6
hokey-cokey   12.3
hold   12.7
Holder   12.7
holder   12.7
holding   12.7
hole   12.7

holed   12.7
holidaymaker   3.3
holier   12.7
holiness   5.11
holing   12.7
holistic   9.11
holler   11.6
Hollow   11.6
hollow   11.6
Holly   11.6
holly   11.6
hollyhock   11.2
Hollyoaks   12.3
Hollywood   16.2
holocaust   14.13
hologram   1.7
holster   12.7
holy   12.7
Holyhead   5.3
home   12.8
homecoming   17.7
home-grown   12.9
home-made   3.4
homeopath   1.15
homeopathic   1.15
homeopathy   6.1
homeowner   12.9
Homer   12.8
homer   12.8
homesickness   9.2
hom(e)y   12.8
homicidal   10.4
homicide   10.4
homily   6.1
homing   12.8
homogenize   10.17
homogenizer   10.17
homogenizing   10.17
homogenous   11.3
homonym   9.7
honcho   11.8
Honda   11.8
hone   12.9
honestly   6.1
honey   17.8
honeycomb   12.8
honeycombing   12.8
honeymoon   18.9
honeymooned   18.9
honeymooner   18.9
honeysuckle   17.2
Hong Kong   11.8
honing   12.9
honk   11.8
honker   11.8
honky-tonk   11.8

Honolulu   18.7
Honor   11.8
honorary   6.1
honour   11.8
hooch   18.14
hood   16.2
hoof   18.5
hook   16.1
hooked   16.1
hooker   16.1
hook(e)y   16.1
hooking   16.1
hooligan   17.8
hooliganism   9.18
hoop   18.10
hooper   18.10
hooray   3.1
hoot   18.14
hooted   18.14
hooter   18.14
hooting   18.14
Hoover®   18.17
hop   11.9
Hope   12.10
hope   12.10
hopefully   6.1
hopelessly   6.1
hoper   12.10
hopper   11.9
hopping   11.9
hops   11.9
Horace   11.10
horde   14.4
horizontally   6.1
horn   14.10
hornet   14.10
hornier   14.10
horny   14.10
horoscope   12.10
horrendous   5.8
horrendously   5.8
horrible   16.3
horribly   6.1
horrid   11.10
horrific   9.4
horrified   10.4
horrify   10.1
horrifying   10.1
horror   11.10
horror-stricken   9.2
horse   14.13
horsemanship   9.9
horsepower   13.1
hors(e)y   14.13
horticulture   17.6
hose   12.19

hosiery 6.1
hosing 12.19
hospitable 9.14
hospitably 6.1
hospital 16.3
hospitality 1.6
hospitalize 10.17
hospitalizing 10.17
host 12.11
hostility 9.6
hosting 12.11
hot 11.13
hot-blooded 17.3
hotel 5.6
hotfoot 16.5
hotheaded 5.3
hotly 11.13
hotter 11.13
hot-water 14.15
hound 13.4
hounded 13.4
hounding 13.4
hour 13.1
hourglass 2.13
hourglasses 2.13
hourly 13.1
house 13.6, 13.9
housebreaker 3.3
housebreaking 3.3
householder 12.7
housekeeper 6.10
housekeeping 6.10
housemaster 2.13
house-sitter 9.14
house-to-house 13.6
housewarming 14.9
housing 13.9
hove 12.17
hovel 11.15
hovercraft 2.5
how 13.1
Howard 13.1
however 5.17
howl 13.3
howler 13.3
howling 13.3
HP 6.1
HQ 18.1
HRT 6.1
HTML 5.6
HTTP 6.1
hub 17.1
Hubble 17.1
hubby 17.1
Huckleberry Finn 9.8
Huddersfield 6.7

huddle 17.3
hue 18.1
huff 17.4
huffed 17.4
huffy 17.4
hug 17.5
huge 18.4
hugger 17.5
Hugh 18.1
Hughes 18.19
Hughie 18.1
Hulk 17.6
hulk 17.6
Hull 17.6
hull 17.6
hullabaloo 18.1
hum 17.7
human 18.8
humane 3.9
humanely 3.9
humanism 9.18
humanistic 9.11
humanitarian 4.6
humanitarianism 4.6
humanity 1.8
humanize 10.17
humanizing 10.17
humankind 10.9
humanly 6.1
humanoid 15.2
human rights 10.13
Humberside 10.4
humble 17.7
humbler 17.7
humbling 17.7
humbly 17.7
humdinger 9.8
humdrum 17.7
Hume 18.8
humerus 18.8
humidifier 10.1
humidity 9.3
humiliate 9.6
humiliating 3.14
humiliation 3.13
humility 9.6
hummer 17.7
humming 17.7
hummingbird 8.4
hummus 17.7
humorous 18.8
humorously 6.1
humour 18.8
humourless 5.11
humourlessly 6.1
hump 17.7

humper 17.7
humping 17.7
Hun 17.8
hunch 17.8
hunches 17.8
hundredfold 12.7
hundredweight 3.14
hung 17.8
Hungarian 4.6
Hungary 6.1
hunger 17.8
hungrily 6.1
hunk 17.8
hunky 17.8
Hunt 17.8
hunt 17.8
hunted 17.8
hunter 17.8
hunting 17.8
Hurd 8.4
hurdle 8.4
hurdy-gurdy 8.4
hurl 8.7
hurled 8.7
Hurley 8.7
hurling 8.7
hurly-burly 8.7
hurrah 2.1
hurrahing 2.12
hurricane 3.9, 17.8
hurried 17.10
hurriedly 6.1
hurry 17.10
Hurst 8.12
Hurt 8.14
hurt 8.14
hurter 8.14
hurtle 8.14
hurts 8.14
husbandry 6.1
hush 17.12
hushed 17.12
husher 17.12
hushing 17.12
husk 17.11
hussar 2.1
Hussein 3.9
hussy 17.11
hustle 17.11
hustler 17.11
hustles 17.11
hut 17.13
hutch 17.13
Hutton 17.13
hyacinth 9.8
Hyde 10.4

Index

Hyderabad 2.4
hydrangea 3.9
hydrocortisone 12.9
hydroelectricity 9.11
hydrofoil 15.3
hydrogen 17.8
hydrolysis 11.6
hydroplane 3.9
hydroxide 10.4
hyena 6.9
hygienic 6.9
hygienics 6.9
hymn 9.7
hymned 9.7
hype 10.10
hyped 10.10
hyper 10.10
hyperactive 1.2
hyperbole 8.2
hypercritical 9.14
hyperinflation 3.13
hyperlink 9.8
hyperlinked 9.8
hypertension 5.8
hypertext 5.2
hyphen 10.5
hyphenate 3.14
hyping 10.10
hypnosis 12.11
hypnotic 11.13
hypnotism 9.18
hypnotist 9.11
hypnotize 10.17
hypnotizing 10.17
hypoallergenic 5.8
hypochondriac 1.2
hypochondriacs 1.2
hypocrisy 6.1
hypocrite 9.14
hypocritical 9.14
hypotenuse 18.19
hypothesis 9.11
hypothesize 10.17
hypothesizing 10.17
hypothetical 5.14
hypothetically 5.14
hysterectomy 5.2
hysteria 7.5
hysterical 5.10
hysterically 5.10
Hywel 13.1

I

I 10.1
IAEA 3.1

Iago 2.6
Ian 6.1
IBA 3.1
Iberia 7.5
Iberian 7.5
Ibiza 6.16
IBM 5.7
Ibrahim 6.8
Icarus 17.11
ice 10.12
icebreaker 3.3
ice-cold 12.7
ice-cream 6.8
iced 10.12
Icelander 1.8
icer 10.12
ice-skate 3.14
ice-skating 3.14
icicle 10.12
icing 10.12
iconoclastic 1.11
icy 10.12
ID 6.1
I'd 10.4
Idaho 12.1
idea 6.1
ideal 7.4
idealism 7.4
idealist 7.4
idealistic 9.11
idealize 7.4
ideally 7.4
identical 16.3
identification 3.13
identified 10.4
identify 10.1
Identikit® 9.14
identity 5.8
ideological 11.3
ideology 11.6
idiocy 6.1
idiomatic 1.13
idiosyncrasy 6.1
idiosyncratic 1.13
idiotic 11.13
idle 10.4
idleness 5.11
idol 10.4
idolatry 6.1
idolize 10.17
idolizer 10.17
idolizing 10.17
Idomeneo 3.1
idyll 9.3
idyllic 9.6
ie 6.1

if 9.4
IFA 3.1
iffy 9.4
ignite 10.13
ignited 10.13
igniter 10.13
igniting 10.13
ignition 9.13
ignoble 12.2
ignoramus 3.8
ignore 14.1
ignorer 14.12
ignoring 14.12
iguana 2.10
Ike 10.3
ilk 9.6
I'll 10.7
ill 9.6
ill-advised 10.17
ill-bred 5.3
ill-concealed 6.7
ill-disposed 12.19
illegal 6.6
illegality 1.6
illegally 6.6
illegitimacy 6.1
illegitimately 6.1
ill-fated 3.14
ill-founded 13.4
ill-gotten 11.13
ill-health 5.6
illiberally 6.1
illicit 9.11
ill-informed 14.9
Illinois 15.1
ill-intentioned 5.8
illiterate 17.13
illness 9.6
illogical 11.3
illogically 6.1
ill-suited 18.14
ill-timed 10.8
ill-treat 6.14
ill-treated 6.14
ill-treating 6.14
ill-treats 6.14
illuminate 18.8
illuminating 3.14
illumination 3.13
ill-use 18.11, 18.19
ill-using 18.19
illusion 18.12
illusory 6.1
illustrate 3.14
illustration 3.13
illustrator 3.14

illustrious 17.11
ILO 12.1
I'm 10.8
image 9.7
imagery 6.1
imaginable 16.3
imaginary 6.1
imagination 3.13
imaginative 9.17
imbalance 1.6
imbecile 6.7
imbibe 10.2
imbiber 10.2
imbue 18.1
Imelda 5.6
IMF 5.4
imitate 3.14
imitation 3.13
imitative 9.17
imitator 3.14
immaculate 17.13
immaterial 7.5
immature 19.1
immaturely 19.3
immaturity 19.4
immeasurable 5.12
immediacy 6.1
immediate 6.4
immediately 6.1
immemorial 14.12
immense 5.8
immensely 5.8
immensity 5.8
immerse 8.12
immersed 8.12
immerser 8.12
immersion 8.13
immigrate 3.14
immigration 3.13
imminent 5.8
immobility 9.6
immobilize 10.17
immobilizer 10.17
immobilizing 10.17
immoderate 17.13
immodest 11.3
immodestly 6.1
immodesty 6.1
immoral 11.10
immorality 1.6
immorally 6.1
immortal 14.15
immortality 1.6
immovable 18.17
immune 18.9
immunity 18.9

immunization 3.13
immunize 10.17
immunizer 10.17
immunizing 10.17
immunosuppression
  5.13
immutable 18.14
Imogen 17.8
imp 9.7
impact 1.2
impacted 1.2
impacting 1.2
impair 4.1
impaired 4.2
impairing 4.6
impale 3.7
impaled 3.7
impaler 3.7
impaling 3.7
impalings 3.7
impart 2.16
imparted 2.16
imparter 2.16
impartial 2.15
impartiality 1.6
imparting 2.16
impassable 2.13
impassioned 1.12
impassive 1.11
impassively 1.11
impeach 6.14
impeaching 6.14
impeccable 16.3
impede 6.4
impediment 5.3
impel 5.6
impelled 5.6
impelling 5.6
impending 5.8
impenetrable 16.3
impenitent 5.8
imperative 9.17
imperceptible 16.3
imperceptibly 6.1
imperfection 5.2
imperfectly 6.1
imperial 7.5
imperialism 7.5
imperialist 9.11
imperil 5.10
imperious 7.5
imperiously 7.5
impersonally 6.1
impersonate 3.14
impersonation 3.13
impersonator 3.14

impertinence 5.8
imperturbable 16.3
impetus 17.11
impinge 9.8
impish 9.7
implacable 16.3
implant 2.10
implanting 2.10
implausible 16.3
implement 5.8
implementation 3.13
implicate 3.14
implication 3.13
implicit 9.11
implied 10.4
implore 14.1
implorer 14.12
imploring 14.12
implosion 12.12
imply 10.1
impolite 10.13
impoliteness 10.13
imponderable 16.3
import 14.15
important 14.15
importantly 6.1
importation 3.13
importer 14.15
importing 14.15
impose 12.19
imposer 12.19
imposing 12.19
imposition 9.13
impossibility 9.6
impostor 11.11
impotence 5.8
impotency 6.1
impotent 5.8
impound 13.4
impounded 13.4
impounding 13.4
impractical 1.2
impracticality 1.6
imprecise 10.12
imprecisely 10.12
imprecision 9.12
impregnable 16.3
impregnate 3.14
impregnation 3.13
impresario 2.12
impress 5.11
impressed 5.11
impression 5.13
impressionable 16.3
impressionism 9.18
impressionist 9.11

impressionistic 9.11
impressive 5.11
impressively 5.11
imprint 9.8
imprinting 9.8
imprison 9.18
imprisonment 5.8
improbability 9.6
improper 11.9
improperly 11.9
impropriety 10.1
improve 18.17
improved 18.17
improvement 18.17
improvident 5.8
improving 18.17
improvisation 3.13
improvise 10.17
improviser 10.17
improvising 10.17
imprudent 18.4
impudence 5.8
impudent 5.8
impugn 18.9
impugned 18.9
impugner 18.9
impulsive 17.6
impunity 18.9
impure 19.1
impurest 19.4
impurity 19.4
impute 18.14
imputed 18.14
imputer 18.14
imputing 18.14
in 9.8
inability 9.6
inaccessibility 9.6
inaccessible 5.11
inaction 1.2
inactive 1.2
inactivity 9.17
inadequacy 6.1
inadequately 6.1
inadmissible 9.11
inadvertently 6.1
inadvisable 10.17
inalienable 16.3
inane 3.9
inanimate 17.13
inanity 1.8
inapplicable 16.3
inapt 1.9
inattention 5.8
inattentive 5.8
inaudible 16.3

inaugural 16.3
inaugurate 3.14
inauguration 3.13
inaugurator 3.14
inauspicious 9.13
inauspiciously 9.13
in-between 6.9
Inc 9.8
Inca 9.8
incandescence 5.11
incandescent 5.11
incantation 3.13
incapability 9.6
incapable 3.10
incapacitate 1.11
incapacity 1.11
incarcerate 3.14
incarceration 3.13
incarcerator 3.14
incarnate 2.10
incarnation 3.13
incendiary 6.1
incense 5.8
incentive 5.8
inception 5.9
incessant 5.11
incestuous 5.11
inch 9.8
inching 9.8
incident 5.8
incidental 5.8
incidentally 5.8
incinerate 3.14
incineration 3.13
incinerator 3.14
incision 9.12
incisive 10.12
incisor 10.17
incite 10.13
incited 10.13
incitement 10.13
inciter 10.13
inciting 10.13
incivility 9.6
inclemency 6.1
inclinable 10.9
inclination 3.13
incline 10.9
inclining 10.9
include 18.4
including 18.4
inclusive 18.11
incognito 6.14
incoherence 7.5
incoming 17.7
incommunicado 2.4

incompatibility 9.6
incompatible 16.3
incomplete 6.14
incomprehensible 5.8
incomprehensibly 5.8
incomprehension 5.8
inconceivable 6.17
inconclusive 18.11
incongruity 18.1
inconsequential 5.8
inconsequentially 5.8
inconsistent 9.11
inconsistently 9.11
inconsolable 12.7
incontestable 16.3
incontinence 5.8
incontrovertible 16.3
inconvenient 6.9
incorporate 3.14
incorporator 3.14
incorrect 5.2
incorrectly 5.2
incorrigible 16.3
incorruptible 16.3
increase 6.11
increased 6.11
increasing 6.11
increasingly 6.1
incredible 5.3
incredibly 6.1
increment 5.8
incremental 5.8
incrementally 5.8
incriminate 9.7
incriminating 9.7
incubate 3.14
incubation 3.13
incubator 3.14
inculcate 3.14
inculcator 3.14
incur 8.1
incurable 19.4
incurious 19.4
incurred 8.4
incurring 8.11
incurs 8.18
incursion 8.13
indebted 5.14
indebtedness 5.11
indecent 6.11
indecently 6.11
indecipherable 16.3
indecision 9.12
indecisive 10.12
indeed 6.4
indefatigable 16.3

indefensible 5.8
indefensibly 5.8
indefinable 10.9
indelible 16.3
indemnify 10.1
indemnity 5.7
indent 5.8
indentation 3.13
independence 5.8
independent 5.8
independently 6.1
indescribable 16.3
indestructible 17.2
indeterminate 17.13
index-linked 9.8
India 9.8
Indiana 1.8
Indianapolis 9.11
indicate 9.8
indication 3.13
indicative 9.17
indicator 3.14
indict 10.13
indictable 10.13
indicted 10.13
indicter 10.13
indicting 10.13
indictment 10.13
indie 9.8
indigenous 17.11
indigestible 16.3
indigestion 5.11
indignant 9.5
indignation 3.13
indigo 12.1
indirect 5.2
indirectly 5.2
indiscipline 9.8
indisciplined 9.8
indiscreet 6.14
indiscreetly 6.14
indiscretion 5.13
indispensable 16.3
indisposed 12.19
indisputable 18.14
indissoluble 11.6
indistinct 9.8
indistinguishable 16.3
individual 9.3
individualist 9.11
individuality 1.6
individually 6.1
indivisible 9.18
Indochina 10.9
indoctrinate 3.14
indoctrination 3.13

indoctrinator 3.14
indolent 5.8
indomitable 16.3
Indonesia 6.12
Indonesian 6.12
induce 18.11
induct 17.2
induction 17.2
inductive 17.2
indulge 17.6
industrialist 9.11
industrialize 10.17
industrializing 10.17
industrious 17.11
industry 6.1
inebriated 3.14
inedible 5.3
ineffable 16.3
ineffective 5.2
ineffectual 5.2
inefficacy 6.1
inefficiency 6.1, 9.13
inefficient 9.13
inefficiently 9.13
ineligibility 9.6
ineligible 5.6
ineluctable 17.2
inept 5.9
ineptitude 18.4
inequality 11.6
inert 8.14
inescapable 3.10
inessential 5.8
inestimable 16.3
inevitability 9.6
inevitable 16.3
inevitably 6.1
inexact 1.2
inexcusable 18.19
inexhaustible 16.3
inexorable 16.3
inexpensive 5.8
inexpensively 5.8
inexplicable 9.2
inexpressible 5.11
inexpressive 5.11
inexpressively 5.11
inextricably 6.1
infallibility 9.6
infamous 17.11
infamy 6.1
infancy 6.1
infanticide 10.4
infantile 10.7
infantry 6.1
infatuated 3.14

infatuation 3.13
infect 5.2
infected 5.2
infecting 5.2
infection 5.2
infer 8.1
inference 5.8
inferior 7.5
inferiority 11.10
infernal 8.9
inferno 8.9
inferred 8.4
inferring 8.11
infers 8.18
infertility 9.6
infest 5.11
infested 5.11
infesting 5.11
infighting 10.13
infiltrate 3.14
infiltration 3.13
infiltrator 3.14
infinite 9.14
infinitely 6.1
infinitesimal 5.11
infinitive 9.17
infinity 9.8
infirm 8.8
infirmary 6.1
infirmity 6.1
inflame 3.8
inflamed 3.8
inflames 3.8
inflammable 1.7
inflammation 3.13
inflammatory 6.1
inflatable 3.14
inflate 3.14
inflated 3.14
inflation 3.13
inflationary 3.13, 6.1
inflator 3.14
inflect 5.2
inflected 5.2
inflecting 5.2
inflexibility 9.6
inflict 9.2
inflictable 9.2
inflicted 9.2
inflicter 9.2
in-flight 10.13
influence 17.8
influential 5.8
influenza 5.8
infomercial 8.13
inform 14.9

informal 14.9
informality 1.6
informally 14.9
informant 14.9
information 3.13
informative 14.9
informed 14.9
informer 14.9
infra dig 9.5
infrared 5.3
infringe 9.8
infuriate 3.14
infuriating 3.14
infuse 18.19
infuser 18.19
infusing 18.19
infusion 18.12
ingenious 17.11
ingenuity 18.1
ingenuous 5.8
inglorious 14.12
ingrained 3.9
ingratiate 3.13
ingratiating 3.14
ingratitude 1.13
ingredient 6.4
ingrowing 12.1
inhabit 1.1
inhabited 9.3
inhalation 3.13
inhale 3.7
inhaled 3.7
inhaler 3.7
inhaling 3.7
inherent 5.10
inherit 5.10
inhibit 9.1
inhibited 9.3
inhibition 9.13
inhospitable 9.14
inhospitably 6.1
in-house 13.6
inhuman 18.8
inhumane 3.9
inhumanely 3.9
inhumanity 1.8
inhumanly 6.1
inimical 16.3
inimitable 16.3
iniquitous 9.2
iniquity 9.2
initial 9.13
initially 9.13
initiate 9.13
initiation 3.13
initiative 9.17

inject 5.2
injectable 5.2
injected 5.2
injecting 5.2
injection 5.2
injector 5.2
injudicious 9.13
injudiciously 9.13
injunction 17.8
injure 9.8
injury 6.1
ink 9.8
inked 9.8
inker 9.8
inking 9.8
inkling 9.8
inky 9.8
inlaid 3.4
inland 1.8
in lieu 18.1
inmost 12.11
inn 9.8
innate 3.14
inner 9.8
innermost 12.11
innkeeper 6.10
innocence 5.8
innocent 5.8
innovate 3.14
innovation 3.13
innovative 9.17
innovator 3.14
innuendo 5.8
innumerable 16.3
innumeracy 6.1
inoculate 3.14
inoculation 3.13
inoculator 3.14
inoffensive 5.8
inoffensively 5.8
inopportune 18.9
inordinate 14.4
inorganic 1.8
inquire 10.1
inquirer 10.1
inquiring 10.1
inquiry 10.1
Inquisition 9.13
inquisition 9.13
insalubrious 18.2
insane 3.9
insanely 3.9
insanitary 6.1
insanity 1.8
insatiable 16.3
inscribe 10.2

inscription 9.9
inscrutable 18.14
insecticide 10.4
insecure 19.1
insecurely 19.3
insecurity 19.4
insemination 3.13
insensible 5.8
insensibly 5.8
insensitivity 9.17
inseparable 5.9
insert 8.14
inserted 8.14
inserter 8.14
insertion 8.13
inserts 8.14
inshore 14.1
inside 10.4
insider 10.4
insidious 9.3
insightful 10.13
insightfully 10.13
insignificantly 6.1
insincere 7.1
insincerely 7.4
insincerity 5.10
insinuate 3.14
insinuation 3.13
insist 9.11
insisted 9.11
insistence 9.11
insistent 9.11
insistently 9.11
insisting 9.11
insolence 5.8
insolent 5.8
insoluble 11.6
insolvency 6.1
insomniac 1.2
insomniacs 1.2
inspect 5.2
inspectable 5.2
inspected 5.2
inspecting 5.2
inspection 5.2
inspector 5.2
inspiration 3.13
inspire 10.1
inspired 10.1
inspiring 10.1
instability 9.6
install 14.8
installation 3.13
installed 14.8
instantaneous 3.9
instantly 6.1

instead 5.3
instigate 3.14
instigation 3.13
instigator 3.14
instil 9.6
instilled 9.6
instilling 9.6
instilment 9.6
institute 18.14
instituted 18.14
instituting 18.14
institution 18.13
institutional 18.13
institutionalize 10.17
institutionalizing 10.17
instruct 17.2
instruction 17.2
instructive 17.2
instructor 17.2
instrument 5.8
instrumental 5.8
instrumentalist 5.8
instrumentally 5.8
instrumentation 3.13
insubordinate 14.4
insubordination 3.13
insubstantial 1.8
insufferable 16.3
insufficiency 9.13
insufficient 9.13
insufficiently 9.13
insular 9.8
insulate 3.14
insulation 3.13
insulator 3.14
insulin 9.8
insult 17.6
insuperable 16.3
insurable 19.4
insurance 19.4
insure 19.1
insured 19.2
insurer 19.4
insurgency 8.4
insurgent 8.4
insuring 19.4
insurmountable 13.4
insurrection 5.2
intact 1.2
intangibly 6.1
in tears 7.7
integral 16.3
integrate 3.14
integrated 3.14
integration 3.13
integrator 3.14

integrity 6.1
intellect 5.2
intellectual 5.2
intelligent 5.8
intelligible 5.6
intend 5.8
intended 5.8
intending 5.8
intense 5.8
intensely 5.8
intensify 10.1
intensity 5.8
intensive 5.8
intensively 5.8
intent 5.8
intention 5.8
intentional 5.8
intentionally 6.1
intentioned 5.8
intently 5.8
inter 8.1
interact 1.2
interacted 1.2
interacting 1.2
interaction 1.2
interactive 1.2
intercede 6.4
intercept 5.9
interception 5.9
intercession 5.13
interchange 3.9
interchangeable 3.9
interchanged 3.9
interchanging 3.9
intercom 11.7
interconnect 5.2
interconnected 5.2
interconnecting 5.2
interconnector 5.2
intercontinental 5.8
intercourse 14.13
interdependent 5.8
interest 5.11
interested 5.11
interest-free 6.1
interesting 5.11
interface 3.11
interfacing 3.11
interfere 7.1
interference 7.5
interferer 7.5
interfering 7.5
interim 9.7
interior 7.5
interject 5.2
interjected 5.2

interjecting 5.2
interjection 5.2
interlocking 11.2
interloper 12.10
interlude 18.4
intermarry 1.10
intermediary 6.1
intermediate 6.4
interminable 16.3
intermingle 9.8
intermission 9.13
intern 8.9
internal 8.9
internalize 10.17
internalizing 10.17
internally 8.9
international 1.12
internationally 1.12
interned 8.9
internee 6.1
Internet 5.14
interning 8.9
internment 8.9
interplanetary 1.8
interplay 3.1
Interpol 11.6
interpolate 3.14
interpolator 3.14
interpose 12.19
interposing 12.19
interpretation 3.13
interracial 3.13
interred 8.4
interrelated 3.14
interring 8.11
interrogate 3.14
interrogation 3.13
interrogator 3.14
interrupt 17.9
interruption 17.9
inters 8.18
intersect 5.2
intersected 5.2
intersecting 5.2
intersection 5.2
intersperse 8.12
interspersed 8.12
intertwine 10.9
intertwining 10.9
interval 16.3
intervene 6.9
intervening 6.9
intervention 5.8
interview 18.1
interviewee 6.1
interviewer 18.1

intestinal 10.9
intestine 5.11
intimacy 6.1
intimate 3.14, 17.13
intimately 6.1
intimidate 3.14
intimidating 3.14
intimidation 3.13
intimidator 3.14
intonation 3.13
intone 12.9
intoning 12.9
intoxicated 3.14
intoxication 3.13
intractable 1.2
Intranet 5.14
intransigence 5.8
intransigent 5.8
intravenous 6.9
intravenously 6.1
intrepid 5.9
intricacy 6.1
intricate 17.13
intrigue 6.6
introduce 18.11
introduction 17.2
introductory 6.1
introspection 5.2
introspective 5.2
introvert 8.14
introverted 8.14
introverts 8.14
intrude 18.4
intruder 18.4
intruding 18.4
intrusion 18.12
intrusive 18.11
intrusively 18.11
intuition 9.13
intuitive 9.17
Inuit 9.14
inundate 3.14
invade 3.4
invaded 3.4
invader 3.4
invading 3.4
invalid 1.6
invalidate 3.14
invariably 6.1
invasion 3.12
invasive 3.11
invective 5.2
inveigh 3.1
inveigle 3.6
invent 5.8
inventable 5.8

invention 5.8
inventive 5.8
inventiveness 5.11
inventor 5.8
inventory 6.1
Inverclyde 10.4
Inverness 5.11
invert 8.14
inverted 8.14
inverter 8.14
inverts 8.14
invest 5.11
invested 5.11
investigate 3.14
investigation 3.13
investigative 9.17
investigator 3.14
investing 5.11
investor 5.11
inveterate 17.13
invidious 9.3
invigilate 3.14
invigilator 3.14
invigorate 3.14
invigorated 3.14
invigorating 3.14
invincible 16.3
inviolable 16.3
inviolate 10.1
invisible 9.18
invisibly 6.1
invitation 3.13
invite 10.13
invited 10.13
inviting 10.13
in vitro fertilization 3.13
invoke 12.3
invoker 12.3
invoking 12.3
involuntary 6.1
involve 11.6
involved 11.6
invulnerable 16.3
inward-looking 16.1
inwardly 6.1
in-your-face 3.11
iodine 6.9
ion 10.1
Iona 12.9
Ionian 12.9
ionize 10.17
ionizer 10.17
ionizing 10.17
iota 12.14
IOU 18.1
IPA 3.1

iPod® 11.3
IQ 18.1
IRA 3.1
Ira 10.1
Iran 2.10
Iranian 3.9
Iraq 2.3
Iraqi 2.3
irascible 16.3
irate 3.14
irately 3.14
irateness 3.14
ire 10.1
Irene 10.11
Iris 10.11
Irishman 17.8
irk 8.3
irking 8.3
Irma 8.8
iron 10.1
ironic 11.8
ironical 11.8
ironmonger 17.8
irony 6.1, 10.1
irradiate 3.14
irradiation 3.13
irrational 1.12
irrationally 1.12
Irrawaddy 11.3
irreconcilable 16.3
irredeemable 16.3
irrefutable 18.14
irregularity 1.10
irreligious 9.3
irremediable 16.3
irreparable 5.9
irreplaceable 16.3
irrepressible 5.11
irreproachable 12.14
irresistible 16.3
irresolute 18.14
irrespective 5.2
irresponsibility 9.6
irretrievable 6.17
irreverence 5.17
irreverent 5.8
irreversible 16.3
irrevocable 16.3
irrigate 3.14
irrigation 3.13
irrigator 3.14
irritable 16.3
irritate 3.14
irritating 3.14
irritation 3.13
irritator 3.14

IRS 5.11
is 9.18
ISA 10.12
Isabella 5.6
Isabel(le) 5.6
Isaiah 10.1
ISBN 5.8
Isis 10.12
Isla 10.7
Islamabad 2.4
Islamic 1.7
island 10.7
islander 10.7
islands 10.7
Islay 10.7
isle 10.7
Isle of Man 1.8
Isle of Wight 10.13
Ismail 6.7
ISO 12.1
isobar 2.1
isolate 3.14
isolated 3.14
isolation 3.13
isolator 3.14
Isolde 12.7
isotope 12.10
ISP 6.1
I-spy 10.1
Israeli 3.7
Israelite 10.13
issue 9.13
Istanbul 16.3
isthmus 9.11
IT 6.1
it 9.14
Italian 1.6
italic 1.6
Italy 9.14
itch 9.14
itchy 9.14
it'd 9.14
item 10.13
itemize 10.17
itemizer 10.17
itemizing 10.17
iterative 9.17
itinerary 6.1
it'll 9.14
ITN 5.8
its 9.14
it's 9.14
itself 5.6
ITV 6.1
Ivan 10.15
Ivana 2.10

Ivanhoe 12.1
I've 10.15
Ives 10.15
IVF 5.4
Ivor 10.15
ivory 6.1
Iwo Jima 6.8

J

J 3.1
jab 1.1
jabber 1.1
Jack 1.2
jack 1.2
jackal 1.2
jackass 1.11
jackdaw 14.1
jacked 1.2
jacket 1.2
Jackie 1.2
jack-in-the-box 11.2
jackpot 1.2
jacks 1.2
Jackson 1.2
Jacobean 6.1
Jacobite 10.13
Jacqueline 6.9
Jacuzzi® 18.19
Jade 3.4
jade 3.4
jaded 3.4
jade-green 6.9
Jaffa 1.4
Jag 1.5
jag 1.5
jagged 1.5
jagging 1.5
jaggy 1.5
jaguar 1.5
jail 3.7
jailed 3.7
jailer 3.7
jailhouse 13.6
jailing 3.7
jailings 3.7
Jakarta 2.16
Jake 3.3
jalop(p)y 11.9
jam 1.7
Jamaica 3.3
Jamaican 3.3
Jamal 2.8
jamb 1.7
jamboree 6.1
James 3.8

Jamie 3.8
Jamila 6.7
jammily 1.7
jamming 1.7
jammy 1.7
jam-packed 1.2
Jan 1.8
Jane 3.9
Janet 1.8
jangle 1.8
jangled 1.8
jangling 1.8
Janine 6.9
January 6.1
Janus 3.9
Japan 1.8
Japanese 6.19
jape 3.10
jar 2.1
jargon 2.6
jarred 2.4
jarring 2.12
Jarrow 1.10
Jasmine 1.17
jasmine 1.17
Jason 3.11
jaunt 14.10
jaunted 14.10
jauntiness 5.11
jaunting 14.10
Java 2.19
Javanese 6.19
jaw 14.1
jawbreaker 14.2
jawing 14.12
Jay 3.1
jay 3.1
jaywalker 14.3
jaywalking 14.3
jazz 1.17
jazzy 1.17
jealous 5.6
jealously 6.1
jealousy 6.1
Jean 6.9
Jean(n)ette 5.14
Jean(n)ie 6.9
jeans 6.9
Jeep® 6.10
jeer 7.1
jeerer 7.5
jeering 7.5
Jeeves 6.17
jeez 6.19
Jehovah 12.17
Jekyll 5.2

jell   5.6
jelled   5.6
jelling   5.6
jelly   5.6
jellybean   6.9
jellyfish   9.13
Jemima   10.8
jemmy   5.7
Jenna   5.8
Jenny   5.8
jeopardize   10.17
jeopardizing   10.17
jeopardy   6.1
Jeremiah   10.1
Jeremy   6.1
Jericho   12.1
jerk   8.3
jerker   8.3
jerkily   6.1
jerking   8.3
jerky   8.3
Jerome   12.8
jerrican   1.8
jerry-built   9.6
Jersey   8.18
jersey   8.18
Jerusalem   5.7
Jess   5.11
Jesse   5.11
Jessie   5.11
jest   5.11
jested   5.11
jester   5.11
jesting   5.11
Jesuit   9.14
Jesuitical   9.14
jet   5.14
jet-powered   13.1
jet-propelled   5.6
jet-setter   5.14
jetted   5.14
jetting   5.14
jettison   17.8
jetty   5.14
Jew   18.1
jewel   18.1
jeweller   18.1
jewellery   6.1
Jewess   18.1
Jewry   19.4
Jezebel   5.6
jib   9.1
jiffy   9.4
jig   9.5
jigger   9.5
jiggle   9.5

jigs   9.5
jihad   1.3
Jill   9.6
jilt   9.6
Jim   9.7
Jimmy   9.7
jingle   9.8
jingoism   9.18
jingoistic   9.11
jinx   9.8
jitney   9.14
jitterbug   17.5
jittery   6.1
jive   10.15
jived   10.15
jiver   10.15
J K Rowling   12.7
J M Barrie   1.10
Jo   12.1
Joan   12.9
Joanie   12.9
Joanna   1.8
Joanne   1.8
Joan of Arc   2.3
job   11.1
jobber   11.1
jobbing   11.1
Jobcentre   5.8
Jock   11.2
jockey   11.2
Jodie   12.4
Joe   12.1
Joel   12.1
Joey   12.1
joey   12.1
jog   11.5
joggle   11.5
Johannesburg   8.6
John   11.8
Johnny   11.8
John o'Groats   12.14
join   15.5
joint   15.5
jointed   15.5
joist   15.6
joke   12.3
joker   12.3
jokily   6.1
joking   12.3
jokingly   6.1
joky   12.3
Jolene   6.9
jollification   3.13
jolly   11.6
jolt   12.7
Jonah   12.9

Jonathan   17.8
Jones   12.9
Jordan   14.4
Jordanian   3.9
Josephine   6.9
josh   11.12
josher   11.12
jostle   11.11
jot   11.13
jotter   11.13
joule   18.7
journal   8.9
journalese   6.19
journalism   9.18
journalist   9.11
journalistic   9.11
journey   8.9
joust   13.6
jovially   6.1
jowl   13.3
Joy   15.1
joy   15.1
Joyce   15.6
joyfully   6.1
joyrider   10.4
joys   15.8
JP   6.1
Juan   2.10
jubilation   3.13
jubilee   6.1
Judaic   3.1
Judaism   9.18
judder   17.3
Jude   18.4
judge   17.3
judg(e)mental   5.8
judg(e)mentally   5.8
judging   17.3
judicial   9.13
judiciary   6.1
judicious   9.13
judiciously   9.13
judiciousness   5.11
judo   18.4
Judy   18.4
jug   17.5
juggernaut   14.15
juggle   17.5
juggler   17.5
juice   18.11
juicer   18.11
juicy   18.11
Julia   18.7
Juliana   2.10
Julie   18.7
Juliet   5.14

July   10.1
jumble   17.7
jumbling   17.7
jumbo   17.7
jump   17.7
jumped-up   17.9
jumper   17.7
jumping   17.7
jump-start   17.7
jumpy   17.7
junction   17.8
juncture   17.8
June   18.9
jungle   17.8
junior   18.9
junk   17.8
junkie   17.8
junta   17.8
Jurassic   1.11
jurisdiction   9.2
jurist   19.4
juror   19.4
jury   19.4
just   17.11
justifiable   10.1, 16.3
justifiably   6.1, 10.1
justification   3.13
justified   10.4
justify   10.1
Justin   17.11
Justine   6.9
jut   17.13
jute   18.14
jutting   17.13
juvenile   10.7
juxtapose   12.19
juxtaposing   12.19
juxtaposition   9.13

K

K   3.1
K2   18.1
Kabul   2.2
Kalahari   1.10
kalashnikov   11.4
kale   3.7
kaleidoscope   12.10
Kali   2.8
Kamal   2.8
kamikaze   2.21
Kampala   2.8
Kampuchea   7.1
Kandahar   2.1
Kane   3.9
kangaroo   18.1

Kansas   1.8
Kant   2.10
kaolin   9.8
kaput   16.5
Karachi   2.16
karate   2.16
Karen   1.10
Karl   2.8
Kashmir   7.1
Kashmiri   7.5
Kate   3.14
Kath   1.15
Kathleen   6.9
Kat(h)mandu   18.1
Katie   3.14
Katrina   6.9
Kay   3.1
Kay(e)   3.1
Kazak(h)stan   2.10
KB   6.1
Keane   6.9
Keaton   6.14
Keats   6.14
kebab   1.1
Keble   6.2
kedgeree   6.1
keel   6.7
keeled   6.7
keeling   6.7
keen   6.9
keener   6.9
keening   6.9
keenly   6.9
keep   6.10
keeper   6.10
keep-fit   9.14
keeping   6.10
keg   5.5
kegs   5.5
Keith   6.16
Kelly   5.6
Kelvin   5.6
Ken   5.8
ken   5.8
kendo   5.8
Kennedy   6.1
kennel   5.8
Kenneth   5.8
Kenny   5.8
Kent   5.8
Kentucky   17.2
Kenya   6.9
Kenyatta   1.13
kept   5.9
kerb   8.2
kerbed   8.2

kerfuffle   17.4
kerfuffled   17.4
Kermit   8.8
kernel   8.9
kerosene   6.9
Kerouac   1.2
Kerry   5.10
kestrel   5.11
kettle   5.14
kettledrum   17.7
Kevin   5.17
key   6.1
keyboard   6.2
keyboarder   14.4
keyboarders   14.4
keycard   6.3
keyed   6.4
keying   6.1
KGB   6.1
khaki   2.3
Khan   2.10
Khartoum   18.8
Khomeini   3.9
kibbutzim   6.8
kick   9.2
kicked   9.2
kicker   9.2
kicking   9.2
kicks   9.2
kid   9.3
kidder   9.3
kidding   9.3
kidney   9.3
Kiel   6.7
Kilda   9.6
Kildare   4.1
Kilimanjaro   2.12
Kilkenny   5.8
kill   9.6
Killarney   2.10
killed   9.6
killer   9.6
killing   9.6
kilobyte   10.13
kilogram(me)   1.7
kilohertz   8.14
kilometre   11.7
kilowatt   11.13
kilt   9.6
kilter   9.6
Kim   9.7
Kim Jong Il   6.7
kimono   12.9
kin   9.8
Kincardineshire   10.1
kind   10.9

kinda 10.9
kinder 10.9
kindergarten 2.16
kind-hearted 2.16
kindle 9.8
kindly 10.9
kindness 10.9
kinetic 5.14
kinetics 5.14
King 9.8
king 9.8
kingfisher 9.13
King Kong 11.8
king-size 10.17
kink 9.8
kinked 9.8
kinking 9.8
kinky 9.8
kip 9.9
Kipling 9.9
kipper 9.9
Kirg(h)izia 9.18
Kirg(h)izstan 1.8
Kiribati 2.16
Kirk 8.3
kirk 8.3
Kirkcudbrightshire 10.1
kirking 8.3
Kirsty 8.12
kiss 9.11
kissable 9.11
kissed 9.11
kisser 9.11
kissogram 1.7
kit 9.14
kitchenette 5.14
kitchenware 4.1
kite 10.13
kith 9.16
kitsch 9.14
kitschy 9.14
kitten 9.14
Kitts 9.14
Kitty 9.14
kitty 9.14
kiwi 6.18
Klammer 1.7
klaxon 1.2
Klein 10.9
kleptomania 3.9
kleptomaniac 3.9
knack 1.2
knacker 1.2
knave 3.17
knead 6.4
knee 6.1

kneecap 6.3
kneed 6.4
knee-deep 6.10
knee-high 10.1
kneel 6.7
kneeled 6.7
kneeler 6.7
kneeling 6.7
knell 5.6
knelled 5.6
knelling 5.6
knelt 5.6
knew 18.1
knickers 9.2
knife 10.5
knight 10.13
knighted 10.13
knighting 10.13
knit 9.14
knitted 9.14
knitter 9.14
knitting 9.14
knives 10.15
knob 11.1
knobbly 11.1
knobby 11.1
knock 11.2
knocked 11.2
knocker 11.2
knocking 11.2
knock-kneed 6.4
knockout 11.2
knot 11.13
knotty 11.13
know 12.1
knower 12.1
knowing 12.1
knowingly 6.1
know-it-all 14.8
knowledge 11.6
knowledgeable 16.3
known 12.9
knuckle 17.2
knuckle-duster 17.11
knuckling 17.2
KO 3.1, 12.1
koala 2.8
KO'd 12.4
kookaburra 17.10
kopeck 12.10
Koran 2.10
Koranic 1.8
Korea 7.1
Korean 6.1
kosher 12.13
Kosovan 17.8

Kosovo 12.1
kowtow 13.1
kowtowed 13.2
Kramer 3.8
Krankie 1.8
Krays 3.18
Kremlin 5.7
krona 12.9
krone 12.9
kroner 12.9
kudos 11.11
Kurd 8.4
Kurdistan 1.8
Kurt 8.14
Kuwait 3.14
Kuwaiti 3.14
Kwai 10.1
Kyle 10.7
Kylie 10.7
Kyoto 12.14
Kyrgyzstan 2.10

L
L 5.6
LA 3.1
lab 1.1
label 3.2
labelled 3.2
La Bohème 5.7
laboratory 6.1
laborious 14.12
laboriously 14.12
labour 3.2
labouring 3.2
labour-intensive 5.8
labrador 14.1
laburnum 8.9
labyrinth 9.8
lace 3.11
lacerate 3.14
laceration 3.13
lachrymose 12.11
lacing 3.11
lack 1.2
lackadaisical 16.3
lackey 1.2
lacking 1.2
laconic 11.8
lacquer 1.2
lacrosse 11.11
lacuna 18.9
lacy 3.11
lad 1.3
Lada 2.4
ladder 1.3

laddie   1.3
laddish   1.3
laden   3.4
ladle   3.4
lady   3.4
ladybird   8.4
lady-in-waiting   3.14
lady-killer   9.6
ladylike   10.3
ladyship   9.9
Lafayette   5.14
lag   1.5
lager   2.6
laggard   1.5
lagging   1.5
lagoon   18.9
la(h)   2.1
Lahore   14.1
laid   3.4
laid-back   1.2
lain   3.9
Laine   3.9
lair   4.1
laird   4.2
laisser-faire   4.1
laity   3.1
lake   3.3
Lamarr   2.1
lamb   1.7
lambast   1.11
lambing   1.7
Lamborghini   6.9
lame   3.8
lamé   3.1
lamely   3.8
lament   5.8
lamentable   5.8, 16.3
lamentably   6.1
lamentation   3.13
laminate   1.7
lamp   1.7
lampoon   18.9
lampooned   18.9
lampooner   18.9
LAN   5.8
Lanarkshire   10.1
Lancashire   10.1
Lancaster   2.13
lance   2.10
Lancelot   11.13
lancer   2.10
lancing   2.10
land   1.8
landed   1.8
lander   1.8
landing   1.8

landmine   10.9
landowner   12.9
landowning   12.9
Land Rover   12.17
Land's End   5.8
lane   3.9
languidly   6.1
languish   1.8
languor   1.8
languorous   17.11
lank   1.8
lanker   1.8
lankly   1.8
lanky   1.8
lanolin(e)   9.8
Lanza   1.8
Lanzarote   11.13
Laos   13.6
lap   1.9
laparotomy   11.13
La Paz   1.17
lapel   5.6
Laplander   1.8
Lapp   1.9
lapping   1.9
lapse   1.9
Lara   2.12
larceny   6.1
larch   2.16
lard   2.4
larded   2.4
larder   2.4
large   2.4
larger   2.4
largesse   5.11
largo   2.6
lark   2.3
larked   2.3
larker   2.3
larking   2.3
Larry   1.10
larva   2.19
laryngitis   10.13
lascivious   9.17
laser   3.18
lash   1.12
lashed   1.12
lasher   1.12
lashing   1.12
lass   1.11
lassitude   18.4
lasso   18.1
last   2.13
last-ditch   9.14
lasting   2.13
lastly   2.13

last-minute   9.8
Las Vegas   3.6
latch   1.13
latched   1.13
latching   1.13
late   3.14
latecomer   17.7
lately   3.14
lateness   3.14
latent   3.14
latently   3.14
later   3.14
lateral   16.3
lath   2.18
lathe   3.15
lather   1.14
Latin   1.13
latitude   1.13, 18.4
latitudinal   16.3
La Traviata   2.16
latrine   6.9
latte   1.13
latter   1.13
latter-day   3.1
latterly   1.13
latticework   8.3
laud   14.4
laudable   14.4
laudanum   17.7
lauded   14.4
lauding   14.4
laugh   2.5
laughable   16.3
laughed   2.5
laughing   2.5
laughter   2.5
launch   14.10
laundrette   5.14
Laura   14.12
Laurel   11.10
laurel   11.10
Lauren   11.10
Laurie   11.10
lava   2.19
lavatory   6.1
Lavinia   9.8
lavish   1.16
lavishly   6.1
Law   14.1
law   14.1
law-abiding   10.4
lawbreaker   14.2
lawcourt   14.3
lawful   14.5
lawless   14.8
lawlessness   5.11

lawmaker   3.3
lawn   14.10
lawnmower   12.1
lawyer   14.19
lax   1.2
laxative   9.17
laxity   6.1
lay   3.1
layabout   13.7
layer   3.1
layette   5.14
laying   3.1
layman   3.8
lay-off   3.1
Lazarus   17.11
laze   3.18
lazed   3.18
lazier   3.18
laziness   5.11
lazy   3.18
lazybones   12.9
LCD   6.1
LEA   3.1
lea   6.1
lead   5.3, 6.4
leaded   5.3
leaden   5.3
leader   6.4
leadership   9.9
lead-free   6.1
lead-in   6.4
leading   5.3, 6.4
leaf   6.5
leafing   6.5
leafy   6.5
league   6.6
Lea(h)   6.1
leak   6.3
leaker   6.3
leaking   6.3
leaky   6.3
Lean   6.9
lean   6.9
leaner   6.9
leaning   6.9
Leanne   1.8
leant   5.8
leap   6.10
leaper   6.10
leaping   6.10
leapt   5.9
Lear   7.1
learn   8.9
learned   8.9
learner   8.9
learning   8.9

learnt   8.9
lease   6.11
leased   6.11
leaseholder   12.7
leash   6.13
leasing   6.11
least   6.11
leather   5.15
leather-bound   13.4
leathery   5.15
leave   6.17
leaven   5.17
leaver   6.17
leaves   6.17
leave-taking   3.3
Lebanese   6.19
Lebanon   11.8
lech   5.14
lecher   5.14
lecherous   5.14
lechery   5.14
leching   5.14
Lecter   5.2
lecture   5.2
LED   6.1
led   5.3
ledge   5.3
ledged   5.3
ledger   5.3
Lee   6.1
leech   6.14
leeching   6.14
Leeds   6.4
leek   6.3
leer   7.1
leering   7.5
leeway   6.18
left   5.4
left-field   6.7
left-handed   1.8
left-hander   1.8
leftover   12.17
left-wing   9.8
left-winger   9.8
leg   5.5
legacy   6.1
legal   6.6
legalese   6.19
legality   1.6, 6.1
legalization   3.13
legalize   10.17
legalizing   10.17
legally   6.1, 6.6
legation   3.13
leggy   5.5
legible   16.3

legion   6.4
legionnaire   4.1
legislate   3.14
legislation   3.13
legislative   9.17
legislator   3.14
legislature   19.1
legitimacy   6.1
legitimate   3.14
legitimately   6.1
legs   5.5
Leicester   5.11
Leicestershire   10.1
Leiden   10.4
Leigh   6.1
Leila   3.7
leisure   5.12
leisurely   6.1
Lemmon   5.7
lemon   5.7
lemonade   3.4
lemony   5.7
lemur   6.8
Len   5.8
Lena   6.9
lend   5.8
lender   5.8
lending   5.8
length   5.8
lengthen   5.8
lengthily   6.1
lenient   6.9
Leningrad   1.3
Lenny   5.8
lens   5.8
Lent   5.8
lent   5.8
lentil   5.8
lento   5.8
Leo   6.1
Leonora   14.12
leopard   5.9
leotard   2.4
leper   5.9
leprechaun   14.10
leprosy   6.1
lesion   6.12
Lesley   5.18
Leslie   5.18
less   5.11
lessen   5.11
lesser   5.11
lesson   5.11
lest   5.11
Lester   5.11
let   5.14

lethargy   6.1
Letitia   9.13
letter   5.14
letterhead   5.3
letting   5.14
let-up   5.14
leukaemia   6.8
level   5.17
level-headed   5.3
leveller   5.17
lever   6.17
levitate   3.14
levitation   3.13
levitator   3.14
levity   5.17
levy   5.17
lewd   18.4
Lewis   18.1
lexical   16.3
lexicographer   11.5
Lexington   17.8
liability   9.6
liable   10.1
liaise   3.18
liaised   3.18
liaising   3.18
liaison   11.8
liaisons   11.8
Liam   6.1
liar   10.1
Lib Dem   5.7
libel   10.2
liberal   16.3
liberalism   9.18
liberalize   10.17
liberalizing   10.17
liberally   6.1
liberate   3.14
liberated   3.14
liberating   3.14
liberation   3.13
liberator   3.14
Liberia   7.5
Liberian   7.5
libertarian   4.6
libertarianism   4.6
liberty   6.1
libido   6.4
Libra   6.2
librarian   4.6
library   6.1
libretto   5.14
Libya   9.1
Libyan   9.1
lice   10.12
licentious   5.8

licit   9.11
lick   9.2
licked   9.2
licker   9.2
licking   9.2
licks   9.2
lid   9.3
lido   6.4
lie   10.1
Liechtenstein   10.9
liege   6.4
Liège   3.12
lie-in   9.8
lieutenant   5.8
life   10.5
life-giving   9.17
lifelessly   6.1
lifer   10.5
life-saver   3.17
life-saving   3.17
life-support   14.15
lift   9.4
lifter   9.4
lifting   9.4
ligament   9.5
light   10.13
lighted   10.13
lighten   10.13
lightened   10.13
lightening   10.13
lighter   10.13
light-headed   5.3
light-hearted   2.16
lighting   10.13
lightly   10.13
lightness   10.13
lightning   10.13
like   10.3
likeable   16.3
likelihood   16.2
like-minded   10.9
liking   10.3
Lille   6.7
Lillee   9.6
Lil(l)ian   9.6
Lilliput   16.5
Lilo®   10.7
lilt   9.6
Lily   9.6
lily   9.6
Lima   6.8
limb   9.7
limbed   9.7
limber   9.7
limbo   9.7
lime   10.8

Limerick   9.2
limerick   9.2
limericks   9.2
limey   10.8
limit   9.7
limitation   3.13
limited   9.3
limitless   5.11
limousine   6.9
limp   9.7
limply   9.7
Lincolnshire   10.1
Linda   9.8
linden   9.8
line   10.9
lineage   9.3
linear   9.8
lined   10.9
liner   10.9
linger   9.8
lingerie   6.1
lingo   9.8
lingua franca   1.8
linguistic   9.11
linguistics   9.11
lining   10.9
link   9.8
linked   9.8
linker   9.8
linking   9.8
lino   10.9
linoleum   12.7
Linus   10.9
lion   10.1
Lionel   16.3
lioness   5.11
lion-hearted   2.16
lip   9.9
liposuction   17.2
lipstick   9.9
liquefy   10.1
liqueur   19.1
liquidate   3.14
liquidation   3.13
liquidator   3.14
liquidity   9.3
liquidize   10.17
liquidizer   10.17
liquidizing   10.17
liquor   9.2
liquorice   9.11
lira   7.5
lire   7.5
Lisbon   9.18
lisp   9.11
list   9.11

listed   9.11
listen   9.11
listing   9.11
Liszt   9.11
lit   9.14
litany   9.14
literal   16.3
literally   6.1
literary   6.1
literature   19.1
lithe   10.14
lithograph   2.5
lithographed   2.5
lithographing   2.5
lithosphere   7.1
Lithuania   3.9
Lithuanian   3.9
litigate   9.14
litigation   3.13
litre   6.14
litter   9.14
litterbug   17.5
littered   9.14
little   9.14
liturgy   6.1
Liv   9.17
livable   9.17
live   9.17, 10.15
livelihood   16.2
liveliness   5.11
liven   10.15
liver   9.17
Liverpool   18.7
livery   9.17
lives   10.15
livid   9.17
living   9.17
Livingstone   17.8
Liz   9.18
Liza   10.17
lizard   9.18
Lizzie   9.18
Ljubljana   2.10
llama   2.9
llamas   2.9
Lloyd   15.2
Lloyd-George   14.4
lo   12.1
load   12.4
loaded   12.4
loading   12.4
loaf   12.5
loafer   12.5
loam   12.8
loaming   12.8
loamy   12.8

loan   12.9
loaning   12.9
loath   12.16
loathe   12.15
loathed   12.15
loathes   12.15
loathing   12.15
lob   11.1
lobbing   11.1
lobby   11.1
lobbyist   9.11
lobe   12.2
lobotomy   11.13
lobster   11.1
local   12.3
locale   2.8
locales   2.8
locality   1.6
locally   6.1
locate   3.14
location   3.13
locative   11.2
locator   3.14
loch   11.2
Loch Ness   5.11
lock   11.2
locked   11.2
locker   11.2
locket   11.2
locking   11.2
lock-out   11.2
lockup   11.2
locomotion   12.13
locomotive   12.14
locution   18.13
lodge   11.3
lodger   11.3
loft   11.4
lofty   11.4
log   11.5
loggerheads   5.3
logic   11.3
logical   11.3
logically   6.1
logistic   9.11
logistical   9.11
logistics   9.11
logo   12.6
Lohengrin   9.8
loin   15.5
Loire   2.1
loiter   15.7
Lola   12.7
Lolita   6.14
loll   11.6
lollipop   11.9

lollop   11.6
lolly   11.6
Londonderry   5.10
London Eye   10.1
lone   12.9
loneliness   5.11
lonely   12.9
loner   12.9
long   11.8
long-distance   9.11
longer   11.8
longevity   5.17
Longfellow   5.6
long-forgotten   11.13
long-haired   4.2
long-haul   14.8
longing   11.8
longingly   6.1
longitude   18.4
longitudinal   16.3
long-lasting   2.13
long-life   10.5
long-range   3.9
longshoreman   14.9
long-sighted   10.13
long-sleeved   6.17
long-standing   1.8
loo   18.1
look   16.1
lookalike   10.3
looked   16.1
looker   16.1
looking   16.1
loom   18.8
looming   18.8
loony   18.9
loop   18.10
looper   18.10
loopy   18.10
loose   18.11
loose-fitting   9.14
loose-limbed   9.7
loosely   18.11
looser   18.11
loot   18.14
looted   18.14
looter   18.14
looting   18.14
lope   12.10
loper   12.10
lopsided   10.4
loquacious   3.13
lord   14.4
lorded   14.4
lording   14.4
lordly   14.4

Lord of the Flies   10.17
lore   14.1
Loretta   5.14
Lorna   14.10
Lorraine   3.9
lorry   11.10
Los Angeles   6.19
lose   18.19
loser   18.19
losing   18.19
Loss   11.11
loss   11.11
loss-making   3.3
lost   11.11
lot   11.13
Lothario   2.12
lotion   12.13
lottery   11.13
lotto   11.13
lotus   12.14
Lou   18.1
loud   13.2
louder   13.2
loudhailer   3.7
loudly   13.2
loudspeaker   6.3
Louis   18.1
Louisa   6.19
Louise   6.19
Louisiana   1.8
Louisville   9.6
lounge   13.4
louse   13.6
loused   13.6
lousy   13.9
lout   13.7
Louth   13.8
lovable   16.3
love   17.15
loved   17.15
lovely   6.1
lovemaking   3.3
lover   17.15
loving   17.15
low   12.1
low-budget   17.3
low-calorie   1.6
low-cut   17.13
low-down   12.4
lowed   12.4
lower   12.1, 13.1
lowered   13.1
lowering   13.1
low-flying   10.1
low-heeled   6.7
lowing   12.1

low-key   6.1
lowland   12.7
low-level   5.17
lowlier   12.7
lowly   12.7
low-lying   10.1
lowness   12.9
Lowry   13.5
loyal   15.1
loyalist   15.1
loyally   15.1
loyalty   15.1
LP   6.1
LSD   6.1
lubricate   3.14
lubrication   3.13
lubricator   3.14
Lucan   18.3
Lucas   18.3
Lucerne   8.9
Lucille   6.7
Lucinda   9.8
luck   17.2
luckily   17.2
lucky   17.2
lucrative   9.17
lucre   18.3
Lucy   18.11
ludicrous   17.11
lug   17.5
luge   18.12
lughole   17.5
lugubrious   18.2
Luke   18.3
lull   17.6
lullaby   10.1
Lulu   18.7
lulu   18.7
lumbago   3.6
lumbar   17.7
lumber   17.7
lumberjack   1.2
lumberjacks   1.2
luminary   6.1
luminescence   5.11
luminescent   5.11
luminous   18.8
lump   17.7
lumping   17.7
lumpy   17.7
lunacy   6.1
lunar   18.9
lunatic   9.2
lunatics   9.2
lunch   17.8
luncheon   17.8

lunches   17.8
Lundy   17.8
lung   17.8
lunge   17.8
lupin   18.10
lurch   8.14
lurcher   8.14
lurching   8.14
lure   19.1
lured   19.2
luring   19.4
lurk   8.3
lurker   8.3
lurking   8.3
Lusaka   2.3
lush   17.12
lushed   17.12
lusher   17.12
lushing   17.12
Lusitania   3.9
lust   17.11
lusted   17.11
lustful   17.11
lusting   17.11
lustre   17.11
lustred   17.11
lusty   17.11
lute   18.14
Luton   18.14
Luxembourg   8.6
luxuriant   19.4
luxuriate   3.14
luxurious   19.4
luxury   6.1
lychee   6.1
lye   10.1
lying   10.1
Lyme Regis   6.4
lymph   9.7
lymphatic   1.13
lymphoma   12.8
lynch   9.8
lynching   9.8
Lynette   5.14
Lynn(e)   9.8
lynx   9.8
lyre   10.1
lyrical   9.10
lyricism   9.10
lyricist   9.11

M
M   5.7
MA   3.1
ma   2.1

ma'am 2.9
Mabel 3.2
mac 1.2
macabre 2.2
macaque 2.3
macaroni 12.9
macaroon 18.9
MacArthur 2.18
macaw 14.1
Macbeth 5.16
MacColl 14.8
Mace® 3.11
mace 3.11
Macedonia 12.9
Macedonian 12.9
Mach 1.2
machete 5.14
Machiavelli 5.6
machinations 3.13
machine 6.9
machine-knitted 9.14
machine-readable 6.4
machinery 6.9
machining 6.9
machismo 9.18
mac(k)intosh 11.12
Mack the Knife 10.5
Macmillan 9.6
macramé 2.9
macrobiotics 11.13
macroeconomics 11.7
mad 1.3
Madagascar 1.11
madam 1.3
madden 1.3
madder 1.3
made 3.4
Madeira 7.5
Madel(e)ine 9.8
made-up 17.9
Madge 1.3
Mad Hatter 1.13
madly 1.3
madman 1.3
madness 1.3
Madonna 11.8
madonna 11.8
Madras 2.13
Madrid 9.3
Mae 3.1
Mafia 1.4
mag 1.5
magazine 6.9
Magellan 5.6
magenta 5.8
Maggie 1.5

Maggiore 14.12
maggot 1.5
Maghreb 5.1
magic 1.3
magical 16.3
magically 1.3
magician 9.13
magisterial 7.5
magistrate 3.14
magnanimity 9.7
magnanimous 1.8
magnetic 5.14
magnetism 9.18
magnification 3.13
magnificence 5.8
magnificent 5.8
magnify 10.1
magnitude 18.4
magnolia 12.7
Magnus 1.5
magpie 10.1
Mahler 2.8
mahogany 6.1
maid 3.4
maiden 3.4
mail 3.7
mailbox 11.2
mailer 3.7
mailing 3.7
mailings 3.7
mailshot 11.13
maim 3.8
maimed 3.8
maims 3.8
main 3.9
Maine 3.9
mainly 3.9
maintain 3.9
Maisie 3.18
maisonette 5.14
maize 3.18
majestic 5.11
majesty 6.1
Major 3.4
major 3.4
Majorca 14.3
Majorcan 14.3
major-domo 12.8
majority 11.10
Makarios 11.11
make 3.3
make-believe 6.17
makeover 3.3
maker 3.3
make-up 3.3
making 3.3

maladjusted 17.11
maladroit 15.7
malady 6.1
Malagasy 6.1
malaise 3.18
Malaprop 11.9
malaria 4.6
Malay 3.1
Malaysia 3.18
Maldives 6.17
male 3.7
malefactor 1.2
malevolence 5.17
malevolent 5.17
malformed 14.9
malfunction 17.8
Mali 2.8
malice 1.6
malicious 9.13
maliciously 9.13
malign 10.9
malignant 9.5
maligner 10.9
malinger 9.8
mall 14.8
malleable 16.3
mallet 1.6
mallow 1.6
malnutrition 9.13
Malo 2.8
malt 14.8
Malta 14.8
malted 14.8
Maltese 6.19
maltreat 6.14
maltreated 6.14
maltreating 6.14
maltreats 6.14
mammal 1.7
Mamma Mia! 7.1
mammary 6.1
mammography 11.5
mammy 1.7
man 1.8
manageable 16.3
management 5.8
manageress 5.11
managerial 7.5
Mandalay 3.1
mandate 3.14
mandator 3.14
mandatory 6.1
Mandela 5.6
mandible 16.3
mandolin 9.8
Mandy 1.8

mane   3.9
man-eater   6.14
man-eating   6.14
manfully   6.1
manganese   6.19
mange   3.9
manger   3.9
mangle   1.8
mangled   1.8
mango   1.8
mangy   3.9
manhandle   1.8
Manhattan   1.13
man-hour   13.1
mania   3.9
maniac   3.9
manic   1.8
manic-depressive   5.11
manicure   19.1
manicured   19.2
manicuring   19.4
manifest   5.11
manifestation   3.13
manifested   5.11
manifesting   5.11
manifestly   6.1
manifold   12.7
Manila   9.6
manipulate   9.9
manipulation   3.13
manipulative   9.17
Manitoba   12.2
mankind   10.9
manky   1.8
manliness   5.11
manly   1.8
man-made   3.4
mannequin   9.8
manner   1.8
mannerism   9.18
Manning   1.8
manoeuvre   18.17
Manon Lescaut   12.1
manor   1.8
manpower   13.1
manse   1.8
mansion   1.8
manslaughter   14.15
manta   1.8
mantelpiece   6.11
man-to-man   1.8
manual   1.8
manually   1.8
manufacture   1.2
manure   19.1
manured   19.2

manuscript   9.9
many   5.8
many-coloured   17.6
Maori   13.5
Mao Zedong   17.8
map   1.9
maple   3.10
maples   3.10
mapper   1.9
mapping   1.9
mar   2.1
maracas   1.2
Maradona   11.8
marathon   11.8
marathons   11.8
marauder   14.4
marauders   14.4
marauding   14.4
Marbella   3.1
marble   2.2
marbled   2.2
March   2.16
march   2.16
marcher   2.16
Marconi   12.9
Marco Polo   12.7
Marcus   2.3
mare   4.1
margarine   6.9
marge   2.4
marginal   16.3
marginalize   10.17
marginalizing   10.17
marginally   6.1
Margo(t)   2.6
Maria   7.1
Marianne   1.8
Marie   2.12, 6.1
marigold   12.7
marijuana   2.10
Marilyn   1.10
Marina   6.9
marina   6.9
marinade   3.4
marinaded   3.4
marinading   3.4
marinate   3.14
marine   6.9
Marion   1.10
marionette   5.14
marital   16.3
maritime   10.8
marjoram   1.7
Marjorie   6.1
Mark   2.3
mark   2.3

marked   2.3
markedly   6.1
marker   2.3
marketable   16.3
marketplace   3.11
marking   2.3
markka   2.3
marl   2.8
Marley   2.8
marling   2.8
Marlon   2.8
marls   2.8
marmalade   3.4
maroon   18.9
marooned   18.9
marquee   6.1
Marquis de Sade   2.4
Marrakesh   5.13
marred   2.4
marriage   1.10
marriageable   16.3
married   1.10
marring   2.12
marrow   1.10
marrowbone   12.9
marry   1.10
Mars   2.21
Marsalis   1.6
Marseilles   3.1
marsh   2.15
marshal   2.15
marshmallow   1.6
Martha   2.18
martial   2.15
Martina   6.9
Martine   6.9
Martinique   6.3
martyr   2.16
marvellous   17.11
Mary   4.6
Maryland   1.8
marzipan   1.8
mascara   2.12
mascot   1.11
masculine   9.8
masculinity   9.8
Maserati   1.13
mash   1.12
mashed   1.12
masher   1.12
mashing   1.12
mask   2.13
masochism   9.18
masochist   9.11
masochistic   9.11
mason   3.11

masonry 6.1
masquerade 3.4
mass 1.11
massage 2.14
massed 1.11
masseur 8.1
masseuse 8.18
massive 1.11
massively 1.11
mass-produce 18.11
mast 2.13
mastectomy 5.2
master 2.13
mastered 2.13
masterful 16.3
masterly 6.1
mastermind 10.9
masterpiece 6.11
masterstroke 12.3
mastery 6.1
masting 2.13
mastitis 10.13
mat 1.13
matador 14.1
match 1.13
matched 1.13
matcher 1.13
matching 1.13
matchmaker 3.3
mate 3.14
mater 3.14
material 7.5
materialism 7.5
materialistic 9.11
materialize 7.5
materially 6.1
maternal 8.9
maternally 8.9
maternity 8.9
matey 3.14
mathematical 1.13
mathematician 9.13
mathematics 1.13
Mat(h)ilda 9.6
matinée 3.1
mating 3.14
Matisse 6.11
matriarch 3.14
matriarchal 2.3
matriarchy 2.3
matricide 10.4
matriculate 9.2
matriculation 3.13
matrimonial 12.9
matrimony 1.13
matron 3.14

Matt 1.13
matt 1.13
matter 1.13
mattered 1.13
Matterhorn 14.10
mattering 1.13
matter-of-fact 1.2
mature 19.1
matured 19.2
maturely 19.3
maturest 19.4
maturing 19.4
maturity 19.4
Maud(e) 14.4
Maui 13.1
maul 14.8
mauled 14.8
Maureen 14.12
Maurice 11.10
Mauritania 3.9
Mauritanian 3.9
Mauritian 9.13
Mauritius 9.13
mausoleum 6.1
mauve 12.17
maverick 9.2
mavericks 9.2
Mavis 3.17
mawkish 14.3
Max 1.2
max 1.2
maximize 10.17
maximizer 10.17
maximizing 10.17
maximum 17.7
Maxine 6.9
May 3.1
may 3.1
Mayan 10.1
maybe 3.2
Mayday 3.4
Mayflower 13.1
Mayo 3.1
mayo 3.1
mayonnaise 3.18
mayor 4.1
mayoress 4.6
maze 3.18
MBA 3.1
MBE 6.1
MBO 12.1
MC 6.1
McCoist 15.6
McGregor 5.5
McQueen 6.9
MD 6.1

ME 6.1
me 6.1
meagre 6.6
meagrely 6.6
meal 6.7
mealy 6.7
mean 6.9
meander 1.8
meandered 1.8
meaner 6.9
meanie 6.9
meaning 6.9
meaningful 16.3
meaningless 5.11
meanly 6.9
means 6.9
meant 5.8
measurable 5.12
measure 5.12
measurement 5.8
meat 6.14
meat-eater 6.14
meat-eating 6.14
Meath 6.15
meats 6.14
meaty 6.14
Mecca 5.2
mechanic 1.8
mechanical 1.8
mechanism 9.18
mechanize 10.17
mechanized 10.17
mechanizing 10.17
MEd 5.3
Med 5.3
medal 5.3
medallion 1.6
meddle 5.3
meddler 5.3
meddlesome 17.7
media 6.4
median 6.4
mediate 3.14
mediation 3.13
mediator 3.14
medical 16.3
medicate 5.3
medicated 5.3
medication 3.13
medicinal 16.3
medicine 9.8
medieval 6.17
mediocre 12.3
mediocrity 6.1
meditate 3.14
meditation 3.13

Mediterranean 3.9
medium 6.4
medium-range 3.9
medley 5.3
Medusa 18.11
meek 6.3
meeker 6.3
meekly 6.3
meet 6.14
meeting 6.14
meets 6.14
Meg 5.5
megabyte 10.13
megahertz 8.14
megalomania 3.9
megalomaniac 3.9
megaphone 12.9
megaton(ne) 17.8
megawatt 11.13
Meir 7.1
Mekong 11.8
Mel 5.6
melancholy 11.6
Melanesia 6.12
Melanie 5.6
melanin 9.8
melanoma 12.8
melee 5.6
Melissa 9.11
mellow 5.6
Melly 5.6
melodeon 12.4
melodic 11.3
melodious 12.4
melodrama 2.9
melodramas 2.9
melodramatic 1.13
melodramatics 1.13
melody 6.1
melon 5.6
melt 5.6
Melvin 5.6
member 5.7
membership 9.9
memento 5.8
memo 5.7
memorable 16.3
memoranda 1.8
memorandum 1.8
memorial 14.12
memorize 10.17
memorizing 10.17
memory 5.7
men 5.8
menace 5.8
menagerie 6.1

mend 5.8
Mendelssohn 17.8
mender 5.8
mending 5.8
Mendip Hills 9.6
menial 6.9
meningitis 10.13
meniscus 9.11
menopause 14.20
menstruate 3.14
menstruation 3.13
mental 5.8
mentality 1.6
mentally 5.8
mention 5.8
mentionable 5.8
mentioned 5.8
menu 5.8
MEP 6.1
MEPs 6.19
mercantile 10.7
mercenary 6.1
merchandise 10.17
merchandising 10.17
merciful 16.3
mercifully 6.1
merciless 5.11
mercurial 19.4
mercy 8.12
mere 7.1
merely 7.4
merge 8.4
merger 8.4
meringue 1.8
merit 5.10
meritorious 14.12
merrily 6.1
merriment 5.10
merry 5.10
merry-go-round 13.4
Mersey 8.18
Merseyside 10.4
Meryl 5.10
mesh 5.13
mesmerize 10.17
mesmerizing 10.17
mess 5.11
message 5.11
Messalina 6.9
messed 5.11
Messiah 10.1
messianic 1.8
messily 6.1
messy 5.11
met 5.14
metabolic 11.6

metabolism 9.18
metal 5.14
metallic 1.6
metallurgy 1.6
metalwork 8.3
metalworker 8.3
metalworking 8.3
metamorphosis 9.11
metaphor 14.1
metaphorical 11.10
metaphysical 9.18
mete 6.14
meted 6.14
meteoric 11.10
meteorite 10.13
meteorological 11.3
meteorology 11.6
meter 6.14
metes 6.14
methodical 11.3
methodically 11.3
Methodism 9.18
Methodist 9.11
methodology 11.6
meticulous 9.2
meting 6.14
metre 6.14
metronome 12.8
metropolis 9.11
metropolitan 11.6
mettle 5.14
mew 18.1
Mexican 17.8
mezzanine 6.9
mg 6.1
mi 6.1
MI5 10.15
MI6 9.2
Mia 6.1
Miami 1.7
miaow 13.1
miaowed 13.2
mica 10.3
mice 10.12
Michael 10.3
Michaela 3.7
Michelangelo 12.1
Michelle 5.6
Michigan 17.8
Mick 9.2
Mick(e)y 9.2
mickey 9.2
microbiology 11.6
microchip 9.9
microcomputer 18.14
microcomputing 18.14

microeconomics 11.7
microfiche 6.13
micrometer 11.7
Micronesia 6.12
microphone 12.9
microscope 12.10
microscopic 11.9
microsurgery 8.4
microwave 3.17
microwaved 3.17
mid 9.3
midair 4.1
midday 3.1
midden 9.3
middle 9.3
middle-aged 3.4
middlebrow 13.1
middle-class 2.13
middle-distance 9.11
middleman 1.8
middle-of-the-road 12.4
middle-sized 10.17
middleweight 3.14
midfield 6.7
midge 9.3
midget 9.3
midmorning 14.10
midstream 6.8
midsummer 17.7
midweek 6.3
Mid-West 5.11
Mid-Western 5.11
midwifery 9.4
midwinter 9.8
might 10.13
mightily 6.1
mighty 10.13
migrate 3.14
migration 3.13
migratory 6.1
Mikado 2.4
Mike 10.3
mike 10.3
Mikonos 11.11
Milan 1.8
mild 10.7
mildly 10.7
mildness 10.7
mile 10.7
mileage 10.7
militarism 9.18
military 6.1
militate 9.6
militia 9.13
milk 9.6
milky 9.6

mill 9.6
milled 9.6
Miller 9.6
miller 9.6
millet 9.6
Millie 9.6
milligram(me) 1.7
millilitre 6.14
millimetre 6.14
milling 9.6
million 9.6
millionaire 4.1
millionairess 4.6
millipede 6.4
milometer 11.7
Milosevic 9.14
Milton Keynes 6.9
Milwaukee 11.2
mime 10.8
mimer 10.8
mimic 9.7
mimicry 6.1
miming 10.8
minaret 5.14
mince 9.8
mincer 9.8
mincing 9.8
mind 10.9
minded 10.9
minder 10.9
minding 10.9
mind-numbing 17.7
mindreader 6.4
mine 10.9
miner 10.9
mineral 16.3
minesweeper 6.10
Ming 9.8
mingle 9.8
Mini 9.8
mini 9.8
miniature 19.1
miniaturize 10.17
miniaturizing 10.17
minibus 17.11
minicab 1.1
MiniDisc® 9.11
minigolf 11.6
minimal 16.3
minimize 10.17
minimizing 10.17
minimum 17.7
mining 10.9
minion 9.8
miniskirt 8.14
miniskirts 8.14

minister 9.8
ministerial 7.5
ministry 6.1
mink 9.8
minke 9.8
Minneapolis 9.11
Minnelli 5.6
Minnesota 12.14
Minnie 9.8
minnow 9.8
minor 10.9
Minorca 14.3
Minorcan 14.3
minority 11.10
minster 9.8
mint 9.8
minting 9.8
minuet 5.14
minus 10.9
minuscule 18.7
minute 9.8, 18.14
minutely 18.14
miracle 16.3
miraculous 17.11
mirage 2.14
Miranda 1.8
mire 10.1
Miriam 9.10
Miró 7.5
mirth 8.16
misadventure 5.8
misanthrope 12.10
misanthropic 11.9
misanthropist 1.8
misapprehension 5.8
misappropriation 3.13
misbehave 3.17
misbehaved 3.17
misbehaviour 3.17
miscalculate 3.14
miscalculation 3.13
miscarriage 1.10
miscarry 1.10
miscast 2.13
miscellaneous 3.9
miscellany 5.6
mischievous 17.11
misconception 5.9
misconduct 17.2
misconstrue 18.1
misdemeanour 6.9
misdiagnose 12.19
misdiagnosing 12.19
misdirect 5.2
misdirected 5.2
misdirecting 5.2

miser 10.17
miserable 16.3
miserably 6.1
miserly 6.1
misery 6.1
misery-guts 17.13
misfire 10.1
misfiring 10.1
misgiving 9.17
misgovern 17.15
misguided 10.4
mishandle 1.8
mishear 7.1
misheard 8.4
mishearing 7.5
misinformation 3.13
misjudge 17.3
misjudging 17.3
mislaid 3.4
mislay 3.1
mislaying 3.1
mislead 6.4
misleading 6.4
misled 5.3
misnomer 12.8
misogynist 9.11
misplace 3.11
misplacing 3.11
mispronounce 13.4
mispronounced 13.4
mispronunciation 3.13
misquote 12.14
misquoted 12.14
misquoting 12.14
misread 5.3, 6.4
misrepresent 5.8
misrepresentation 3.13
misrule 18.7
misruling 18.7
Miss 9.11
miss 9.11
missable 9.11
missal 9.11
missed 9.11
misses 9.11
misshapen 3.10
mission 9.13
missionary 9.13
Mississippi 9.9
Missouri 19.4
misspell 5.6
misspelled 5.6
misspelling 5.6
misspelt 5.6
misspent 5.8
missus 9.11

missy 9.11
mist 9.11
mistakable 3.3
mistake 3.3
mistaken 3.3
mistaking 3.3
misted 9.11
Mister 9.11
mistime 10.8
mistiming 10.8
misting 9.11
mistletoe 12.1
mistook 16.1
mistranslation 3.13
mistreat 6.14
mistreated 6.14
mistreating 6.14
mistreats 6.14
mistrial 10.1
mistrust 17.11
mistrusted 17.11
mistrustful 17.11
mistrusting 17.11
misty 9.11
misunderstand 1.8
misunderstanding 1.8
misunderstood 16.2
misuse 18.11, 18.19
misusing 18.19
mite 10.13
mitigate 9.14
mitigation 3.13
mitre 10.13
mitt 9.14
mitten 9.14
Mitty 9.14
mix 9.2
mixed 9.2
mixed-up 17.9
mixer 9.2
mixture 9.2
MLR 2.1
mnemonic 11.8
mnemonics 11.8
Mo 12.1
moan 12.9
moaner 12.9
moanier 12.9
moaning 12.9
moany 12.9
moat 12.14
mob 11.1
mobbing 11.1
mobility 9.6
mobilize 10.17
mobilizer 10.17

mobster 11.1
moccasin 9.8
mock 11.2
mocked 11.2
mocker 11.2
mockery 11.2
mocking 11.2
mockney 11.2
mock-up 11.2
MOD 6.1
mod cons 11.8
mode 12.4
model 11.3
moderate 3.14, 17.13
moderately 6.1
moderation 3.13
moderator 3.14
modern 11.3
modernism 9.18
modernization 3.13
modernize 10.17
modernizer 10.17
modernizing 10.17
modest 11.3
modestly 6.1
modesty 6.1
modicum 17.7
modification 3.13
modify 10.1
modulate 3.14
modulation 3.13
modulator 3.14
module 11.3
Mogadishu 9.13
mogul 12.6
moist 15.6
moister 15.6
moisturize 10.17
moisturizer 10.17
moisturizing 10.17
molar 12.7
Moldavia 3.17
Moldavian 17.8
Moldova 12.17
Moldovan 12.17
Mole 12.7
mole 12.7
molecular 5.2
molecule 18.7
molest 5.11
molested 5.11
molesting 5.11
molestor 5.11
mollified 11.6
mollify 11.6
Molly 11.6

mollycoddle 11.3
molten 12.7
mom 11.7
Mombasa 1.11
momentary 6.1
momentous 5.8
Mona 12.9
Monaco 12.1
Monaghan 17.8
monarchist 9.11
monarchy 6.1
monastery 6.1
monastic 1.11
Monday 17.8
monetarism 9.18
monetarist 9.11
monetary 6.1
money 17.8
moneybox 11.2
moneylender 5.8
moneymaker 3.3
moneymaking 3.3
moneyspinner 9.8
Mongolia 12.7
Mongolian 12.7
Monica 11.8
moni(c)ker 11.8
monk 17.8
monkey 17.8
Monmouthshire 10.1
monochrome 12.8
monocle 16.3
monogamous 17.11
monogamy 6.1
monogram 1.7
monograph 2.5
monographed 2.5
monographing 2.5
monolithic 9.16
monologue 11.5
monophonic 11.8
monopolize 10.17
monopolizing 10.17
monopoly 11.9
monorail 3.7
monoski 6.1
monoskis 6.19
monosyllable 9.6
monotone 12.9
monotonous 17.11
monotony 11.13
Monroe 12.1
Mons 11.8
Monsignor 6.9
monsoon 18.9
monstrosity 11.11

Montana 1.8
Mont Blanc 11.8
Monte Carlo 2.8
Monterey 3.1
Montevideo 3.1
Montezuma 18.8
Montgomerie 17.7
Montgomery 17.7
Montreal 14.8
Montserrat 1.13
Monty 11.8
monument 5.8
monumental 5.8
monumentally 5.8
moo 18.1
mooch 18.14
moocher 18.14
mood 18.4
moodily 6.1
moody 18.4
moon 18.9
mooned 18.9
mooner 18.9
moonlighting 10.13
moony 18.9
Moor 19.1
moor 19.1
Moore 14.1, 18.1, 19.1
moored 19.2
mooring 19.4
Moorish 19.4
moose 18.11
moot 18.14
mooted 18.14
mooting 18.14
mop 11.9
mope 12.10
moper 12.10
mopper 11.9
moral 11.10
morale 2.8
moralistic 9.11
morality 1.6
moralize 10.17
moralizer 10.17
moralizing 10.17
morally 6.1
morass 1.11
moratoria 14.12
moratorium 14.12
Morayshire 10.1
morbidly 6.1
mordant 14.4
More 14.1
more 14.1
moreover 12.17

moribund 17.8
Moritz 9.14
Mormon 14.9
morning 14.10
moron 14.12
moronic 11.8
morose 12.11
morris 11.10
morrow 11.10
Morse 14.13
morsel 14.13
mortal 14.15
mortality 1.6
mortally 14.15
mortar 14.15
mortician 9.13
mortification 3.13
mortify 14.15
mortuary 6.1
mosaic 3.1
mosquito 6.14
Moss 11.11
moss 11.11
mossed 11.11
mossy 11.11
most 12.11
mostly 12.11
MOT 6.1
motel 5.6
motet 5.14
moth 11.14
moth-eaten 6.14
mother 17.14
motherboard 14.4
motherhood 16.2,
 17.14
mother-in-law 14.1,
 17.14
motherland 1.8
mother-of-pearl 8.7
mother-to-be 6.1
motif 6.5
motion 12.13
motionless 5.11
motivate 3.14
motivation 3.13
motivator 3.14
motive 12.14
motley 11.13
motor 12.14
motorbike 10.3
motorboat 12.14
motorcade 3.4
motorcar 2.1
motorcycle 10.3
motorist 9.11

motorize 10.17
motorized 10.17
motorizing 10.17
motorway 3.1
mottled 11.13
motto 11.13
mould 12.7
moulder 12.7
moulding 12.7
mouldy 12.7
moult 12.7
mound 13.4
mounded 13.4
mounding 13.4
mount 13.4
mountain 13.4
mountaineer 7.1
mountaineering 7.5
mountainous 17.11
Mountbatten 1.13
mounted 13.4
mounting 13.4
mourn 14.10
Mourne 14.10
mourner 14.10
mournful 14.10
mourning 14.10
Mouse 13.6
mouse 13.6
moused 13.6
mousse 18.11
moustache 1.12
mouth 13.8
mouthwatering 14.15
movable 18.17
move 18.17
moved 18.17
movement 18.17
mover 18.17
movie 18.17
moviegoer 12.1
moving 18.17
mow 12.1
mowed 12.4
mower 12.1
mowing 12.1
mown 12.9
Mozambican 6.3
Mozambique 6.3
MP 6.1
mpg 6.1
MPs 6.19
Mr 9.11
Mrs 9.11
Ms 9.18
MSc 6.1

MSG 6.1
MSP 6.1
MSPs 6.19
much 17.13
muck 17.2
mucked 17.2
mucker 17.2
muckraking 3.3
mucks 17.2
mucky 17.2
mucous 18.3
mucus 18.3
mud 17.3
muddied 17.3
muddle 17.3
muddleheaded 5.3
muddy 17.3
mudslinging 9.8
muff 17.4
muffed 17.4
muffin 17.4
muffle 17.4
muffled 17.4
mug 17.5
Mugabe 2.2
mugger 17.5
muggy 17.5
Muhammad 1.7
mulberry 6.1
mulch 17.6
mule 18.7
Mull 17.6
mull 17.6
mullet 17.6
multicoloured 17.6
multifarious 4.6
multifariously 4.6
multi-functional 17.8
multimedia 6.4
multimillionaire 4.1
multinational 1.12
multiparty 2.16
multiple 16.3
multiple-choice 15.6
multiplex 5.2
multiplication 3.13
multiplicity 9.11
multiply 10.1
multiracial 3.13
multistorey 14.12
multitude 18.4
mum 17.7
mumble 17.7
mumbler 17.7
mumbling 17.7
mummer 17.7

mummery 17.7
mummify 10.1
mumming 17.7
mummy 17.7
mumps 17.7
munch 17.8
munches 17.8
munchies 17.8
mundane 3.9
Munich 18.9
municipal 16.3
municipality 1.6
mural 19.4
murder 8.4
Muriel 19.4
murky 8.3
murmur 8.8
Murray 17.10
muscle 17.11
muscleman 1.8
muscles 17.11
Muscovite 10.13
Muse 18.19
muse 18.19
mush 17.12
mushed 17.12
musher 17.12
mushing 17.12
mushy 17.12
musical 16.3
musician 9.13
musicologist 11.6
musing 18.19
musk 17.11
musketeer 7.1
mussel 17.11
mussels 17.11
Mussolini 6.9
must 17.11
mustard 17.11
muster 17.11
mustered 17.11
musty 17.11
mutant 18.14
mutate 3.14
mutation 3.13
mute 18.14
muted 18.14
mutilate 3.14
mutilation 3.13
mutilator 3.14
mutineer 7.1
muting 18.14
mutinous 18.14
mutiny 18.14
mutt 17.13

mutter 17.13
mutton 17.13
mutually 6.1
muzzle 17.16
muzzy 17.16
my 10.1
Myanmar 2.1
My Lai 10.7
mynah 10.9
myopia 12.10
myopic 11.9
Myra 10.1
myrrh 8.1
Myrtle 8.14
myrtle 8.14
myself 5.6
Mysore 14.1
mysterious 7.5
mysteriously 7.5
mystery 9.11
mystic 9.11
mystical 9.11
mysticism 9.18
mystics 9.11
mystify 10.1
mystique 6.3
myth 9.16
mythic 9.16
mythical 16.3
mythological 11.3
mythology 11.6
myxomatosis 12.11

N
N 5.8
naan 2.10
nab 1.1
Nadine 6.9
nadir 3.4
naff 1.4
NAFTA 1.4
nag 1.5
Nagasaki 2.3
nagging 1.5
nail 3.7
nail-biting 10.13
nailed 3.7
nailer 3.7
nailing 3.7
nailings 3.7
Nairn 4.5
Nairobi 12.2
naive 6.17
naivety 6.1
namby-pamby 1.7

name 3.8
name-calling 14.8
named 3.8
name-dropper 11.9
name-dropping 11.9
nameless 3.8
namely 3.8
namer 3.8
names 3.8
Namibia 9.1
Namibian 9.1
Nan 1.8
Nancy 1.8
nancy 1.8
Nanette 5.14
Nanking 9.8
nanny 1.8
nanny-goat 12.14
nanosecond 5.2
nanotechnology 11.6
Nantes 11.8
Nantucket 17.2
nap 1.9
nape 3.10
naphthalene 6.9
Naples 3.10
Napoleon 12.7
Napoleonic 11.8
napper 1.9
napping 1.9
nappy 1.9
narc 2.3
narcosis 12.11
narcotic 11.13
narcotics 11.13
nark 2.3
narked 2.3
narker 2.3
narking 2.3
narky 2.3
narrate 3.14
narrative 1.10
narrator 3.14
narrow 1.10
narrowly 6.1
narrow-minded 10.9
NASA 1.11
nasal 3.18
Nassau 14.1
Nasser 1.11
nastily 6.1
nastiness 5.11
nasty 2.13
Nat 1.13
Natal 2.8
Natalie 1.13

Natasha 1.12
Nathaniel 1.8
nation 3.13
national 1.12
nationalism 1.12
nationalist 1.12
nationalistic 9.11
nationality 1.6
nationalization 3.13
nationalize 1.12
nationalizing 10.17
nationally 1.12
nationwide 10.4
native 3.14
Nativity 9.17
NATO 3.14
natter 1.13
nattered 1.13
nattering 1.13
natty 1.13
natural 16.3
naturalism 9.18
naturalist 9.11
naturalistic 9.11
naturalization 3.13
naturalize 10.17
naturalizing 10.17
naturally 6.1
naturist 9.11
naught 14.15
naughty 14.15
nauseate 3.14
nautical 14.15, 16.3
nave 3.17
navel-gazing 3.18
navigable 16.3
navigate 3.14
navigation 3.13
navigational 3.13
navigator 3.14
Navratilova 12.17
navy 3.17
navy-blue 18.1
Nazareth 5.16
NB 6.1
NCO 12.1
Neanderthal 2.8
Neapolitan 11.6
near 7.1
nearby 10.1
nearer 7.5
nearing 7.5
nearly 7.4
nearly-new 18.1
near-sighted 10.13
neat 6.14

neaten 6.14
neater 6.14
neatly 6.14
neatness 6.14
Nebraska 1.11
nebulous 17.11
necessarily 5.10
necessitate 3.14
neck 5.2
necked 5.2
necklace 5.2
necks 5.2
necromancer 1.8
necromancy 1.8
nectar 5.2
nectarine 6.9
Ned 5.3
née 3.1
need 6.4
needier 6.4
needle 6.4
needlecraft 2.5
needless 6.4
needlessly 6.1
needlework 8.3
needleworker 8.3
need-to-know 12.1
needy 6.4
nefarious 4.6
nefariously 4.6
Nefertiti 6.14
negate 3.14
negation 3.13
negative 9.17
negatively 6.1
negativity 9.17
negator 3.14
neglect 5.2
neglected 5.2
neglectful 5.2
neglecting 5.2
negligée 3.1
negligence 5.8
negligent 5.8
negligently 6.1
negligible 16.3
negotiable 12.13, 16.3
negotiate 3.14
negotiation 3.13
negotiations 3.13
negotiator 3.14
neigh 3.1
neighbour 3.2
neighbourhood 16.2
neighbouring 3.2
neighbourly 6.1

Neil 6.7
neither 6.15
Nell 5.6
Nellie 5.6
neocolonial 12.9
neolithic 9.16
Nepal 14.8
Nepalese 6.19
Nepali 14.8
nepotism 9.18
nerd 8.4
nerdy 8.4
Nero 7.5
Neruda 16.2
nerve 8.17
nerve-(w)racking 1.2
nervously 6.1
nervousness 5.11
nervy 8.17
Nerys 5.10
nest 5.11
nested 5.11
nester 5.11
nesting 5.11
nestle 5.11
nestling 5.11
Net 5.14
net 5.14
Netanyahu 2.7
netiquette 5.14
netted 5.14
netting 5.14
nettle 5.14
neural 19.4
neurologist 11.6
neurology 11.6
neuroses 12.11
neurosis 12.11
neurosurgery 8.4
neurotic 11.13
neurotics 11.13
neuter 18.14
neutrality 1.6
neutralize 10.17
neutralizer 10.17
neutralizing 10.17
neutrino 6.9
Nevada 2.4
never 5.17
never-ending 5.8
never-never 5.17
nevertheless 5.11
Neville 5.17
new 18.1
newbie 18.2
Newcastle 16.3

newcomer 17.7
newer 18.1
newest 18.1
newfangled 1.8
Newfoundland 1.8
newly 18.7
newlyweds 5.3
Newman 18.8
newness 18.9
New Orleans 6.9
Newquay 18.3
newscaster 2.13
newsdealer 6.7
newsletter 5.14
newspaper 3.10
newspaperman 1.8
newsreader 6.4
newsworthy 8.15
newt 18.14
Newton 18.14
New York 14.3
New Yorker 14.3
next 5.2
next-door 14.1
next-of-kin 9.8
NFL 5.6
NGO 12.1
NHS 5.11
NI 10.1
Niamh 6.17
nib 9.1
nibble 9.1
Nicaragua 1.5
Nice 6.11
nice 10.12
nice-looking 16.1
nicely 10.12
nicer 10.12
niche 6.13
Nic(h)olas 17.11
Nick 9.2
nick 9.2
nicked 9.2
nickel 9.2
nickelodeon 12.4
nicker 9.2
nicking 9.2
nicks 9.2
Nicky 9.2
Nicole 12.7
Nicosia 6.1
nicotine 6.9
niece 6.11
Nietzsche 6.14
niff 9.4
nifty 9.4

Nigella   5.6
Nigeria   7.5
Nigerian   7.5
niggardly   6.1
niggle   9.5
nigh   10.1
night   10.13
nightie   10.13
nightingale   3.7
nightly   10.13
nihilistic   9.11
Nike   10.3
Nikki   9.2
nil   9.6
Nile   10.7
nimble   9.7
Nina   6.9
nincompoop   18.10
nine   10.9
nineteen   6.9
Nineteen Eighty-Four
   14.1
Nineveh   3.1
Nintendo®   5.8
nip   9.9
nipper   9.9
nipple   9.9
nippy   9.9
nirvana   2.10
Nisha   6.13
nit   9.14
Nita   6.14
nit-picker   9.2
nit-picking   9.2
nitrogen   17.8
nitroglycerine   6.9
nitty-gritty   9.14
Niven   9.17
Nixon   9.2
Nkrumah   18.8
NME   6.1
no   12.1
Noah   12.1
nobble   11.1
nobby   11.1
nobility   9.6
noble   12.2
nobody   11.3
no-brainer   3.9
nocturnal   8.9
nocturnally   8.9
nod   11.3
nodded   11.3
nodder   11.3
Noddy   11.3
node   12.4

nodule   11.3
Noel   12.1
Noël   5.6
Noel(l)e   5.6
no-frills   9.6
no-hoper   12.10
noise   15.8
noiselessly   6.1
noisily   6.1
nomadic   1.3
nomenclature   19.1
nominal   11.7
nominally   11.7
nominate   3.14, 11.7
nomination   3.13
nominative   9.17
nominator   3.14
nominee   6.1
nonagenarian   4.6
nonalcoholic   11.6
nonaligned   10.9
nonattendance   5.8
noncommittal   9.14
non-denominational
   3.13
nondescript   9.9
none   17.8
nonentity   5.8
nonessential   5.8
nonetheless   5.11
nonevent   5.8
nonexistent   9.11
non-fiction   9.2
nonflammable   1.7
non-invasive   3.11
non-linear   9.8
non-malignant   9.5
non-member   5.7
non-negotiable   12.13,
   16.3
no-no   12.9
non-partisan   1.8
non-payment   3.8
non-person   8.12
non-physical   9.18
nonplussed   17.11
non-profit-making   3.3
non-racist   3.11
nonresident   5.18
non-rhyming   10.8
nonsensical   16.3
non sequitur   8.1
non sequiturs   8.18
non-smoker   12.3
nonstarter   2.16
nonstick   9.2

non-stop   11.9
nonverbal   8.2
nonverbally   8.2
non-viable   10.1
noodles   18.4
nook   16.1
noon   18.9
noose   18.11
nope   12.10
nor   14.1
Nora(h)   14.12
Noreen   14.12
Norm   14.9
norm   14.9
Norma   14.9
normal   14.9
normality   1.6
normalization   3.13
normalize   14.9
normally   14.9
Norman   14.9
Normandy   6.1
normative   14.9
north   14.16
Northamptonshire   10.1
Northants   1.8
northeast   6.11
northerly   6.1
north-facing   3.11
north-northeast   6.11
north-northwest   5.11
north-northwester   5.11
north-northwestern   5.11
northwest   5.11
northwester   5.11
northwestern   5.11
Norway   14.18
Norwegian   6.4
Norwich   11.10
nose   12.19
noser   12.19
nosey   12.19
nosh   11.12
nosher   11.12
no-show   12.1
nosiness   5.11
nosing   12.19
no-smoking   12.3
nostalgically   6.1
nostrum   11.11
nosy parker   2.3
not   11.13
notable   16.3
notably   6.1
notary   12.14
notation   3.13

notch   11.13
note   12.14
noted   12.14
notepaper   3.10
noteworthy   8.15
notice   12.14
noticeable   16.3
noticeably   6.1
noticeboard   14.4
notification   3.13
notify   10.1
noting   12.14
notion   12.13
not on your nelly   5.6
notoriety   10.1
notorious   14.12
notoriously   14.12
Nottinghamshire   10.1
notwithstanding   1.8
nought   14.15
noun   13.4
nourish   17.10
nourishing   17.10
nourishment   5.8
nous   13.6
Nova Scotia   12.13
novel   11.15
novelist   9.11
Novello   5.6
novelty   6.1
November   5.7
now   13.1
nowadays   3.18
NRA   3.1
NSPCC   6.1
nth   5.8
nub   17.1
nude   18.4
nudge   17.3
nudging   17.3
nudity   6.1
nugatory   6.1
nuke   18.3
null   17.6
nullify   10.1
NUM   5.7
numb   17.7
number   17.7
numberplate   3.14
numbing   17.7
numeracy   6.1
numeral   16.3
numerate   17.13
numerator   3.14
numerical   5.10
numerically   5.10

numerous   18.8
nun   17.8
Nunn   17.8
Nuremberg   8.6
Nureyev   5.4
nurse   8.12
nursed   8.12
nursery   8.12
nurture   8.14
NUS   5.11
NUT   6.1
nut   17.13
nutcrackers   1.2
nutrition   9.13
nutritional   9.13
nutritious   9.13
nuts   17.13
nutter   17.13
nutting   17.13
nutty   17.13
nuzzle   17.16
NVQ   18.1
NY   10.1
nylon   10.7
nymph   9.7
nymphomania   3.9
nymphomaniac   3.9

O
O   12.1
oaf   12.5
Oahu   2.7
oak   12.3
oaking   12.3
OAP   6.1
oar   14.1
OAS   5.11
oases   3.11
oasis   3.11
Oates   12.14
oath   12.16
oats   12.14
OBE   6.1
obedient   6.4
obelisk   9.11
obese   6.11
obesity   6.1
obey   3.1
obeying   3.1
obfuscation   3.13
obituary   6.1
object   5.2
objected   5.2
objectify   5.2
objecting   5.2

objection   5.2
objectionable   16.3
objective   5.2
objectively   5.2
objectivity   9.17
objector   5.2
obligation   3.13
obligatory   6.1
oblique   6.3
obliterate   9.14
oblivion   9.17
oblivious   9.17
oboist   9.11
obscene   6.9
obscenely   6.9
obscenity   5.8
obscure   19.1
obscured   19.2
obscurely   19.3
obscuring   19.4
obscurity   19.4
observable   16.3
observant   8.17
observation   3.13
observatory   6.1
observe   8.17
observed   8.17
observer   8.17
observing   8.17
obsess   5.11
obsessed   5.11
obsession   5.13
obsessional   5.13
obsessive   5.11
obsessively   5.11
obsolescence   5.11
obsolete   6.14
obstacle   16.3
obstetrician   9.13
obstinacy   6.1
obstinate   17.13
obstreperous   17.11
obstruct   17.2
obstruction   17.2
obstructive   17.2
obtain   3.9
obtainable   3.9
obtainer   3.9
obtrusive   18.11
obtrusively   18.11
obtuse   18.11
obviate   3.14
obviously   6.1
occasion   3.12
occasional   16.3
occasionally   6.1

occidental   5.8
occidentally   5.8
occult   17.6
occupation   3.13
occupational   3.13
occupied   10.4
occupy   10.1
occur   8.1
occurred   8.4
occurring   8.11
occurs   8.18
ocean   12.13
ocean-going   12.1
oceanic   1.8
ocelot   11.13
ochre   12.3
o'clock   11.2
OCR   2.1
octagon   17.8
octagonal   1.5
Octavia   3.17
octet   5.14
October   12.2
octogenarian   4.6
octopus   17.11
OD   6.1
odd   11.3
odder   11.3
oddest   11.3
oddity   11.3
oddly   11.3
odds-on   11.8
ode   12.4
Odessa   5.11
Odette   5.14
odious   12.4
odium   12.4
odour   12.4
odourless   5.11
odyssey   6.1
OECD   6.1
Oedipal   16.3
Oedipus   17.11
oesophagi   11.4
oesophagus   11.4
off   11.4
offal   11.4
Offaly   6.1
Offa's Dyke   10.3
off-colour   17.6
off-duty   18.14
offence   5.8
offend   5.8
offended   5.8
offender   5.8
offending   5.8

offensive   5.8
offensively   5.8
offer   11.4
offhand   1.8
officeholder   12.7
official   9.13
officialese   6.19
officially   9.13
officiate   9.13
officious   9.13
officiously   9.13
off-key   6.1
off-line   10.9
off-load   12.4
off-loading   12.4
off-peak   6.3
off-putting   16.5
off-season   6.19
offshore   14.1
offside   10.4
offstage   3.4
off-the-cuff   17.4
off-the-wall   14.8
off-white   10.13
ogle   12.6
ogre   12.6
oh   12.1
ohm   12.8
OHMS   5.11
oho   12.1
OHP   6.1
oi   15.1
oil   15.3
oil-fired   10.1
oily   15.3
ointment   15.5
OK   3.1
O'Keefe   6.5
okey-dokey   12.3
Okinawa   2.20
Oklahoma   12.8
old   12.7
old as the hills   9.6
older   12.7
old-fashioned   1.12
oldie   12.7
Old MacDonald   11.8
Old Man of Hoy   15.1
old stager   3.4
old-timer   10.8
oleander   1.8
olfactory   1.2
Olga   11.6
oligarchy   2.3
oligopoly   11.9
Olive Oyl   15.3

Olivia   9.17
Ollie   11.6
Omagh   12.8
Omaha   2.1
Oman   1.8
Omani   1.8
Omar Khayyám   1.7
ombudsman   17.8
omen   12.8
ominous   17.11
ominously   6.1
omission   9.13
omit   9.14
omnibus   17.11
omnipotence   5.8
omnipotent   5.8
omnipresent   5.18
omnivore   14.1
omnivorous   9.17
on   11.8
once   11.8, 17.8
once-over   12.17
oncoming   17.7
one   17.8
one-dimensional   5.8
one-liner   10.9
one of these days   3.18
one-party   2.16
onerous   17.11
oneself   5.6
one-sided   10.4
one-to-one   17.8
one-upmanship   9.9
one-way   17.8
ongoing   12.1
onion   17.8
on-line   10.9
onlooker   16.1
only   12.9
ono   12.1
on-stage   3.4
onus   12.9
oodles   18.4
oops   18.10
ooze   18.19
oozing   18.19
oozy   18.19
op   11.9
opaque   3.3
op cit   9.14
OPEC   12.10
open-air   4.1
opencast   2.13
open-ended   5.8
openly   6.1
open-minded   10.9

openness   5.11
open-plan   1.8
operate   3.14
operatic   1.13
operating   3.14
operation   3.13
operational   3.13
operative   9.17
operator   3.14
operetta   5.14
Ophelia   6.7
ophthalmology   11.6
opinion   9.8
opinionated   3.14
Oporto   14.15
opossum   11.11
opportune   18.9
opportunism   9.18
opportunist   18.9
opportunity   18.9
oppose   12.19
opposer   12.19
opposing   12.19
opposite   9.14
opposition   9.13
oppress   5.11
oppressed   5.11
oppression   5.13
oppressive   5.11
oppressively   5.11
oppressor   5.11
opt   11.9
optical   16.3
optician   9.13
optimism   9.18
optimist   9.11
optimistic   9.11
optimize   10.17
optimizer   10.17
optimizing   10.17
optimum   17.7
option   11.9
optional   16.3
opulent   5.8
OR   2.1
or   14.1
oracle   16.3
oral   14.12
orally   6.1
Oran   1.8
orang-outan(g)   1.8
oration   3.13
oratory   11.10
orb   14.2
orchestral   5.11
orchestrate   3.14

orchestrator   3.14
ordain   3.9
ordeal   7.4
order   14.4
ordered   14.4
orderly   6.1
orders   14.4
ordinal   16.3
ordinarily   5.10, 6.1
ordinary   6.1
ordination   3.13
ore   14.1
oregano   2.10
Oregon   17.8
organ   14.6
organ-grinder   10.9
organic   1.8
organism   9.18
organist   9.11
organization   3.13
organize   10.17
organized   10.17
organizer   10.17
organizing   10.17
orient   5.8
oriental   5.8
Orientalist   5.8
orientally   5.8
orientate   3.14
orientation   3.13
orienteering   7.5
orifice   9.11
origami   2.9
origin   9.8
original   16.3
originality   1.6
originally   6.1
originate   3.14
ornament   5.8
ornamental   5.8
ornamentally   5.8
ornate   3.14
ornithologist   11.6
ornithology   11.6
orris   11.10
orthodox   11.2
orthodoxy   11.2
orthop(a)edic   6.4
Osaka   2.3
Osama   2.9
Osama bin Laden   2.4
Oscar   11.11
oscillate   3.14
oscillator   3.14
osmosis   12.11
Osnabrück   16.1

ossify   10.1
Ostend   5.8
ostensible   5.8
ostensibly   5.8
ostentation   3.13
ostentatious   3.13
osteoarthritis   10.13
osteopath   1.15
osteopathic   1.15
osteoplasty   1.11
osteoporosis   12.11
ostracism   9.18
ostracize   10.17
ostracizing   10.17
OTC   6.1
Othello   5.6
other   17.14
otherwise   10.17
OTT   6.1
otter   11.13
Otto   11.13
ouch   13.7
ought   14.15
oughtn't   14.15
ounce   13.4
our   13.1
ourselves   5.6
oust   13.6
out   13.7
out-and-out   13.7
outbid   9.3
outbidding   9.3
outclass   2.13
outclassed   2.13
outdated   3.14
outdid   9.3
outdistance   9.11
outdo   18.1
outdone   17.8
outdoors   14.20
outermost   12.11
outflank   1.8
outflanking   1.8
outgoing   12.1
outgrew   18.1
outgrow   12.1
outgrowing   12.1
outgrown   12.9
outing   13.7
outlandish   1.8
outlast   2.13
outlasting   2.13
outlive   9.17
outliving   9.17
outlying   10.1
outmoded   12.4

oversaw 14.1
overseas 6.19
oversee 6.1
overseeing 6.1
overseen 6.9
overseer 6.1, 7.1
overshadow 1.3
overshoe 18.1
overshoot 18.14
overshooting 18.14
overshot 11.13
oversight 10.13
oversimplify 10.1
oversized 10.17
oversleep 6.10
oversleeping 6.10
overslept 5.9
overspend 5.8
overspending 5.8
overspent 5.8
overspill 9.6
overspilled 9.6
overstaffed 2.5
overstaffing 2.5
overstate 3.14
overstatement 3.14
overstay 3.1
overstaying 3.1
overstep 5.9
overstepped 5.9
overt 8.14
overtake 3.3
overtaken 3.3
overtaking 3.3
overtaxed 1.2
over-the-top 11.9
overthrew 18.1
overthrow 12.1
overthrowing 12.1
overthrown 12.9
overtime 10.8
overtone 12.9
overtook 16.1
overture 19.1
overturn 8.9
overturned 8.9
overturning 8.9
overuse 18.11, 18.19
overusing 18.19
overview 18.1
overweight 3.14
overwhelm 5.6
overwhelmingly 6.1
overwork 8.3
overworking 8.3
overwrite 10.13

overwriter 10.13
overwriting 10.13
overwritten 9.14
overwrote 12.14
overwrought 14.15
ovulate 3.14
ovulation 3.13
ow 13.1
owe 12.1
owed 12.4
oweing 12.1
owl 13.3
own 12.9
owner 12.9
owner-occupier 10.1
ownership 9.9
owning 12.9
ox 11.2
oxen 11.2
Oxfordshire 10.1
oxidize 10.17
oxidizer 10.17
oxidizing 10.17
oxyacetylene 6.9
oxygen 17.8
oxymoron 14.12
oyster 15.6
oystercatcher 1.13
Oz 11.16

P
P 6.1
PA 3.1
pa 2.1
pace 3.11
pacemaker 3.3
pac(e)y 3.11
Pacific 9.4
pacifism 9.18
pacifist 9.11
pacify 1.11
pacing 3.11
Pacino 6.9
pack 1.2
packed 1.2
packer 1.2
packet 1.2
packing 1.2
packs 1.2
pact 1.2
pad 1.3
paddle 1.3
paddock 1.3
Paddy 1.3
paddy 1.3

paean 6.1
paediatric 1.13
paediatrician 9.13
paediatrics 1.13
paedophile 10.7
pagan 3.6
paganism 9.18
page 3.4
pageantry 6.1
paged 3.4
pager 3.4
pagination 3.13
paging 3.4
pagoda 12.4
paid 3.4
Pa(i)ge 3.4
pail 3.7
pain 3.9
pained 3.9
painful 3.9
painfully 3.9
painkiller 9.6
painless 3.9
painstaking 3.3
paint 3.9
painted 3.9
pair 4.1
paired 4.2
pairing 4.6
Pakistan 2.10
Pakistani 2.10
pal 1.6
palace 1.6
palatable 16.3
palate 1.6
palatial 3.13
palaver 2.19
pale 3.7
paled 3.7
paler 3.7
Palestine 10.9
Palestinian 9.8
palette 1.6
palisade 3.4
pall 14.8
pallbearer 4.6
palled 14.8
pallet 1.6
palliative 9.17
pallid 1.6
pally 1.6
palm 2.9
Palma 1.6
palmed 2.9
palmer 2.9
palming 2.9

palmistry 6.1
palms 2.9
Paloma 12.8
palomino 6.9
palpable 16.3
palpate 3.14
palpitate 3.14
palpitations 3.13
Pam 1.7
pamper 1.7
Pamplona 12.9
Pan 1.8
pan 1.8
panacea 7.1
panache 1.12
Panamanian 3.9
panda 1.8
pandemonium 12.9
pander 1.8
pandered 1.8
Pandora 14.12
pane 3.9
panel 1.8
panelling 1.8
panellist 1.8
pang 1.8
panhandle 1.8
panic 1.8
panicky 6.1
panic-stricken 9.2
panned 1.8
pannier 1.8
panoply 6.1
panorama 2.9
panoramas 2.9
panoramic 1.7
pant 1.8
panther 1.8
pantomime 10.8
pantry 1.8
pants 1.8
pantyhose 12.19
panzer 1.8
panzers 1.8
pap 1.9
papa 2.1
papacy 6.1
Papa Doc 11.2
papal 3.10
paper 3.10
paperback 1.2
paperbacks 1.2
paperclip 9.9
paperknife 10.5
paperweight 3.14
paperwork 8.3

papery 6.1
papier-mâché 1.12
papyrus 10.11
par 2.1
parable 1.10
parabolic 11.6
paracetamol 11.6
parachute 18.14
parachuted 18.14
parachuting 18.14
parade 3.4
paraded 3.4
paradigm 10.8
parading 3.4
paradise 10.12
paradox 11.2
paradoxical 16.3
paraffin 9.8
paragliding 10.4
paragon 1.10
paragraph 2.5
paragraphed 2.5
paragraphing 2.5
Paraguay 10.1
Paraguayan 10.1
parakeet 6.14
parakeets 6.14
parallel 5.6
parallelling 5.6
parallelogram 1.7
paralyse 10.17
paralysed 10.17
paralysing 10.17
paralysis 1.6
paralytic 9.14
parameter 1.7
paramilitary 6.1
paramount 13.4
paranoia 15.1
paranoid 15.2
paranormal 14.9
parapet 5.14
paraphernalia 3.7
paraphrase 3.18
paraplegic 6.4
parascending 5.8
parasite 10.13
parasitic 9.14
parasitical 9.14
parasol 11.6
paratrooper 18.10
parboil 15.3
parcel 2.13
parch 2.16
pardon 2.4
pardonable 2.4

pardoned 2.4
pare 4.1
pared 4.2
parental 5.8
parentally 5.8
parenthesis 9.11
parenthood 16.2
pariah 10.1
paring 4.6
Paris 1.10
parishioner 9.13
Parisian 9.18
parity 1.10
park 2.3
parka 2.3
parked 2.3
Parker 2.3
parking 2.3
parley 2.8
parliament 5.8
parliamentarian 4.6
parliamentarianism 4.6
parliamentary 5.8
parlour 2.8
Parma 2.9
Parmesan 1.8
Parnell 5.6
parody 6.1
parole 12.7
paroled 12.7
paroling 12.7
paroxysm 9.18
parquet 3.1
parred 2.4
parried 1.10
parrot 1.10
parrot-fashion 1.12
parry 1.10
parse 2.21
parsimonious 12.9
parsley 2.13
parson 2.13
part 2.16
partake 3.3
partaken 3.3
partaker 3.3
partaking 3.3
partial 2.15
partiality 1.6
partially 6.1
participate 9.11
participation 3.13
participle 16.3
particle 2.16
particular 9.2
particularly 6.1

parting 2.16
partisan 1.8
partisanship 9.9
partition 9.13
partitioned 9.13
partitioning 9.13
partly 2.16
partnership 9.9
partook 16.1
partridge 2.16
part-time 10.8
part-timer 10.8
party 2.16
Pasadena 6.9
pass 2.13
passable 2.13
passageway 3.1
passé 3.1
passer-by 10.1
passion 1.12
passionate 1.12, 17.13
passive 1.11
passively 1.11
past 2.13
pasta 1.11
paste 3.11
paster 3.11
Pasteur 8.1
pasteurize 10.17
pasteurizer 10.17
pasteurizing 10.17
pastiche 6.13
pasting 3.11
pastings 3.11
pastor 2.13
pastoral 16.3
pastrami 2.9
pasty 1.11, 3.11
Pat 1.13
pat 1.13
Patagonia 12.9
patch 1.13
patched 1.13
patcher 1.13
patching 1.13
patchy 1.13
pate 3.14
pâté 1.13
patent 3.14
patently 3.14
pater 3.14
paternal 8.9
paternally 8.9
paternity 8.9
path 2.18
pathetic 5.14

pathetically 5.14
pathological 11.3
pathologist 11.6
pathology 11.6
pathos 3.16
patiently 6.1
patio 12.1
patriarch 3.14
patriarchal 2.3
patriarchy 2.3
Patricia 9.13
patricide 10.4
Patrick 1.13
patrimony 1.13
patriot 17.13
patriotic 11.13
patriotism 9.18
patrol 12.7
patrolled 12.7
patroller 12.7
patrolling 12.7
patrolman 12.7
patron 3.14
patronize 10.17
patronizing 10.17
patter 1.13
pattered 1.13
pattering 1.13
pattern 1.13
Patton 1.13
Patty 1.13
Paul 14.8
Paula 14.8
Paulette 5.14
paunch 14.10
pauper 14.11
pause 14.20
Pavarotti 11.13
pave 3.17
paved 3.17
paver 3.17
pavilion 9.6
paving 3.17
Pavlova 12.17
pavlova 12.17
paw 14.1
pawing 14.12
pawn 14.10
pawnbroker 12.3
pawning 14.10
pax 1.2
pay 3.1
payable 3.1
pay-as-you-earn 8.9
payday 3.4
PAYE 6.1

payee 6.1
paying 3.1
paymaster 2.13
payment 3.8
payoff 3.1
pay-per-view 18.1
PC 6.1
PE 6.1
pea 6.1
peace 6.11
peaceable 16.3
peacekeeping 6.10
peace-loving 17.15
peach 6.14
peak 6.3
peaking 6.3
peaky 6.3
peal 6.7
pealed 6.7
pealing 6.7
pear 4.1
Pearl 8.7
pearl 8.7
pearled 8.7
Pearl Harbor 2.2
pearling 8.7
pearly 8.7
peasant 5.18
peashooter 18.14
pea-souper 18.10
peat 6.14
pebble 5.1
pebbledash 1.12
pebbledashed 1.12
pebbledashing 1.12
pecan 6.3
peccary 6.1
Peck 5.2
peck 5.2
pecked 5.2
pecks 5.2
pecs 5.2
pectoral 5.2
peculiar 18.7
peculiarity 1.10
peculiarly 6.1
pecuniary 6.1
pedagogic 11.3
pedagogical 11.3
pedal 5.3
pedalo 12.1
pedantic 1.8
pedantry 5.3
peddle 5.3
peddler 5.3
pedestal 16.3

pedestrian 5.11
pedestrianize 10.17
pedestrianizing 10.17
pedicure 19.1
pedicured 19.2
pedigree 6.1
pedlar 5.3
Peeblesshire 10.1
peek 6.3
peeking 6.3
Peel 6.7
peel 6.7
peeled 6.7
peeler 6.7
peeling 6.7
peelings 6.7
peep 6.10
peeper 6.10
peeping 6.10
peer 7.1
peeress 5.11
Peer Gynt 9.8
peering 7.5
peerless 7.4
peeve 6.17
peeved 6.17
peeves 6.17
Peg 5.5
peg 5.5
Pegasus 17.11
Peggy 5.5
pegs 5.5
pejorative 9.17
Pekinese 6.19
Peking 9.8
Pele 5.6
pelican 17.8
pellet 5.6
pell-mell 5.6
pelmet 5.6
pelt 5.6
pelvis 5.6
Pembrokeshire 10.1
pen 5.8
penal 6.9
penalize 10.17
penalizing 10.17
penalty 6.1
pence 5.8
pencil 5.8
pendant 5.8
pending 5.8
pendragon 1.5
pendulum 17.7
Penelope 6.1
penetrate 3.14

penetrating 3.14
penetration 3.13
penetrator 3.14
penicillin 9.6
peninsula 9.8
peninsular 9.8
penitence 5.8
penitent 5.8
penitentiary 6.1
Penn 5.8
pennant 5.8
penniless 5.11
Pennsylvania 3.9
Pennsylvanian 3.9
Penny 5.8
penny 5.8
penny-pinching 9.8
pens 5.8
pension 5.8
pensionable 5.8
pensioned 5.8
pensive 5.8
pensively 5.8
pentagon 17.8
pentameter 1.7
Pentecoste 11.11
pent-up 17.9
penury 6.1
Penzance 1.8
peony 6.1
people 6.10
PEP 5.9
pep 5.9
Pepe le Pew 18.1
pepped 5.9
pepper 5.9
peppercorn 14.10
peppermint 9.8
peppery 6.1
per 8.1
perceive 6.17
perceived 6.17
perceives 6.17
percent 5.8
perceptible 16.3
perceptibly 6.1
perception 5.9
perch 8.14
percher 8.14
perching 8.14
Percival 16.3
percolate 3.14
percolator 3.14
percussion 17.12
percussionist 9.11
Percy 8.12

peremptory 6.1
perennial 5.8
perfect 5.2
perfected 5.2
perfecting 5.2
perfection 5.2
perfectionist 5.2
perfectly 6.1
perfidious 9.3
perforate 3.14
perforated 3.14
perforation 3.13
perforator 3.14
perform 14.9
performance-related
3.14
performed 14.9
performer 14.9
performing 14.9
perfume 18.8
perfumer 18.8
perfuming 18.8
perfunctory 6.1
perhaps 1.9
peril 5.10
perilous 17.11
perilously 6.1
perimeter 9.7
periodic 11.3
periodical 11.3
periodically 11.3
peripheral 16.3
periphery 9.4
periscope 12.10
perish 5.10
perishable 16.3
peritonitis 10.13
periwinkle 9.8
perjure 8.4
perjury 8.4
perk 8.3
perking 8.3
perky 8.3
perm 8.8
permanence 5.8
permanent 5.8
permeate 3.14
permed 8.8
permissible 9.11
permission 9.13
permit 8.8, 9.14
permutation 3.13
pernicious 9.13
perniciously 9.13
pernickety 9.2
Perón 11.8

Index

perpendicular   9.2
perpetrate   3.14
perpetrator   3.14
perpetually   6.1
perpetuate   3.14
perpetuator   3.14
perpetuity   18.1
perplex   5.2
perplexed   5.2
perplexity   5.2
Perry   5.10
persecute   18.14
persecuted   18.14
persecuting   18.14
persecution   18.13
persecutor   18.14
perseverance   7.5
persevere   7.1
persevering   7.5
Persian   8.13
persimmon   9.7
persist   9.11
persisted   9.11
persistence   9.11
persistent   9.11
persistently   9.11
persisting   9.11
person   8.12
personable   16.3
personal   16.3
personality   1.6
personally   6.1
personification   3.13
personify   10.1
personnel   5.6
perspective   5.2
perspicacious   3.13
perspiration   3.13
perspire   10.1
perspiring   10.1
persuade   3.4
persuaded   3.4
persuader   3.4
persuading   3.4
persuasion   3.12
persuasive   3.11
persuasively   6.1
pert   8.14
pertain   3.9
perter   8.14
Perth   8.16
perturb   8.2
perturbed   8.2
Peru   18.1
perusal   18.19
peruse   18.19

perusing   18.19
pervade   3.4
pervaded   3.4
pervading   3.4
pervasive   3.11
perverse   8.12
perversely   8.12
perversion   8.13
pervert   8.14
perverted   8.14
perverts   8.14
peseta   3.14
Peshawar   2.20
peso   3.11
pessary   5.11
pessimism   9.18
pessimist   9.11
pessimistic   9.11
pest   5.11
pester   5.11
pesticide   10.4
pestilence   5.8
pestle   5.11
pet   5.14
petal   5.14
Pete   6.14
Peter   6.14
peter   6.14
Peterhead   5.3
Petersburg   8.6
Peterson   17.8
petite   6.14
petition   9.13
petitioned   9.13
petitioner   9.13
petitioning   9.13
Petra   5.14
petrify   10.1
petrochemical   5.7
petroleum   12.7
petted   5.14
petticoat   12.14
petting   5.14
Petty   5.14
petty   5.14
Petula   18.7
pew   18.1
pewter   18.14
PG   6.1
phantom   1.8
Pharaoh   4.6
pharmaceutical   18.14
pharmacist   9.11
pharmacologist   11.6
pharmacology   11.6
pharmacy   6.1

phase   3.18
phased   3.18
phasing   3.18
PhD   6.1
pheasant   5.18
phenomenal   11.7
phenomenally   11.7
phenomenon   17.8
phew   18.1
phial   10.1
Phil   9.6
philander   1.8
philanthropic   11.9
philanthropist   1.8, 9.11
philanthropy   6.1
philately   1.13
philharmonic   11.8
Philippines   6.9
philologist   11.6
philology   11.6
philosophize   10.17
philosophizing   10.17
philosophy   6.1
phlegm   5.7
phlegmatic   1.13
Phnom Penh   5.8
phobic   12.2
phobics   12.2
Phoenix   6.9
phoenix   6.9
phone   12.9
phone-in   12.9
phoner   12.9
phonetic   5.14
phonetically   5.14
phonetics   5.14
phon(e)y   12.9
phonic   11.8
phonics   11.8
phonier   12.9
phoning   12.9
phosphorescence   5.11
phosphorescent   5.11
phosphorus   11.11
photo   12.14
photocopier   11.9
photocopy   11.9
photogenic   5.8
photograph   2.5
photographed   2.5
photographer   11.5
photographic   1.4
photographing   2.5
photography   11.5
Photostat®   1.13
photosynthesis   9.11

photosynthesize 10.17
photosynthesizing 10.17
phrase 3.18
phrased 3.18
phraseology 11.6
phrasing 3.18
Phuket 5.14
Phyllis 9.6
physical 9.18
physically 6.1
physician 9.13
physicist 9.11
physiognomy 11.8
physiological 11.3
physiology 11.6
physiotherapist 9.11
physique 6.3
pi 10.1
pianist 9.11
Picasso 1.11
piccolo 12.1
piccy 9.2
pick 9.2
picked 9.2
picker 9.2
picket 9.2
picking 9.2
pickle 9.2
pick-me-up 17.9
pickpocket 11.2
picks 9.2
pick-up 9.2
picky 9.2
picnicker 9.2
Pict 9.2
pictorial 14.12
picturesque 5.11
pidgin 9.3
pie 10.1
piece 6.11
pieced 6.11
piecing 6.11
pier 7.1
pierce 7.6
Piers 7.7
piety 10.1
pig 9.5
pigeon 9.3
pigeonhole 12.7
pigeonholed 12.7
pigeonholing 12.7
pigeon-toed 12.4
piggy 9.5
piggyback 1.2
piggybacking 1.2

piggybacks 1.2
pig-headed 5.3
pigment 9.5
pigmentation 3.13
pigpen 5.8
pigpens 5.8
pigs 9.5
Pike 10.3
pike 10.3
Pilate 10.7
pile 10.7
piled 10.7
pile-driver 10.15
piles 10.7
piling 10.7
pill 9.6
pillage 9.6
pillar 9.6
pillion 9.6
pillory 9.6
pillow 9.6
pillowcase 3.11
pilot 10.7
pimento 5.8
pimp 9.7
pimple 9.7
pimply 9.7
PIN 9.8
pin 9.8
pinafore 14.1
pincer 9.8
pinch 9.8
pinching 9.8
Pine 10.9
pine 10.9
pineapple 16.3
ping 9.8
pinging 9.8
pining 10.9
pinion 9.8
pink 9.8
pinked 9.8
pinkie 9.8
pinking 9.8
pinnacle 16.3
pinned 9.8
pinning 9.8
Pinocchio 12.3
Pinochet 3.1
Pinter 9.8
pioneer 7.1
pioneering 7.5
pious 10.1
piously 6.1
Pip 9.9
pip 9.9

pipe 10.10
piped 10.10
piper 10.10
pipette 5.14
piping 10.10
Pippa 9.9
pique 6.3
piracy 6.1
piranha 2.10
pirouette 5.14
Pisa 6.19
Pisces 10.12
pistachio 12.1
pistol 9.11
piston 9.11
pit 9.14
pit-a-pat 1.13
Pitcairn 4.5
pitch 9.14
pith 9.16
pitiable 16.3
pitiful 16.3
pitifully 6.1
pitiless 5.11
Pitt 9.14
pittance 9.14
pity 9.14
pivotal 16.3
pixelize 10.17
pixelizing 10.17
placate 3.14
place 3.11
placement 3.11
placenta 5.8
placid 1.11
placing 3.11
plagiarism 9.18
plagiarize 10.17
plagiarizing 10.17
plague 3.6
plaice 3.11
plaid 1.3
plain 3.9
plainer 3.9
plainly 3.9
plain-spoken 12.3
plaintively 6.1
plait 1.13
plan 1.8
plane 3.9
planet 1.8
planetaria 4.6
planetarium 4.6
planetary 1.8, 6.1
plank 1.8
planking 1.8

planned   1.8
planner   1.8
planning   1.8
Plant   2.10
plant   2.10
plantation   3.13
planting   2.10
plaque   2.3
plaster   2.13
plasterboard   14.4
plastered   2.13
plastic   1.11
plate   3.14
plateau   1.13
plateaux   1.13
platinum   17.7
platitude   1.13
Plato   3.14
platonic   11.8
platoon   18.9
platter   1.13
plausible   16.3
play   3.1
playable   3.1
play-acting   1.2
player   3.1
playing   3.1
play-off   3.1
playpen   5.8
playpens   5.8
playtime   3.14
plaza   2.21
plc   6.1
plea   6.1
plead   6.4
pleadable   6.4
pleader   6.4
pleasant   5.18
pleasantly   5.18, 6.1
pleasantry   6.1
please   6.19
pleased   6.19
pleasing   6.19
pleasurable   5.12
pleasure   5.12
pleat   6.14
pleated   6.14
pleating   6.14
pleats   6.14
pleb   5.1
plebeian   6.1
plebiscite   9.14
plectrum   5.2
pledge   5.3
pledged   5.3
plenary   6.9

plentiful   16.3
plenty   5.8
pleurisy   6.1
pliable   10.1
plight   10.13
plinth   9.8
PLO   12.1
plod   11.3
plodded   11.3
plodder   11.3
plonk   11.8
plop   11.9
plot   11.13
plotter   11.13
plough   13.1
ploughed   13.2
plover   17.15
ploy   15.1
ploys   15.8
pluck   17.2
plucked   17.2
plucker   17.2
pluckily   17.2
plucks   17.2
plucky   17.2
plug   17.5
plugger   17.5
plughole   17.5
plum   17.7
plumb   17.7
plumber   17.7
plumbing   17.7
plume   18.8
pluming   18.8
plummet   17.7
plummy   17.7
plump   17.7
plumper   17.7
plumping   17.7
plunder   17.8
plunge   17.8
plunger   17.8
plural   19.4
pluralism   9.18
plurality   1.6
plus   17.11
plush   17.12
plusher   17.12
Pluto   18.14
plutonium   12.9
ply   10.1
PM   5.7
pm   5.7
PMT   6.1
pneumatic   1.13
pneumonia   12.9

PO   12.1
poach   12.14
poachable   12.14
pocket   11.2
pocketbook   16.1
pocketknife   10.5
pod   11.3
podgy   11.3
podiatrist   10.1
podiatry   10.1
podium   12.4
Poe   12.1
poetic   5.14
poetical   5.14
poetically   5.14
poetics   5.14
poetry   6.1
pogo   12.6
poignancy   6.1
point   15.5
point-blank   1.8
pointed   15.5
pointedly   6.1
pointillism   9.18
Poirot   1.10
poise   15.8
poisonous   17.11
poke   12.3
poker   12.3
poker-faced   3.11
poking   12.3
poky   12.3
Poland   12.7
polar   12.7
polarity   1.10
polarization   3.13
polarize   10.17
polarizer   10.17
polarizing   10.17
Polaroid®   15.2
Pole   12.7
pole   12.7
polemic   5.7
polemical   5.7
pole-vaulter   14.8
police   6.11
policing   6.11
policy   6.1
polio   12.7
polish   11.6
polished   11.6
polite   10.13
politely   10.13
politeness   10.13
politer   10.13
politic   9.2

political 9.14
politically 6.1
politician 9.13
politicize 9.14
politicking 9.2
politics 9.2
poll 12.7
polled 12.7
pollen 11.6
pollinate 3.14
pollination 3.13
pollinator 3.14
polling 12.7
pollutant 18.14
pollute 18.14
polluted 18.14
polluter 18.14
polluting 18.14
pollution 18.13
Polly 11.6
Pollyanna 1.8
polo 12.7
polonaise 3.18
Pol Pot 11.13
poltergeist 10.12
poly 11.6
polyester 5.11
polygamy 6.1
polyglot 11.13
polygon 11.8
polygons 11.8
Polynesia 6.12
polyphonic 11.8
polystyrene 10.11
polythene 6.9
polyunsaturated 3.14
polyurethane 3.9
pom 11.7
pomegranate 1.8
pommy 11.7
pomp 11.7
pomposity 11.11
ponce 11.8
poncho 11.8
pond 11.8
ponder 11.8
ponderous 17.11
pong 11.8
ponging 11.8
pontificate 3.14
pontificator 3.14
Pontius 11.8
pontoon 18.9
Pontypool 18.7
pony 12.9
ponytail 3.7

poodle 18.4
poodles 18.4
Pooh 18.1
pooh-pooh 18.1
pool 18.7
pooling 18.7
pooper-scooper 18.10
poor 19.1
poorer 19.4
poorest 19.4
poorhouse 14.7
poorly 19.3
pop 11.9
pope 12.10
Popocatepetl 5.14
pop one's clogs 11.5
popper 11.9
poppy 11.9
poppycock 11.2
populace 17.11
popularity 1.10
popularize 10.17
popularizer 10.17
popularizing 10.17
popularly 6.1
populate 11.9
population 3.13
populist 9.11
populous 17.11
porch 14.15
porcupine 10.9
pore 14.1
pork 14.3
porker 14.3
porky 14.3
pornographer 11.5
pornographic 1.4
pornography 11.5
porous 14.12
porridge 11.10
port 14.15
portable 16.3
Portadown 13.4
portal 14.15
Port-au-Prince 9.8
portend 5.8
portending 5.8
portentous 5.8
Porter 14.15
porter 14.15
portfolio 12.7
portion 14.14
portly 14.15
portray 3.1
portrayable 3.1
portrayal 3.1

portraying 3.1
Portrush 17.12
Port Said 10.4
Portugal 16.3
Portuguese 6.19
POS 5.11
pose 12.19
poser 12.19
posh 11.12
posher 11.12
posing 12.19
posit 11.16
position 9.13
positioned 9.13
positioning 9.13
positive 9.17
positively 6.1
posse 11.11
possess 5.11
possessed 5.11
possession 5.13
possessive 5.11
possessively 5.11
possessor 5.11
possibility 9.6
possum 11.11
post 12.11
postal 12.11
poster 12.11
posterior 7.5
posterity 5.10
posthaste 3.11
posthumous 17.11
posthumously 6.1
posting 12.11
postmaster 2.13
post-modernism 9.18
postnatal 3.14
postpone 12.9
postponement 12.9
postponing 12.9
postulate 3.14
postulator 3.14
postviral 10.11
postwar 14.1
posy 12.19
pot 11.13
potato 3.14
potency 6.1
potentate 3.14
potential 5.8
potentially 5.8
potholer 12.7
potholing 12.7
potion 12.13
potluck 17.2

potpourri 19.4
pottage 11.13
potted 11.13
Potter 11.13
potter 11.13
pottery 11.13
potty 11.13
potty-trained 3.9
pouch 13.7
pouf(fe) 18.5
pounce 13.4
pounced 13.4
pound 13.4
pounded 13.4
pounder 13.4
pounding 13.4
pour 14.1
pourer 14.12
pouring 14.12
pout 13.7
pouting 13.7
poverty 6.1
poverty-stricken 9.2
POW 18.1
powder 13.2
powdery 6.1
Powell 13.1
power 13.1
powered 13.1
powerful 16.3
powerhouse 13.6
powering 13.1
powerless 5.11
Powys 13.1
poxy 11.2
p & p 6.1
PR 2.1
practicable 16.3
practical 1.2
practicality 1.6
practically 6.1
pragmatic 1.13
pragmatics 1.13
pragmatism 9.18
pragmatist 9.11
prairie 4.6
praise 3.18
praised 3.18
praiseworthy 8.15
praising 3.18
pram 1.7
prance 2.10
prancer 2.10
prancing 2.10
prank 1.8
prat 1.13

prattle 1.13
prawn 14.10
praxis 1.2
pray 3.1
prayer 3.1, 4.1
praying 3.1
preach 6.14
preacher 6.14
preaching 6.14
preamble 1.7
prearranged 3.9
precarious 4.6
precariously 4.6
precaution 14.14
precede 6.4
precedence 5.8
precedent 5.8
preceding 6.4
precipice 9.11
precipitate 3.14, 17.13
precipitately 6.1
precipitation 3.13
precipitator 3.14
precipitous 17.11
précis 3.11
precise 10.12
precisely 10.12
preciser 10.12
precision 9.12
preclude 18.4
precluding 18.4
precocious 12.13
precociousness 5.11
precocity 11.11
preconceived 6.17
preconception 5.9
precondition 9.13
precooked 16.1
precursor 8.12
predate 3.14
predatory 6.1
predecessor 5.11
predestination 3.13
predestine 5.11
predetermine 8.8
predicament 5.8
predicate 5.3, 17.13
predicated 5.3
predict 9.2
predictability 6.1
predictable 9.2
predictably 6.1
predicted 9.2
prediction 9.2
predictor 9.2
predispose 12.19

predisposing 12.19
predisposition 9.13
predominance 11.7
predominant 11.7
predominantly 6.1
predominate 3.14, 11.7
pre-empt 5.7
preen 6.9
preening 6.9
prefabricated 3.14
prefect 6.5
prefer 8.1
preferable 16.3
preferably 6.1
preference 5.4
preferential 5.8
preferred 8.4
preferring 8.11
prefers 8.18
prefigure 9.5
pregnancy 6.1
preheat 6.14
preheated 6.14
preheating 6.14
preheats 6.14
prehistoric 11.10
prehistory 9.11
prejudge 17.3
prejudging 17.3
prejudice 9.11
prejudiced 9.11
prejudicial 9.13
preliminary 6.1
premature 19.1
prematurely 19.3
premeditated 3.14
premiere 4.1
premiered 4.2
premonition 9.13
prenatal 3.14
preoccupation 3.13
preoccupied 10.4
preoccupy 10.1
prep 5.9
prepaid 3.4
preparation 3.13
preparatory 6.1
prepare 4.1
prepared 4.2
preparing 4.6
prepayment 3.8
preposition 9.13
prepositional 9.13
prepossessing 5.11
preposterous 17.11
prepped 5.9

prerecorded   14.4
prerogative   9.17
presage   5.11
Presbyterian   7.5
preschool   18.7
preschooler   18.7
prescribe   10.2
prescription   9.9
present   5.8, 5.18
presentable   5.8
presentation   3.13
present-day   3.1
presenter   5.8
presentiment   5.8
presently   5.18
preservation   3.13
preservative   9.17
preserve   8.17
preserved   8.17
preserver   8.17
preserving   8.17
preset   5.14
presetting   5.14
preshrunk   17.8
preside   10.4
presided   10.4
presidency   6.1
president   5.18
presidential   5.8
presiding   10.4
Presley   5.18
press   5.11
pressed   5.11
pressing   5.11
pressure   5.13
pressurize   10.17
pressurizing   10.17
prestigious   9.3
Preston   5.11
presumably   6.1
presume   18.8
presuming   18.8
presumption   17.7
presumptuous   17.7
presuppose   12.19
presupposing   12.19
presupposition   9.13
pretence   5.8
pretend   5.8
pretender   5.8
pretending   5.8
pretension   5.8
pretentious   5.8, 17.11
pretentiousness   5.11
Pretoria   14.12
pretty   9.14

prevail   3.7
prevailed   3.7
prevailing   3.7
prevalence   5.17
prevalent   5.17
prevaricate   3.14
prevarication   3.13
prevent   5.8
preventable   5.8
preventative   5.8
preventer   5.8
prevention   5.8
preventive   5.8
previous   6.17
previously   6.1
prewar   14.1
prey   3.1
preying   3.1
price   10.12
price-cutting   17.13
priced   10.12
pricer   10.12
pricey   10.12
pricing   10.12
prick   9.2
pricked   9.2
pricker   9.2
pricking   9.2
prickle   9.2
prickly   9.2
pricks   9.2
pride   10.4
prided   10.4
priest   6.11
prig   9.5
prigs   9.5
prim   9.7
primacy   6.1
primarily   6.1
primary   6.1
prime   10.8
primer   10.8
primeval   6.17
priming   10.8
primitive   9.17
primly   9.7
primmer   9.7
primordial   14.4
prince   9.8
princess   5.11
Princeton   9.8
principality   1.6
print   9.8
printer   9.8
printing   9.8
prior   10.1

prioritize   10.17
prioritizing   10.17
priority   11.10
priory   10.1
Priscilla   9.6
prise   10.17
prising   10.17
prism   9.18
prison   9.18
prissy   9.11
Pristina   6.9
pristine   9.11
privacy   6.1
privately   6.1
privation   3.13
privatization   3.13
privatize   10.17
privatizer   10.17
privatizing   10.17
privet   9.17
privy   9.17
prize   10.17
prizefighter   10.13
prizegiving   9.17
prizer   10.17
prizewinner   9.8
pro   12.1
proactive   1.2
pro-am   1.7
probability   9.6
probably   6.1
probation   3.13
probationary   3.13
probationer   3.13
probe   12.2
probiotics   11.13
probity   6.1
problematic   1.13
problematical   1.13
proceed   6.4
process   12.11
procession   5.13
processional   5.13
proclaim   3.8
proclaimed   3.8
proclaimer   3.8
proclaims   3.8
proclamation   3.13
proclivity   9.17
procrastinate   3.14
procrastination   3.13
procreate   3.14
procreation   3.13
procurable   19.4
procure   19.1
procured   19.2

procurer   19.4
procuring   19.4
prod   11.3
prodded   11.3
prodder   11.3
prodigal   16.3
prodigious   9.3
prodigy   6.1
produce   18.11
producer   18.11
production   17.2
productive   17.2
productivity   9.17
profane   3.9
profanity   1.8
profess   5.11
professed   5.11
profession   5.13
professional   5.13
professionalism   9.18
professor   5.11
proffer   11.4
proficiency   9.13
proficient   9.13
proficiently   9.13
profiling   10.7
profit   11.4
profitability   9.6
profitably   6.1
profiteer   7.1
profiteering   7.5
profit-making   3.3
profit-sharing   4.6
profligate   17.13
profound   13.4
profoundly   13.4
profundity   6.1
profuse   18.11
profusely   18.11
profusion   18.12
progeny   6.1
prognoses   12.11
prognosis   12.11
programmable   1.7
progress   5.11
progressed   5.11
progression   5.13
progressive   5.11
progressively   5.11
prohibit   9.1
prohibited   9.3
prohibition   9.13
prohibitive   9.17
prohibitively   6.1
project   5.2
projected   5.2

projecting   5.2
projection   5.2
projectionist   5.2
projector   5.2
proletarian   4.6
proletariat   4.6
proliferate   3.14
proliferation   3.13
prolific   9.4
prolong   11.8
prolonging   11.8
prom   11.7
promenade   2.4
promenaded   2.4
prominence   11.7
prominent   11.7
prominently   6.1
promiscuity   18.1
promise   11.7
prommer   11.7
promontory   11.7
promote   12.14
promoted   12.14
promoter   12.14
promoting   12.14
promotion   12.13
promotional   12.13
prone   12.9
prong   11.8
pronging   11.8
pronounce   13.4
pronounced   13.4
pronouncement   13.4
pronto   11.8
pronunciation   3.13
proof   18.5
proofreader   6.4
prop   11.9
propaganda   1.8
propagate   3.14
propagation   3.13
propagator   3.14
propel   5.6
propelled   5.6
propeller   5.6
propellers   5.6
propelling   5.6
propensity   5.8
proper   11.9
properly   11.9
property   6.1
prophecy   6.1
prophesy   10.1
prophet   11.4
prophetic   5.14
prophetically   5.14

prophylactic   1.2
propitiate   9.13
propitious   9.13
propitiously   9.13
proportion   14.14
proportional   16.3
proportionate   14.14
propose   12.19
proposer   12.19
proposing   12.19
proposition   9.13
propositioned   9.13
propositioning   9.13
propound   13.4
propounded   13.4
propounding   13.4
proprietary   6.1, 10.1
proprietor   10.1
propriety   10.1
propulsion   17.6
pro rata   2.16
prosaic   3.1
proscribe   10.2
prose   12.19
prosecute   18.14
prosecuted   18.14
prosecuting   18.14
prosecution   18.13
prosecutor   18.14
prospect   5.2
prospected   5.2
prospecting   5.2
prospective   5.2
prospector   5.2
prosperity   5.10
prosperous   17.11
prostheses   6.11
prosthesis   6.11
prostitute   18.14
prostituted   18.14
prostituting   18.14
prostitution   18.13
prostrate   3.14
protagonist   1.5
protect   5.2
protected   5.2
protecting   5.2
protection   5.2
protectionism   9.18
protectionist   5.2
protective   5.2
protector   5.2
protégé   3.1
protest   5.11
Protestantism   9.18
protestation   3.13

protested 5.11
protesting 5.11
protestor 5.11
protocol 11.6
prototype 10.10
protracted 1.2
protractor 1.2
protrude 18.4
protruding 18.4
protuberance 18.2
proud 13.2
prouder 13.2
proudly 13.2
Proust 18.11
prove 18.17
proved 18.17
proven 12.17
provide 10.4
provided 10.4
providence 5.8
providential 5.8
providentially 5.8
provider 10.4
providing 10.4
proving 18.17
provision 9.12
provisional 16.3
provisionally 6.1
proviso 10.17
provocation 3.13
provocative 11.2
provoke 12.3
provoking 12.3
prow 13.1
prowess 13.1
prowl 13.3
prowler 13.3
prowling 13.3
proximity 9.7
proxy 11.2
prude 18.4
prudent 18.4
Pru(e) 18.1
prune 18.9
pruned 18.9
Prunella 5.6
pruner 18.9
prurient 19.4
Prussia 17.12
Prussian 17.12
pry 10.1
PS 5.11
psalm 2.9
psalms 2.9
pseud 18.4
pseudo 18.4

pseudonym 9.7
psych 10.3
psyche 10.3
psychedelic 5.6
psychiatric 1.13
psychiatrist 9.11, 10.1
psychiatry 6.1, 10.1
psychoanalyse 10.17
psychoanalysing 10.17
psychoanalysis 1.6
psychoanalyst 1.8
psychological 11.3
psychologist 11.6
psychology 11.6
psychopath 1.15
psychopathic 1.15
psychoses 12.11
psychosis 12.11
psychosomatic 1.13
psychotic 11.13
psychotics 11.13
PT 6.1
PTA 3.1
ptarmigan 17.8
PTO 12.1
pub 17.1
puberty 6.1
pubic 18.2
publican 17.1
publication 3.13
publicity 9.11
publicize 10.17
publicizing 10.17
publicly 6.1
Puccini 6.9
Puck 17.2
pucker 17.2
puddle 17.3
pudgy 17.3
puff 17.4
puffed 17.4
puffer 17.4
puffin 17.4
puffy 17.4
pug 17.5
pugnacious 3.13
puke 18.3
puker 18.3
pukka 17.2
pull 16.3
pullet 16.3
pulley 16.3
pullover 12.17
pulmonary 6.1
pulp 17.6
pulsate 3.14

pulsator 3.14
pulse 17.6
pulverize 10.17
pulverizer 10.17
pulverizing 10.17
puma 18.8
pumice 17.7
pump 17.7
pumper 17.7
pumping 17.7
pumpkin 17.7
pun 17.8
Punch 17.8
punch 17.8
punches 17.8
punchy 17.8
punctilious 9.6
punctuality 1.6
punctually 6.1
punctuate 3.14
punctuation 3.13
punctuator 3.14
puncture 17.8
punishment 5.8
punitive 9.17
punk 17.8
punky 17.8
punned 17.8
punnet 17.8
punning 17.8
punt 17.8
punted 17.8
punter 17.8
punting 17.8
puny 18.9
pup 17.9
pupil 18.10
pupped 17.9
puppy 17.9
pure 19.1
purely 19.3
purer 19.4
purgatory 6.1
purge 8.4
purification 3.13
purify 10.1
purifying 10.1
purist 19.4
puritan 17.8
puritanical 1.8
purity 19.4
purl 8.7
purled 8.7
purling 8.7
purloin 15.5
purport 14.15

purporting   14.15
purpose-built   9.6
purposeful   16.3
purposely   6.1
purr   8.1
purred   8.4
purring   8.11
purrs   8.18
purse   8.12
pursed   8.12
purser   8.12
pursue   18.1
pursuer   18.1
pursuit   18.14
purveyor   3.1
pus   17.11
push   16.4
push-button   17.13
pushed   16.4
pushover   12.17
pushy   16.4
pussy   17.11
pussyfoot   16.5
pussyfooting   16.5
put   16.5
putative   9.17
putrefy   10.1
putsch   16.5
putt   17.13
putter   17.13
putting   16.5, 17.13
putty   17.13
puzzle   17.16
PVC   6.1
Pygmalion   3.7
pyjamas   2.9
pylon   10.7
pyorrhoea   7.1
pyramid   9.3
pyre   10.1
Pyrenean   6.1
Pyrenees   6.19
pyromania   3.9
pyromaniac   3.9

Q
Q   18.1
Qatar   1.13
Qatari   1.13
QC   6.1
QE2   18.1
QED   6.1
quack   1.2
quacked   1.2
quacking   1.2

quacks   1.2
quad   11.3
quadrangle   1.8
quadraphonic   11.8
quadraphonics   11.8
quadriplegic   6.4
quadruped   5.3
quadruplet   5.14
quaff   11.4
quaffer   11.4
quagmire   10.1
quail   3.7
quailed   3.7
quailing   3.7
quaint   3.9
quaintly   3.9
quake   3.3
quaked   3.3
Quaker   3.3
quaker   3.3
quaking   3.3
qualification   3.13
qualified   11.6
qualify   10.1, 11.6
qualifying   10.1
qualitative   9.17
quality   11.6
qualm   2.9
qualms   2.9
quandary   6.1
quango   1.8
Quant   11.8
quantify   10.1
quantifying   10.1
quantitative   9.17
quantity   6.1
quarantine   6.9
quarantining   6.9
quark   2.3
quarrel   11.10
quarrelsome   17.7
quarry   11.10
quart   14.15
quarter   14.15
quarterback   1.2
quarterbacks   1.2
quarterdeck   5.2
quarterdecks   5.2
quarterfinal   10.9
quartering   14.15
quarterly   14.15
quartermaster   2.13
quarter-pounder   13.4
quartet   5.14
quarto   14.15
quartz   14.15

quash   11.12
quaver   3.17
quavering   3.17
quavery   3.17
quay   6.1
quayside   6.11
queasier   6.19
queasily   6.19
queasy   6.19
Quebec   5.2
Queen   6.9
queen   6.9
Queenie   6.9
Queens   6.9
queen-size   10.17
queer   7.1
queerer   7.5
queerly   7.4
quell   5.6
quelled   5.6
quelling   5.6
quench   5.8
querulous   17.11
query   7.5
quest   5.11
quested   5.11
questing   5.11
question   5.11
questionable   16.3
questionnaire   4.1
questor   5.11
queue   18.1
quibble   9.1
quiche   6.13
quick   9.2
quicken   9.2
quicker   9.2
quickie   9.2
quickly   9.2
quickness   9.2
quick-witted   9.14
quid   9.3
quiescence   5.11
quiescent   5.11
quiet   10.1
quieten   17.8
quieter   10.1
quietly   6.1
quietness   5.11
quiff   9.4
quill   9.6
quilt   9.6
quince   9.8
quinine   6.9
quintessence   5.11
quintessential   5.8

quintessentially 5.8
quintet 5.14
Quintin 9.8
quip 9.9
quirk 8.3
quirky 8.3
Quisling 9.18
quisling 9.18
quit 9.14
quite 10.13
Quito 6.14
quits 9.14
quitter 9.14
quiver 9.17
quivery 9.17
quixotic 11.13
quiz 9.18
quizzical 9.18
quoit 15.7
Quorn® 14.10
quorum 14.12
quota 12.14
quotation 3.13
quote 12.14
quoted 12.14
quoting 12.14

R

R 2.1
RA 3.1
Rabat 1.13
rabbi 10.1
rabbit 1.1
rabble 1.1
rabid 1.1
rabies 3.2
Rabin 6.9
RAC 6.1
rac(c)oon 18.9
race 3.11
racer 3.11
racial 3.13
racing 3.11
racist 3.11
rack 1.2
racked 1.2
racket 1.2
racketeer 7.1
racketeering 7.5
racks 1.2
racy 3.11
rad 1.3
radiant 3.4
radiate 3.14
radiation 3.13

radiator 3.14
radical 16.3
radicalism 9.18
radio 12.1
radioactive 1.2
radioactivity 9.17
radio-controlled 12.7
radioed 12.4
radiographer 11.5
radiography 11.5
radioing 12.1
radiologist 11.6
radiology 11.6
radish 1.3
radium 3.4
RAF 5.4
raffia 1.4
raffle 1.4
raft 2.5
rafter 2.5
rag 1.5
ragamuffin 17.4
rage 3.4
raged 3.4
ragga 1.5
ragged 1.5
ragging 1.5
raging 3.4
raid 3.4
raided 3.4
raider 3.4
raiding 3.4
rail 3.7
railed 3.7
railing 3.7
railings 3.7
railway 3.1
rain 3.9
raining 3.9
rainslicker 9.2
rainstorm 3.9
rainwater 14.15
rainy 3.9
raise 3.18
raised 3.18
raisin 3.18
raising 3.18
Rajiv 6.17
rake 3.3
raked 3.3
raker 3.3
raking 3.3
Raleigh 14.8
rallied 1.6
rally 1.6
Ralph 1.6, 3.5

RAM 1.7
ram 1.7
Ramadan 2.10
ramble 1.7
rambler 1.7
rambling 1.7
Rameses 6.19
ramification 3.13
rammer 1.7
ramming 1.7
ramp 1.7
rampage 3.4
rampaged 3.4
rampager 3.4
rampaging 3.4
ramshackle 1.2
ran 1.8
ranch 2.10
rancour 1.8
rand 1.8
Randall 1.8
random 1.8
Randy 1.8
rang 1.8
range 3.9
ranged 3.9
rangefinder 10.9
Ranger 3.9
ranger 3.9
ranging 3.9
Rangoon 18.9
rangy 3.9
Rank 1.8
rank 1.8
rank-and-file 10.7
ranker 1.8
ranking 1.8
rankle 1.8
rankly 1.8
ransom 1.8
rant 1.8
ranter 1.8
rants 1.8
rap 1.9
rapacious 3.13
rape 3.10
rapid 1.9
rapidity 9.3
rapidly 6.1
rapper 1.9
rapping 1.9
rapport 14.1
rapt 1.9
raptor 1.9
rapture 1.9
rapturous 17.11

Raquel 5.6
rare 4.1
rarefied 10.4
rarely 4.3
rarer 4.6
raring 4.6
rarity 6.1
rash 1.12
rasher 1.12
rashly 1.12
rasp 2.13
raspberry 6.1
rat 1.13
rat-a-tat 1.13
ratchet 1.13
rate 3.14
ratepayer 3.1
rater 3.14
rather 2.17
ratification 3.13
ratify 1.13
rating 3.14
ratio 12.1
ration 1.12
rationable 1.12
rational 1.12
rationalism 1.12
rationalist 1.12
rationalization 3.13
rationalize 1.12
rationally 1.12
rationed 1.12
ratter 1.13
rattle 1.13
rattlesnake 3.3
ratty 1.13
raucous 14.3
ravage 1.16
rave 3.17
raved 3.17
Ravel 5.6
raven 3.17
ravenous 1.16
raver 3.17
Ravi 2.19
ravine 6.9
raving 3.17
ravish 1.16
raw 14.1
Rawalpindi 9.8
Ray 3.1
ray 3.1
rayon 3.1
raze 3.18
razed 3.18
razing 3.18

razor 3.18
razor-sharp 2.11
razor-shell 5.6
razzmatazz 1.17
RC 6.1
RDA 3.1
RE 6.1
re 6.1
reach 6.14
reachable 16.3
reaching 6.14
react 1.2
reacted 1.2
reacting 1.2
reaction 1.2
reactionary 6.1
reactivate 3.14
reactor 1.2
read 5.3, 6.4
readable 6.4
reader 6.4
readily 5.3
reading 6.4
readjust 17.11
readjusted 17.11
readjustment 17.11
readmit 9.14
read-only 12.9
readvertise 10.17
readvertising 10.17
ready 5.3
ready-made 3.4
reaffirm 8.8
reaffirmed 8.8
reafforestation 3.13
Reagan 3.6
real 7.4
realign 10.9
realism 7.4
realist 7.4
realistic 9.11
reality 1.6
realize 7.4
really 7.4
realm 5.6
ream 6.8
reamer 6.8
reaming 6.8
reanimate 3.14
reap 6.10
reaper 6.10
reaping 6.10
reappear 7.1
reappearance 7.5
reappearing 7.5
reapply 10.1

reappraise 3.18
reappraised 3.18
reappraising 3.18
rear 7.1
rearer 7.5
rearing 7.5
rearm 2.9
rearmed 2.9
rearmer 2.9
rearmers 2.9
rearming 2.9
rearms 2.9
rearrange 3.9
rearranged 3.9
rearranger 3.9
rearranging 3.9
reason 6.19
reasonable 6.19
reasonably 6.1
reasoning 6.19
reassemble 5.7
reassess 5.11
reassessed 5.11
reassurance 19.4
reassure 19.1
reassured 19.2
reassuring 19.4
reawaken 3.3
Rebecca 5.2
rebel 5.1, 5.6
rebelled 5.6
rebelling 5.6
rebirth 8.16
reborn 14.10
rebound 13.4
rebounded 13.4
rebounder 13.4
rebounding 13.4
rebuff 17.4
rebuffed 17.4
rebuild 9.6
rebuilding 9.6
rebuilt 9.6
rebuke 18.3
rebut 17.13
rebuttal 17.13
rebutting 17.13
recall 14.8
recalled 14.8
recant 1.8
recanter 1.8
recap 6.3
recapitulate 3.14
recapture 1.9
recede 6.4
receipt 6.14

receipts   6.14
receive   6.17
received   6.17
receiver   6.17
receivership   9.9
receives   6.17
receiving   6.17
recent   6.11
recently   6.11
receptacle   16.3
reception   5.9
receptionist   9.11
recession   5.13
recharge   2.4
rechargeable   16.3
recharger   2.4
recidivism   9.18
recipe   6.1
recipient   5.8
reciprocal   16.3
reciprocate   3.14
reciprocator   3.14
recital   10.13
recitation   3.13
recite   10.13
recited   10.13
reciter   10.13
reciting   10.13
reckless   5.2
reckon   5.2
reckoned   5.2
reclaim   3.8
reclaimed   3.8
reclaimer   3.8
reclaims   3.8
reclamation   3.13
recline   10.9
recliner   10.9
reclining   10.9
recluse   18.11
recognition   9.13
recognizable   10.17
recognize   10.17
recognized   10.17
recognizing   10.17
recoil   15.3
recollect   5.2
recollected   5.2
recollecting   5.2
recollection   5.2
recommend   5.8
recommendation   3.13
recommending   5.8
recompense   5.8
reconcile   10.7
reconciled   10.7

reconciler   10.7
reconciliation   3.13
reconditioned   9.13
reconquer   11.8
reconsider   9.3
reconstruct   17.2
reconstruction   17.2
record   14.4
record-breaking   3.3
recorded   14.4
recorder   14.4
recorders   14.4
record-holder   12.7
recording   14.4
recount   13.4
recounted   13.4
recounting   13.4
recoup   18.10
recourse   14.13
recoursed   14.13
recover   17.15
recoverable   16.3
recovery   17.15
re-create   3.14
recreation   3.13
recreational   3.13
recrimination   3.13
recruit   18.14
recruited   18.14
recruiter   18.14
recruiting   18.14
rectangle   1.8
rectangular   1.8
rectify   5.2
rectitude   18.4
rector   5.2
rectory   5.2
recuperate   3.14
recuperation   3.13
recuperator   3.14
recur   8.1
recurred   8.4
recurring   8.11
recurs   8.18
recycle   10.3
Red   5.3
red   5.3
red-blooded   17.3
redden   5.3
redecorate   3.14
redeem   6.8
Redeemer   6.8
redeeming   6.8
redemption   5.7
redeploy   15.1
redeploying   15.1

redeployment   15.4
redeploys   15.8
red-faced   3.11
red-haired   4.2
red-handed   1.8
red-hot   11.13
redial   10.1
redid   9.3
redirect   5.2
redirected   5.2
redirecting   5.2
rediscover   17.15
redo   18.1
redolent   5.8
redone   17.8
redraft   2.5
redress   5.11
redressed   5.11
reduce   18.11
reduced   18.11
reduction   17.2
redundancy   6.1
redundant   17.8
Reed   6.4
reed   6.4
reef   6.5
reek   6.3
reeking   6.3
reel   6.7
re-elect   5.2
re-elected   5.2
re-electing   5.2
re-election   5.2
reeled   6.7
reeler   6.7
reeling   6.7
re-enact   1.2
re-enacted   1.2
re-enacting   1.2
re-enter   5.8
re-entry   5.8
Reeves   6.17
re-examine   1.7
ref   5.4
refectory   5.2
refer   8.1
referee   6.1
refereed   6.4
refereeing   6.1
reference   5.4
referred   8.4
referring   8.11
refers   8.18
refill   9.6
refillable   9.6
refilled   9.6

refilling   9.6
refinable   10.9
refine   10.9
refined   10.9
refinement   10.9
refiner   10.9
refinery   10.9
refining   10.9
refit   9.14
refitter   9.14
reflate   3.14
reflation   3.13
reflect   5.2
reflected   5.2
reflecting   5.2
reflection   5.2
reflective   5.2
reflector   5.2
reflexologist   11.6
reflexology   11.6
reforestation   3.13
re-form   14.9
reform   14.9
re-format   14.9
reformation   3.13
reformatory   6.1
reformed   14.9
re-formed   14.9
reformer   14.9
refract   1.2
refractable   1.2
refracted   1.2
refracting   1.2
refractory   1.2
refrain   3.9
re-freeze   6.19
refresh   5.13
refresher   5.13
refried   10.4
refrigerate   3.14
refrigeration   3.13
refrigerator   3.14
re-frozen   12.19
refuel   18.1
refuelling   18.1
refugee   6.1
refund   17.8
refusal   18.19
refuse   18.19
refusing   18.19
refutation   3.13
refute   18.14
refuted   18.14
refuter   18.14
refuting   18.14
Reg   5.3

regain   3.9
regal   6.6
regale   3.7
regaled   3.7
regalia   3.7
regaling   3.7
regally   6.6
regard   2.4
regarded   2.4
regarder   2.4
regatta   1.13
regency   6.1
regenerate   5.8
regeneration   3.13
Reggie   5.3
regime   6.8
regiment   5.8
regimental   5.8
regimentally   5.8
regimentation   3.13
regimented   5.8
Regina   10.9
region   6.4
regional   16.3
regionalism   9.18
regionalization   3.13
registrar   2.1
registration   3.13
regress   5.11
regressed   5.11
regression   5.13
regressive   5.11
regressively   5.11
regret   5.14
regretful   5.14
regrettable   5.14
regretted   5.14
regretting   5.14
regroup   18.10
regularity   1.10
regulate   3.14
regulation   3.13
regulator   3.14
regulatory   3.14
regurgitate   3.14
rehabilitate   9.6
rehabilitation   3.13
rehash   1.12
rehashed   1.12
rehasher   1.12
rehashing   1.12
rehearsal   8.12
rehearse   8.12
rehearsed   8.12
rehearser   8.12
reheats   6.14

rehouse   13.9
rehousing   13.9
reign   3.9
reigning   3.9
reimburse   8.12
reimbursed   8.12
rein   3.9
reincarnation   3.13
reinforce   14.13
reinforced   14.13
reinforcement   14.13
reinsert   8.14
reinserted   8.14
reinserts   8.14
reinstate   3.14
reinstatement   3.14
reinsurance   19.4
reinsure   19.1
reinsured   19.2
reinterpretation   3.13
reintroduction   17.2
reinvent   5.8
reinvest   5.11
reinvested   5.11
reinvesting   5.11
reissue   9.13
reiterate   9.14
reiteration   3.13
reject   5.2
rejected   5.2
rejecting   5.2
rejection   5.2
rejoice   15.6
rejoiced   15.6
rejoin   15.5
rejuvenate   3.14
rejuvenator   3.14
rekindle   9.8
relaid   3.4
relapse   1.9
relate   3.14
related   3.14
relation   3.13
relationship   9.9
relative   9.17
relatively   6.1
relativity   9.17
relax   1.2
relaxation   3.13
relaxed   1.2
relaxing   1.2
relay   3.1
relaying   3.1
release   6.11
released   6.11
releasing   6.11

relegate   5.6
relegation   3.13
relent   5.8
reliability   9.6
reliable   10.1
reliably   10.1
reliance   10.1
reliant   10.1
relic   5.6
relief   6.5
relieve   6.17
relieved   6.17
relieves   6.17
religious   9.3
religiously   6.1
relish   5.6
relivable   9.17
relive   9.17
reliving   9.17
relocate   3.14
relocation   3.13
rely   10.1
REM   5.7
remade   3.4
remain   3.9
remaining   3.9
remains   3.9
remake   3.3
remaker   3.3
remaking   3.3
remand   2.10
remander   2.10
remanding   2.10
remark   2.3
remarkable   16.3
remarkably   6.1
remarked   2.3
remarker   2.3
remarking   2.3
remarry   1.10
remedy   6.1
remember   5.7
remind   10.9
reminded   10.9
reminder   10.9
reminding   10.9
reminisce   9.11
reminisced   9.11
remiss   9.11
remission   9.13
remit   9.14
remittable   9.14
remittal   9.14
remittance   9.14
remonstrate   5.7
remorse   14.13

remorseful   14.13
remote   12.14
remote-controlled   12.7
removable   18.17
removal   18.17
remove   18.17
removed   18.17
remover   18.17
removing   18.17
remunerate   3.14
remuneration   3.13
remunerative   9.17
remunerator   3.14
renal   6.9
rename   3.8
renamed   3.8
renames   3.8
Renata   2.16
rend   5.8
render   5.8
rendezvous   18.1, 18.19
rending   5.8
rendition   9.13
Rene   6.9
renegade   3.4
renege   3.6
renew   18.1
renewable   16.3
renewal   18.1
Renfrewshire   10.1
rennet   5.8
Reno   6.9
renounce   13.4
renounced   13.4
renovate   3.14
renovation   3.13
renovator   3.14
renown   13.4
renowned   13.4
rent   5.8
rentable   5.8
rental   5.8
rent-a-mob   11.1
renter   5.8
rent-free   6.1
reorder   14.4
reordered   14.4
reorders   14.4
reorganization   3.13
reorganize   10.17
reorganizing   10.17
rep   5.9
repaid   3.4
repaint   3.9
repainted   3.9
repair   4.1

repairable   4.6
repaired   4.2
repairing   4.6
repairman   4.4
reparation   3.13
repartee   6.1
repast   2.13
repatriate   3.14
repatriation   3.13
repatriator   3.14
repay   3.1
repayable   3.1
repaying   3.1
repayment   3.8
repeal   6.7
repealed   6.7
repealer   6.7
repeat   6.14
repeated   6.14
repeatedly   6.1
repeater   6.14
repeating   6.14
repeats   6.14
repel   5.6
repelled   5.6
repelling   5.6
repent   5.8
repentance   5.8
repenter   5.8
repercussion   17.12
repertoire   2.1
repertory   6.1
repetition   9.13
repetitive   9.17
rephrase   3.18
rephrased   3.18
rephrasing   3.18
replace   3.11
replacement   3.11
replacing   3.11
replay   3.1
replaying   3.1
replete   6.14
replicate   3.14
replicator   3.14
reply   10.1
report   14.15
reportedly   6.1
reporter   14.15
reporting   14.15
repose   12.19
reposing   12.19
repository   6.1
repossess   5.11
repossessed   5.11
reprehensible   5.8

reprehensibly   5.8
represent   5.8
representation   3.13
representational   3.13
representative   5.8
repress   5.11
repressed   5.11
repression   5.13
repressive   5.11
repressively   5.11
reprieve   6.17
reprieved   6.17
reprieves   6.17
reprimand   2.10
reprimander   2.10
reprimanding   2.10
reprint   9.8
reprinting   9.8
reproach   12.14
reprobate   3.14
reproduce   18.11
reproduction   17.2
reproductive   17.2
reproof   18.5
reprove   18.17
reproved   18.17
reproving   18.17
reptilian   9.6
Republican   17.1
republican   17.1
repudiate   3.14
repudiation   3.13
repudiator   3.14
repulse   17.6
repulsion   17.6
repulsive   17.6
reputable   16.3
reputation   3.13
repute   18.14
reputed   18.14
reputedly   6.1
reputing   18.14
request   5.11
requested   5.11
requesting   5.11
require   10.1
requirement   10.1
requiring   10.1
requisition   9.13
requisitioned   9.13
requisitioning   9.13
requited   10.13
reran   1.8
rerun   17.8
rerunning   17.8
Reservoir Dogs   11.5

resale   3.7
resat   1.13
rescind   9.8
research   8.14
researcher   8.14
researching   8.14
resemble   5.7
resent   5.8
resenter   5.8
resentful   5.8
resentment   5.8
reservation   3.13
reserve   8.17
reserved   8.17
reserving   8.17
reservoir   2.1
reset   5.14
resetting   5.14
reshape   3.10
reshuffle   17.4
reshuffled   17.4
reside   10.4
residence   5.8
resident   5.18
residential   5.8
residing   10.4
residual   9.3
residue   18.1
resign   10.9
resignation   3.13
resigning   10.9
resist   9.11
resistance   9.11
resistant   9.11
resisted   9.11
resisting   9.11
resistor   9.11
resit   9.14
resolute   18.14
resolutely   18.14
resolution   18.13
resolve   11.6
resolved   11.6
resonate   3.14
resort   14.15
resorting   14.15
resound   13.4
resounding   13.4
resource   14.13
resourced   14.13
resourceful   14.13
respect   5.2
respectability   9.6
respectable   5.2
respectably   6.1
respected   5.2

respecter   5.2
respectful   5.2
respecting   5.2
respective   5.2
respectively   5.2
respiration   3.13
respirator   3.14
respiratory   6.1
resplendence   5.8
resplendency   5.8
resplendent   5.8
respond   11.8
respondent   11.8
responder   11.8
responding   11.8
response   11.8
responsibility   9.6
rest   5.11
rested   5.11
resting   5.11
restive   5.11
restoration   3.13
restore   14.1
restorer   14.12
restoring   14.12
restrain   3.9
restrained   3.9
restrainer   3.9
restraint   3.9
restrict   9.2
restricted   9.2
restriction   9.2
restrictive   9.2
result   17.6
resultant   17.6
resume   18.8
résumé   3.1
resuming   18.8
resumption   17.7
resurgency   8.4
resurgent   8.4
resurrect   5.2
resurrected   5.2
resurrecting   5.2
resurrection   5.2
resuscitate   3.14
resuscitation   3.13
resuscitator   3.14
retail   6.14
retain   3.9
retainable   3.9
retainer   3.9
retake   3.3
retaken   3.3
retaker   3.3
retaking   3.3

retaliate 3.14
retaliation 3.13
retard 2.4
retarded 2.4
retarder 2.4
retch 5.14
retching 5.14
retention 5.8
retentive 5.8
rethink 9.8
rethinking 9.8
rethought 14.15
reticent 5.8
retinue 18.1
retiral 10.11
retire 10.1
retired 10.1
retirement 10.1
retiring 10.1
retort 14.15
retorting 14.15
retrace 3.11
retracing 3.11
retract 1.2
retractable 1.2
retracted 1.2
retracting 1.2
retrain 3.9
retrainable 3.9
retrainer 3.9
retraining 3.9
retreat 6.14
retreated 6.14
retreating 6.14
retreats 6.14
retrench 5.8
retrial 10.1
retribution 18.13
retrievable 6.17
retrieve 6.17
retrieved 6.17
retriever 6.17
retrieves 6.17
retroactive 1.2
retrograde 3.4
retrospect 5.2
retrospecting 5.2
retrospective 5.2
retrospectively 5.2
retrovirus 10.11
retsina 6.9
return 8.9
returnable 8.9
returned 8.9
returner 8.9
returning 8.9

Reuben 18.2
reunification 3.13
reunify 10.1
reunion 18.9
reunite 10.13
reunited 10.13
reuniting 10.13
reusable 18.19
reuse 18.19
reusing 18.19
revamp 1.7
revamper 1.7
reveal 6.7
revealed 6.7
revealer 6.7
revealing 6.7
revel 5.17
revelation 3.13
reveller 5.17
revenge 5.8
revenue 18.1
reverberate 3.14
reverberation 3.13
revere 7.1
reverence 5.17
reverential 5.8
reverentially 5.8
reverie 6.1
revering 7.5
reversal 8.12
reverse 8.12
reversed 8.12
reverser 8.12
reversible 16.3
reversion 8.13
revert 8.14
reverted 8.14
reverts 8.14
review 18.1
reviewer 18.1
revile 10.7
reviled 10.7
reviler 10.7
reviling 10.7
revise 10.17
reviser 10.17
revising 10.17
revision 9.12
revisionism 9.18
revitalize 10.17
revitalizing 10.17
revival 10.15
revive 10.15
revived 10.15
reviving 10.15
revoke 12.3

revoking 12.3
revolt 12.7
revolution 18.13
revolutionary 18.13
revolutionize 10.17
revolutionizing 10.17
revolve 11.6
revolved 11.6
revue 18.1
revulsion 17.6
reward 14.4
rewarded 14.4
rewarding 14.4
rewind 10.9
rewinding 10.9
rewire 10.1
rewiring 10.1
reword 8.4
rework 8.3
reworkable 8.3
reworking 8.3
rewound 13.4
rewrite 10.13
rewriter 10.13
rewriting 10.13
rewritten 9.14
rewrote 12.14
Rex 5.2
Reykjavik 9.2
RFU 18.1
rhapsodic 11.3
rhapsodically 11.3
rhapsodize 10.17
rhapsodizing 10.17
rhapsody 6.1
rhesus 6.11
rhetoric 9.2
rhetorical 11.10
rheumatic 1.13
rheumatics 1.13
rheumatism 9.18
Rhiannon 1.8
Rhine 10.9
rhino 10.9
rhinoceros 17.11
rhinoplasty 1.11
Rhoda 12.4
rhodium 12.4
rhombi 10.1
Rhona 12.9
Rhonda 11.8
Rhondda 11.8
Rhone 12.9
Rhyl 9.6
rhyme 10.8
rhymer 10.8

rhyming   10.8
Rhys   6.11
Ria   6.1
rib   9.1
RIBA   6.2
ribbon   9.1
Ribena®   6.9
Rican   6.3
rice   10.12
ricer   10.12
rich   9.14
Richard III   8.4
Richie   9.14
Rick   9.2
rick   9.2
ricked   9.2
ricker   9.2
rickety   9.2
ricking   9.2
ricks   9.2
Ricky   9.2
ricochet   3.1
ricotta   11.13
rid   9.3
ridden   9.3
riddle   9.3
riddler   9.3
ride   10.4
rider   10.4
ridge   9.3
ridged   9.3
ridicule   18.7
ridiculing   18.7
ridiculous   9.2
riding   10.4
rife   10.5
riff   9.4
rifle   10.5
rifling   10.5
rift   9.4
rifting   9.4
rig   9.5
Riga   6.6
rigger   9.5
right   10.13
righted   10.13
righter   10.13
rightful   10.13
rightfully   10.13
right-handed   1.8
right-hander   1.8
righting   10.13
rightly   10.13
right-minded   10.9
right-thinking   9.8
right-wing   9.8

right-winger   9.8
rigid   9.3
rigidity   9.3
rigmarole   12.7
Rigoletto   5.14
rigorous   9.5
rigour   9.5
rigs   9.5
rile   10.7
riled   10.7
riling   10.7
rim   9.7
rime   10.8
rimmed   9.7
rimming   9.7
rind   10.9
ring   9.8
ringing   9.8
ringleader   6.4
ringmaster   2.13
rink   9.8
rinked   9.8
rinking   9.8
rinse   9.8
rinser   9.8
rinsing   9.8
Rio   6.1
Rio de Janeiro   4.6, 7.5
Rio Grande   1.8
riot   10.1
rioter   10.1
riotous   17.11
RIP   6.1
rip   9.9
ripe   10.10
riper   10.10
rip-off   9.9
riposte   11.11
Ripper   9.9
ripper   9.9
ripple   9.9
rippling   9.9
Rip Van Winkle   9.8
rise   10.17
risen   9.18
riser   10.17
risible   9.18
rising   10.17
risk   9.11
risky   9.11
risotto   11.13
risqué   9.11
Rita   6.14
rite   10.13
ritual   9.14
Ritz   9.14

ritzy   9.14
rival   10.15
rivalry   6.1
river   9.17
riverbed   5.3
riverside   10.4
rivet   9.17
Riviera   4.6
Riyadh   1.3
RN   5.8
RNA   3.1
RNLI   10.1
roach   12.14
road   12.4
roadie   12.4
roadrunner   17.8
roadworthy   8.15
roam   12.8
roamer   12.8
roaming   12.8
roar   14.1
roarer   14.12
roaring   14.12
roast   12.11
roaster   12.11
roasting   12.11
Rob   11.1
rob   11.1
robber   11.1
robbery   11.1
Robbie   11.1
robbing   11.1
robe   12.2
Robert   11.1
Roberta   8.14
Robin   11.1
robin   11.1
Robin Hood   16.2
Robocop   11.9
robotics   11.13
robust   17.11
rock   11.2
rocked   11.2
rocker   11.2
rockery   11.2
rocket   11.2
rock-hard   2.4
rocking   11.2
rock'n'roll   12.7
Rocky   11.2
rocky   11.2
Rod   11.3
rod   11.3
Roddy   11.3
rode   12.4
rodeo   12.1

Roderick 9.2
roe 12.1
Roger 11.3
rogue 12.6
Roisin 6.9
Roland 12.7
role 12.7
Rolf 11.6
roll 12.7
rolled 12.7
roller 12.7
Rollerblade® 3.4
Rollerblades® 3.4
roller-coaster 12.11
roller-skate 3.14
roller-skating 3.14
rolling 12.7
roll-on 11.8
rollover 12.17
Rolls-Royce 15.6
roly-poly 12.7
ROM 11.7
Roman 12.8
roman 12.8
romance 1.8
romancer 1.8
Romania 3.9
Romanian 3.9
romantic 1.8
romanticism 9.18
romanticize 10.17
romanticizing 10.17
Romany 6.1
Rome 12.8
Romeo 12.1
romp 11.7
Romulus 17.11
Ron 11.8
Ronald 11.8
Ronnie 11.8
roof 18.5
rook 16.1
rookery 16.1
rookie 16.1
room 18.8
rooming 18.8
roomy 18.8
Rooney 18.9
Roosevelt 5.6
roost 18.11
rooster 18.11
root 18.14
rooted 18.14
rooting 18.14
rope 12.10
roper 12.10

rop(e)y 12.10
Rory 14.12
Ros 11.16
Rosa 12.19
Rosalie 6.1
Rosalind 9.8
Rosamund 17.8
rosary 6.1
Rose 12.19
rose 12.19
rosé 12.19
Roseanne 1.8
rose-coloured 17.6
Rosemary 6.1
rosemary 6.1
rosette 5.14
Rosie 12.19
Ross 11.11
Rossellini 6.9
Rossini 6.9
roster 11.11
rostrum 11.11
rosy 12.19
rot 11.13
rota 12.14
rotary 12.14
rotate 3.14
rotation 3.13
rotator 3.14
rote 12.14
rotor 12.14
rotten 11.13
rotter 11.13
Rotterdam 1.7
rottweiler 10.7
rotund 17.8
rouge 18.12
rough 17.4
rough-and-ready 5.3
rough-and-tumble 17.7
roughed 17.4
rougher 17.4
roughly 17.4
roughness 17.4
roulette 5.14
round 13.4
roundabout 13.7
rounded 13.4
rounder 13.4
rounding 13.4
roundly 13.4
round-trip 9.9
rouse 13.9
rousing 13.9
Rousseau 12.1
rout 13.7

route 18.14
routed 18.14
router 18.14
routine 6.9
routinely 6.9
routing 13.7, 18.14
Roux 18.1
rove 12.17
rover 12.17
row 12.1, 13.1
rowdy 13.2
rowed 12.4, 13.2
Rowena 6.9
rower 12.1
rowing 12.1
Roxan(n)e 1.8
Roxburghshire 10.1
Roy 15.1
royal 15.1
royal-blue 18.1
royalist 15.1
royally 15.1
royalty 15.1
RP 6.1
RPI 10.1
rpm 5.7
RRP 6.1
RS 5.11
RSA 3.1
RSI 10.1
RSPB 6.1
RSPCA 3.1
RSPCC 6.1
RSVP 6.1
rub 17.1
rubber 17.1
rubber-stamp 1.7
rubber-stamper 1.7
rubbery 17.1
rubble 17.1
rubella 5.6
Ruby 18.2
ruby 18.2
RUC 6.1
ruck 17.2
rucked 17.2
rucks 17.2
rudder 17.3
ruddy 17.3
rude 18.4
ruder 18.4
rudimentary 5.8
rue 18.1
ruff 17.4
ruffle 17.4
ruffled 17.4

rug   17.5
rugby-tackle   1.2
rugger   17.5
ruinous   17.11
rule   18.7
ruler   18.7
ruling   18.7
Rum   17.7
rum   17.7
rumble   17.7
rumbling   17.7
ruminate   18.8
rummer   17.7
rump   17.7
rumple   17.7
rumpus   17.7
run   17.8
run-around   13.4
runaway   3.1
run-down   13.4
rundown   17.8
rung   17.8
run-in   9.8
runner   17.8
runner-up   17.9
running   17.8
runny   17.8
run-of-the-mill   9.6
runt   17.8
runway   17.8
Runyon   17.8
rupee   6.1
rural   19.4
Ruritania   3.9
Ruritanian   3.9
ruse   18.19
rush   17.12
rushed   17.12
rusher   17.12
rushing   17.12
rusk   17.11
Russell   17.11
russet   17.11
Russia   17.12
Russian   17.12
rust   17.11
rusted   17.11
rusting   17.11
rustle   17.11
rustler   17.11
rustles   17.11
rusty   17.11
rut   17.13
Ruth   18.16
ruthless   18.16
rutting   17.13

RV   6.1
Rwanda   1.8
Rwandan   1.8
Ryan   10.1
Rye   10.1
rye   10.1

S

S   5.11
sabbatical   1.13
sable   3.2
sabotage   2.14
saboteur   8.1
saboteurs   8.18
sabre   3.2
Sabrina   6.9
sac   1.2
sachet   1.12
sack   1.2
sacked   1.2
sacker   1.2
sacking   1.2
sacks   1.2
sacrament   5.8
Sacramento   5.8
sacrifice   10.12
sacrificed   10.12
sacrificer   10.12
sacrificial   9.13
sacrificing   10.12
sacrilegious   9.3
sacristan   17.8
sacs   1.2
SAD   1.3
sad   1.3
Sadat   1.13
sadden   1.3
sadder   1.3
saddish   1.3
saddle   1.3
saddlebag   1.5
saddo   1.3
Sadie   3.4
sadistic   9.11
sadly   1.3
sadness   1.3
SAE   6.1
safari   2.12
safe   3.5
safe-keeping   6.10
safer   3.5
sag   1.5
saga   2.6
sagacious   3.13
sagacity   1.11

sage   3.4
sagging   1.5
saggy   1.5
Sagittarius   4.6
sago   3.6
Sahara   2.12
said   5.3
Saigon   11.8
sail   3.7
sailed   3.7
sailing   3.7
sailor   3.7
saint   3.9
Saint Helena   6.9
saintly   3.9
sake   3.3
Sal   1.6
salacious   3.13
salad   1.6
salamander   1.8
salami   2.9
salary   1.6
sale   3.7
saleable   3.7
Salerno   8.9
salesmanship   9.9
salesperson   8.12
Salisbury   6.1
saliva   10.15
salivate   3.14
sallied   1.6
sallow   1.6
Sally   1.6
sally   1.6
salmon   1.7
salmonella   5.6
Salome   12.8
saloon   18.9
salt   14.8
saltcellar   5.6
saltcellars   5.6
salted   14.8
salter   14.8
saltpetre   6.14
saltwater   14.15
salty   14.8
salubrious   18.2
salutary   6.1
salute   18.14
saluted   18.14
saluting   18.14
salvation   3.13
salve   1.6
Sam   1.7
Samantha   1.8
Samaritan   17.8

samba 1.7
same 3.8
Sammy 1.7
Samoa 12.1
samosa 12.11
sample 2.9
San Antonio 12.1
sanatoria 14.12
sanatorium 14.12
sanctify 10.1
sanctimonious 12.9
sanctity 6.1
sanctuary 6.1
sand 1.8
sandal 1.8
sandbag 1.8
San Diego 3.6
sandpaper 3.10
Sandra 1.8
Sandy 1.8
sandy 1.8
sane 3.9
sanely 3.9
saner 3.9
San Francisco 9.11
sang 1.8
sanitary 1.8, 6.1
sanitation 3.13
sanitize 10.17
sanitizer 10.17
sanitizing 10.17
sanity 1.8
San Juan 2.10
sank 1.8
San Marino 6.9
San Miguel 5.6
San Salvador 14.1
Santa 1.8
Santa Barbara 2.2
Santa Claus 14.20
Santa Fe 3.1
Santiago 2.6
Santorini 6.9
sap 1.9
sapper 1.9
sapphire 10.1
sappily 1.9
sappiness 1.9
sapping 1.9
sappy 1.9
Sara 2.12
Sara(h) 4.6
sarcastic 1.11
sarcastically 1.11
sarcophagi 11.4

sarcophagus 11.4, 17.11
sardine 6.9
Sardinia 9.8
Sardinian 9.8
sardonic 11.8
sari 2.12
Sark 2.3
Sarkozy 12.19
sarnie 2.10
sarong 11.8
sartorial 14.12
Sartre 2.16
SAS 5.11
sash 1.12
Sassenach 1.2
Sassenachs 1.2
sat 1.13
Satan 3.14
satanic 1.8
satay 1.13
sate 3.14
satellite 10.13
satiate 3.13
satiety 10.1
satin 1.13
satire 10.1
satirical 9.10
satirist 9.11
satirize 10.17
satirizing 10.17
satisfaction 1.2
satisfactory 1.2
satisfied 10.4
satisfier 10.1
satisfy 10.1
satisfying 10.1
saturate 3.14
saturation 3.13
sauce 14.13
sauced 14.13
saucer 14.13
saucy 14.13
Saudi 13.2
sauerkraut 13.7
Saul 14.8
sauna 14.10
savage 1.16
savagely 6.1
Savannah 1.8
savanna(h) 1.8
save 3.17
saved 3.17
saver 3.17
saving 3.17
saviour 3.17

savour 3.17
savouring 3.17
savourless 3.17
savoury 3.17
saw 14.1
sawing 14.12
sawn 14.10
Sawyer 14.19
sax 1.2
Saxon 1.2
Saxony 6.1
saxophone 12.9
saxophonist 9.11
say 3.1
saying 3.1
say-so 3.11
scab 1.1
scabby 1.1
scabies 3.2
Scafell 5.6
scald 14.8
scalding 14.8
scale 3.7
scaled 3.7
scaler 3.7
scales 3.7
scaling 3.7
scalings 3.7
scallop 11.6
scallywag 1.5
scaly 3.7
scam 1.7
scammer 1.7
scamming 1.7
scamp 1.7
scamper 1.7
scan 1.8
scandal 1.8
scandalize 1.8
scandalous 17.11
Scandinavia 3.17
Scandinavian 17.8
scanned 1.8
scanner 1.8
scant 1.8
scanter 1.8
scantily 6.1
scanty 1.8
scar 2.1
scarcity 6.1
scare 4.1
scared 4.2
scarer 4.6
scarf 2.5
scarfed 2.5
scarfing 2.5

scaring   4.6
Scarlet   2.8
scarlet   2.8
Scarlett   2.8
scarred   2.4
scarring   2.12
scart   2.16
scarves   2.19
scary   4.6
scat   1.13
scathing   3.15
scatological   11.3
scatter   1.13
scatterbrain   3.9
scatterbrained   3.9
scattered   1.13
scattering   1.13
scatty   1.13
scenario   2.12
scene   6.9
scenery   6.9
scenic   6.9
scent   5.8
sceptic   5.9
sceptical   16.3
scepticism   9.18
schematic   1.13
scheme   6.8
schemer   6.8
scheming   6.8
schilling   9.6
schism   9.18
schizophrenia   6.9
schizophrenic   5.8
scholar   11.6
scholarly   6.1
scholarship   9.9
scholastic   1.11
school   18.7
schoolfellow   5.6
schooling   18.7
schoolmaster   2.13
schoolteacher   6.14
schoolteaching   6.14
schooner   18.9
Schumacher   1.2
Schwarzenegger   5.5
science   10.1
scientific   9.4
scientist   9.11
Scilly   9.6
scimitar   9.7
scintillating   3.14
sclerosis   12.11
scoff   11.4
scoffer   11.4

scold   12.7
scolding   12.7
scone   11.8
scones   11.8
Scooby Doo   18.1
scoop   18.10
scooper   18.10
scoot   18.14
scooted   18.14
scooter   18.14
scooting   18.14
scope   12.10
scorch   14.15
scorcher   14.15
score   14.1
scoreboard   14.2
scorer   14.12
scoring   14.12
scorn   14.10
scornful   14.10
scorning   14.10
Scorpio   12.1
Scot   11.13
Scotch   11.13
scotch   11.13
scot-free   6.1
Scots   11.13
Scotsman   11.13
Scotswoman   11.13
Scott   11.13
Scotticism   9.18
scour   13.1
scoured   13.1
scourge   8.4
scouring   13.1
scout   13.7
scouting   13.7
scoutmaster   2.13
scowl   13.3
scowler   13.3
scowling   13.3
scrabble   1.1
scraggy   1.5
scram   1.7
scramble   1.7
scrambler   1.7
scrambling   1.7
scramming   1.7
scrap   1.9
scrape   3.10
scraper   3.10
scrapper   1.9
scrappily   1.9
scrapping   1.9
scrappy   1.9
scratch   1.13

scratched   1.13
scratcher   1.13
scratching   1.13
scratchy   1.13
scrawl   14.8
scrawled   14.8
scrawler   14.8
scrawnier   14.10
scrawny   14.10
scream   6.8
screamer   6.8
screaming   6.8
screamingly   6.8
scree   6.1
screech   6.14
screecher   6.14
screeching   6.14
screen   6.9
screening   6.9
screenwriter   10.13
screw   18.1
screwdriver   10.15
scribble   9.1
scribe   10.2
scrimmage   9.7
scrimp   9.7
scrimper   9.7
script   9.9
scriptwriter   10.13
scroll   12.7
scrolled   12.7
scrolling   12.7
Scrooge   18.4
scrounge   13.4
scrub   17.1
scrubber   17.1
scrubby   17.1
scruff   17.4
scruffily   6.1
scruffy   17.4
scrum   17.7
scrumming   17.7
scrummy   17.7
scrumptious   17.7
scrunch   17.8
scrunches   17.8
scrunchie   17.8
scrunchies   17.8
scruple   18.10
scrupulous   17.11
scrupulously   6.1
scrutineer   7.1
scrutinize   10.17
scrutinizing   10.17
scrutiny   18.14
scuba   18.2

scuff 17.4
scuffed 17.4
scuffle 17.4
scuffled 17.4
scull 17.6
sculler 17.6
scullery 6.1
scum 17.7
scupper 17.9
scurried 17.10
scurrilous 17.11
scurry 17.10
scurvy 8.17
scuttle 17.13
scuzzy 17.16
scythe 10.14
SDLP 6.1
SDP 6.1
SE 6.1
SEA 3.1
sea 6.1
seaboard 6.2
seafarer 4.6
seafaring 4.6
seagoing 12.1
seal 6.7
sealed 6.7
sealer 6.7
sealing 6.7
seam 6.8
seaman 6.8
seamanship 9.9
seamer 6.8
seamier 6.8
seaming 6.8
Seamus 3.8
seamy 6.8
Sean 14.10
sear 7.1
search 8.14
searcher 8.14
searching 8.14
searing 7.5
seasickness 9.2
seaside 6.11
season 6.19
seasonable 6.19
seasonal 16.3
seasoning 6.19
Seat 6.14
seat 6.14
seated 6.14
seater 6.14
seating 6.14
SEATO 6.14
seats 6.14

Seattle 1.13
seaway 6.18
seaworthy 8.15
sebaceous 3.13
Sebastopol 11.6
secateurs 8.18
secede 6.4
secession 5.13
seclusion 18.12
second 5.2, 11.8
secondary 6.1
second-best 5.11
second-class 2.13
second-guess 5.11
second-guessed 5.11
second-hand 1.8
seconding 11.8
secondly 6.1
second-rate 3.14
secrecy 6.1
secretarial 4.6
secretariat 4.6
secrete 6.14
secreted 6.14
secretes 6.14
secreting 6.14
secretion 6.13
secretive 9.17
secretly 6.1
secretor 6.14
sect 5.2
sectarian 4.6
sectarianism 4.6
section 5.2
sector 5.2
secular 5.2
secure 19.1
secured 19.2
securely 19.3
securing 19.4
security 19.4
sedan 1.8
sedate 3.14
sedately 3.14
sedateness 3.14
sedation 3.13
sedative 9.17
sedentary 5.3
sedge 5.3
sedged 5.3
sediment 5.3
sedition 9.13
seditious 9.13
seditiously 9.13
seduce 18.11
seducer 18.11

seduction 17.2
seductive 17.2
see 6.1
seed 6.4
seeder 6.4
seedier 6.4
seedily 6.4
seedless 6.4
seedy 6.4
seeing 6.1
seek 6.3
seeker 6.3
seeking 6.3
seem 6.8
seeming 6.8
seemingly 6.8
seemly 6.8
seen 6.9
seep 6.10
seeping 6.10
seer 6.1, 7.1
seethe 6.15
seething 6.15
segment 5.8
segmentation 3.13
segregate 3.14
segregation 3.13
Seine 3.9
seismograph 2.5
seismology 11.6
seize 6.19
seized 6.19
seizing 6.19
seizure 6.12
select 5.2
selected 5.2
selecting 5.2
selection 5.2
selective 5.2
selector 5.2
self 5.6
self-appointed 15.5
self-assured 19.2
self-coloured 17.6
self-confessed 5.11
self-conscious 11.8
self-contained 3.9
self-contradictory 9.2
self-control 12.7
self-controlled 12.7
self-deception 5.9
self-defeating 6.14
self-defence 5.8
self-denial 10.1
self-deprecation 3.13
self-destruct 17.2

self-destruction 17.2
self-determination 3.13
self-discipline 9.8
self-disciplined 9.8
self-doubt 13.7
self-effacing 3.11
self-employed 15.2
self-esteem 6.8
self-expression 5.13
self-harmer 2.9
self-harmers 2.9
self-harming 2.9
self-help 5.6
self-inflicted 9.2
selfish 5.6
selfishness 5.11
self-knowledge 11.6
self-pity 9.14
self-possessed 5.11
self-possession 5.13
self-preservation 3.13
self-reliance 10.1
self-reliant 10.1
self-respect 5.2
self-respecting 5.2
self-restraint 3.9
self-satisfied 10.4
self-starter 2.16
self-sufficient 9.13
self-taught 14.15
Selina 6.9
Selkirkshire 10.1
sell 5.6
seller 5.6
sellers 5.6
selling 5.6
Sellotape® 3.10
selves 5.6
semantic 1.8
semantics 1.8
semaphore 14.1
semester 5.11
semi 5.7
semiautomatic 1.13
semiautomatics 1.13
semicolon 12.7
semiconductor 17.2
semiconscious 11.8
semidetached 1.13
semifinal 10.9
seminal 16.3
seminar 2.1
semiquaver 3.17
semi-skimmed 9.7
Semitic 9.14
semitone 12.9

semitropical 11.9
semolina 6.9
Senate 5.8
send 5.8
sender 5.8
sending 5.8
Senegal 14.8
Senegalese 6.19
senility 9.6
senior 6.9
seniority 11.10
Senna 5.8
sensation 3.13
sensational 3.13
sensationalism 9.18
sense 5.8
senseless 5.8
sensible 5.8
sensibly 5.8
sensitive 9.17
sensor 5.8
sensory 5.8
sensuality 1.6
sent 5.8
sentence 5.8
sententious 5.8
sentiment 5.8
sentimental 5.8
sentimentalist 5.8
sentimentality 1.6
sentimentally 5.8
sentry 5.8
Seoul 12.7
separable 5.9
separate 3.14, 17.13
separation 3.13
separatist 9.11
separator 3.14
September 5.7
septet 5.14
septic 5.9
septicaemia 6.8
septuagenarian 4.6
sequel 6.3
sequential 5.8
sequester 5.11
sequestration 3.13
sequoia 15.1
Serb 8.2
Serbia 8.2
Serena 6.9
serenade 3.4
serenaded 3.4
serenading 3.4
serene 6.9
serenely 6.9

Serengeti 5.14
serenity 5.8
serf 8.5
Serge 8.4
serge 8.4
sergeant-major 3.4
serial 7.5
serialize 7.5
serious 7.5
seriously 7.5
sermon 8.8
serotonin 12.9
serpentine 8.10
serrated 3.14
serum 7.5
servant 8.17
serve 8.17
served 8.17
server 8.17
serviceable 16.3
serviette 5.14
serving 8.17
servitude 18.4
sesame 6.1
session 5.13
SET 6.1
set 5.14
Seth 5.16
settee 6.1
setter 5.14
setting 5.14
settle 5.14
settlement 5.8
set-to 18.1
set-up 5.14
seven 5.17
seventeen 6.9
seventh 5.17
seventy 6.1
sever 5.17
several 16.3
severance 5.17
severe 7.1
severely 7.4
severity 5.10
Severn 5.17
Seville 9.6
sew 12.1
sewed 12.4
sewer 18.1
sewing 12.1
sewn 12.9
sex 5.2
sexagenarian 4.6
sexier 5.2
sextet 5.14

sexuality   1.6
sexually   6.1
sexy   5.2
Seychelles   5.6
Seymour   6.8
SFA   3.1
shabbily   6.1
shabbiness   5.11
shabby   1.1
shack   1.2
shackle   1.2
Shackleton   17.8
shacks   1.2
shaddock   1.3
shade   3.4
shaded   3.4
shades   3.4
shading   3.4
shadow   1.3
shadowy   6.1
Shady   3.4
shady   3.4
shaft   2.5
shaggy   1.5
shah   2.1
shake   3.3
shakeable   3.3
shaken   3.3
shaker   3.3
Shakespearean   7.5
shake-up   3.3
shakily   6.1
shaking   3.3
shaky   3.3
shale   3.7
shall   1.6
shallot   11.13
shallow   1.6
shallow-fried   10.4
shallow-fry   10.1
sham   1.7
shaman   3.8
shamanism   9.18
shamble   1.7
shambolic   11.6
shame   3.8
shamed   3.8
shamefaced   3.11
shamefully   6.1
shameless   3.8
shamelessly   6.1
shamer   3.8
shames   3.8
shamming   1.7
shampoo   18.1
shandy   1.8

Shane   3.9
Shanghai   10.1
Shangri-La   2.1
shank   1.8
Shankar   1.8
shanker   1.8
Shankly   1.8
Shannon   1.8
shan't   2.10
shanty   1.8
shapable   3.10
shape   3.10
Sharapova   12.17
shard   2.4
share   4.1
shared   4.2
shareholder   12.7
shareholding   12.7
sharer   4.6
sharing   4.6
shark   2.3
Sharon   1.10
sharp   2.11
sharpshooter   18.14
sharp-sighted   10.13
shatter   1.13
shattered   1.13
shattering   1.13
shatterproof   18.5
shave   3.17
shaved   3.17
shaven   3.17
shaver   3.17
shaving   3.17
Shaw   14.1
shawl   14.8
she   6.1
sheaf   6.5
shear   7.1
Shearer   7.5
shearer   7.5
shearing   7.5
shears   7.7
sheath   6.16
sheathe   6.15
sheathing   6.15
sheaves   6.17
Sheba   6.2
shed   5.3
she'd   6.4
shedded   5.3
shedding   5.3
Sheen   6.9
sheen   6.9
Sheena   6.9
sheep   6.10

sheer   7.1
Sheerness   5.11
sheet   6.14
sheeting   6.14
sheets   6.14
sheik(h)   3.3
Sheila   6.7
shekel   5.2
shelf   5.6
shell   5.6
she'll   6.7
shelled   5.6
Shelley   5.6
shellfish   5.6
shelling   5.6
shelter   5.6
shelve   5.6
shelves   5.6
shepherd   5.9
shepherdess   5.11
sherbet   8.2
Shereen   6.9
sherry   5.10
she's   6.19
Shetty   5.14
shield   6.7
shift   9.4
shifter   9.4
shifting   9.4
shiftless   9.4
shifty   9.4
shilling   9.6
Shiloh   10.7
shimmer   9.7
shimmy   9.7
shin   9.8
shindy   9.8
shine   10.9
shiner   10.9
shingle   9.8
shining   10.9
shinned   9.8
shinning   9.8
Shintoism   9.18
shiny   10.9
ship   9.9
shipboard   9.9
shipment   9.9
shipowner   12.9
shipper   9.9
shipping   9.9
shire   10.1
shirk   8.3
shirkable   8.3
shirker   8.3
shirking   8.3

Shirley   8.7
shirt   8.14
shirtmaker   3.3
shirts   8.14
shirty   8.14
shiver   9.17
shivery   9.17
shoal   12.7
shock   11.2
shocked   11.2
shocker   11.2
shocking   11.2
shod   11.3
shoddy   11.3
shoe   18.1
shoemaker   3.3
Shona   12.9
shone   11.8
shoo   18.1
shook   16.1
shoot   18.14
shooter   18.14
shooting   18.14
shop   11.9
shopaholic   11.6
shopkeeper   6.10
shoplifter   9.4
shopper   11.9
shopping   11.9
shore   14.1
shorn   14.10
short   14.15
short-change   3.9
short-changing   3.9
short-circuit   8.3
shorten   14.15
shorter   14.15
short-haired   4.2
short-haul   14.8
shorting   14.15
shortly   14.15
short-range   3.9
shorts   14.15
short-sighted   10.13
short-sleeved   6.17
shot   11.13
shotgun   17.8
should   16.2
shoulder   12.7
shouldn't   16.2
shout   13.7
shouting   13.7
shove   17.15
shoved   17.15
shovelful   16.3
shoving   17.15

show   12.1
showdown   12.4
showed   12.4
shower   13.1
showered   13.1
showering   13.1
shower-proof   18.5
showery   6.1
showing   12.1
showman   12.8
showmanship   9.9
shown   12.9
showstopping   11.9
showy   12.1
shrank   1.8
shrapnel   1.9
shred   5.3
shredded   5.3
shredder   5.3
shredding   5.3
Shrek   5.2
shrew   18.1
shrewd   18.4
shrewder   18.4
Shrewsbury   6.1
shriek   6.3
shrieking   6.3
shrift   9.4
shrill   9.6
shriller   9.6
shrillness   9.6
shrimp   9.7
shrimper   9.7
shrine   10.9
shrink   9.8
shrinker   9.8
shrinking   9.8
shrivel   9.17
shrivelling   9.17
shroud   13.2
shrub   17.1
shrubbery   17.1
shrug   17.5
shrunk   17.8
shrunken   17.8
shucks   17.2
shudder   17.3
shuffle   17.4
shuffled   17.4
shun   17.8
shunned   17.8
shunning   17.8
shunt   17.8
shunted   17.8
shunter   17.8
shunting   17.8

shush   16.4
shushed   16.4
shut   17.13
shutter   17.13
shutting   17.13
shuttle   17.13
shuttlecock   11.2
shy   10.1
shyly   10.7
shyness   10.9
Siamese   6.19
Sian   2.10
Siberia   7.5
Siberian   7.5
Sibyl   9.1
sic   9.2
Sicilian   9.6
Sicily   6.1
sick   9.2
sicked   9.2
sicken   9.2
sicker   9.2
sicking   9.2
sickle   9.2
sickly   9.2
sickness   9.2
side   10.4
sided   10.4
sideline   10.4
side-saddle   1.3
side-splitting   9.14
siding   10.4
sidle   10.4
Sidney   9.3
Sidon   10.4
siege   6.4
Siena   5.8
sierra   5.10
Sierra Leone   12.9
sieve   9.17
sieving   9.17
sift   9.4
sifter   9.4
sifting   9.4
sigh   10.1
sight   10.13
sighted   10.13
sighter   10.13
sighting   10.13
sightless   10.13
sights   10.13
sightseeing   6.1
sightseer   6.1
sign   10.9
signalman   1.8
signatory   6.1

signature   19.1
significantly   6.1
signified   9.5
signify   9.5
signing   10.9
sign of the times   10.8
Sikh   6.3
silage   10.7
silently   6.1
silhouette   5.14
silhouetting   5.14
silica   9.6
silicon   17.8
silk   9.6
silky   9.6
sill   9.6
silliness   5.11
silly   9.6
silly-billy   9.6
silo   10.7
silt   9.6
silver-plated   3.14
silversmith   9.16
silverware   4.1
silverwork   8.3
silvery   6.1
Sim   9.7
similarity   1.10
similarly   6.1
simile   6.1
simmer   9.7
Simone   12.9
simper   9.7
simple   9.7
simple-minded   10.9
simpleton   17.8
simplicity   9.11
simplification   3.13
simplify   10.1
simplistic   9.11
simply   9.7
simulate   9.7
simulated   3.14
simulation   3.13
simultaneous   3.9
simultaneously   6.1
sin   9.8
Sinatra   2.16
since   9.8
sincere   7.1
sincerely   7.4
sincerity   5.10
sine   10.9
Sinéad   3.4
sinecure   19.1
sinecured   19.2

sinew   9.8
sinewy   6.1
sing   9.8
Singapore   14.1
Singaporean   14.12
singe   9.8
singeing   9.8
singer   9.8
singing   9.8
single   9.8
single-breasted   5.11
single-decker   5.2
single-handedly   1.8
single-minded   10.9
singularly   6.1
Sinhalese   6.19
sinister   9.8
sink   9.8
sinker   9.8
sinking   9.8
sinned   9.8
sinner   9.8
sinning   9.8
sinter   9.8
sinuous   9.8
sinus   10.9
sinusitis   10.13
Siobhán   14.10
sip   9.9
siphon   10.5
sipper   9.9
sir   8.1
sire   10.1
siren   10.1
siring   10.1
sister   9.11
sisterhood   16.2
sister-in-law   14.1
sisterly   6.1
sit   9.14
site   10.13
sited   10.13
siting   10.13
sitter   9.14
sitting   9.14
situate   9.14
situated   3.14
situation   3.13
six   9.2
sixer   9.2
six-shooter   18.14
sixteen   6.9
size   10.17
siz(e)able   10.17
sizer   10.17
sizing   10.17

sizzle   9.18
sizzling   9.18
skate   3.14
skater   3.14
skating   3.14
Skegness   5.11
skeletal   16.3
skeleton   17.8
sketch   5.14
sketcher   5.14
sketchily   6.1
sketching   5.14
sketchy   5.14
skew   18.1
skewer   18.1
ski   6.1
ski'd   6.4
skid   9.3
skidder   9.3
skidding   9.3
skier   6.1
skiing   6.1
skilful   9.6
skilfully   9.6
skill   9.6
skilled   9.6
skillet   9.6
skilling   9.6
skim   9.7
skimmed   9.7
skimmer   9.7
skimming   9.7
skimp   9.7
skin   9.8
skinned   9.8
Skinner   9.8
skinner   9.8
skinnier   9.8
skinning   9.8
skinny   9.8
skint   9.8
skip   9.9
skipper   9.9
skipping   9.9
skirt   8.14
skirted   8.14
skirter   8.14
skirts   8.14
skit   9.14
skitter   9.14
skittered   9.14
skittish   9.14
skittle   9.14
skive   10.15
skived   10.15
skiver   10.15

skiving 10.15
skivvy 9.17
Skoda 12.4
skulk 17.6
skull 17.6
skunk 17.8
sky 10.1
sky-blue 18.1
skydiver 10.15
skydiving 10.15
Skye 10.1
Skylab 1.1
skylight 10.7
skyline 10.7
skyscraper 3.10
slab 1.1
slack 1.2
slacken 1.2
slacker 1.2
slackers 1.2
slacking 1.2
slackness 1.2
slacks 1.2
Slade 3.4
slag 1.5
slagging 1.5
slain 3.9
slake 3.3
slaked 3.3
slaker 3.3
slaking 3.3
slalom 2.8
slam 1.7
slammer 1.7
slander 2.10
slanderous 17.11
slang 1.8
slant 2.10
slanting 2.10
slanty 2.10
slap 1.9
slapdash 1.12
slapper 1.9
slapping 1.9
slash 1.12
slashed 1.12
slasher 1.12
slashing 1.12
slat 1.13
slate 3.14
slater 3.14
slatey 3.14
slaughter 14.15
slaughterhouse 13.6
Slav 2.19
slave 3.17

slaved 3.17
slaver 1.16, 3.17
slavering 3.17
slavery 3.17
Slavonic 11.8
slay 3.1
slaying 3.1
sleaze 6.19
sleazier 6.19
sleazily 6.19
sleazy 6.19
sled 5.3
sledded 5.3
sledding 5.3
sledge 5.3
sledged 5.3
sleek 6.3
sleeker 6.3
sleekly 6.3
sleep 6.10
sleeper 6.10
sleepily 6.1
sleeping 6.10
sleepwalker 14.3
sleepy 6.10
sleet 6.14
sleeted 6.14
sleeting 6.14
sleets 6.14
sleeve 6.17
sleeved 6.17
sleeves 6.17
sleigh 3.1
sleight 10.13
slender 5.8
slept 5.9
sleuth 18.16
slew 18.1
slice 10.12
sliced 10.12
slicer 10.12
slicing 10.12
slick 9.2
slicked 9.2
slicker 9.2
slid 9.3
slide 10.4
slider 10.4
sliding 10.4
slight 10.13
slighted 10.13
slighter 10.13
slighting 10.13
slightly 10.13
Slim 9.7
slim 9.7

slime 10.8
slimmed 9.7
slimmer 9.7
slimming 9.7
slimy 10.8
sling 9.8
slinger 9.8
slinging 9.8
slink 9.8
slinker 9.8
slinking 9.8
slinky 9.8
slip 9.9
slip-on 9.9
slipper 9.9
slippery 6.1
slippy 9.9
slit 9.14
slither 9.15
slithering 9.15
slitter 9.14
sliver 9.17
slob 11.1
slobber 11.1
slobbery 11.1
slobbing 11.1
slobby 11.1
sloe 12.1
sloe-eyed 10.4
slog 11.5
slo-mo 12.8
sloop 18.10
slop 11.9
slope 12.10
sloppier 11.9
sloppily 11.9
sloppy 11.9
slosh 11.12
slot 11.13
sloth 12.16
slouch 13.7
slough 17.4
sloughed 17.4
Slovakia 1.2
Slovene 6.9
Slovenia 6.9
Slovenian 6.9
slovenly 6.1
slow 12.1
slow-down 12.4
slowed 12.4
slower 12.1
slowing 12.1
slowly 12.7
slowness 12.9
slow-witted 9.14

slow-worm   12.18
SLR   2.1
sludge   17.3
slug   17.5
slugger   17.5
sluice   18.11
slum   17.7
slumber   17.7
slumming   17.7
slump   17.7
slumping   17.7
slung   17.8
slunk   17.8
slur   8.1
slurp   8.10
slurred   8.4
slurring   8.11
slurs   8.18
slush   17.12
slushed   17.12
slushing   17.12
slushy   17.12
slut   17.13
slutty   17.13
sly   10.1
slyly   10.7
smack   1.2
smacked   1.2
smacker   1.2
smackers   1.2
smacking   1.2
smacks   1.2
small   14.8
smaller   14.8
smallholder   12.7
smallholding   12.7
small-minded   10.9
smarmy   2.9
smart   2.16
smarted   2.16
smarten   2.16
smartening   2.16
smarter   2.16
smarting   2.16
smartly   2.16
smarty-pants   1.8
smash   1.12
smashed   1.12
smasher   1.12
smashing   1.12
smattering   1.13
smear   7.1
smearer   7.5
smearing   7.5
smell   5.6
smelled   5.6

smelling   5.6
smelly   5.6
smelt   5.6
smelter   5.6
smidgen   9.3
smile   10.7
smiled   10.7
smiler   10.7
smiley   10.7
smiling   10.7
smirk   8.3
smirker   8.3
smirking   8.3
smite   10.13
smiter   10.13
Smith   9.16
smith   9.16
smithereens   6.9
smiting   10.13
smitten   9.14
smock   11.2
smog   11.5
smoke   12.3
smoked   12.3
smoker   12.3
smoking   12.3
smoky   12.3
smolt   12.7
smooch   18.14
smoocher   18.14
smooth   18.15
smooth-talking   14.3
smote   12.14
smother   17.14
smoulder   12.7
smudge   17.3
smudging   17.3
smug   17.5
smugger   17.5
smuggle   17.5
smuggler   17.5
smugly   17.5
smut   17.13
smutty   17.13
snack   1.2
snacked   1.2
snacker   1.2
snacking   1.2
snacks   1.2
snaffle   1.4
snag   1.5
snagging   1.5
snail   3.7
snake   3.3
snaked   3.3
snaking   3.3

snap   1.9
snapper   1.9
snappily   1.9
snappiness   1.9
snapping   1.9
snappy   1.9
snare   4.1
snared   4.2
snarer   4.6
snaring   4.6
snarl   2.8
snarled   2.8
snarling   2.8
snarls   2.8
snatch   1.13
snatched   1.13
snatcher   1.13
snatching   1.13
snazzy   1.17
sneak   6.3
sneaker   6.3
sneaking   6.3
sneaky   6.3
sneer   7.1
sneerer   7.5
sneering   7.5
sneeze   6.19
sneezed   6.19
sneezer   6.19
sneezing   6.19
sneezy   6.19
snicker   9.2
Snickers®   9.2
snide   10.4
sniff   9.4
sniffer   9.4
sniffy   9.4
snifter   9.4
snigger   9.5
snip   9.9
snipe   10.10
sniped   10.10
sniper   10.10
sniping   10.10
snipper   9.9
snippet   9.9
snitch   9.14
snivel   9.17
snivelling   9.17
snob   11.1
snobbery   11.1
snog   11.5
snooker   18.3
snoop   18.10
snooper   18.10
Snoopy   18.10

snooty 18.14
snooze 18.19
snoozer 18.19
snoozing 18.19
snoozy 18.19
snore 14.1
snorer 14.12
snoring 14.12
snort 14.15
snorter 14.15
snorting 14.15
snot 11.13
snotty 11.13
snout 13.7
snow 12.1
snowboarding 14.4
snowed 12.4
snowing 12.1
snowman 1.8
snowmobile 6.7
snow-white 10.13
snowy 12.1
SNP 6.1
snub 17.1
snuck 17.2
snuff 17.4
snuffed 17.4
snuffer 17.4
snuffle 17.4
snuffled 17.4
snug 17.5
snugger 17.5
snuggle 17.5
snugly 17.5
so 12.1
soak 12.3
soaked 12.3
soaking 12.3
so-and-so 12.1
soap 12.10
soapy 12.10
soar 14.1
soarer 14.12
soaring 14.12
sob 11.1
sobbing 11.1
sober 12.2
sobriety 10.1
so-called 14.8
soccer 11.2
sociable 12.13
socialism 9.18
socialist 9.11
socialite 10.13
socialize 10.17
socializer 10.17

socializing 10.17
socially 6.1
society 10.1
socioeconomic 11.7
sociological 11.3
sociologist 11.6
sociology 11.6
sock 11.2
socked 11.2
socket 11.2
socking 11.2
Socrates 6.19
sod 11.3
soda 12.4
sodden 11.3
sodium 12.4
sofa 12.5
Sofia 7.1
soft 11.4
softhearted 2.16
softly 11.4
softly-softly 11.4
soft-pedal 5.3
soft-spoken 12.3
softy 11.4
soggy 11.5
soh 12.1
soil 15.3
Sol 11.6
solace 11.6
solar 12.7
solar-powered 13.1
sold 12.7
solder 12.7
sole 12.7
solely 12.7
solemn 11.6
solemnity 5.7
solicit 9.11
solicitous 9.11
solid 11.6
solidarity 1.10
solidify 10.1
solidity 9.3
solidly 6.1
solid-state 3.14
Solihull 17.6
soliloquy 6.1
solitaire 4.1
solitary 6.1
solitude 18.4
solo 12.7
soloist 9.11
Solomon 17.8
soluble 11.6
solution 18.13

solve 11.6
solved 11.6
solvency 6.1
Somali 2.8
sombrero 4.6
some 17.7
somebody 11.3
somersault 14.8
somersaulted 14.8
Somerset 5.14
Somme 11.7
somnolent 5.8
son 17.8
sonata 2.16
song 11.8
songwriter 10.13
sonic 11.8
sonics 11.8
son-in-law 14.1
sonnet 11.8
sonny 17.8
sonorous 17.11
soon 18.9
sooner 18.9
soot 16.5
sooth 18.16
soothe 18.15
soothsayer 3.1
sooting 16.5
Sooty 18.14
sop 11.9
Sophia 6.1
Sophie 12.5
sophisticated 3.14
sophistication 3.13
sophistry 6.1
sophomore 14.1
soporific 9.4
soppier 11.9
soppily 11.9
soppy 11.9
soprano 2.10
sorceress 5.11
sorcery 6.1
sordid 14.4
sore 14.1
sorely 14.8
sorrel 11.10
sorrow 11.10
sorrowful 16.3
sorry 11.10
sort 14.15
sorted 14.15
sorter 14.15
sorting 14.15
SOS 5.11

sought 14.15
sought-after 2.5
soul 12.7
soul-destroying 15.1
soulful 12.7
soulless 12.7
sound 13.4
soundalike 10.3
sounded 13.4
sounder 13.4
sounding 13.4
soundings 13.4
soundless 13.4
soundly 13.4
soup 18.10
sour 13.1
source 14.13
sourced 14.13
soured 13.1
souring 13.1
sourly 13.1
souse 13.6
soused 13.6
south 13.8
southeast 6.11
Southend 5.8
southerly 6.1
south-facing 3.11
south-southeast 6.11
south-southwest 5.11
south-southwester 5.11
south-southwestern 5.11
southwest 5.11
southwester 5.11
southwestern 5.11
souvenir 7.1
sou'-wester 5.11
sovereignty 6.1
sow 12.1, 13.1
sowed 12.4
sower 12.1
Soweto 5.14
sowing 12.1
sown 12.9
soya 15.1
spa 2.1
space 3.11
spaceless 3.11
Spacey 3.11
spacey 3.11
spacing 3.11
spacious 3.13
spade 3.4
spaghetti 5.14
Spain 3.9

spam 1.7
spammer 1.7
spamming 1.7
span 1.8
spangle 1.8
spangled 1.8
spaniel 1.8
Spanish 1.8
spank 1.8
spanker 1.8
spanking 1.8
spanned 1.8
spanner 1.8
spanning 1.8
spar 2.1
spare 4.1
spared 4.2
sparer 4.6
sparing 4.6
sparingly 4.6
spark 2.3
sparked 2.3
sparker 2.3
sparking 2.3
sparkle 2.3
sparky 2.3
sparred 2.4
sparring 2.12
sparrow 1.10
sparrowhawk 14.3
sparse 2.13
sparsely 2.13
Sparta 2.16
Spartacus 17.11
spartan 2.16
spasm 1.17
spasmodic 11.3
spasmodically 11.3
spastic 1.11
spat 1.13
spate 3.14
spatial 3.13
spatter 1.13
spattered 1.13
spattering 1.13
spawn 14.10
spawning 14.10
spay 3.1
spaying 3.1
speak 6.3
speaker 6.3
speaking 6.3
spear 7.1
spearing 7.5
spearmint 9.8
Spears 7.7

spec 5.2
speciality 1.6
specialization 3.13
specialize 10.17
specializing 10.17
specific 9.4
specifically 6.1
specification 3.13
specified 10.4
specify 10.1
specious 6.13
speck 5.2
speckle 5.2
specs 5.2
spectacle 16.3
spectacular 1.2
spectator 3.14
Spector 5.2
spectra 5.2
spectre 5.2
spectrum 5.2
speculate 3.14
speculation 3.13
speculative 9.17
speculator 3.14
sped 5.3
speech 6.14
speechwriter 10.13
speed 6.4
speeder 6.4
speedier 6.4
speedily 6.4
speeding 6.4
speedo 6.4
speedometer 11.7
speedy 6.4
spell 5.6
spell-checker 5.2
spelled 5.6
speller 5.6
spellers 5.6
spelling 5.6
spelt 5.6
spend 5.8
spender 5.8
spending 5.8
spent 5.8
sperm 8.8
spermicidal 10.4
spermicide 10.4
spew 18.1
Speyside 3.11
sphere 7.1
spherical 5.10
sphinx 9.8
spice 10.12

spiced 10.12
spicer 10.12
spicing 10.12
spick-and-span 1.8
spicy 10.12
spider 10.4
spiel 6.7
spieler 6.7
spike 10.3
spiking 10.3
spiky 10.3
spill 9.6
spillage 9.6
spilled 9.6
spiller 9.6
spilling 9.6
spilt 9.6
spin 9.8
spinal 10.9
spindle 9.8
spindly 9.8
spin-drier 10.1
spin-dry 10.1
spine 10.9
spine-chilling 9.6
spinner 9.8
spinney 9.8
spinning 9.8
spinster 9.8
spiny 10.9
spiral 10.11
spire 10.1
spiritualism 9.18
spirituality 1.6
spit 9.14
spite 10.13
spited 10.13
spiteful 10.13
spitefully 10.13
spiting 10.13
spitter 9.14
spittle 9.14
spiv 9.17
splash 1.12
splashed 1.12
splasher 1.12
splashing 1.12
splatter 1.13
splattered 1.13
splattering 1.13
splay 3.1
splaying 3.1
spleen 6.9
splendid 5.8
splendour 5.8
splice 10.12

spliced 10.12
splicer 10.12
splicing 10.12
splint 9.8
splinter 9.8
splinting 9.8
Split 9.14
split 9.14
split hairs 4.8
split-second 5.2
splitter 9.14
splitting 9.14
splodge 11.3
splodgy 11.3
splutter 17.13
spoil 15.3
spoke 12.3
spoken 12.3
spokesperson 8.12
sponge 17.8
sponger 17.8
sponsorship 9.9
spontaneity 3.1
spontaneous 3.9
spoof 18.5
spook 18.3
spooky 18.3
spool 18.7
spooler 18.7
spooling 18.7
spoon 18.9
spooned 18.9
Spooner 18.9
spoonful 18.9
sporadic 1.3
spore 14.1
sporran 11.10
sport 14.15
sporting 14.15
sportive 14.15
sports 14.15
sportsmanlike 10.3
sportsmanship 9.9
sportsperson 8.12
sporty 14.15
spot 11.13
spot-on 11.8
spotter 11.13
spotty 11.13
spousal 13.9
spouse 13.6
spout 13.7
spouting 13.7
sprain 3.9
sprang 1.8
sprat 1.13

sprawl 14.8
sprawled 14.8
sprawler 14.8
sprawling 14.8
spray 3.1
spraying 3.1
spray-on 3.1
spread 5.3
spreading 5.3
spree 6.1
sprig 9.5
sprightly 10.13
sprigs 9.5
spring 9.8
spring-clean 6.9
spring-cleaning 6.9
springer 9.8
springing 9.8
springy 9.8
sprinkle 9.8
sprinkling 9.8
sprint 9.8
sprinter 9.8
sprinting 9.8
sprite 10.13
sprocket 11.2
sprout 13.7
sprouting 13.7
spruce 18.11
sprung 17.8
spry 10.1
spryly 10.7
spud 17.3
spun 17.3
spunk 17.8
spur 8.1
spurious 19.4
spurn 8.9
spurned 8.9
spurning 8.9
spurred 8.4
spurring 8.11
spurs 8.18
spurt 8.14
spurted 8.14
spurts 8.14
sputter 17.13
spy 10.1
squabble 11.1
squad 11.3
squaddie 11.3
squalid 11.6
squall 14.8
squalled 14.8
squally 14.8
squalor 11.6

squander 11.8
square 4.1
squared 4.2
squarely 4.3
squareness 4.5
squarer 4.6
squaring 4.6
squash 11.12
squasher 11.12
squat 11.13
squatter 11.13
squaw 14.1
squawk 14.3
squawked 14.3
squawker 14.3
squawking 14.3
squeak 6.3
squeaker 6.3
squeaking 6.3
squeaky 6.3
squeal 6.7
squealed 6.7
squealer 6.7
squealing 6.7
squeegee 6.4
squeeze 6.19
squeezed 6.19
squeezer 6.19
squeezing 6.19
squelch 5.6
squib 9.1
squid 9.3
squiggle 9.5
squint 9.8
squinting 9.8
squire 10.1
squiring 10.1
squirm 8.8
squirmed 8.8
squirmer 8.8
squirrel 9.10
squirt 8.14
squirted 8.14
squirter 8.14
squirts 8.14
Sri Lanka 1.8
stab 1.1
stability 9.6
stabilize 10.17
stabilizer 10.17
stabilizing 10.17
stable 3.2
Stac(e)y 3.11
stack 1.2
stacked 1.2
stacking 1.2

stacks 1.2
stadia 3.4
stadium 3.4
staff 2.5
Staffa 1.4
staffed 2.5
staffing 2.5
Staffordshire 10.1
stag 1.5
stage 3.4
staged 3.4
stagehand 1.8
stagflation 3.13
stagger 1.5
staggered 1.5
staging 3.4
stagnate 3.14
stagnation 3.13
staid 3.4
stain 3.9
stained 3.9
Staines 3.9
stair 4.1
stairlift 4.3
stairway 4.7
stake 3.3
stakeout 3.3
staking 3.3
stalactite 10.13
stalagmite 10.13
stale 3.7
staler 3.7
Stalingrad 1.3
stalk 14.3
stalked 14.3
stalker 14.3
stalking 14.3
stall 14.8
stalled 14.8
stallion 1.6
Stallone 12.9
stamen 3.8
stamina 1.7
stammer 1.7
stammered 1.7
Stamp 1.7
stamp 1.7
stampede 6.4
stamper 1.7
Stan 1.8
stance 2.10
stand 1.8
standard 1.8
standardization 3.13
standardize 10.17
standardizer 10.17

standardizing 10.17
stander 1.8
stand-in 9.8
standing 1.8
stank 1.8
Stanley 1.8
stanza 1.8
stanzas 1.8
staple 3.10
staples 3.10
Star 2.1
star 2.1
starch 2.16
starchy 2.16
stare 4.1
stared 4.2
starer 4.6
staring 4.6
stark 2.3
starker 2.3
starlet 2.8
starling 2.8
starlit 2.8
starred 2.4
starrier 2.12
starring 2.12
starry 2.12
starry-eyed 10.4
start 2.16
started 2.16
starter 2.16
starting 2.16
starvation 3.13
starve 2.19
starving 2.19
stash 1.12
stashed 1.12
stasher 1.12
stashing 1.12
state 3.14
stateless 3.14
stately 3.14
statement 3.14
Staten 1.13
state-of-the-art 2.16
state-owned 12.9
statesmanlike 10.3
static 1.13
station 3.13
stationary 3.13
stationer 3.13
stationery 3.13
statistic 9.11
statistical 9.11
statistician 9.13
statistics 9.11

stative   3.14
statuesque   5.11
statuette   5.14
status   3.14
status quo   12.1
statutory   6.1
staunch   14.10
stave   3.17
staved   3.17
staving   3.17
stay   3.1
staying   3.1
stead   5.3
steadily   5.3
steading   5.3
steady   5.3
steak   3.3
steal   6.7
stealer   6.7
stealing   6.7
stealth   5.6
stealthily   6.1
stealthy   5.6
steam   6.8
steamer   6.8
steamier   6.8
steaming   6.8
steamroller   12.7
steamy   6.8
steel   6.7
steelier   6.7
steeling   6.7
steely   6.7
steep   6.10
steepen   6.10
steeper   6.10
steeple   6.10
steeplechase   3.11
steeplechaser   3.11
steeplechasing   3.11
steeplejack   1.2
steeplejacks   1.2
steer   7.1
steerer   7.5
steering   7.5
Stein   6.9, 10.9
Stella   5.6
stem   5.7
stench   5.8
stencil   5.8
stenographer   11.5
step   5.9
stepbrother   17.14
stepdaughter   14.15
Stephanie   6.1
Stephen   6.17

stepladder   1.3
stepmother   17.14
steppe   5.9
stepped   5.9
stepsister   9.11
stereo   12.1
stereophonic   11.8
stereoscopic   11.9
stereotype   10.10
stereotyped   10.10
stereotyper   10.10
sterility   9.6
sterilization   3.13
sterilize   10.17
sterilizer   10.17
sterilizing   10.17
sterling   8.7
stern   8.9
sterner   8.9
sternest   8.9
sternum   8.9
stethoscope   12.10
Steve   6.17
stevedore   14.1
Steven   6.17
stew   18.1
stewardess   5.11
stick   9.2
sticker   9.2
sticking   9.2
stick-in-the-mud   17.3
stickleback   1.2
sticklebacks   1.2
stick-on   11.8
sticks   9.2
stick-up   9.2
sticky   9.2
stiff   9.4
stiffen   9.4
stiffer   9.4
stifle   10.5
stifling   10.5
stigma   9.5
stigmata   2.16
stigmatize   10.17
stigmatizing   10.17
stile   10.7
Stiles   10.7
stiletto   5.14
still   9.6
stillness   9.6
stilt   9.6
stimulate   9.7
stimulating   3.14
stimulation   3.13
stimulus   17.11

Sting   9.8
sting   9.8
stinger   9.8
stinging   9.8
stingy   9.8
stink   9.8
stinker   9.8
stinking   9.8
stinky   9.8
stint   9.8
stinting   9.8
stipulate   9.9
stipulation   3.13
stir   8.1
stir-fried   10.4
stir-fry   10.1
Stirling   8.7
Stirlingshire   10.1
stirred   8.4
stirring   8.11
stirrup   9.10
stirs   8.18
stitch   9.14
stoat   12.14
stock   11.2
stockade   3.4
stockbroker   12.3
stocked   11.2
stocker   11.2
stockholder   12.7
stocking   11.2
stock-still   9.6
stocktaking   3.3
stocky   11.2
stodge   11.3
stodgy   11.3
stoic   12.1
stoical   16.3
stoicism   9.18
stoke   12.3
Stoke-on-Trent   5.8
Stoker   12.3
stoker   12.3
stoking   12.3
stole   12.7
stolen   12.7
stolid   11.6
stomp   11.7
Stone   12.9
stone   12.9
stone-cold   12.7
stoned   12.9
stone-dead   5.3
stone-deaf   5.4
Stonehenge   5.8
stonemason   3.11

stuck-up   17.9
stud   17.3
studded   17.3
studding   17.3
student   18.4
studied   17.3
studio   12.1
study   17.3
stuff   17.4
stuffed   17.4
stuffer   17.4
stuffy   17.4
stultifying   10.1
stumble   17.7
stumbling   17.7
stump   17.7
stumper   17.7
stumping   17.7
stumpy   17.7
stun   17.8
stung   17.8
stunk   17.8
stunned   17.8
stunner   17.8
stunning   17.8
stunt   17.8
stunted   17.8
stunting   17.8
stupefy   10.1
stupefying   10.1
stupendous   5.8
stupendously   5.8
stupid   18.10
stupidity   9.3
stupidly   6.1
stupor   18.10
sturdy   8.4
sturgeon   8.4
stutter   17.13
stye   10.1
style   10.7
styled   10.7
styli   10.7
styling   10.7
stylistic   9.11
stylistics   9.11
stylized   10.17
stymie   10.8
styptic   9.9
Styx   9.2
suave   2.19
sub   17.1
subaltern   17.8
subcommittee   9.14
subconscious   11.8
subcontract   1.2

subcontracted   1.2
subcontracting   1.2
subcontractor   1.2
subculture   17.6
subdivision   9.12
subdue   18.1
subedit   5.3
subeditor   5.3
subhuman   18.8
subject   5.2
subjected   5.2
subjecting   5.2
subjective   5.2
subjectivity   9.17
sub judice   6.1
subjugate   3.14
subjugator   3.14
sublet   5.14
subletter   5.14
subletting   5.14
sublimate   3.14
sublime   10.8
sublimely   10.8
subliminal   9.7
submarine   6.9
submerge   8.4
submersion   8.13
submission   9.13
submit   9.14
submitter   9.14
subnormal   14.9
subordinate   3.14, 14.4
subordination   3.13
subpoena   6.9
subscribe   10.2
subscriber   10.2
subscription   9.9
subsection   5.2
subsequent   5.8
subsequently   6.1
subside   10.4
subsided   10.4
subsidence   10.4
subsidiarity   1.10
subsidiary   6.1
subsiding   10.4
subsidize   10.17
subsidizing   10.17
subsidy   6.1
subsist   9.11
subsisted   9.11
subsistence   9.11
substandard   1.8
substantial   1.8
substantially   1.8
substantiate   3.14

substitutable   18.14
substitute   18.14
substituted   18.14
substitution   18.13
subsume   18.8
subsuming   18.8
subterfuge   18.4
subterranean   3.9
subtitle   10.13
subtle   17.13
subtlety   6.1
subtly   17.13
subtotal   12.14
subtract   1.2
subtracted   1.2
subtracting   1.2
subtraction   1.2
subtropical   11.9
suburban   8.2
suburbia   8.2
subversion   8.13
subversive   8.12
subvert   8.14
subverted   8.14
subverter   8.14
subverts   8.14
sub-zero   7.5
succeed   6.4
succeeding   6.4
success   5.11
successful   5.11
successfully   6.1
succession   5.13
successive   5.11
successively   5.11
successor   5.11
succinct   9.8
succulent   17.2
succumb   17.7
succumbing   17.7
such   17.13
suck   17.2
sucked   17.2
sucker   17.2
suckle   17.2
suckling   17.2
sucks   17.2
suction   17.2
Sudan   1.8
Sudanese   6.19
suddenly   6.1
suddenness   5.11
Sue   18.1
sue   18.1
suede   3.4
suet   18.1

suffer 17.4
suffice 10.12
sufficed 10.12
sufficiency 9.13
sufficient 9.13
sufficiently 9.13
sufficing 10.12
suffix 9.2
suffixed 9.2
suffocate 3.14
suffocation 3.13
suffragette 5.14
suffuse 18.19
suffusing 18.19
sugar-coated 12.14
sugar-free 6.1
sugary 6.1
suggest 5.11
suggested 5.11
suggestible 16.3
suggesting 5.11
suggestion 5.11
suggestive 5.11
suicidal 10.4
suicide 10.4
suit 18.14
suitability 9.6
suitable 18.14
suitably 6.1
suite 6.14
suited 18.14
suites 6.14
suiting 18.14
suitor 18.14
sulk 17.6
sulky 17.6
Sullivan 17.8
sully 17.6
sulphate 3.14
sulphuric 19.4
sultana 2.10
sum 17.7
Sumatra 2.16
summarily 6.1
summarize 10.17
summarizer 10.17
summarizing 10.17
summary 17.7
summer 17.7
summerhouse 13.6
summertime 10.8
summery 17.7
summing 17.7
summing-up 17.9
summit 17.7
summon 17.7

sump 17.7
sumptuous 17.7
sun 17.8
sundae 17.8
Sunday 17.8
sundown 17.8
sun-dried 10.4
sun-dry 10.1
sunflower 13.1
sung 17.8
sunglasses 2.13
Sunil 6.7
sunk 17.8
sunken 17.8
sunned 17.8
sunning 17.8
sunny 17.8
sup 17.9
super 18.10
superannuation 3.13
superb 8.2
Super Bowl® 12.7
supercharger 2.4
supercilious 9.6
superconductor 17.2
super-duper 18.10
superficial 9.13
superficiality 1.6
superficially 9.13
supergrass 2.13
supergrasses 2.13
superhuman 18.8
superimpose 12.19
superimposing 12.19
superintend 5.8
superintendent 5.8
superintending 5.8
Superior 7.5
superior 7.5
superiority 11.10
superlative 9.17
superman 1.8
supermodel 11.3
supernova 12.17
superpower 13.1
supersede 6.4
supersonic 11.8
superstar 2.1
superstition 9.13
superstitious 9.13
superstitiously 9.13
superstore 14.1
supertanker 1.8
supervise 10.17
supervising 10.17
supervision 9.12

supervisor 10.17
supervisory 10.17
supped 17.9
supper 17.9
supplant 2.10
supplanting 2.10
supple 17.9
supplement 5.8
supplementary 5.8
supplication 3.13
supply 10.1
support 14.15
supporter 14.15
supporting 14.15
supportive 14.15
suppose 12.19
supposed 12.19
supposing 12.19
supposition 9.13
suppository 6.1
suppress 5.11
suppressed 5.11
suppression 5.13
suppurate 3.14
supranational 1.12
supremacy 6.1
supreme 6.8
supremely 6.8
surd 8.4
sure 19.1
surely 19.3
surer 19.4
surest 19.4
surety 19.4
surf 8.5
surfing 8.5
surge 8.4
surgeon 8.4
surgery 8.4
surgical 16.3
Surinam 1.7
surly 8.7
surmise 10.17
surmiser 10.17
surmising 10.17
surmount 13.4
surmountable 13.4
surmounted 13.4
surmounting 13.4
surpass 2.13
surpassable 2.13
surpassed 2.13
surpasses 2.13
surprise 10.17
surprising 10.17
surprisingly 6.1

surreal 7.4
surrealism 7.4
surrealist 7.4
surrender 5.8
surreptitious 9.13
surreptitiously 9.13
Surrey 17.10
surrogate 17.13
surround 13.4
surrounded 13.4
surrounding 13.4
surroundings 13.4
survey 3.1
surveyable 3.1
surveying 3.1
surveyor 3.1
survival 10.15
survive 10.15
survived 10.15
surviving 10.15
survivor 10.15
Susanna(h) 1.8
susceptible 16.3
Susie 18.19
suspect 5.2
suspected 5.2
suspecting 5.2
suspend 5.8
suspended 5.8
suspender 5.8
suspending 5.8
suspense 5.8
suspenser 5.8
suspension 5.8
suspicion 9.13
suspicious 9.13
suspiciously 9.13
suss 17.11
sussed 17.11
sustain 3.9
sustainable 3.9
sustained 3.9
sustainer 3.9
suture 18.14
svelte 5.6
Svengali 2.8
swab 11.1
swabber 11.1
swabbing 11.1
swag 1.5
swagger 1.5
swaggered 1.5
swallow 11.6
swam 1.7
swamp 11.7
swan 11.8

swank 1.8
swanky 1.8
swanned 11.8
swans 11.8
swap 11.9
swarf 14.5
swarm 14.9
swarmed 14.9
swarmer 14.9
swashbuckling 17.2
SWAT 11.13
swat 11.13
swatch 11.13
swathe 3.15
swatter 11.13
sway 3.1
swayable 3.1
swaying 3.1
Swayze 3.18
Swazi 2.21
Swaziland 1.8
swear 4.1
swearer 4.6
swearing 4.6
sweat 5.14
sweated 5.14
sweater 5.14
sweating 5.14
sweaty 5.14
Swede 6.4
swede 6.4
Sweden 6.4
sweep 6.10
sweeper 6.10
sweeping 6.10
sweet 6.14
sweet-and-sour 13.1
sweeten 6.14
sweeter 6.14
sweetie 6.14
sweetly 6.14
sweetness 6.14
sweets 6.14
sweet-smelling 5.6
swell 5.6
swelled 5.6
swelling 5.6
swelter 5.6
swept 5.9
swerve 8.17
swerved 8.17
swerver 8.17
swerving 8.17
swift 9.4
swifter 9.4
swig 9.5

swigger 9.5
swigs 9.5
swill 9.6
swilled 9.6
swiller 9.6
swilling 9.6
swim 9.7
swimmer 9.7
swimming 9.7
swimmingly 6.1
swindle 9.8
Swindon 9.8
swine 10.9
swing 9.8
swingeing 9.8
swinger 9.8
swinging 9.8
swipe 10.10
swiped 10.10
swiper 10.10
swiping 10.10
swirl 8.7
swirled 8.7
swirling 8.7
swish 9.13
swisher 9.13
swishing 9.13
swishy 9.13
Swiss 9.11
Switch® 9.14
switch 9.14
Switzerland 1.8
swivel 9.17
swivelling 9.17
swizz 9.18
swollen 12.7
swoon 18.9
swooned 18.9
swoop 18.10
sword 14.4
swore 14.1
sworn 14.10
swot 11.13
swum 17.7
swung 17.8
sycamore 14.1
sycophant 1.8
sycophantic 1.8
sycophants 1.8
Sydney 9.3
syllable 9.6
syllabus 17.11
Sylvester 5.11
symbiotic 11.13
symbol 9.7
symbolic 11.6

symbolism 9.18
symbolist 9.11
symbolize 10.17
symbolizing 10.17
symmetrical 16.3
sympathetic 5.14
sympathetically 5.14
sympathize 10.17
sympathizer 10.17
sympathizing 10.17
sympathy 6.1
symphony 6.1
symptomatic 1.13
synagogue 11.5
sync(h) 9.8
sync(h)ed 9.8
sync(h)ing 9.8
synchronization 3.13
synchronize 10.17
synchronizer 10.17
synchronizing 10.17
syncopation 3.13
syndicalism 9.18
syndicalist 9.11
syndicate 9.8, 17.13
synergy 6.1
synonym 9.7
synonymous 11.8
synthesis 9.11
synthesize 10.17
synthesizer 10.17
synthesizing 10.17
synthetic 5.14
synthetically 5.14
synthetics 5.14
Syracuse 18.19
syringe 9.8
syrup 9.10
syrupy 6.1
systematic 1.13
systematize 10.17
systematizer 10.17
systematizing 10.17

T

T 6.1
TA 3.1
ta 2.1
tab 1.1
tabby 1.1
tabernacle 1.2
table 3.2
tablecloth 11.14
tabled 3.2
tablespoon 18.9

tableware 4.1
taboo 18.1
tabulate 3.14
tachometer 11.7
tacit 1.11
tacitly 6.1
taciturn 8.9
tack 1.2
tacked 1.2
tackier 1.2
tacking 1.2
tackle 1.2
tacks 1.2
tacky 1.2
tact 1.2
tactfully 6.1
tactic 1.2
tactical 1.2
tactician 9.13
tactlessly 6.1
tad 1.3
Tadzhikistan 2.10
tag 1.5
tagger 1.5
tagging 1.5
tagliatelle 5.6
Tagus 3.6
Tahiti 6.14
Tahitian 6.13
tail 3.7
tailed 3.7
tailing 3.7
tailor 3.7
tailor-made 3.4
taint 3.9
tainted 3.9
Taiwan 2.10
Taiwanese 6.19
take 3.3
takeaway 3.3
taken 3.3
takeout 3.3
takeover 3.3
taker 3.3
Take That 1.13
take-up 3.3
taking 3.3
tale 3.7
talent 1.6
talented 9.3
talisman 17.8
talk 14.3
talkative 9.17
talked 14.3
talker 14.3
talking 14.3

talking-to 18.1
tall 14.8
Tallahassee 1.11
taller 14.8
tallied 1.6
tallow 1.6
tally 1.6
talon 1.6
Tam 1.7
Tamara 2.12
tamarind 9.8
tambourine 6.9
tame 3.8
tamed 3.8
tamely 3.8
tamer 3.8
tames 3.8
Tamil 1.7
Tammy 1.7
Tam o'Shanter 1.8
Tampa 1.7
tamper 1.7
tampon 1.7
tan 1.8
tandem 1.8
tang 1.8
Tanganyika 6.3
tangerine 6.9
tangible 16.3
tangibly 6.1
Tangier 7.1
Tangiers 7.7
tangle 1.8
tangled 1.8
tango 1.8
tank 1.8
tanker 1.8
tanking 1.8
tanned 1.8
tanner 1.8
tannery 1.8
tanning 1.8
tantalize 10.17
tantalizer 10.17
tantalizing 10.17
tantamount 13.4
tantrum 1.8
Tanya 1.8
Tanzania 7.1
Tanzanian 6.1
tap 1.9
tape 3.10
taper 3.10
tape-record 14.4
tape-recorded 14.4
tape-recorder 14.4

Index

tapestry 6.1
tapioca 12.3
tapir 3.10
tapper 1.9
tapping 1.9
tar 2.1
Tara 2.12
Tarantella 5.6
Tarantino 6.9
tardily 6.1
tardy 2.4
Tariq 1.10
tarnish 2.10
tarot 1.10
tarpaulin 14.8
tarragon 1.10
tarred 2.4
tarried 1.10
tarring 2.12
tarry 1.10, 2.12
tart 2.16
tartan 2.16
Tartar 2.16
tartar 2.16
tartly 2.16
tarty 2.16
taser 3.18
Tashkent 5.8
task 2.13
taskmaster 2.13
Tasmania 3.9
Tasmanian 3.9
tassel 1.11
taste 3.11
tasteful 3.11
tastefully 6.1
tastelessly 6.1
taster 3.11
tasty 3.11
tat 1.13
ta-ta 2.1
tatter 1.13
tattered 1.13
tattering 1.13
tattle 1.13
tattoo 18.1
tattooist 18.1
tatty 1.13
taught 14.15
taunt 14.10
taunted 14.10
taunting 14.10
Taurus 14.12
taut 14.15
tauten 14.15
tautological 11.3

tautology 11.6
tavern 1.16
tawdry 14.4
tawny 14.10
tax 1.2
taxation 3.13
tax-deductible 17.2
tax-free 6.1
taxing 1.2
taxonomy 11.8
taxpayer 3.1
Tayside 3.11
TB 6.1
te 6.1
tea 6.1
teach 6.14
teacher 6.14
teaching 6.14
teak 6.3
team 6.8
teaming 6.8
tear 4.1, 7.1
tearaway 3.1
tearer 4.6
tearful 7.3
tearfully 6.1
tearing 4.6
tearjerker 8.3
tear to shreds 5.3
tease 6.19
teased 6.19
teasel 6.19
teaser 6.19
teasing 6.19
teat 6.14
teats 6.14
technical 16.3
technicality 1.6
technically 6.1
technician 9.13
technique 6.3
technological 11.3
technology 11.6
Ted 5.3
Teddy 5.3
teddy 5.3
tedium 6.4
tee 6.1
teed 6.4
teeing 6.1
teem 6.8
teeming 6.8
teen 6.9
teenager 3.4
teens 6.9
teeny 6.9

teeny-bopper 11.9
teeny-weeny 6.9
Teesside 6.11
teeter 6.14
teeth 6.16
teethe 6.15
teething 6.15
teetotal 12.14
Teh(e)ran 2.10
Tel Aviv 6.17
telebanking 1.8
telecommunications 3.13
telecommuting 18.14
telegenic 5.8
telegram 1.7
telegraph 2.5
telegraphed 2.5
telegraphic 1.4
telegraphing 2.5
telepathic 1.15
telepathically 6.1
telepathy 6.1
telephone 12.9
telephoner 12.9
telephoning 12.9
telephonist 9.11
telephoto 12.14
teleprinter 9.8
telesales 3.7
telescope 12.10
telescopic 11.9
teleshopping 11.9
teletext 5.2
televangelist 9.11
televise 10.17
televising 10.17
television 9.12
tell 5.6
teller 5.6
tellers 5.6
telling 5.6
telly 5.6
temerity 5.10
temp 5.7
temperament 5.8
temperamental 5.8
temperamentally 5.8
temperature 19.1
tempestuous 5.11
temporal 16.3
temporarily 5.10
temporary 6.1
tempt 5.7
temptation 3.13
ten 5.8

tenacious   3.13
tenacity   1.11
tenancy   6.1
tenant   5.8
ten-a-penny   5.8
tench   5.8
tend   5.8
tendency   5.8
tendentious   5.8
tender   5.8
tenderhearted   2.16
tenderly   6.1
tenderness   5.11
tending   5.8
tendon   5.8
tenement   5.8
Tenerife   6.5
tenet   5.8
tenner   5.8
Tennessee   6.1
tennis   5.8
Tennyson   5.8
tenor   5.8
tense   5.8
tensely   5.8
tenser   5.8
tension   5.8
tent   5.8
tentacle   16.3
tentative   5.8
tentatively   6.1
tenth   5.8
tenuous   5.8
tepid   5.9
tequila   6.7
tercentenary   6.9
Teresa   6.19
term   8.8
termed   8.8
terminal   16.3
terminally   6.1
terminate   8.8
termination   3.13
terminological   11.3
terminology   11.6
terminus   17.11
tern   8.9
terrace   5.10
terracotta   11.13
terrain   3.9
terrapin   9.8
terrible   16.3
terribly   6.1
terrific   9.4
terrifically   6.1
terrified   10.4

terrify   5.10
terrifying   10.1
terrine   6.9
territorial   14.12
territory   6.1
terror   5.10
terrorism   9.18
terrorist   9.11
terrorize   10.17
terrorizer   10.17
terrorizing   10.17
terror-stricken   9.2
Terry   5.10
terse   8.12
tersely   8.12
terser   8.12
tertiary   6.1
Tesco   5.11
TESL   5.11
Tess   5.11
TESSA   5.11
Tessa   5.11
test   5.11
testament   5.8
testamentary   5.8
tested   5.11
tester   5.11
testicle   16.3
testify   10.1
testily   6.1
testimonial   12.9
testimony   6.1
testing   5.11
testosterone   12.9
tetanus   17.11
tetchy   5.14
tête-à-tête   3.14
tether   5.15
Tex-Mex   5.2
text   5.2
Thai   10.1
Thailand   10.7
than   1.8
thank   1.8
thankfully   6.1
thanklessly   6.1
thanksgiving   9.17
that   1.13
thatch   1.13
thatched   1.13
Thatcher   1.13
thatcher   1.13
thatching   1.13
thaw   14.1
thawing   14.12
theatre-goer   12.1

theatrical   16.3
thee   6.1
theft   5.4
their   4.1
theirs   4.8
them   5.7
thematic   1.13
theme   6.8
theming   6.8
themselves   5.6
then   5.8
thence   5.8
Theo   6.1
Theodore   14.1
theologian   12.4
theological   11.3
theology   11.6
theorem   7.5
theoretical   5.14
theoretically   5.14
theoretician   9.13
theorist   9.11
theorize   10.17
theorizing   10.17
theory   7.5
therapist   9.11
therapy   6.1
there   4.1
thereabouts   13.7
thereafter   2.5
T(h)eresa   6.19
thereupon   11.8
thermal   8.8
thermodynamics   1.7
thermometer   11.7
thermostat   1.13
thesauri   10.1
thesaurus   14.12
these   6.19
theses   6.11
thesis   6.11
they   3.1
they'd   3.4
they'll   3.7
they're   4.1
they've   3.17
thick   9.2
thicken   9.2
thicker   9.2
thicket   9.2
thickly   9.2
thickness   9.2
thickset   5.14
thick-skinned   9.8
thief   6.5
thieve   6.17

thieved 6.17
thieves 6.17
thieving 6.17
thigh 10.1
thimble 9.7
thin 9.8
thing 9.8
thingummy 6.1
thingy 9.8
think 9.8
thinker 9.8
thinking 9.8
thinly 9.8
thinned 9.8
thinner 9.8
thinning 9.8
thin-skinned 9.8
third 8.4
third-rate 3.14
thirst 8.12
thirsty 8.12
thirteen 6.9
thirty 8.14
this 9.11
thistle 9.11
thither 9.15
Thomas 11.7
thong 11.8
Thora 14.12
thoracic 1.11
thorn 14.10
thornier 14.10
thorny 14.10
thorough 17.10
thoroughbred 5.3
thoroughfare 4.1
thoroughgoing 12.1
thoroughly 6.1
thoroughness 5.11
those 12.19
though 12.1
thought 14.15
thoughtfully 6.1
thoughtlessly 6.1
thought-out 13.7
thought-provoking 12.3
thrash 1.12
thrashed 1.12
thrasher 1.12
thrashing 1.12
thread 5.3
threaded 5.3
threading 5.3
threat 5.14
threaten 5.14
three 6.1

three-dimensional 5.8
three-wheeled 6.7
three-wheeler 6.7
thresh 5.13
thresher 5.13
threw 18.1
thrice 10.12
thrift 9.4
thriftless 9.4
thrifty 9.4
thrill 9.6
thrilled 9.6
thriller 9.6
thrilling 9.6
thrillingness 9.6
thrive 10.15
thrived 10.15
thriver 10.15
thriving 10.15
throat 12.14
throaty 12.14
throb 11.1
throbbing 11.1
throes 12.19
thrombosis 12.11
throne 12.9
throng 11.8
thronging 11.8
throning 12.9
throttle 11.13
throttled 11.13
through 18.1
throughout 13.7
throve 12.17
throw 12.1
throwaway 12.1
Thrower 12.1
thrower 12.1
throwing 12.1
thrown 12.9
thrush 17.12
thrust 17.11
thrusting 17.11
thruway 18.18
thud 17.3
thudded 17.3
thudding 17.3
thug 17.5
Thumb 17.7
thumb 17.7
thumbing 17.7
thump 17.7
thumper 17.7
thumping 17.7
thunder 17.8
thunderbolt 12.7

thunderclap 1.9
thundercloud 13.2
thunderous 17.11
thunderstorm 14.9
thunderstruck 17.2
thus 17.11
thwart 14.15
thwarting 14.15
thyme 10.8
tiara 2.12
Tiber 10.2
Tibet 5.14
Tibetan 5.14
tibia 9.1
tic 9.2
tick 9.2
ticked 9.2
ticker 9.2
ticket 9.2
ticketless 5.11
ticking 9.2
tickle 9.2
ticks 9.2
tics 9.2
tidal 10.4
tiddler 9.3
tiddly 9.3
tiddlywinks 9.8
tide 10.4
tided 10.4
tideline 10.4
tidy 10.4
tie 10.1
tie-dye 10.1
tier 7.1
tiered 7.2
tiering 7.5
Tierra del Fuego 3.6
tiff 9.4
Tiffany 9.4
tiger 10.6
Tiggy-Winkle 9.8
tight 10.13
tighten 10.13
tightened 10.13
tightening 10.13
tighter 10.13
tight-fisted 9.11
tight-fitting 9.14
tightknit 9.14
tightly 10.13
tightness 10.13
tights 10.13
Tijuana 2.10
Tilbury 9.6
tile 10.7

tiled   10.7
tiler   10.7
tiling   10.7
till   9.6
tillable   9.6
tilled   9.6
tiller   9.6
tilling   9.6
Tilly   9.6
tilt   9.6
Tim   9.7
timber   9.7
Timbuktu   18.1
time   10.8
time-consuming   18.8
timekeeper   6.10
timekeeping   6.10
timely   10.8
timer   10.8
Times   10.8
time-saving   3.17
time-wasting   3.11
timidity   9.3
timidly   6.1
timing   10.8
Timmy   9.7
Timor   6.8
timorous   17.11
Timothy   6.1
tin   9.8
Tina   6.9
tinder   9.8
tinderbox   11.2
tine   10.9
ting-a-ling   9.8
tinge   9.8
tingle   9.8
tinker   9.8
Tinkerbell   5.6
tinkle   9.8
tinkling   9.8
tinned   9.8
tinnier   9.8
tinning   9.8
tinnitus   17.11
tinny   9.8
tint   9.8
tinting   9.8
tiny   10.9
tip   9.9
tip-off   9.9
tipper   9.9
Tipperary   4.6
Tippett   9.9
tipple   9.9
tippling   9.9

tipsy   9.9
tirade   3.4
Tirana   2.10
tire   10.1
tired   10.1
Tiree   6.1
tireless   10.1
tiresome   17.7
tiring   10.1
tissue   9.13
tit   9.14
Titanic   1.8
titanic   1.8
titanium   3.9
ti(t)ch   9.14
ti(t)chy   9.14
tit-for-tat   1.13
Titian   9.13
titillate   3.14
titillation   3.13
titillator   3.14
title   10.13
titleholder   12.7
Tito   6.14
titter   9.14
tittered   9.14
tit(t)ivate   3.14
tit(t)ivation   3.13
tittle-tattle   1.13
tizzy   9.18
T-junction   17.8
TLC   6.1
TNT   6.1
to   18.1
toad   12.4
toady   12.4
toast   12.11
toaster   12.11
toasting   12.11
tobacconist   9.11
Tobago   3.6
Tobias   10.1
Tobruk   16.1
Toby   12.2
today   3.1
Todd   11.3
toddle   11.3
to-do   18.1
toe   12.1
toes   12.19
toff   11.4
toffee   11.4
toga   12.6
together   5.15
togetherness   5.11
toggle   11.5

Togo   12.6
Togolese   6.19
togs   11.5
toil   15.3
token   12.3
Tokyo   12.3
told   12.7
Toledo   3.4
tolerate   3.14
toleration   3.13
tolerator   3.14
toll   12.7
tolled   12.7
toll-free   6.1
tolling   12.7
Tom   11.7
tom   11.7
tomahawk   14.3
Tom and Jerry   5.10
tomb   18.8
tombing   18.8
tome   12.8
tomfoolery   6.1
Tommy   11.7
tomorrow   11.10
tone   12.9
tone-deaf   5.4
toner   12.9
Tong   11.8
Tonga   11.8
tongue   17.8
Toni   12.9
tonic   11.8
tonics   11.8
tonight   10.13
toning   12.9
ton(ne)   17.8
tonsil   11.8
tonsillitis   10.13
Tony   12.9
too   18.1
took   16.1
tool   18.7
tooler   18.7
tooling   18.7
toot   18.14
tooted   18.14
tooth   18.16
toothless   18.16
tooting   18.14
top   11.9
Topeka   6.3
top-heavy   5.17
topic   11.9
topical   11.9
top-level   5.17

topography   11.5
topper   11.9
topping   11.9
topsy-turvy   8.17
torch   14.15
torchbearer   4.6
tore   14.1
toreador   14.1
Torfaen   10.9
torment   5.8
torn   14.10
tornado   3.4
Toronto   11.8
torpedo   6.4
torpor   14.11
Torquay   6.1
Torquemada   2.4
torrent   11.10
torrential   5.8
torrid   11.10
tortoiseshell   5.6
torture   14.15
Tory   14.12
Tosca   11.11
Tosh   11.12
tosh   11.12
toss   11.11
tossed   11.11
tot   11.13
total   12.14
totalitarian   4.6
totalitarianism   4.6
totality   1.6
totally   6.1
tote   12.14
toting   12.14
totter   11.13
tottery   11.13
totty   11.13
toucan   18.3
touch   17.13
touched   17.13
touchy   17.13
touchy-feely   6.7
tough   17.4
toughed   17.4
tougher   17.4
toughie   17.4
toughly   17.4
toughness   17.4
Toulouse   18.19
Toulouse-Lautrec   5.2
tour   19.1
toured   19.2
tourer   19.4
touring   19.4

tourist   19.4
tournament   5.8
tourniquet   3.1
tousle   13.9
tout   13.7
touting   13.7
tow   12.1
toward   14.4
towbar   12.2
towed   12.4
towel   13.1
tower   13.1
towering   13.1
towing   12.1
town   13.4
townspeople   6.10
towny   13.4
toxin   11.2
toy   15.1
toyed   15.2
toying   15.1
toys   15.8
trace   3.11
traceless   3.11
tracer   3.11
Trac(e)y   3.11
trachea   6.1
tracing   3.11
track   1.2
tracked   1.2
tracker   1.2
trackers   1.2
tracking   1.2
tracks   1.2
tract   1.2
tractable   1.2
traction   1.2
tractor   1.2
trade   3.4
traded   3.4
trademark   2.3
trademarked   2.3
trademarking   2.3
trader   3.4
trading   3.4
tradition   9.13
traditional   9.13
traditionalist   9.11
traffic   1.4
tragedian   6.4
tragedy   6.1
tragic   1.3
tragically   1.3, 6.1
trail   3.7
trailed   3.7
trailer   3.7

trailing   3.7
train   3.9
trainable   3.9
trained   3.9
trainee   6.1
trainer   3.9
training   3.9
trainspotter   11.13
trainspotting   11.13
trait   3.14
traitor   3.14
trajectory   5.2
Tralee   6.1
tram   1.7
tramp   1.7
tramper   1.7
trample   1.7
trampoline   6.9
trance   2.10
trancey   1.8
trannie   1.8
tranquillity   9.6
tranquillizer   10.17
transaction   1.2
transatlantic   1.8
transcend   5.8
transcendence   5.8
transcendency   5.8
transcendental   5.8
transcendentally   5.8
transcending   5.8
transcontinental   5.8
transcontinentally   5.8
transcribe   10.2
transcript   9.9
transcription   9.9
transfer   8.1
transferred   8.4
transferring   8.11
transfers   8.18
transfigure   9.5
transfix   9.2
transfixed   9.2
transform   14.9
transformation   3.13
transformed   14.9
transformer   14.9
transfusion   18.12
transgenic   5.8
transgress   5.11
transgressed   5.11
transistor   9.11
transition   9.13
transitional   9.13
transitive   9.17
transitory   6.1

Index

translatable   3.14
translate   3.14
translation   3.13
translator   3.14
transliterate   9.14
transmission   9.13
transmit   9.14
transmitter   9.14
transom   1.8
transparent   1.10
transpire   10.1
transplant   2.10
transplantation   3.13
transplanting   2.10
transport   14.15
transportation   3.13
transporter   14.15
transporting   14.15
transpose   12.19
transposer   12.19
transposing   12.19
Transvaal   2.8
transverse   8.12
transversed   8.12
Transylvania   3.9
Transylvanian   3.9
trap   1.9
trapeze   6.19
trapper   1.9
trapping   1.9
trash   1.12
trashed   1.12
trashing   1.12
trashy   1.12
trauma   14.9
traumatic   1.13
traumatize   10.17
traumatized   10.17
traumatizing   10.17
travail   3.7
travailed   3.7
travailing   3.7
travel   1.16
traveller   1.16
travelling   1.16
travel-sick   9.2
travel-sickness   9.2
traverse   8.12
traversed   8.12
traverser   8.12
travesty   6.1
trawl   14.8
trawled   14.8
trawler   14.8
tray   3.1
treacherous   5.14

treachery   5.14
tread   5.3
treading   5.3
treadle   5.3
treason   6.19
treasonable   6.19
treasure   5.12
treasure-trove   12.17
treasury   6.1
treat   6.14
treated   6.14
treating   6.14
treats   6.14
treaty   6.14
treble   5.1
Tree   6.1
tree   6.1
trek   5.2
trekked   5.2
trekker   5.2
treks   5.2
trellis   5.6
tremble   5.7
tremendous   5.8
tremendously   5.8
tremor   5.7
tremulous   17.11
trench   5.8
trend   5.8
trendsetter   5.14
trendy   5.8
trepidation   3.13
trestle   5.11
Trevino   6.9
Trevor   5.17
trial   10.1
triangular   1.8
Triassic   1.11
tribal   10.2
tribalism   9.18
tribe   10.2
tribulation   3.13
trice   10.12
triceps   10.12
trick   9.2
tricked   9.2
tricker   9.2
trickery   9.2
tricking   9.2
trickle   9.2
trickly   9.2
tricks   9.2
tricky   9.2
tricycle   10.12
trident   10.4
tried   10.4

tried-and-tested   5.11
Trieste   5.11
trifle   10.5
trifling   10.5
trigger   9.5
trigonometry   11.7
trike   10.3
trill   9.6
trilled   9.6
triller   9.6
trilling   9.6
trillion   9.6
trilogy   6.1
trim   9.7
trimaran   1.8
Trimble   9.7
trimester   5.11
trimmed   9.7
trimmer   9.7
trimming   9.7
Trinidad   1.3
Trinity   9.8
trio   6.1
triolet   10.1
trip   9.9
tripe   10.10
triple   9.9
triplicate   17.13
Tripoli   6.1
tripper   9.9
trippy   9.9
triptych   9.9
Trisha   9.13
Tristan da Cunha   18.9
trite   10.13
trivet   9.17
trivia   9.17
trivial   9.17
trivialize   10.17
trivializing   10.17
trod   11.3
trodden   11.3
Trojan   12.4
troll   12.7
trolley   11.6
trollop   11.6
trombone   12.9
Troon   18.9
troop   18.10
trooper   18.10
trophy   12.5
tropic   11.9
tropical   11.9
trot   11.13
Trotskyism   9.18
Trotskyist   9.11

trotter   11.13
trouble   17.1
troubled   17.1
trouble-free   6.1
troublemaker   3.3
troubleshooter   18.14
troublesome   17.7
trough   11.4
trounce   13.4
trounced   13.4
troupe   18.10
trousseau   18.11
trout   13.7
trowel   13.1
Troy   15.1
truancy   18.1
truant   18.1
truce   18.11
truck   17.2
trucked   17.2
trucker   17.2
trucks   17.2
truculent   17.2
Trudeau   18.4
trudge   17.3
trudging   17.3
Trudi(e)   18.4
true   18.1
truer   18.1
truest   18.1
truffle   17.4
truffled   17.4
trug   17.5
truly   18.7
Truman   18.8
Trump   17.7
trump   17.7
trumpet   17.7
trumping   17.7
truncate   3.14
truncheon   17.8
trundle   17.8
trunk   17.8
Truro   19.4
truss   17.11
trussed   17.11
trust   17.11
trusted   17.11
trustee   6.1
trustful   17.11
trusting   17.11
trustworthy   8.15
trusty   17.11
truth   18.16
truthful   18.16
try   10.1

trying   10.1
try-out   10.1
tryst   9.11
tsar   2.1
tsarist   2.12
tsetse   5.14
tub   17.1
tuba   18.2
tubby   17.1
tube   18.2
tuber   18.2
tuberculosis   12.11
Tuck   17.2
tuck   17.2
tucked   17.2
tucker   17.2
tucks   17.2
Tucson   11.8
Tudor   18.4
tuft   17.4
tug   17.5
tugger   17.5
tug-of-love   17.15
tug-of-war   14.1
tuition   9.13
Tull   17.6
Tulsa   17.6
tum   17.7
tumble   17.7
tumbledown   13.4
tumble-drier   10.1
tumble-dry   10.1
tumbler   17.7
tumbling   17.7
tummy   17.7
tumour   18.8
tuna   18.9
tune   18.9
tuned   18.9
tuneful   18.9
tuner   18.9
tunic   18.9
Tunis   18.9
Tunisia   9.18
Tunisian   9.18
Tunnel   17.8
tunnel   17.8
turban   8.2
turbo-charger   2.4
turbojet   5.14
turboprop   11.9
turbot   8.2
turbulence   5.8
turbulent   5.8
tureen   6.9
turf   8.5

turfing   8.5
Turin   9.8
Turk   8.3
Turkey   8.3
turkey   8.3
turkey baster   3.11
Turkmenistan   2.10
turmeric   9.2
turn   8.9
turnabout   13.7
turnaround   13.4
turned   8.9
Turner   8.9
turner   8.9
turning   8.9
turnover   12.17
turpentine   8.10
turtle   8.14
turtleneck   5.2
turtle-necked   5.2
turtlenecks   5.2
Tuscan   17.11
Tuscany   6.1
tusk   17.11
tussle   17.11
tussles   17.11
Tutankhamen   2.9
Tutankhamun   18.9
tutor   18.14
tutorial   14.12
Tuvalu   18.1
tux   17.2
tuxedo   6.4
TV   6.1
TVP   6.1
twaddle   11.3
Twain   3.9
twang   1.8
tweak   6.3
tweaker   6.3
tweaking   6.3
twee   6.1
tweed   6.4
Tweedledee   6.1
Tweedledum   17.7
tweeds   6.4
tweely   6.7
tweet   6.14
tweeted   6.14
tweeter   6.14
tweeting   6.14
tweets   6.14
twelve   5.6
twenty   5.8
twenty-one   17.8
twerp   8.10

twice 10.12
twiddle 9.3
twiddly 9.3
twig 9.5
Twiggy 9.5
twigs 9.5
twilight 10.7
twilit 10.7
twin 9.8
twine 10.9
twinge 9.8
twinkle 9.8
twinkling 9.8
twinkly 9.8
twinned 9.8
twinning 9.8
twirl 8.7
twirled 8.7
twirling 8.7
Twist 9.11
twist 9.11
twisted 9.11
twister 9.11
twisting 9.11
twisty 9.11
twit 9.14
twitch 9.14
twitchy 9.14
twitter 9.14
twittered 9.14
two 18.1
two-bit 9.14
two-dimensional 5.8
twopence 17.9
two-pin 18.10
twosome 18.11
two-way 18.18
two-wheeled 6.7
tycoon 18.9
Tyler 10.7
Tyne 10.9
type 10.10
typed 10.10
typesetter 5.14
typewriter 10.13
typhoon 18.9
typically 6.1
typify 10.1
typing 10.10
typographic 1.4
typographical 1.4
typography 11.5
tyrannical 1.8
tyrannize 10.17
tyrannizing 10.17
tyranny 6.1

Tyre 10.1
tyre 10.1
tyro 10.11
Tyrone 12.9

U
U 18.1
UAE 6.1
UB40 14.15
ubiquitous 9.2
ubiquity 9.2
UDA 3.1
udder 17.3
UDI 10.1
UEFA 3.5
UFO 12.1
Uganda 1.8
Ugandan 1.8
ugly 17.5
UHF 5.4
UHT 6.1
Uist 18.1
UK 3.1
Ukraine 3.9
Ukrainian 3.9
ukulele 3.7
ulcer 17.6
ulcerate 3.14
Ullapool 18.7
Ulrika 6.3
ulterior 7.5
ultimate 17.13
ultimately 6.1
ultimatum 3.14
ultramarine 6.9
ultramodern 11.3
ultrasound 13.4
ultraviolet 10.1
Ulysses 6.19
um and aah 2.1
umbrella 5.6
umbrellas 5.6
umpteen 6.9
UN 5.8
Una 18.9
unabashed 1.12
unable 3.2
unabridged 9.3
unacceptable 16.3
unaccountable 13.4
unaccounted 13.4
unacquainted 3.9
unadulterated 3.14
unaffected 5.2
unaffiliated 3.14

unaffordable 14.4
unafraid 3.4
unaided 3.4
unalike 10.3
unambitious 9.13
unambitiously 9.13
unanimity 9.7
unanimous 1.8
unanimously 6.1
unannounced 13.4
unapologetic 5.14
unapologetically 5.14
unappealing 6.7
unappetizing 10.17
unappreciated 3.14
unapproachable 12.14
unarmed 2.9
unashamed 3.8
unassailable 3.7
unassuming 18.8
unattached 1.13
unattainable 3.9
unattractive 1.2
unauthorized 10.17
unavailability 9.6
unavailable 3.7
unavailing 3.7
unaware 4.1
unawareness 4.5
unbalanced 1.6
unbearable 4.6
unbeatable 16.3
unbeaten 6.14
unbecoming 17.7
unbelievable 6.17
unbeliever 6.17
unbending 5.8
unbidden 9.3
unblock 11.2
unblocked 11.2
unblocking 11.2
unbounded 13.4
unbreakable 3.3
unbroken 12.3
unbusinesslike 10.3
unbutton 17.13
uncanny 1.8
uncaring 4.6
unceasing 6.11
uncertain 8.14
unchanged 3.9
unchanging 3.9
unchaperoned 12.9
uncharacteristic 9.11
uncharted 2.16
unchecked 5.2

Index

uncivil 9.17
uncivilized 10.17
unclaimed 3.8
uncle 17.8
unclean 6.9
unclear 7.1
unclearly 7.4
unclothed 12.15
uncoil 15.3
uncomfortable 16.3
uncommitted 9.14
uncomplicated 3.14
uncomplimentary 5.8
uncomprehending 5.8
uncompromising 10.17
unconcealed 6.7
unconcerned 8.9
unconditional 9.13
unconditionally 6.1
unconfirmed 8.8
unconnected 5.2
unconscious 11.8
unconsciously 6.1
unconstitutional 18.13
uncontainable 3.9
uncontaminated 3.14
uncontested 5.11
uncontrollable 12.7
uncontrolled 12.7
uncontroversial 8.13
unconventional 5.8
unconvincing 9.8
uncooked 16.1
uncool 18.7
uncoordinated 3.14
uncork 14.3
uncorked 14.3
uncorking 14.3
uncorroborated 3.14
uncountable 13.4
uncouth 18.16
uncover 17.15
uncritical 9.14
unction 17.8
uncultivated 3.14
uncut 17.13
undated 3.14
undaunted 14.10
undecided 10.4
undefeated 6.14
undefended 5.8
undemanding 2.10
undemocratic 1.13
undeniable 10.1
undeniably 10.1
under 17.8

underachieve 6.17
underachieved 6.17
underachievement 6.17
underachiever 6.17
underachieves 6.17
underactive 1.2
under-age 3.4
undercarriage 1.10
undercharge 2.4
undercharger 2.4
underclass 2.13
underclasses 2.13
underclothes 12.15
underclothing 12.15
undercoat 12.14
undercook 16.1
undercooked 16.1
undercooking 16.1
undercover 17.15
undercut 17.13
undercutting 17.13
underdog 11.5
underestimate 3.14
underexposed 12.19
underfed 5.3
underfoot 16.5
undergo 12.1
undergoing 12.1
undergone 11.8
underground 13.4
undergrowth 12.16
underhand 1.8
underhanded 1.8
underlain 3.9
underlay 3.1
underlie 10.1
underline 10.9
underlining 10.9
underlying 10.1
undermanning 1.8
undermentioned 5.8
undermine 10.9
undermining 10.9
underneath 6.16
underpaid 3.4
underpants 1.8
underpass 2.13
underpasses 2.13
underpayment 3.8
underperform 14.9
underperformed 14.9
underperformer 14.9
underpin 9.8
underpinned 9.8
underpinning 9.8
underpopulated 3.14

underproduction 17.2
underqualified 11.6
underrate 3.14
underside 10.4
underskirt 8.14
underskirts 8.14
understaffed 2.5
understaffing 2.5
understand 1.8
understandable 16.3
understandably 6.1
understanding 1.8
understatement 3.14
understood 16.2
understudy 17.3
undertake 3.3
undertaken 3.3
undertaker 3.3
undertaking 3.3
undertone 12.9
undertook 16.1
undertow 12.1
underwater 14.15
underwear 4.1
underweight 3.14
underwent 5.8
underworld 8.7
underwrite 10.13
underwriter 10.13
underwriting 10.13
underwritten 9.14
underwrote 12.14
undeserved 8.17
undeserving 8.17
undesirable 10.1
undetected 5.2
undeterred 8.4
undid 9.3
undigested 5.11
undignified 9.5
undiluted 18.14
undiminished 9.8
undiplomatic 1.13
undisciplined 9.8
undisclosed 12.19
undiscriminating 9.7
undisputed 18.14
undisturbed 8.2
undo 18.1
undoing 18.1
undone 17.8
undoubtedly 6.1
undress 5.11
undressed 5.11
undrinkable 9.8
undue 18.1

undulate   3.14
undulation   3.13
unduly   18.7
unearned   8.9
unearth   8.16
unease   6.19
uneasily   6.19
uneasy   6.19
uneaten   6.14
uneconomical   11.7
uneconomically   6.1
uneducated   3.14
unemotional   12.13
unemphatic   1.13
unemployable   15.1
unemployed   15.2
unemployment   15.4
unending   5.8
unendurable   19.4
unenjoyable   15.1
unenlightened   10.13
unenlightening   10.13
unenterprising   10.17
unenthusiastic   1.11
unequal   6.3
unerring   8.11
UNESCO   5.11
uneven   6.17
uneventful   5.8
unexciting   10.13
unexpected   5.2
unexplained   3.9
unfailing   3.7
unfair   4.1
unfairly   4.3
unfairness   4.5
unfamiliar   9.6
unfashionable   1.12
unfasten   2.13
unfathomable   16.3
unfazed   3.18
unfeasibility   9.6
unfeeling   6.7
unfinished   9.8
unfit   9.14
unflagging   1.5
unflappable   16.3
unflattering   1.13
unflinching   9.8
unfold   12.7
unforced   14.13
unforeseeable   6.1
unforeseen   6.9
unforgettable   5.14
unforgivable   9.17
unforgiving   9.17

unforthcoming   17.7
unfortunately   6.1
unfounded   13.4
unfreeze   6.19
unfrock   11.2
unfrocked   11.2
unfrocking   11.2
unfulfilled   9.6
unfunny   17.8
unfurl   8.7
unfurled   8.7
unfurling   8.7
ungainly   3.9
ungodly   11.3
ungovernable   16.3
ungracious   3.13
ungrateful   3.14
ungrudging   17.3
unguarded   2.4
unhappily   1.9
unhappiness   1.9
unhappy   1.9
unharmed   2.9
UNHCR   2.1
unhealthy   5.6
unhesitating   3.14
unhip   9.9
unholy   12.7
unhurriedly   6.1
unhurt   8.14
unhygienic   6.9
UNICEF   5.4
unicorn   14.10
unidentified   10.4
unification   3.13
uniform   14.9
uniformed   14.9
uniformity   14.9
uniformly   14.9
unify   10.1
unifying   10.1
unimaginable   16.3
unimpaired   4.2
unimportant   14.15
unimportantly   6.1
unimpressed   5.11
uninhibited   9.3
uninitiated   3.14
uninspired   10.1
uninspiring   10.1
uninsurable   19.4
uninsured   19.2
unintelligible   5.6
unintended   5.8
unintentional   5.8
unintentionally   6.1

uninvited   10.13
uninviting   10.13
union   18.9
unionist   9.11
unionize   10.17
unionizing   10.17
unique   6.3
unisex   5.2
UNISON   17.8
unison   17.8
unitary   6.1
unite   10.13
united   10.13
uniter   10.13
uniting   10.13
unity   18.9
universal   8.12
universally   6.1
universe   8.12
university   6.1
unjust   17.11
unjustifiable   10.1
unjustifiably   10.1
unjustified   10.4
unkempt   5.7
unkind   10.9
unkindly   10.9
unkindness   10.9
unknowingly   6.1
unknown   12.9
unlace   3.11
unlacing   3.11
unlawful   14.5
unleaded   5.3
unleash   6.13
unless   5.11
unlike   10.3
unlisted   9.11
unlit   9.14
unlivable   9.17
unload   12.4
unloaded   12.4
unloading   12.4
unlock   11.2
unlocked   11.2
unlocking   11.2
unlovable   16.3
unloved   17.15
unlovely   6.1
unluckily   17.2
unlucky   17.2
unmade   3.4
unmanly   1.8
unmanned   1.8
unmarked   2.3
unmarried   1.10

unmask 2.13
unmelodious 12.4
unmentionable 5.8
unmissable 9.11
unmistakable 3.3
unmoved 18.17
unnamed 3.8
unnatural 16.3
unnaturally 6.1
unnerve 8.17
unnerved 8.17
unnerving 8.17
UNO 12.1
unobservant 8.17
unobserved 8.17
unobtainable 3.9
unobtrusive 18.11
unobtrusively 18.11
unoccupied 10.4
unofficial 9.13
unofficially 9.13
unopposed 12.19
unorthodox 11.2
unpack 1.2
unpacked 1.2
unpacking 1.2
unpaid 3.4
unparalleled 5.6
unpardonable 2.4
unparliamentary 5.8
unpatriotic 11.13
unperturbed 8.2
unplanned 1.8
unplayable 3.1
unpleasant 5.18
unpleasantly 5.18
unpleasantness 5.11
unplug 17.5
unpolished 11.6
unpolluted 18.14
unpopularity 1.10
unpredictability 6.1
unpredictable 9.2
unprepared 4.2
unprepossessing 5.11
unpresentable 5.8
unpretentious 5.8
unprintable 16.3
unproductive 17.2
unprofessional 5.13
unprofitability 9.6
unpronounceable 16.3
unprotected 5.2
unprovoked 12.3
unpunctuality 1.6
unqualified 11.6

unquestionable 16.3
unquote 12.14
unquoted 12.14
unravel 1.16
unraveller 1.16
unravelling 1.16
unreadable 6.4
unreal 7.4
unrealistic 9.11
unreasonable 6.19
unreasonably 6.1
unrecognizable 10.17
unrecognized 10.17
unrecorded 14.4
unrefined 10.9
unrelated 3.14
unrelenting 5.8
unreliability 9.6
unreliable 10.1
unreliably 10.1
unrelieved 6.17
unremitting 9.14
unremorseful 14.13
unreported 14.15
unrepresentative 5.8
unrepresented 5.8
unreserved 8.17
unrest 5.11
unrested 5.11
unresting 5.11
unrestricted 9.2
unrewarding 14.4
unrhymed 10.8
unripe 10.10
unromantic 1.8
unruffled 17.4
unrulier 18.7
unruly 18.7
unsaddle 1.3
unsafe 3.5
unsaid 5.3
unsalted 14.8
unsatisfactory 1.2
unsatisfied 10.4
unsatisfying 10.1
unsavoury 3.17
unsayable 3.1
unscientific 9.4
unscramble 1.7
unscrambler 1.7
unscrambling 1.7
unscrew 18.1
unscrupulous 17.11
unscrupulously 6.1
unseasonable 6.19
unseat 6.14

unseated 6.14
unseating 6.14
unseats 6.14
unseemly 6.8
unseen 6.9
unselfconscious 11.8
unselfish 5.6
unsentimental 5.8
unsentimentally 5.8
unsettle 5.14
unshakeable 3.3
unshaven 3.17
unsheathe 6.15
unsheathing 6.15
unshed 5.3
unsightly 10.13
unsigned 10.9
unsinkable 9.8
unskilful 9.6
unskilfully 9.6
unskilled 9.6
unsociable 12.13
unsold 12.7
unsolved 11.6
unsophisticated 3.14
unsound 13.4
unsparing 4.6
unspeakable 16.3
unspecified 10.4
unspoken 12.3
unsporting 14.15
unsportsmanlike 10.3
unstable 3.2
unsteadily 5.3
unsteady 5.3
unstinting 9.8
unstressed 5.11
unstuck 17.2
unsubstantiated 3.14
unsubtlety 6.1
unsuccessful 5.11
unsuccessfully 6.1
unsuitability 9.6
unsuitable 18.14
unsuitably 6.1
unsuited 18.14
unsupervised 10.17
unsupported 14.15
unsupportive 14.15
unsure 19.1
unsurpassable 2.13
unsurpassed 2.13
unsurprising 10.17
unsurprisingly 6.1
unsuspected 5.2
unsuspecting 5.2

unsustainable 3.9
unswerving 8.17
unsympathetic 5.14
unsympathetically 5.14
unsystematic 1.13
untainted 3.9
untalkative 9.17
untamed 3.8
untangle 1.8
untangled 1.8
untested 5.11
unthinkable 9.8
untidiness 5.11
untidy 10.4
untie 10.1
until 9.6
untimely 10.8
untiring 10.1
untold 12.7
untouchable 16.3
untouched 17.13
untoward 14.4
untrained 3.9
untranslatable 3.14
untried 10.4
untroubled 17.1
untrue 18.1
untrustworthy 8.15
untruth 18.16
untruthful 18.16
untypically 6.1
unusable 18.19
unused 18.11, 18.19
unusually 6.1
unveil 3.7
unveiled 3.7
unveiler 3.7
unveiling 3.7
unveilings 3.7
unverifiable 10.1, 16.3
unverifiably 10.1
unvoiced 15.6
unwaged 3.4
unwary 4.6
unwavering 3.17
unwell 5.6
unwilling 9.6
unwillingly 6.1
unwillingness 9.6
unwind 10.9
unwinding 10.9
unwise 10.17
unwitting 9.14
unwittingly 6.1
unworkable 8.3
unworthy 8.15

unwound 13.4
unwrap 1.9
unwrapped 1.9
unwrapping 1.9
unwritten 9.14
unzip 9.9
up 17.9
up-and-coming 17.7
upbeat 6.14
upbraid 3.4
upbringing 9.8
update 3.14
upend 5.8
upending 5.8
upfront 17.8
upgradable 3.4
upgrade 3.4
upgraded 3.4
upgrading 3.4
upheaval 6.17
upheld 5.6
uphill 9.6
uphold 12.7
upholster 12.7
upholstery 6.1
uplift 9.4
uplifter 9.4
uplifting 9.4
upon 11.8
upped 17.9
upper 17.9
upper-class 2.13
upper-crust 17.11
uppermost 12.11
uppity 6.1
uprising 10.17
uproarious 14.12
uproariously 14.12
uproot 18.14
uprooted 18.14
uprooting 18.14
upset 5.14
upsetting 5.14
upstage 3.4
upstaged 3.4
upstaging 3.4
upstanding 1.8
upstream 6.8
uptight 10.13
up-to-date 3.14
up-to-the-minute 9.8
uptown 13.4
uranium 3.9
Uranus 3.9
urban 8.2
urbane 3.9

urbanely 3.9
urbanity 1.8
urbanization 3.13
urge 8.4
urgency 8.4
urgent 8.4
urgently 6.1
Uriah Heep 6.10
urinal 10.9
urinary 6.1
urinate 3.14
URL 5.6
URLs 5.6
urn 8.9
urology 11.6
Uruguay 10.1
Uruguayan 10.1
US 5.11
us 17.11
USA 3.1
usable 18.19
USAF 5.4
use 18.11, 18.19
used 18.11, 18.19
used to 18.11
usefully 6.1
usefulness 5.11
uselessly 6.1
user 18.19
usher 17.12
usherette 5.14
using 18.19
USN 5.8
USP 6.1
USS 5.11
USSR 2.1
usually 6.1
usurp 8.10
usury 6.1
utensil 5.8
uterus 17.11
utilitarian 4.6
utilitarianism 4.6
utility 9.6
utilize 10.17
utilizer 10.17
utilizing 10.17
Utopia 12.10
Utopian 12.10
Utrecht 5.2
utter 17.13
utterly 17.13
uttermost 12.11
UV 6.1
Uzbekistan 2.10

V

V   6.1
V&A   3.1
vacancy   6.1
vacantly   6.1
vacate   3.14
vacation   3.13
vacationer   3.13
vaccinate   3.14
vaccination   3.13
vaccinator   3.14
vaccine   6.9
vacillate   3.14
vacuum-packed   1.2
vagabond   11.8
vagary   6.1
vagrancy   6.1
vagrant   3.6
vague   3.6
vain   3.9
vainer   3.9
vainly   3.9
Val   1.6
valance   1.6
valanced   1.6
vale   3.7
valency   6.1
Valentine   10.9
valentine   10.9
Valentino   6.9
Valerie   1.6
valet   1.6
Valetta   5.14
Valhalla   1.6
valiantly   6.1
valid   1.6
validate   3.14
validation   3.13
validity   9.3
valise   6.19
Valkyries   6.19
valley   1.6
valour   1.6
Valparaíso   10.17
valuable   16.3
valuation   3.13
valueless   5.11
valve   1.6
vamp   1.7
vampire   10.1
van   1.8
Van Cleef   6.5
Vancouver   18.17
vandal   1.8
vandalism   9.18
vandalize   1.8

Van Damme   1.7
vane   3.9
Vanessa   5.11
Van Gogh   11.4
vanilla   9.6
vanish   1.8
vanity   1.8
vanned   1.8
Vanuatu   18.1
vapid   1.9
vaporize   10.17
vaporizer   10.17
vaporizing   10.17
vapour   3.10
variable   16.3
variation   3.13
varicose veins   3.9
variegated   3.14
variety   10.1
varifocal   12.3
various   4.6
variously   4.6
varnish   2.10
vary   4.6
Vasco da Gama   2.9
vase   2.21
vasectomy   5.2
Vaseline®   1.11
vast   2.13
vaster   2.13
vastly   2.13
VAT   1.13, 6.1
vat   1.13
Vatican   17.8
vaudeville   9.6
vault   14.8
vaulted   14.8
vaulter   14.8
vaunt   14.10
vaunted   14.10
vaunting   14.10
VC   6.1
vCJD   6.1
VCR   2.1
VDU   18.1
veal   6.7
vector   5.2
veer   7.1
veering   7.5
veg   5.3
vegetable   16.3
vegetarian   4.6
vegetarianism   4.6
vegetate   3.14
vegetation   3.13
vegged   5.3

veggie   5.3
vehemence   5.8
vehement   5.8
vehicle   16.3
vehicular   9.2
veil   3.7
veiled   3.7
veiling   3.7
veilings   3.7
vein   3.9
vellum   5.6
velocity   11.11
velveteen   6.9
velvety   6.1
venal   6.9
vendetta   5.14
veneer   7.1
veneered   7.2
venerable   16.3
venerate   5.8
veneration   3.13
Venetian   6.13
Venezuela   3.7
venial   6.9
Venice   5.8
venison   5.8
venomous   17.11
vent   5.8
ventilate   3.14
ventilation   3.13
ventilator   3.14
ventriloquism   9.18
ventriloquist   9.11
venture   5.8
venue   5.8
Venus   6.9
Vera   7.5
veracity   1.11
veranda(h)   1.8
verb   8.2
verbal   8.2
verbalize   10.17
verbalizing   10.17
verbally   8.2
verbatim   3.14
verbose   12.11
verbosity   11.11
Verdi   8.4
verge   8.4
verger   8.4
verifiable   10.1, 16.3
verifiably   10.1
verification   3.13
verify   5.10
verisimilitude   18.4
veritable   16.3

Vermeer 7.1
vermilion 9.6
vermin 8.8
Vermont 11.8
vernacular 1.2
Verne 8.9
Verona 12.9
Veronica 11.8
verruca 18.3
versatile 10.7
versatility 9.6
verse 8.12
versed 8.12
version 8.13
vertical 16.3
vertically 6.1
vertigo 12.1
verve 8.17
very 5.10
vessel 5.11
vest 5.11
vested 5.11
vestibule 18.7
vet 5.14
vetch 5.14
veteran 17.8
veterinarian 4.6
veterinary 6.1
veto 6.14
vetted 5.14
vetting 5.14
vex 5.2
vexation 3.13
vexed 5.2
VHF 5.4
VHS 5.11
via 10.1
viability 9.6
viable 10.1
viaduct 17.2
vibrate 3.14
vibration 3.13
vibrator 3.14
Vic 9.2
vicar 9.2
vicarious 4.6
vicariously 4.6
vice 10.12
vice-chairman 4.4
vice-president 5.18
vice-presidential 5.8
vice versa 8.12
vicinity 9.8
vicious 9.13
viciously 9.13
Vickers 9.2

Vicki 9.2
victimization 3.13
victimize 10.17
victimizer 10.17
victimizing 10.17
Victor 9.2
victor 9.2
Victoria 14.12
Victorian 14.12
victorious 14.12
victoriously 14.12
victory 9.2
video 12.1
videoed 12.4
videoing 12.1
vie 10.1
vied 10.4
Vienna 5.8
Viennese 6.19
Vietnam 1.7
Vietnamese 6.19
view 18.1
viewer 18.1
viewfinder 10.9
vigilante 1.8
vignette 5.14
vigorous 9.5
vigour 9.5
Vijay 6.4
Viking 10.3
vile 10.7
vilification 3.13
villa 9.6
village 9.6
villain 9.6
villainous 17.11
villainy 6.1
villus 9.6
Vilnius 17.11
vindicate 9.8
vindication 3.13
vindictive 9.2
Vine 10.9
vine 10.9
vino 6.9
vinyl 10.9
viola 12.7
violate 10.1
violation 3.13
violence 5.8
violently 6.1
Violet 10.1
violet 10.1
violin 9.8
VIP 6.1
viper 10.10

viral 10.11
virgin 8.4
Virginia 9.8
Virginian 9.8
virginity 9.8
virility 9.6
virology 11.6
virtually 6.1
virtuosi 6.1
virulent 5.8
virus 10.11
visa 6.19
vis-à-vis 6.1
visceral 16.3
viscous 9.11
visibility 9.6
visible 9.18
visibly 6.1
vision 9.12
visionary 6.1
visit 9.18
visor 10.17
vista 9.11
visualization 3.13
visualize 10.17
visualizer 10.17
visualizing 10.17
visually 6.1
vital 10.13
vitality 1.6
vitally 6.1
vitamin 9.8
vitriolic 11.6
vituperative 9.17
Viv 9.17
viva 10.15
vivacious 3.13
vivacity 1.11
vivid 9.17
vividly 6.1
Vivien 9.17
vivisection 5.2
vivisectionist 5.2
vixen 9.2
Viz 9.18
viz 9.18
V-neck 5.2
V-necks 5.2
VOA 3.1
vocabulary 1.1
vocal 12.3
vocalist 9.11
vocation 3.13
vocational 3.13
vocative 11.2
vociferous 9.4

vociferously   6.1
Vogue   12.6
vogue   12.6
voice   15.6
voiced   15.6
voice-over   12.17
void   15.2
volatile   10.7
volcanic   1.8
vole   12.7
Volga   11.6
Volgograd   1.3
volition   9.13
volley   11.6
volleyball   14.8
volt   12.7
Voltaire   4.1
voluble   11.6
volubly   6.1
voluminous   18.8
voluntarily   5.10
voluntary   6.1
volunteer   7.1
volunteering   7.5
vomit   11.7
voracious   3.13
vortex   14.15
vortices   14.15
Vorticism   9.18
votary   12.14
vote   12.14
voted   12.14
voter   12.14
voting   12.14
votive   12.14
vouch   13.7
vow   13.1
vowed   13.2
vowel   13.1
voyeur   8.1
voyeuristic   9.11
voyeurs   8.18
VSO   12.1
VTR   2.1
vulgarity   1.10
vulnerability   9.6
vulnerable   16.3
vulture   17.6

W

W   18.1
WAAF   1.4
wackier   1.2
wacky   1.2
wad   11.3

Waddle   11.3
waddle   11.3
wade   3.4
waded   3.4
wader   3.4
wadi   11.3
wading   3.4
wafer   3.5
wafer-thin   9.8
waffle   11.4
waft   11.4
wag   1.5
wage   3.4
waged   3.4
wager   3.4
waggle   1.5
wag(g)on   1.5
waging   3.4
waif   3.5
waifs and strays   3.18
wail   3.7
wailed   3.7
wailer   3.7
wailing   3.7
waist   3.11
wait   3.14
Waite   3.14
waiter   3.14
waiting   3.14
waive   3.17
waived   3.17
waiver   3.17
waiving   3.17
wake   3.3
waken   3.3
waker   3.3
wakey wakey   3.3
waking   3.3
Wales   3.7
Walesa   5.8
walk   14.3
walkabout   13.7
walked   14.3
walker   14.3
walkie-talkie   14.3
walking   14.3
walkover   12.17
wall   14.8
wallaby   6.1
Wallace   11.6
walled   14.8
Waller   11.6
wallflower   13.1
Wallis   11.6
Walloon   18.9
wallop   11.6

wallow   11.6
wallpaper   3.10
wall-to-wall   14.8
Wally   11.6
wally   11.6
Walt   14.8
Walter   14.8
waltz   14.8
WAN   5.8
wan   11.8
wand   11.8
Wanda   11.8
wander   11.8
wanderlust   17.11
wane   3.9
wangle   1.8
wangled   1.8
wanna   11.8
wanner   11.8
want   11.8
war   14.1
warble   14.2
ward   14.4
warded   14.4
warden   14.4
warder   14.4
warders   14.4
warding   14.4
warhead   14.7
wariness   5.11
warm   14.9
warm-blooded   17.3
warmed   14.9
warmer   14.9
warm-hearted   2.16
warmly   14.9
warmonger   17.8
warn   14.10
Warne   14.10
warning   14.10
warp   14.11
warrant   11.10
warranty   6.1
Warren   11.10
warren   11.10
warring   14.12
wart   14.15
Warwick   11.10
Warwickshire   10.1
wary   4.6
was   11.16
wash   11.12
washbasin   3.11
washer   11.12
washer-drier   10.1
washing-up   17.9

Index

waste 3.11
wasteful 3.11
wastepaper 3.10
waster 3.11
wasting 3.11
watch 11.13
watchmaker 3.3
watchtower 13.1
water 14.15
waterborne 14.10
watercolour 17.6
watercourse 14.13
watercress 5.11
waterfall 14.8
waterfowl 13.3
waterfront 17.8
watering 14.15
Waterloo 18.1
watermark 2.3
watermarked 2.3
watermarking 2.3
watermelon 5.6
waterproof 18.5
water-resistant 9.11
Waters 14.15
watershed 5.3
waterside 10.4
water-ski 6.1
water-ski'd 6.4
water-skiing 6.1
watertight 10.13
waterway 3.1
waterways 3.18
watery 6.1
Watt 11.13
watt 11.13
wattage 11.13
wave 3.17
waved 3.17
waver 3.17
wavering 3.17
waving 3.17
wavy 3.17
wax 1.2
waxed 1.2
waxen 1.2
waxing 1.2
Way 3.1
way 3.1
wayfarer 4.6
waylaid 3.4
waylay 3.1
waylaying 3.1
Wayne 3.9
way-out 13.7
wayside 3.11

WBA 3.1
WC 6.1
we 6.1
WEA 3.1
weak 6.3
weaken 6.3
weaker 6.3
weak-kneed 6.4
weakly 6.3
weak-willed 9.6
weal 6.7
wealth 5.6
wealthy 5.6
wean 6.9
weaning 6.9
Wear 7.1
wear 4.1
wearer 4.6
wearier 7.5
wearily 7.5
weariness 5.11
wearing 4.6
wearisome 17.7
weary 7.5
weasel 6.19
weather 5.15
weatherbeaten 6.14
weathercock 11.2
weatherman 1.8
weatherproof 18.5
weave 6.17
weaved 6.17
weaver 6.17
weaves 6.17
weaving 6.17
web 5.1
wed 5.3
we'd 6.4
wedded 5.3
wedding 5.3
wedding bells 5.6
wedge 5.3
wedged 5.3
wedge-heeled 6.7
wedlock 5.3
wee 6.1
weed 6.4
weeder 6.4
weedier 6.4
weeding 6.4
weedkiller 9.6
weeds 6.4
weedy 6.4
weeing 6.1
week 6.3
weekend 5.8

weekender 5.8
weekending 5.8
weekly 6.3
weep 6.10
weeping 6.10
weepy 6.10
wee(-)wee 6.18
Wee Willie Winkie 9.8
weft 5.4
weigh 3.1
weighable 3.1
weight 3.14
weighting 3.14
weightless 3.14
weightlifter 9.4
weighty 3.14
weir 7.1
weird 7.2
weld 5.6
welder 5.6
welding 5.6
well 5.6
we'll 6.7
well-adjusted 17.11
well-advised 10.17
well-appointed 15.5
well-balanced 1.6
well-behaved 3.17
wellbeing 6.1
well-bred 5.3
well-built 9.6
well-chosen 12.19
well-disposed 12.19
well-dressed 5.11
well-earned 8.9
welled 5.6
Welles 5.6
well-fed 5.3
well-founded 13.4
well-heeled 6.7
well-informed 14.9
welling 5.6
Wellington 5.6
wellington 5.6
well-intentioned 5.8
well-kept 5.9
well-known 12.9
well-loved 17.15
well-made 3.4
well-meaning 6.9
well-off 11.4
well-paid 3.4
well-read 5.3
well-respected 5.2
Wells 5.6
well-spoken 12.3

well-thought-out 13.7
well-timed 10.8
well-to-do 18.1
wellwisher 9.13
well-worn 14.10
welly 5.6
Welshman 17.8
Welshwoman 17.8
welt 5.6
welter 5.6
welterweight 3.14
Wenceslas 17.11
wench 5.8
wend 5.8
wending 5.8
Wendy 5.8
went 5.8
wept 5.9
we're 7.1
were 8.1
weren't 8.9
Wesley 5.18
West 5.11
west 5.11
westerly 6.1
western 5.11
westernized 10.17
Westmeath 6.15
Weston-super-Mare 4.1
wet 5.14
wetted 5.14
wetter 5.14
wetting 5.14
WEU 18.1
we've 6.17
whack 1.2
whacked 1.2
whacker 1.2
whacking 1.2
whacks 1.2
whale 3.7
whaler 3.7
whaling 3.7
Wham! 1.7
wham 1.7
wharf 14.5
wharves 14.17
what 11.13
what-d'ye-call-her 14.8
whatever 5.17
what's-her-name 3.8
what's-his-name 3.8
whatsoever 5.17
wheat 6.14
wheaten 6.14
wheedle 6.4

wheel 6.7
wheelbarrow 1.10
wheeled 6.7
wheeler 6.7
wheelie 6.7
wheeling 6.7
Wheen 6.9
wheeze 6.19
wheezed 6.19
wheezer 6.19
wheezing 6.19
whelk 5.6
whelp 5.6
when 5.8
whence 5.8
whenever 5.17
where 4.1
whereabouts 13.7
whereas 1.17
whereby 10.1
whereupon 11.8
wherever 5.17
wherewithal 14.8
whet 5.14
whether 5.15
whetted 5.14
whetting 5.14
whew 18.1
whey 3.1
which 9.14
whichever 5.17
Whicker 9.2
whiff 9.4
while 10.7
whiled 10.7
whiling 10.7
whim 9.7
whimper 9.7
whimsical 16.3
whine 10.9
whiner 10.9
whinge 9.8
whingeing 9.8
whinger 9.8
whining 10.9
whinny 9.8
whiny 10.9
whip 9.9
whipper 9.9
whippersnapper 1.9
whippet 9.9
whirl 8.7
whirled 8.7
whirling 8.7
whirr 8.1
whirred 8.4

whirring 8.11
whirrs 8.18
whisk 9.11
whiskers 9.11
whiskey 9.11
whisky 9.11
whist 9.11
whistle 9.11
whistle-stop 11.9
Whit 9.14
whit 9.14
White 10.13
white 10.13
white-collar 11.6
whited 10.13
white-haired 4.2
white-hot 11.13
whiten 10.13
whitened 10.13
whiteness 10.13
whitening 10.13
whiter 10.13
whither 9.15
whiting 10.13
Whitney 9.14
whittle 9.14
whizz 9.18
whizzy 9.18
WHO 12.1
who 18.1
who'd 18.4
whodun(n)it 17.8
whoever 5.17
whole 12.7
wholehearted 2.16
wholesaler 3.7
wholly 12.7
whom 18.8
whoop 18.10
whoopee 6.1
whooper 18.10
whoops 18.10
whopper 11.9
whopping 11.9
whose 18.19
whosoever 5.17
why 10.1
WI 10.1
Wichita 14.1
wick 9.2
wicked 9.2
wickedness 5.11
wicker 9.2
wickerwork 8.3
wicket 9.2
wicketkeeper 6.10

wicking   9.2
wicks   9.2
wide   10.4
wide-angle   1.8
widen   10.4
wider   10.4
wide-ranging   3.9
wield   6.7
wife   10.5
wig   9.5
wigeon   9.3
wiggle   9.5
wigs   9.5
Wigtownshire   10.1
wild   10.7
Wilde   10.7
wilderness   5.11
wildly   10.7
wildness   10.7
wiles   10.7
wilful   9.6
wilfully   6.1, 9.6
Wilhelmina   6.9
Will   9.6
will   9.6
willed   9.6
Willie   9.6
willing   9.6
willingly   6.1
willingness   9.6
will-o'-the-wisp   9.11
willow   9.6
willowy   9.6
willpower   13.1
willy-nilly   9.6
wilt   9.6
wily   10.7
Wimbledon   17.8
wimp   9.7
wimpish   9.7
wimple   9.7
win   9.8
wince   9.8
winch   9.8
winching   9.8
wincing   9.8
wind   9.8, 10.9
windcheater   6.14
winder   10.9
Windermere   7.1
windier   9.8
winding   10.9
window   12.1
window-dressing   5.11
windowpane   3.9
window-shopping   11.9

windowsill   9.6
windsurfing   8.5
windy   9.8
wine   10.9
wing   9.8
winger   9.8
winging   9.8
wink   9.8
winked   9.8
winker   9.8
winking   9.8
winkle   9.8
Winner   9.8
winner   9.8
Winnie   9.8
winning   9.8
Winnipeg   5.5
winnow   9.8
wino   10.9
Winona   12.9
Winston   9.8
winter   9.8
wintertime   10.8
wipe   10.10
wiped   10.10
wiper   10.10
wiping   10.10
wire   10.1
wired   10.1
wireless   10.1
wiring   10.1
wiry   10.1
Wise   10.17
wise   10.17
wiser   10.17
wish   9.13
wishing   9.13
wisp   9.11
wistful   9.11
wit   9.14
witch   9.14
withal   14.8
withdraw   14.1
withdrawer   14.12
withdrawing   14.12
withdrawn   14.10
withdrew   18.1
wither   9.15
withering   9.15
withheld   5.6
withhold   12.7
within   9.8
without   13.7
withstand   1.8
withstood   16.2
witness   9.14

witter   9.14
wittered   9.14
witticism   9.14, 9.18
wittily   6.1
wittingly   6.1
witty   9.14
wives   10.15
wizard   9.18
wobble   11.1
wobbly   11.1
woe   12.1
woebegone   11.8
woggle   11.5
wok   11.2
woke   12.3
woken   12.3
womanizer   10.17
womanly   6.1
womb   18.8
women   9.7
womenfolk   12.3
women's lib   9.1
women's libber   9.1
won   17.8
Wonder   17.8
wonder   17.8
wonderful   16.3
Wonderland   1.8
wonky   11.8
won't   12.9
wont   12.9
woo   18.1
Wood   18.4
wood   16.2
woodcutter   17.13
woodpecker   5.2
woody   16.2
wool   16.3
woolly   16.3
woozy   18.19
Worcestershire   10.1
word   8.4
wordy   8.4
wore   14.1
work   8.3
workable   8.3
workaday   3.1
workaholic   11.6
worker   8.3
working   8.3
working-class   2.13
workmanlike   10.3
workmanship   9.9
work-to-rule   18.7
world   8.7
world-beater   6.14

world-famous 3.8
worldly-wise 10.17
world-weary 7.5
worm 8.8
worm-eaten 6.14
wormer 8.8
worn 14.10
worried 17.10
worry 17.10
worse 8.12
worsen 8.12
worst 8.12
worth 8.16
worthwhile 10.7
worthy 8.15
would 16.2
wouldn't 16.2
wound 13.4, 18.9
wove 12.17
woven 12.17
wow 13.1
wowed 13.2
WP 6.1
WPC 6.1
wpm 5.7
WRAC 1.2
wraith 3.16
wrangle 1.8
wrangling 1.8
wrap 1.9
wrapper 1.9
wrapping 1.9
wrath 11.14
wreak 6.3
wreaking 6.3
wreath 6.16
wreathe 6.15
wreathing 6.15
wreck 5.2
wrecked 5.2
wrecker 5.2
wrecks 5.2
Wren 5.8
wren 5.8
wrench 5.8
wrens 5.8
wrest 5.11
wrested 5.11
wresting 5.11
wrestle 5.11
wrestling 5.11
wretch 5.14
wriggle 9.5
Wright 10.13
wring 9.8
wringer 9.8

wringing 9.8
wrinkle 9.8
wrinkling 9.8
wrinkly 9.8
wrist 9.11
writ 9.14
write 10.13
write-protected 5.2
writer 10.13
writhe 10.14
writing 10.13
written 9.14
wrong 11.8
wrongdoer 18.1
wrongdoing 18.1
wrong-headed 5.3
wronging 11.8
wrongly 11.8
wrote 12.14
wrought-iron 10.1
wrung 17.8
wry 10.1
wryly 10.7
Wuthering Heights
10.13
WWF 5.4
Wyoming 12.8
WYSIWYG 9.5

X
X 5.2
Xanadu 18.1
xenophobic 12.2
xenophobics 12.2
XL 5.6
xylophone 12.9

Y
Y 10.1
yacht 11.13
yachting 11.13
yachtsman 11.13
yachtswoman 11.13
yack 1.2
yak 1.2
yam 1.7
yammer 1.7
yammered 1.7
Yank 1.8
yank 1.8
Yankee 1.8
yanker 1.8
yap 1.9
yapping 1.9

yard 2.4
Yardie 2.4
yarn 2.10
yarned 2.10
Yasmin 1.17
yawn 14.10
yawner 14.10
yawning 14.10
ye 6.1
yea 3.1
yeah 4.1
year 7.1
yearly 7.4
yearn 8.9
yearned 8.9
yearner 8.9
yearning 8.9
yeast 6.11
yell 5.6
yelled 5.6
yeller 5.6
yelling 5.6
yellow 5.6
yelp 5.6
Yemen 5.7
Yemeni 5.7
yen 5.8
yep 5.9
Yerevan 1.8
yes 5.11
yes-man 5.11
yesterday 3.1
yesterdays 3.18
yet 5.14
yeti 5.14
yew 18.1
yield 6.7
yippee 6.1
YMCA 3.1
yob 11.1
yoga 12.6
yoke 12.3
yokel 12.3
yoking 12.3
Yokohama 2.9
yolk 12.3
yomp 11.7
yonder 11.8
Yorick 11.10
York 14.3
yorker 14.3
yorking 14.3
you 18.1
you'd 18.4
you-know-who 18.1
you'll 18.7

Index

Young 17.8
young 17.8
younger 17.8
your 14.1
you're 14.1
yourself 5.6
yourselves 5.6
youth 18.16
youthful 18.16
YouTube 18.2
you've 18.17
yowl 13.3
yowling 13.3
yuan 1.8
yucca 17.2
yu(c)k 17.2
yucky 17.2
Yugoslav 2.19
yummy 17.7
yuppie 17.9
Yvette 5.14
Yvonne 11.8
YWCA 3.1

Z
Z 5.3, 6.1
Zachary 6.1

Za(c)k 1.2
Zagreb 5.1
Zaire 7.1
Zairean 7.5
Zambezi 6.19
Zambia 1.7
zany 3.9
Zanzibar 2.1
zap 1.9
zapper 1.9
zapping 1.9
zappy 1.9
Zara 2.12
zeal 6.7
zealot 5.6
zealous 5.6
Zebedee 6.1
zebra 5.1, 6.2
zeds 5.3
Zelda 5.6
Zen 5.8
Zena 6.9
zenith 5.8
Zephaniah 10.1
zephyr 5.4
zero 7.5
zero-rated 3.14
zest 5.11

zesting 5.11
zilch 9.6
Zimbabwean 17.8
Zimmer® 9.7
zinc 9.8
Zion 10.1
Zionism 9.18
Zionist 9.11
zip 9.9
zipper 9.9
zippy 9.9
zit 9.14
zither 9.15
zodiac 1.2
Zoë 12.1
Zola 12.7
zone 12.9
zoning 12.9
zoo 18.1
zoological 11.3
zoologist 11.6
zoology 11.6
zoom 18.8
zooming 18.8
zucchini 6.9
Zulu 18.7
Zurich 19.4

Some Common Non-Rhyming Words

We have tried to find rhymes for all the words that you might want to look up in this book. However, there are some words for which no common rhyme exists. That is not to say that you cannot use these words in rhymes. You may find ways of accommodating these words by using near-rhymes or by imaginative manipulation of the language.

Here is a list of the most common words that defeated our attempts to find rhymes for them. Perhaps you can do better:

advantage	fertile	patient
agent	friendly	perfect
agreement	garment	phobia
aircraft	good-natured	physics
American	hazard	platform
angel	hostile	playboy
anxious	icon	product
assessment	interpret	profile
backbone	labourer	public
banjo	licence	purpose
basic	manage	secret
bilingual	mannered	service
burger	market	social
capsule	mayhem	solvent
carbon	metric	structure
catering	mistress	sugar
chaos	mobile	sure-footed
chaplain	nature	surfer
charcoal	nothing	tabloid
circle	office	tadpole
climax	officer	temper
dais	orange	temple
decoy	padlock	theatre
eastern	pancake	thermal
electric	parent	treatment
enchantment	partner	tribute
establish	passport	utmost
established	pastel	value
fascist	patience	worship